S. Teresa, David Lewis

The Life of S. Teresa of Jesus

Of the Order of our Lady of Carmel

S. Teresa, David Lewis

The Life of S. Teresa of Jesus
Of the Order of our Lady of Carmel

ISBN/EAN: 9783337118990

Printed in Europe, USA, Canada, Australia, Japan

Cover: Foto ©ninafisch / pixelio.de

More available books at **www.hansebooks.com**

THE LIFE

OF

S. TERESA OF JESUS,

Of the Order of our Lady of Carmel.

WRITTEN BY HERSELF.

TRANSLATED FROM THE SPANISH BY

DAVID LEWIS.

DECOR CARMELI ET SARON.

LONDON:
BURNS, OATES, & CO., 17 & 18 PORTMAN STREET,
AND 63 PATERNOSTER ROW.

1870.

PREFACE.

S. TERESA was born in Avila on Wednesday, March 28, 1515. Her father was Don Alfonso Sanchez de Cepeda, and her mother Doña Beatriz Davila y Ahumada. The name she received in her baptism was common to both families, for her great-grandmother on the father's side was Teresa Sanchez, and her grandmother on her mother's side was Teresa de las Cuevas. While she remained in the world, and even after she had become a nun in the monastery of the Incarnation, which was under the mitigated rule, she was known as Doña Teresa Sanchez Cepeda Davila y Ahumada; for in those days children took the name either of the father or of the mother, as it pleased them. The two families were noble, but that of Ahumada was no longer in possession of its former wealth and power.[1] Doña Beatriz was the second wife of Don Alfonso, and was related in the fourth degree to the first wife, as appears from the dispensation granted to make the marriage valid on the 16th of October 1509. Of this marriage Teresa was the third child.

Doña Beatriz died young, and the eldest daughter, Maria de Cepeda, took charge of her younger sisters—they were two—and was as a second mother to them till her marriage, which took place in 1531, when the Saint was in her sixteenth year. But as she was too young to be left in charge of her father's house, and as her education was not finished, she was sent to the Augustinian monastery, the nuns of which received young girls, and brought them up in the fear of God.[2] The Saint's own account is that she was too giddy and careless to be trusted at home, and that it was necessary to put her under the care of those who would watch over her and correct her ways. She remained a year and a half with the Augustinian nuns,

[1] Fr. Anton. de S. Joseph, in his note on letter 16, but letter 41, vol. iv. ed. Doblado.
[2] Reforma de los Descalços, lib. i. ch. vii. § 3.

and all the while God was calling her to Himself. She was not willing to listen to His voice ; she would ask the nuns to pray for her that she might have light to see her way ; "but for all this," she writes, " I wished not to be a nun."[1] By degrees her will yielded, and she had some inclination to become a religious at the end of the eighteen months of her stay, but that was all. She became ill ; her father removed her, and the struggle within herself continued,—on the one hand, the voice of God calling her ; on the other, herself labouring to escape from her vocation.

At last, after a struggle which lasted three months, she made up her mind, and against her inclination, to give up the world. She asked her father's leave, and was refused. She besieged him through her friends, but to no purpose. " The utmost I could get from him," she says, " was that I might do as I pleased after his death."[2] How long this contest with her father lasted is not known, but it is probable that it lasted many months, for the Saint was always most careful of the feelings of others, and would certainly have endured much rather than displease a father whom she loved so much, and who also loved her more than his other children.[3]

But she had to forsake her father, and so she left her father's house by stealth, taking with her one of her brothers, whom she had persuaded to give himself to God in religion. The brother and sister set out early in the morning, the former for the monastery of the Dominicans, and the latter for the Carmelite monastery of the Incarnation, in Avila. The nuns received her into the house, but sent word to her father of his child's escape. Don Alfonso, however, yielded at once, and consented to the sacrifice which he was compelled to make.

In the monastery of the Incarnation the Saint was led on, without her own knowledge, to states of prayer so high that she became alarmed about herself. In the purity and simplicity of her soul, she feared that the supernatural visitations of God might after all be nothing else but delusions of Satan.[4] She was so humble, that she could not believe graces so great could be given to a sinner like herself. The first person she consulted in her trouble seems to have been a layman, related to her family, Don Francisco de Salcedo. He was a married man, given to prayer, and a diligent frequenter of the theological lectures in the monastery of the Dominicans. Through him she obtained the help of a holy priest, Gaspar Daza, to whom she made known the state of her soul. The priest, hindered by his other labours, declined to be her director, and the Saint

[1] Ch. iii. § 2.   [2] Ch. iii. § 9.   [3] Ch. i. § 3.   [4] Ch. xxiii. § 2.

admits that she could have made no progress under his guidance.[1] She now placed herself in the hands of Don Francis, who encouraged her in every way, and, for the purpose of helping her onwards in the way of perfection, told her of the difficulties he himself had met with, and how by the grace of God he had overcome them.

But when the Saint told him of the great graces which God bestowed upon her, Don Francis became alarmed; he could not reconcile them with the life the Saint was living, according to her own account. He never thought of doubting the Saint's account, and did not suspect her of exaggerating her imperfections in the depths of her humility: "he thought the evil spirit might have something to do" with her,[2] and advised her to consider carefully her way of prayer.

Don Francis now applied again to Gaspar Daza, and the two friends consulted together; but, after much prayer on their part and on that of the Saint, they came to the conclusion that she "was deluded by an evil spirit," and recommended her to have recourse to the fathers of the Society of Jesus, lately settled in Avila.

The Saint, now in great fear, but still hoping and trusting that God would not suffer her to be deceived, made preparations for a general confession, and committed to writing the whole story of her life, and made known the state of her soul to F. Juan de Padranos, one of the fathers of the Society. F. Juan understood it all, and comforted her by telling her that her way of prayer was sound and the work of God. Under his direction she made great progress, and for the further satisfaction of her confessor, and of Don Francis, who seems to have still retained some of his doubts, she told every thing to S. Francis de Borja, who on one point changed the method of direction observed by F. Juan. That father recommended her to resist the supernatural visitations of the spirit as much as she could, but she was not able, and the resistance pained her;[3] S. Francis told her she had done enough, and that it was not right to prolong that resistance.[4]

The account of her life which she wrote before she applied to the Jesuits for direction has not been preserved; but it is possible that it was made more for her own security than for the purpose of being shown to her confessor.

The next account is Relation I., made for S. Peter of Alcantara, and was probably seen by many; for that Saint had to defend her, and maintain that the state of her soul was the work of God, against

[1] Ch. xxiii. § 9.   [2] *Id.* § 12.   [3] Ch. xxiv. § 1.   [4] *Id.* § 4.

those who thought that she was deluded by Satan. Her own confessor was occasionally alarmed, and had to consult others, and thus, by degrees, her state became known to many; and there were some who were so persuaded of her delusions, that they wished her to be exorcised as one possessed of an evil spirit,[1] and at a later time her friends were afraid that she might be denounced to the Inquisitors.[2]

During the troubles that arose when it became known that the Saint was about to found the monastery of S. Joseph, and therein establish the original rule of her Order in its primitive simplicity and austerity, she went for counsel to the Father Fra Pedro Ibañez, the Dominican, a most holy and learned priest. That father not only encouraged her, and commended her work, but also ordered her to give him in writing the story of her spiritual life. The Saint readily obeyed, and began it in the monastery of the Incarnation, and finished it in the house of Doña Luisa de la Cerda, in Toledo, in the month of June 1562. On the 24th of August, the feast of S. Bartholomew, in the same year, the Reform of the Carmelites began in the new monastery of S. Joseph in Avila.

What the Saint wrote for Fra Ibañez has not been found. It is, no doubt, substantially preserved in her Life, as we have it now, and is supposed to have reached no further than the end of ch. xxxi. What follows was added by direction of another Dominican father, confessor of the Saint in the new monastery of S. Joseph, Fra Garcia of Toledo, who, in 1562, bade her " write the history of that foundation, and other matters."

But as the Saint carried a heavy burden laid on her by God, a constant fear of delusion, she had recourse about the same time to the Inquisitor Soto, who advised her to write a history of her life, send it to Juan of Avila, the " Apostle of Andalucia," and abide by his counsel. As the direction of Fra Garcia of Toledo and the advice of the Inquisitor must have been given, according to her account, about the same time, the Life, as we have it now, must have occupied her nearly six years in the writing of it, which may well be owing to her unceasing care in firmly establishing the new monastery of S. Joseph. The book at last was sent to Juan

---

[1] Ch. xxix. § 4.   [2] Ch. xxxiii. § 6.

[3] The Saint held him in great reverence, and in one of her letters—lett. 355, but lett. 100, vol. ii. ed. Doblado—calls him a founder of her Order, because of the great services he had rendered her, and told her nuns of Seville that they need not be veiled in his presence, though they must be so in the presence of every body else, and especially the friars of the Reform.

of Avila by her friend Doña Luisa de la Cerda, and that great master of the spiritual life wrote the following censure of it:

"The grace and peace of Jesus Christ be with you always.

"1. When I undertook to read the book sent me, it was not so much because I thought myself able to judge of it, as because I thought I might, by the grace of our Lord, learn something from the teachings it contains: and praised be Christ; for, though I have not been able to read it with the leisure it requires, I have been comforted by it, and might have been edified by it, if the fault had not been mine. And although, indeed, I may have been comforted by it, without saying more, yet the respect due to the subject and to the person who has sent it will not allow me, I think, to let it go back without giving my opinion on it, at least in general.

"2. The book is not fit to be in the hands of every body, for it is necessary to correct the language in some places, and explain it in others; and there are some things in it useful for your spiritual life, and not so for others who might adopt them, for the special ways by which God leads some souls are not meant for others. These points, or the greater number of them, I have marked for the purpose of arranging them when I shall be able to do so, and I shall not fail to send them to you; for if you were aware of my infirmities and necessary occupations, I believe they would make you pity me rather than blame me for the omission.

"3. The doctrine of prayer is for the most part sound, and you may rely on it, and observe it; and the raptures I find to possess the tests of those which are true. What you say of God's way of teaching the soul, without respect to the imagination and without interior locutions, is safe, and I find nothing to object to it. S. Augustine speaks well of it.

"4. Interior locutions in these days have been a delusion of many, and exterior locutions are the least safe. It is easy enough to see when they proceed from ourselves, but to distinguish between those of a good and those of an evil spirit is more difficult. There are many rules given for finding out whether they come from our Lord or not, and one of them is, that they should be sent us in a time of need, or for some good end, as for the comforting a man under temptation or in doubt, or as a warning of coming danger. As a good man will not speak unadvisedly, neither will God; so, considering this, and that the locutions are agreeable to the holy writings and the teaching of the Church, my opinion is that the locutions mentioned in the book came from God.

"5. Imaginary or bodily visions are those which are most doubtful, and should in no wise be desired, and if they come undesired still they should be shunned as much as possible, yet not by treating them with contempt, unless it be certain that they come from an evil spirit; indeed, I was filled with horror, and greatly distressed, when I read of the gestures of contempt that were made.[1] People ought to entreat our Lord not to lead them by the way of visions, but to reserve for them in heaven the blessed vision of Himself and the Saints, and to guide them here along the beaten path as He guides His faithful servants, and they must take other good measures for avoiding these visions.

"6. But if the visions continue after all this is done, and if the soul derives good from them, and if they do not lead to vanity, but to deeper humility, and if the locutions be at one with the teaching of the Church, and if they continue for any time, and that with inward satisfaction—better felt than described—there is no reason then for avoiding them. But no one ought to rely on his own judgment herein; he should make every thing known to him who can give him light. That is the universal remedy to be had recourse to in such matters, together with hope in God, who will not let a soul that wishes to be safe lie under a delusion, if it be humble enough to yield obedience to the opinion of others.

"7. Nor should any one cause alarm by condemning them forthwith, because he sees that the person to whom they are granted is not perfect, for it is nothing new that our Lord in His goodness makes wicked people just, yea, even grievous sinners, by giving them to taste most deeply of His sweetness. I have seen it so myself. Who will set bounds to the goodness of our Lord?—especially when these graces are given, not for merit, nor because one is stronger; on the contrary, they are given to one because he is weaker; and as they do not make one more holy, they are not always given to the most holy.

"8. They are unreasonable who disbelieve these things merely because they are most high things, and because it seems to them incredible that infinite Majesty humbles Himself to these loving relations with one of His creatures. It is written, God is love, and if He is love, then infinite love and infinite goodness, and we must not be surprised if such a love and such a goodness breaks out into such excesses of love as disturb those who know nothing of it. And though many know of it by faith, still, as to that special experience of the loving, and more than loving, converse of God with whom He will, if not had, how deep it reaches can never be known; and so I

---

[1] See Life, ch. xxix. § 6.

have seen many persons scandalised at hearing of what God in His love does for His creatures. As they are themselves very far away from it, they cannot think that God will do for others what He is not doing for them. As this is an effect of love, and that a love which causes wonder, reason requires we should look upon it as a sign of its being from God, seeing that He is wonderful in His works, and most especially in those of His compassion; but they take occasion from this to be distrustful, which should have been a ground of confidence, when other circumstances combine as evidences of these visitations being good.

"9. It seems from the book, I think, that you have resisted, and even longer than was right. I think, too, that these locutions have done your soul good, and in particular that they have made you see your own wretchedness and your faults more clearly, and amend them. They have lasted long, and always with spiritual profit. They move you to love God, and to despise yourself, and to do penance. I see no reasons for condemning them, I incline rather to regard them as good, provided you are careful not to rely altogether on them, especially if they are unusual, or bid you do something out of the way, or are not very plain. In all these and the like cases you must withhold your belief in them, and at once seek for direction.

"10. Also it should be considered that, even if they do come from God, Satan may mix with them suggestions of his own; you should therefore be always suspicious of them. Also, when they are known to be from God, men must not rest much on them, seeing that holiness does not lie in them, but in a humble love of God and our neighbour: every thing else, however good, must be feared, and our efforts directed to the gaining of humility, goodness, and the love of our Lord. It is seemly, also, not to worship what is seen in these visions, but only Jesus Christ, either as in heaven or in the Sacrament, or, if it be a vision of the Saints, then to lift up the heart to the Holy One in heaven, and not to that which is presented to the imagination: let it suffice that the imagination may be made use of for the purpose of raising me up to that which it makes me see.

"11. I say, too, that the things mentioned in this book befall other persons even in this our day, and that there is great certainty that they come from God, whose arm is not shortened that He cannot do now what He did in times past, and that in weak vessels, for His own glory.

"12. Go on your road, but always suspecting robbers, and asking for the right way; give thanks to our Lord, who has given you His love, the knowledge of yourself, and a love of penance and the cross, making no account of these other things. However, do not despise them either, for there are signs that most of them come from our Lord, and those that do not come from Him will not hurt you if you ask for direction.

"13. I cannot believe that I have written this in my own strength, for I have none, but it is the effect of your prayers. I beg of you, for the love of Jesus Christ our Lord, to burden yourself with a prayer for me; He knows that I am asking this in great need, and I think that is enough to make you grant my request. I ask your permission to stop now, for I am bound to write another letter. May Jesus be glorified in all and by all! Amen.

"Your servant, for Christ's sake,

"JUAN DE AVILA.

"*Montilla*, 12*th Sept.* 1568."

Her confessors, having seen the book, "commanded her to make copies of it,"[1] one of which has been traced into the possession of the Duke and Duchess of Alva.

The Princess of Eboli in 1569 obtained a copy from the Saint herself, after much importunity; but it was more out of vanity or curiosity, it is to be feared, than from any real desire to learn the story of the Saint's spiritual life, that the Princess desired the boon. She and her husband promised to keep it from the knowledge of others, but the promise given was not kept. The Saint heard within a few days later that the book was in the hands of the servants of the Princess, who was angry with the Saint because she had refused to admit, at the request of the Princess, an Augustinian nun into the Order of Carmel in the new foundation of Pastrana. The contents of the book were bruited abroad, and the visions and revelations of the Saint were said to be of a like nature with those of Magdalene of the Cross, a deluded and deluding nun. The gossip in the house of the Princess was carried to Madrid, and the result was that the Inquisition began to make a search for the book.[2] It is not quite clear, however, that it was seized at this time.

The Princess became a widow in July 1573, and insisted on becoming a Carmelite nun in the house she and her husband Ruy Gomez had founded in Pastrana. When the news of her resolve reached the monastery, the mother-prioress, Isabel of S. Dominic, exclaimed, "The Princess a nun! I look on the house as ruined." The Princess came and insisted on her right as foundress; she had

[1] Rel. vii. § 9.
[2] *Reforma de los Descalços*, lib. ii. c. xxviii. § 6.

compelled a friar to give her the habit before her husband was buried, and when she came to Pastrana she began her religious life by the most complete disobedience and disregard of common propriety. Don Vicente's description of her is almost literally correct, though intended only for a general summary of her most childish conduct:

"On the death of the Prince of Eboli, the Princess would become a nun in her monastery of Pastrana. The first day she had a fit of violent fervour; on the next she relaxed the rule; on the third she broke it, and conversed with secular people within the cloisters. She was also so humble that she required the nuns to speak to her on their knees, and insisted upon their receiving into the house as religious whomsoever she pleased. Hereupon complaints were made to S. Teresa, who remonstrated with the Princess, and showed her how much she was in the wrong, whereupon she replied that the monastery was hers; but the Saint proved to her that the nuns were not, and had them removed at once to Segovia."[1]

The nuns were withdrawn from Pastrana in April 1574, and then the anger of the Princess prevailed; she sent the Life of the Saint, which she had still in her possession, to the Inquisition, and denounced it as a book containing visions, revelations, and dangerous doctrines, which the Inquisitors should look into and examine. The book was forthwith given to theologians for examination, and two Dominican friars, of whom Bañes was one, were delegated censors of it by the Inquisition.[2]

Fra Bañes did not know the Saint when he undertook her defence in Avila against the authorities of the city, eager to destroy the monastery of S. Joseph;[3] but from that time forth he was one of her most faithful friends, strict and even severe, as became a wise director who had a great Saint for his penitent. He testifies in the process of her beatification that he was stern and sharp with her; while she herself was the more desirous of his counsel, the more he humbled her, and the less he appeared to esteem her.[4] When he found that copies of her Life were in the hands of secular people,—he had probably also heard of the misconduct of the Princess of Eboli,—he

[1] Introduccion al libro de la Vida, vol. i. p. 3.
[2] Jerome Gratian, *Lucidario*, c. iv.
[3] Life, ch. xxxvi. § 15.
[4] The Saint says of herself, Rel. vii. § 18, that "she took the greatest pains not to submit the state of her soul to any one who she thought would believe that these things came from God, for she was instantly afraid that the devil would deceive them both."

showed his displeasure to the Saint, and told her he would burn the book, it being unseemly that the writings of women should be made public. The Saint left it in his hands, but Fra Bañes, struck with her humility, had not the courage to burn it; he sent it to the Holy Office in Madrid.[1] Thus the book was in a sense denounced twice,—once by an enemy, the second time by a friend, to save it. Both the Saint and her confessor, Fra Bañes, state that the copy given up by the latter was sent to the Inquisition in Madrid, and Fra Bañes says so twice in his deposition. The Inquisitor Soto returned the copy to Fra Bañes, desiring him to read it, and give his opinion thereon. Fra Bañes did so, and wrote his "censure" of the book on the blank leaves at the end. That censure still remains, and is one of the most important, because given during the lifetime of the Saint, and while many persons were crying out against her. Bañes wished it had been published when the Saint's Life was given to the world by Fra Luis de Leon; but notwithstanding its value, and its being preserved in the book, which is in the handwriting of the Saint, no one before Don Vicente made it known. It was easy enough to praise the writings of S. Teresa, and to admit her sanctity, after her death. Fra Bañes had no external help in the applause of the many, and he had to judge the book as a theologian, and the Saint as one of his ordinary penitents. What he wrote, he wrote like a man whose whole life was spent, as he tells us himself, " in lecturing and disputing."[2]

That censure is as follows :

" 1. This book, wherein Teresa of Jesus, Carmelite nun, and foundress of the Barefooted Carmelites, gives a plain account of the state of her soul, in order to be taught and directed by her confessors, has been examined by me, and with much attention, and I have not found any where in it any thing which, in my opinion, is erroneous in doctrine. On the contrary, there are many things in it highly edifying and instructive for those who give themselves to prayer. The great experience of this religious, her discretion also and her humility, which made her always seek for light and learning in her confessors, enabled her to speak with an accuracy on the subject of prayer that the most learned men, through their want of experience, have not always attained to. One thing only there is about the book that may reasonably cause any hesitation till it shall be very carefully

---

[1] Rel. vii. § 16.
[2] " Como hombre criado toda mi vida en leer y disputar" (*De la Fuente*, ii. p. 376).

examined: it contains many visions and revelations, matters always to be afraid of, especially in women, who are very ready to believe of them that they come from God, and to look on them as proofs of sanctity, though sanctity does not lie in them. On the contrary, they should be regarded as dangerous trials for those who are aiming at perfection, because Satan is wont to transform himself into an angel of light,[1] and to deceive souls which are curious and of scant humility, as we have seen in our day: nevertheless, we must not therefore lay down a general rule that all revelations and visions come from the devil. If it were so, S. Paul could not have said that Satan transforms himself into an angel of light, if the angel of light did not sometimes enlighten us.

"2. Saints, both men and women, have had revelations, not only in ancient, but also in modern times; such were S. Dominic, S. Francis, S. Vincent Ferrer, S. Catherine of Siena, S. Gertrude, and many others that might be named; and as the Church of God is, and is to be, always holy to the end, not only because her profession is holiness, but because there are in her just persons and perfect in holiness, it is unreasonable to despise visions and revelations, and condemn them in one sweep, seeing they are ordinarily accompanied with much goodness and a Christian life. On the contrary, we should follow the saying of the Apostle in 1 Thess. v. 19-22: 'Spiritum nolite extinguere. Prophetias nolite spernere. Omnia [autem] probate: quod bonum est tenete. Ab omni specie mala abstinete vos.' He who will read S. Thomas on that passage will see how carefully they are to be examined who, in the Church of God, manifest any particular gift that may be profitable or hurtful to our neighbour, and how watchful the examiners ought to be lest the fire of the Spirit of God should be quenched in the good, and others cowed in the practices of the perfect Christian life.

"3. Judging by the revelations made to her, this woman, even though she may be deceived in something, is at least not herself a deceiver, because she tells all the good and the bad so simply, and with so great a wish to be correct, that no doubt can be made as to her good intention; and the greater the reason for trying spirits of this kind, because there are persons in our day who are deceivers with the appearance of piety, the more necessary it is to defend those who, with the appearance, have also the reality, of piety. For it is a strange thing to see how lax and worldly people delight in seeing those discredited who have an appearance of goodness. God complained of old, by the Prophet Ezekiel, ch. xiii., of those false

[1] 2 Cor. xi. 14: "Ipse enim Satanas transfigurat se in angelum lucis."

prophets who made the just to mourn, and who flattered sinners, saying: 'Mœrere fecistis cor justi mendaciter, quem Ego non contristavi: et confortastis manus impii.' In a certain sense, this may be said of those who frighten souls who are going on by the way of prayer and perfection, telling them that this way is singular and full of danger, that many who went by it have fallen into delusions, and that the safest way is that which is plain and common, travelled by all.

"4. Words of this kind, clearly, sadden the hearts of those who would observe the counsels of perfection in continual prayer, so far as it is possible for them, and in much fasting, watching, and disciplines; and, on the other hand, the lax and the wicked take courage and lose the fear of God, because they consider the way on which they are travelling as the safer: and this is their delusion,—they call that a plain and safe road which is the absence of the knowledge and consideration of the dangers and precipices amidst which we are all of us journeying in this world. Nevertheless, there is no other security than that which lies in our knowing our daily enemies, and in humbly imploring the compassion of God, if we would not be their prisoners. Besides, there are souls whom God, in a way, constrains to enter on the way of perfection, and who, if they relaxed in their fervour, could not keep a middle course, but would immediately fall into the other extreme of sins, and for souls of this kind it is of the utmost necessity that they should watch and pray without ceasing; and, in short, there is nobody whom lukewarmness does not injure. Let every man examine his own conscience, and he will find this to be the truth.

"5. I firmly believe that if God for a time bears with the lukewarm, it is owing to the prayers of the fervent, who are continually crying, 'et ne nos inducas in tentationem.' I have said this, not for the purpose of honouring those whom we see walking in the way of contemplation; for it is another extreme into which the world falls, and a covert persecution of goodness, to pronounce those holy forthwith who have the appearance of it. For that would be to furnish them with motives for vain-glory, and would do little honour to goodness; on the contrary, it would expose it to great risks, because, when they fall who have been objects of praise, the honour of goodness suffers more than if those people had not been so esteemed. And so I look upon this exaggeration of their holiness who are still living in the world to be a temptation of Satan. That we should have a good opinion of the servants of God is most just, but let us consider them always as people in danger, however good they may be, and that their goodness is not so evident that we can be sure of it even now.

"6. Considering myself that what I have said is true, I have always proceeded cautiously in the examination of this account of the prayer and life of this nun, and no one has been more incredulous than myself as to her visions and revelations,—not so, however, as to her goodness and her good desires, for herein I have had great experience of her truthfulness, her obedience, mortification, patience, and charity towards her persecutors, and of her other virtues, which any one who will converse with her will discern; and this is what may be regarded as a more certain proof of her real love of God than these visions and revelations. I do not, however, undervalue her visions, revelations, and ecstasies; on the contrary, I suspect them to be the work of God, as they have been in others who were Saints. But in this case it is always safer to be afraid and wary; for if she is confident about them, Satan will take occasion to interfere, and that which was once, perhaps, the work of God, may be changed into something else, and that will be the devil's.

"7. I am of opinion that this book is not to be shown to every one, but only to men of learning, experience, and Christian discretion. It perfectly answers the purpose for which it was written, namely, that the nun should give an account of the state of her soul to those who had the charge of it, in order that she might not fall into delusions. Of one thing I am very sure, so far as it is possible for a man to be,—she is not a deceiver; she deserves, therefore, for her sincerity, that all should be favourable to her in her good purposes and good works. For within the last thirteen years she has, I believe, founded a dozen monasteries of Barefooted Carmelite nuns, the austerity and perfection of which are exceeded by none other; of which they who have been visitors of them, as the Dominican Provincial, master in theology,[1] Fra Pedro Fernandez, the master Fra Hernando del Castillo, and many others, speak highly. This is what I think, at present, concerning the censure of this book, submitting my judgment herein to that of Holy Church our mother, and her ministers.

"Given in the College of S. Gregory, Valladolid, on the sixth day of July 1575.

"FRA DOMINGO BAÑES."

The book remained in the keeping of the Inquisition, and the Saint never saw it again. But she heard of it from the Archbishop of Toledo, Cardinal Quiroga, President of the Supreme Court of the In-

---

[1] The other theologian appointed by the Inquisition, with Fra Bañes, to examine the "Life."

quisition, when she applied to him for license to found a monastery in Madrid. Jerome of the Mother of God was with her; and heard the Cardinal's reply. His Eminence said he was glad to see her; that a book of hers had been in the Holy Office for some years, and had been rigorously examined; that he had read it himself, and regarded it as containing sound and wholesome doctrine. He would grant the license, and do whatever he could for the Saint. When she heard this, she wished to present a petition to the Inquisition for the restitution of her book; but Gratian thought it better to apply to the Duke of Alba for the copy which he had, and which the Inquisitors had allowed him to retain and read. The Duke gave his book to Fra Jerome, who had copies of it made for the use of the monasteries both of men and women.[1]

Anne of Jesus, in 1586, founding a monastery of her Order in Madrid,—the Saint had died in 1584,—made inquiries about the book, and applied to the Inquisition for it, for she was resolved to publish the writings of her spiritual mother. The Inquisitors made no difficulty, and consented to the publication. In this she was seconded by the Empress Maria, daughter of Charles V. and widow of Maximilian II., who had obtained one of the copies which Fra Jerome of the Mother of God had ordered to be made. Fra Nicholas Doria, then Provincial, asked Fra Luis de Leon, the Augustinian, to edit the book, who consented. He was allowed to compare the copy furnished him with the original in the keeping of the Inquisition; but his edition has not been considered accurate, notwithstanding the facilities given him, and his great reverence for the Saint. It was published in Salamanca, A.D. 1588.

With the Life of the Saint, Fra Luis de Leon received certain papers in the handwriting of the Saint, which he published as an additional chapter. Whether he printed all he received, or merely made extracts, may be doubtful, but anyhow that chapter is singularly incomplete. Don Vicente de la Fuente, from whose edition (Madrid, 1861, 1862) this translation has been made, omitted the additional chapter of Fra Luis de Leon, contrary to the practice of his predecessors. But he has done more, for he has traced the para-

---

[1] This took place in the year 1580, according to the Chronicler of the Order (*Reforma de los Descalços*, lib. v. c. xxxvi. § 8); and the Bollandists (n. 1536) accept his statement. Fra Jerome says he was Provincial of his Order at the time; and as he was elected only on the 4th of March 1581, according to the Chronicler and the Bollandists, it is more likely that the audience granted to them by the Cardinal took place in 1581.

graphs of that chapter to their sources, and has given us now a collection of papers which form almost another Life of the Saint, to which he has given their old name of Relations,[1] the name which the Saint herself had given them.[2] Some of them are usually printed among the Saint's letters, and portions of some of the others are found in the Lives of the Saint written by Ribera and Yepes, and in the Chronicle of the Order; the rest was published for the first time by Don Vicente: the arrangement of the whole is due to him.

The Relations are ten in the Spanish edition, and eleven in the translation. The last, the eleventh, has hitherto been left among the letters, and Don Vicente, seemingly not without some hesitation, so left it; but as it is of the like nature with the Relations, it has now been added to them.

The original text, in the handwriting of the Saint, is preserved in the Escurial, not in the library, but among the relics of the Church. Don Vicente examined it at his leisure, and afterwards found in the National Library in Madrid an authentic and exact transcript of it, made by order of Ferdinand VI. His edition is, therefore, far better than any of its predecessors; but it is possible that even now there may still remain some verbal errors for future editors to correct. The most conscientious diligence is not a safeguard against mistakes. F. Bouix says that in ch. xxxiv. § 12, the reading of the original differs from that of the printed editions; yet Don Vicente takes no notice of it, and retains the common reading. It is impossible to believe that F. Bouix has stated as a fact that which is not. Again, in ch. xxxix. § 29, the printed editions have after the words, "Thou art Mine, and I am thine," "I am in the habit .... sincerity;" but Don Vicente omits them. This may have been an oversight, for in general he points out in his notes all the discrepancies between the printed editions and the original text.

A new translation of the Life of S. Teresa seems called for now, because the original text has been collated since the previous translations were made, and also because those translations are exceedingly scarce. The first is believed to be this—it is a small quarto:

[1] *Reforma de los Descalços,* lib. v. c. xxxv. § 4: "Relaciones de su espiritu."
[2] Rel. ii. § 18.

"The Lyf of the Mother Teresa of Jesus, Foundresse of the Monasteries of the Descalced or Bare-footed Carmelite Nunnes and Fryers of the First Rule.

"Written by herself at the commaundement of her ghostly father, and now translated into English out of Spanish. By W. M. of the Society of Jesus.

"Imprinted in Antwerp by Henry Jaye. Anno MDCXI."

Some thirty years afterwards, Sir Tobias Matthew, S.J., dissatisfied, as he says, with the former translation, published another, with the following title; the volume is a small octavo in form:

"The Flaming Hart, or the Life of the glorious S. Teresa, Foundresse of the Reformation of the Order of the All-Immaculate Virgin Mother, our B. Lady of Mount Carmel.

"This History of her Life was written by the Saint in Spanish, and is newly translated into English in the year of our Lord God 1642.
'Aut mori aut pati:
Either to dye or else to suffer.'—*Chap.* xl.

"Antwerpe, printed by Johannes Meursius. Anno MDCXLII."

The next translation was made by Abraham Woodhead, and published in 1671, without the name of the translator, or of the printer, or of the place of publication. It is in quarto, and bears the following title:

"The Life of the Holy Mother S. Teresa, Foundress of the Reformation of the Discalced Carmelites according to the Primitive Rule. Printed in the year MDCLXXI."

It is not said that the translation was made from the Spanish, and there are grounds for thinking it to have been made from the Italian. Ch. xxxii. is broken off at the end of § 10; and ch. xxxiii., therefore, is ch. xxxvii. That which is there omitted has been thrown into the Book of the Foundations, which, in the translation of Mr. Woodhead, begins with § 11 of ch. xxxii. of the Life, as it also does in the Italian translation. It is due, however, to Mr. Woodhead to say that he has printed five of the Relations separately, not as letters, but as what they really are, and with that designation.

The last translation is that of the Very Reverend John Dalton,

Canon of Northampton, which is now, though twice published, almost as scarce as its predecessors. The title is :

"The Life of Saint Teresa, written by herself, and translated from the Spanish by the Rev. John Dalton. London, MDCCCLI."

The present translation—the fifth—has not been made because the former translations are inaccurate, or in any way unfaithful to the original ; and he who made it cannot refrain from saying, in his own defence, that it was a task laid upon him by those whom he is bound to obey, and one that he never would have undertaken of his own will, partly because of the nature of the subjects of which the Saint treats, *mirabilibus super me*, and partly because of the extreme difficulty of the work.

Septuagesima, 1870.

ANNALS OF THE SAINT'S LIFE.

BY DON VICENTE DE LA FUENTE.

⁎⁎ *These are substantially the same with those drawn up by the Bollandists, but they are fuller and more minute, and furnish a more detailed history of the Saint.*

1515. S. Teresa is born in Avila, March 28th.[1]
1522. She desires martyrdom, and leaves her father's house with one of her brothers.
1527.[2] Death of her mother.
1529. Writes romances of chivalry, and is misled by a thoughtless cousin.
1531. Her sister Maria's marriage, and her removal from home to the Augustinian monastery, where she remains till the autumn of next year.
1533.[3] Nov. 2, enters the monastery of the Incarnation.

[1] In the same year S. Philip was born in Florence. S. Teresa died in 1582, and S. Philip in 1595; but they were canonised on the same day, with S. Isidore, S. Ignatius, and S. Francis Xavier. The three latter were joined together in the three final consistories held before the solemn proclamation of their sanctity, and S. Teresa and S. Philip were joined together in the same way in the final consistories held specially, as usual, for them.

[2] This must be an error. See ch. i. § 7, note 2.

[3] There is a difficulty about this. The Bollandists maintain that she went to the monastery of the Incarnation in the year 1533. On the other hand Ribera, her most accurate biographer,—with whom Fra Jerome agrees,—says that she left her father's house in 1535, when she was more than twenty years of age; Yepes, that she was not yet twenty; and the Second Relation of the Rota, that she was in her twentieth year. The Bull of Canonisation and the Office in the Breviary also say that she was in her twentieth year, that is, A.D. 1534. The Chronicler of the Order differs from all, and assigns the year 1536 as the year in which she entered the monastery.

1534. Nov. 3, makes her profession.
1535. Goes to Castellanos de la Cañada, to her sister's house, where she remains till the spring of 1536, when she goes to Bezadas.
1537. Returns to Avila on Palm Sunday. In July seriously ill, and in a trance for four days, when in her father's house. Paralysed for more than two years.
1539. Is cured of her paralysis by S. Joseph.
1541. Begins to grow lukewarm, and gives up mental prayer.
1542. Our Lord appears to her in the parlour of the monastery, "stern and grave" [ch. vii. § 11, see note there].
1555. Ceases to converse with secular people, moved thereto by the sight of a picture of our Lord on the cross [ch. ix. § 1]. The Jesuits come to Avila, and the Saint confesses to S. Juan de Padranos.
1556. Beginning of the supernatural visitations.
1557. S. Francis de Borja comes to Avila, and approves of the spirit of the Saint.
1558. First rapture of the Saint [ch. xxiv. § 7]. The vision of hell [ch. xxxii. § 1]. Father Alvarez ordained priest.
1559. She takes F. Alvarez for her confessor. The transpiercing of her heart [ch. xxix. § 17]. Vision of our Lord risen from the dead [ch. xxvii. § 3, ch. xxviii. § 2].
1560. The vow of greater perfection. S. Peter of Alcantara approves of her spirit, and S. Luis Beltran encourages her to proceed with her plan of founding a new monastery.
1561. F. Gaspar de Salazar, S.J., comes to Avila; her sister Doña Juana comes to Avila from Alba de Tormes to help the Saint in the new foundation [ch. xxxiii. § 13]. Restores her nephew to life [ch. xxxv. § 14, note]. Fra Ibañez bids her write her Life. Receives a sum of money from her brother in Peru, which enables her to go on with the building of the new house.
1562. Goes to Toledo, to the house of Doña Luisa de la Cerda, and finishes the account of her Life. Makes the acquaintance of Fra Bañes, afterwards her principal director, and Fra Garcia of Toledo, both Dominicans. Receives a visit from Maria of Jesus. Has a revelation that her sister Doña Maria will die suddenly [ch. xxxiv. § 23]. Returns to Avila and takes possession of the new monastery, August 24. Troubles in Avila. The Saint ordered back to the monastery of the Incarnation. Is commanded by Fra Garcia of Toledo to write the history of the foundation of S. Joseph.

CONTENTS.

CHAP.		PAGE
	Prologue	1
I.	Childhood and early Impressions — The Blessing of pious Parents—Desire of Martyrdom—Death of the Saint's Mother	2
II.	Early Impressions—Dangerous Books and Companions—The Saint is placed in a Monastery	6
III.	The Blessing of being with good People— How certain Illusions were removed	12
IV.	Our Lord helps her to become a Nun—Her many Infirmities	15
V.	Illness and Patience of the Saint—The Story of a Priest whom she rescued from a Life of Sin	22
VI.	The great Debt she owed to our Lord for His Mercy to her—She takes S. Joseph for her Patron	30
VII.	Lukewarmness—The Loss of Grace—Inconvenience of Laxity in Religious Houses	37
VIII.	The Saint ceases not to pray—Prayer the way to recover what is lost—All exhorted to pray—The great Advantage of Prayer, even to those who may have ceased from it	51
IX.	The Means whereby our Lord quickened her Soul, gave her Light in her Darkness, and made her strong in Goodness	58
X.	The Graces she received in Prayer—What we can do ourselves—The great Importance of understanding what our Lord is doing for us—She desires her Confessors to keep her Writings secret, because of the special Graces of our Lord to her, which they had commanded her to describe	63
XI.	Why Men do not attain quickly to the perfect Love of God— Of four Degrees of Prayer—Of the first Degree—The Doctrine profitable for Beginners, and for those who have no sensible Sweetness	70
XII.	What we can ourselves do—The Evil of desiring to attain to supernatural States before our Lord calls us	80
XIII.	Of certain Temptations of Satan — Instructions relating thereto	84
XIV.	The second State of Prayer—Its supernatural Character	96
XV.	Instructions for those who have attained to the Prayer of Quiet—Many advance so far, but few go farther	103

CONTENTS.

CHAP.		PAGE
XVI.	The third State of Prayer—Deep Matters—What the Soul can do that has reached it—Effects of the great Graces of our Lord	113
XVII.	The third State of Prayer—The Effects thereof—The Hindrance caused by the Imagination and the Memory	119
XVIII.	The fourth State of Prayer—The great Dignity of the Soul raised to it by our Lord—Attainable on Earth, not by our Merit, but by the Goodness of our Lord .	124
XIX.	The Effects of this fourth State of Prayer—Earnest Exhortations to those who have attained to it not to go back, nor to cease from Prayer, even if they fall —The great Calamity of going back . . .	132
XX.	The Difference between Union and Rapture—What Rapture is—The Blessing it is to the Soul—The Effects of it	142
XXI.	Conclusion of the Subject—Pain of the Awakening— Light against Delusions	158
XXII.	The Security of Contemplatives lies in their not ascending to high Things if our Lord does not raise them—The Sacred Humanity must be the Road to the highest Contemplation—A Delusion in which the Saint was once entangled	164
XXIII.	The Saint resumes the History of her Life—Aiming at Perfection—Means whereby it may be gained—Instructions for Confessors	176
XXIV.	Progress under Obedience—Her Inability to resist the Graces of God—God multiplies His Graces . .	186
XXV.	Divine Locutions—Delusions on that Subject . .	191
XXVI.	How the Fears of the Saint vanished—How she was assured that her Prayer was the Work of the Holy Spirit	203
XXVII.	The Saint prays to be directed by a different Way—Intellectual Visions	208
XXVIII.	Visions of the Sacred Humanity and of the glorified Bodies—Imaginary Visions — Great Fruits thereof when they come from God	219
XXIX.	Of Visions—The Graces our Lord bestowed on the Saint —The Answers our Lord gave her for those who tried her	230
XXX.	S. Peter of Alcantara comforts the Saint—Great Temptations and Interior Trials	239
XXXI.	Of certain outward Temptations and Appearances of Satan —Of the Sufferings thereby occasioned—Counsels for those who go on unto Perfection . . .	252

CHAP.		PAGE
XXXII.	Our Lord shows S. Teresa the Place which she had by her Sins deserved in Hell—The Torments there—How the Monastery of S. Joseph was founded	265
XXXIII.	The Foundation of the Monastery hindered—Our Lord consoles the Saint	274
XXXIV.	The Saint leaves her Monastery of the Incarnation for a time, at the Command of her Superior—Consoles an afflicted Widow	284
XXXV.	The Foundation of the House of S. Joseph—Observance of holy Poverty therein—How the Saint left Toledo	295
XXXVI.	The Foundation of the Monastery of S. Joseph—Persecution and Temptations—Great interior Trial of the Saint, and her Deliverance	304
XXXVII.	The Effects of the divine Graces in the Soul—The inestimable Greatness of one Degree of Glory	320
XXXVIII.	Certain heavenly Secrets, Visions, and Revelations—The Effects of them in her Soul	327
XXXIX.	Other Graces bestowed on the Saint—The Promises of our Lord to her—Divine Locutions and Visions	342
XL.	Visions, Revelations, and Locutions	356

THE RELATIONS.

REL.		
I.	Sent to S. Peter of Alcantara in 1560 from the Monastery of the Incarnation, Avila	373
II.	To one of her Confessors, from the House of Doña Luisa de la Cerda, in 1562	386
III.	Of various Graces granted to the Saint from the year 1568 to 1571 inclusive	392
IV.	Of the Graces the Saint received in Salamanca at the end of Lent 1571	400
V.	Observations on certain Points of Spirituality	403
VI.	The Vow of Obedience to Father Gratian which the Saint made in 1575	409
VII.	Made for Rodrigo Alvarez, S.J., in the year 1575, according to Don Vicente de la Fuente; but in 1576, according to the Bollandists and F. Bouix	412
VIII.	Addressed to F. Rodrigo Alvarez	421
IX.	Of certain spiritual Graces she received in Toledo and Avila in the years 1576 and 1577	430
X.	Of a Revelation to the Saint at Avila, 1579, and of certain Directions concerning the Government of the Order	439
XI.	Written from Palencia in May 1581, and addressed to Don Alonzo Velasquez, Bishop of Osma, who had been, when Canon of Toledo, one of the Saint's Confessors	440

THE LIFE

OF

THE HOLY MOTHER TERESA OF JESUS.

WRITTEN BY HERSELF.

PROLOGUE.

As I have been commanded and left at liberty to describe at length my way of prayer, and the workings of the grace of our Lord within me, I could wish that I had been allowed at the same time to speak distinctly and in detail of my grievous sins and wicked life. But it has not been so willed; on the contrary, I am laid herein under great restraint; and therefore, for the love of our Lord, I beg of every one who shall read this story of my life[1] to keep in mind how wicked it has been; and how, among the Saints who were converted to God, I have never found one in whom I can have any comfort. For I see that they, after our Lord had called them, never fell into sin again; I not only became worse, but, as it seems to me, deliberately

---

[1] The Saint, in a letter written Nov. 19, 1581, to Don Pedro de Castro, then Canon of Avila, speaking of this book, calls it the book "Of the Compassions of God"—*Y ansi intitulé ese libro De las Misericordias de Dios.* That letter is the 358th in the edition of Don Vicente de la Fuente, and the 8th of the fourth volume of the Doblado edition of Madrid. "Vitam igitur suam internam et supernaturalem magis pandit quam narrat actiones suas mere humanas" (*Bollandists,* § 1).

B

withstood the graces of His Majesty, because I saw that I was thereby bound to serve Him more earnestly, knowing, at the same time, that of myself I could not pay the least portion of my debt.

May He be blessed for ever who waited for me so long! I implore Him with my whole heart to send me His grace, so that in all clearness and truth I may give this account of myself which my confessors command me to give; and even our Lord Himself, I know it, has also willed it should be given for some time past, but I had not the courage to attempt it. And I pray it may be to His praise and glory, and a help to my confessors; who, knowing me better, may succour my weakness, so that I may render to our Lord some portion of the service I owe Him. May all creatures praise Him for ever! Amen.

CHAPTER I.

CHILDHOOD AND EARLY IMPRESSIONS—THE BLESSING OF PIOUS PARENTS—DESIRE OF MARTYRDOM—DEATH OF THE SAINT'S MOTHER.

Piety of the Saint's father

1. I HAD a father and mother, who were devout and feared God. Our Lord also helped me with His grace. All this would have been enough to make me good, if I had not been so wicked. My father was very much given to the reading of good books; and so he had them in Spanish, that his children might read them. These books, with my mother's carefulness to make us say our prayers, and to bring us up devout to our Lady and to certain Saints, began to make me think seriously when I was, I believe, six or seven years old. It helped me, too, that I never saw my father and mother respect any thing but goodness. They were very good themselves. My father was a man of great charity towards the poor, and compassion for the sick, and also for servants; so much so, that he never could be persuaded to keep slaves, for he pitied them so much: and a slave belonging to one of his brothers being once in his house, was treated by him with as

much tenderness as his own children. He used to say that he could not endure the pain of seeing that she was not free. He was a man of great truthfulness; nobody ever heard him swear or speak ill of any one; his life was most pure.

2. My mother also was a woman of great goodness, and her life was spent in great infirmities. She was singularly pure in all her ways. Though possessing great beauty, yet was it never known that she gave reason to suspect that she made any account whatever of it; for, though she was only three-and-thirty years of age when she died, her apparel was already that of a woman advanced in years. She was very calm, and had great sense. The sufferings she went through during her life were grievous, her death most Christian.[1]

And mother.

3. We were three sisters and nine brothers.[2] All, by the mercy of God, resembled their parents in goodness except myself, though I was the most cherished of my father. And, before I began to offend God, I think he had some reason,—for I am filled with sorrow whenever I think of the good desires with which our Lord inspired

Brothers and sisters.

---

[1] See ch. xxxvii. § 1; where the Saint says that she saw them in a vision both in heaven.

[2] Alfonso Sanchez de Cepeda, father of the Saint, married first Catalina del Peso y Henao, and had three children—one daughter, Maria de Cepeda, and two sons. After the death of Catalina, he married Beatriz Davila y Ahumada, by whom he had nine children—seven boys and two girls. The third of these, and the eldest of the daughters, was the Saint, Doña Teresa Sanchez Cepeda Davila y Ahumada. In the monastery of the Incarnation, where she was a professed nun for twenty-eight years, she was known as Doña Teresa; but in the year 1563, when she left her monastery for the new foundation of S. Joseph, of the Reform of the Carmelites, she took for the first time the name of Teresa of Jesus (*De la Fuente*). The Saint was born March 28, 1515, and baptised April 4, in the church of S. John; on which day Mass was said for the first time in the monastery of the Incarnation, where the Saint made her profession. Her godfather was Vela Nuñez, and her godmother Doña Maria del Aguila. The Bollandists and F. Bouix say that she was baptised on the very day of her birth. But the testimony of Doña Maria de Pinel, a nun in the monastery of the Incarnation, is clear; and Don Vicente de la Fuente, quoting it, vol. i. p. 549, says that this delay of baptism was nothing singular in those days, provided there was no danger of death.

me, and what a wretched use I made of them. Besides, my brothers never in any way hindered me in the service of God.

The Saint longs for martyrdom.
4. One of my brothers was nearly of my own age;[1] and he it was whom I most loved, though I was very fond of them all, and they of me. He and I used to read lives of Saints together. When I read of martyrdom undergone by the Saints for the love of God, it struck me that the vision of God was very cheaply purchased; and I had a great desire to die a martyr's death,—not out of any love of Him of which I was conscious, but that I might most quickly attain to the fruition of those great joys of which I read that they were reserved in heaven; and I used to discuss with my brother how we could become martyrs. We settled to go together to the country of the Moors,[2] begging our way for the love of God, that we might be there beheaded;[3] and our Lord, I believe, had given us courage enough, even at so tender an age, if we could have found the means to proceed; but our greatest difficulty seemed to be our father and mother.

Early impressions.
5. It astonished us greatly to find it said in what we were reading that pain and bliss were everlasting. We happened very often to talk about this; and we

---

[1] Rodrigo de Cepeda, four years older than the Saint, entered the army, and, serving in South America, was drowned in the river Plate, Rio de la Plata. S. Teresa always considered him a martyr, because he died in defence of the Catholic faith (*Ribera*, lib. i. ch. iv.). Before he sailed for the Indies, he made his will, and left all his property to the Saint, his sister (*Reforma de los Descalços*, vol. i. lib. i. ch. iii. § 4).

[2] The Bollandists incline to believe that S. Teresa may not have intended to quit Spain, because all the Moors were not at that time driven out of the country. The Bull of the Saint's canonisation, and the Lections of the Breviary, say that she left her father's house, *ut in Africam trajiceret*.

[3] The two children set out on their strange journey—one of them seven, the other eleven, years old—through the Adaja Gate; but when they had crossed the bridge, they were met by one of their uncles, who brought them back to their mother, who had already sent through Avila in quest of them. Rodrigo, like Adam, excused himself, and laid the blame on the woman (*Ribera*, lib. i. ch. iv.). Francisco de Santa Maria, chronicler of the Order, says that the uncle was Francisco Alvarez de Cepeda (*Reforma de los Descalços*, lib. i. ch. v. § 4).

had a pleasure in repeating frequently, "For ever, ever, ever." Through the constant uttering of these words, our Lord was pleased that I should receive an abiding impression of the way of truth when I was yet a child.

6. As soon as I saw it was impossible to go to any place where people would put me to death for the sake of God, my brother and I set about becoming hermits; and in an orchard belonging to the house we contrived, as well as we could, to build hermitages, by piling up small stones one on the other, which fell down immediately; and so it came to pass that we found no means of accomplishing our wish. Even now, I have a feeling of devotion when I consider how God gave me in my early youth what I lost by my own fault. I gave alms as I could—and I could but little. I contrived to be alone, for the sake of saying my prayers,[1]—and they were many,—especially the Rosary, to which my mother had a great devotion, and had made us also in this like herself. I used to delight exceedingly, when playing with other children, in the building of monasteries, as if we were nuns; and I think I wished to be a nun, though not so much as I did to be a martyr or a hermit.

Longings for solitude.

7. I remember that, when my mother died,[2] I was about twelve years old—a little less. When I began to understand my loss, I went in my affliction to an image of our Lady,[3] and with many tears implored her to be my mother. I did this in my simplicity, and I believe that

She recommends herself to our Lady.

---

[1] She was also marvellously touched by the story of the Samaritan woman at the well, of whom there was a picture in her room (*Ribera*, lib. i. ch. iv.). She speaks of this later on. (See ch. xxxi. § 24.)

[2] The last will and testament of Doña Beatriz de Ahumada was made Nov. 24, 1528; and she may have died soon after. If there be no mistake in the copy of that instrument, the Saint must have been more than twelve years old at that time. Don Vicente, in a note, says, with the Bollandists, that Doña Beatriz died at the end of the year 1526, or in the beginning of 1527; but it is probable that, when he wrote that note, he had not read the copy of the will, which he has printed in the first volume of the Saint's writings, p. 550.

[3] Our Lady of Charity, in the church of the hospital where the poor and pilgrims were received in Avila (*Bouix*).

it was of service to me; for I have by experience found the royal Virgin help me whenever I recommended myself to her; and at last she has brought me back to herself. It distresses me now, when I think of, and reflect on, that which kept me from being earnest in the good desires with which I began.

Prayer. 8. O my Lord, since Thou art determined to save me,—may it be the pleasure of Thy Majesty to effect it! —and to bestow upon me so many graces, why has it not been Thy pleasure also,—not for my advantage, but for Thy greater honour,—that this habitation, wherein Thou hast continually to dwell, should not have contracted so much defilement? It distresses me even to say this, O my Lord, because I know the fault is all my own, seeing that Thou hast left nothing undone to make me, even from my youth, wholly Thine. When I would complain of my parents, I cannot do it; for I saw nothing in them but all good, and carefulness for my welfare. Then, growing up, I began to discover the natural gifts which our Lord had given me—they were said to be many; and, when I should have given Him thanks for them, I made use of every one of them, as I shall now explain, to offend Him.

CHAPTER II.

EARLY IMPRESSIONS—DANGEROUS BOOKS AND COMPANIONS— THE SAINT IS PLACED IN A MONASTERY.

Importance of early piety. 1. WHAT I shall now speak of was, I believe, the beginning of great harm to me. I often think how wrong it is of parents not to be very careful that their children should always, and in every way, see only that which is good; for though my mother was, as I have just said, so good herself, nevertheless I, when I came to the use of reason, did not derive so much good from her as I ought to have done —almost none at all; and the evil I learned did me much harm. She was very fond of books of chivalry; but this pastime did not hurt her so much as it hurt me, because she never wasted her time on them; only we, her children, were left at liberty to read them; and perhaps she did this to distract her thoughts from her great sufferings, and occupy her children, that they might not go astray in other ways. It annoyed my father so much, that we had to be careful he never saw us. I contracted a habit of reading these books; and this little fault which I observed in my mother was the beginning of lukewarmness in my good desires, and the occasion of my falling away in other respects. I thought there was no harm in it when I wasted many hours night and day in so vain an occupation, even when I kept it a secret from my father. So completely was I mastered by this passion, that I thought I could never be happy without a new book.

2. I began to make much of dress, to wish to please others by my appearance. I took pains with my hands and my hair, used perfumes, and all vanities within my reach—and they were many, for I was very much given to them. I had no evil intention, because I never wished any one to offend God for me. This fastidiousness of excessive neatness[1] lasted some years; and so also did other practices, which I thought then were not at all sinful: now, I see how wrong all this must have been.

3. I had some cousins; for into my father's house no others were allowed an entrance. In this he was very cautious; and would to God he had been cautious about them!—for I see now the danger of conversing, at an age when virtue should begin to grow, with persons who, knowing nothing themselves of the vanity of the world, provoke others to throw themselves into the midst of it. These cousins were nearly of mine own age—a little older, perhaps. We were

---

[1] The Saint throughout her life was extremely careful of cleanliness. In one of her letters to F. Jerome Gratian of the Mother of God (No. 323, Letter 28, vol. iii., ed. Doblado), she begs him, for the love of God, to see that the fathers had clean cells and table; and the Ven. Mother Anne of S. Bartholomew, in her life (Bruxelles, 1708, p. 40), says that she changed the Saint's linen on the day of her death, and was thanked by her for her carefulness. "Her soul was so pure," says the ven. mother, "that she could not bear any thing that was not clean."

always together; and they had a great affection for me. In every thing that gave them pleasure, I kept the conversation alive,—listened to the stories of their affections and childish follies, good for nothing; and, what was still worse, my soul began to give itself up to that which was the cause of all its disorders. If I were to give advice, I would say to parents that they ought to be very careful whom they allow to mix with their children when young; for much mischief thence ensues, and our natural inclinations are unto evil rather than unto good.

4. So it was with me; for I had a sister much older than myself,[1] from whose modesty and goodness, which were great, I learned nothing; and learned every evil from a relative who was often in the house. She was so light and frivolous, that my mother took great pains to keep her out of the house, as if she foresaw the evil I should learn from her; but she could not succeed, there being so many reasons for her coming. I was very fond of this person's company, gossiped and talked with her; for she helped me in all the amusements I liked, and, what is more, found some for me, and communicated to me her own conversations and her vanities. Until I knew her, I mean, until she became friendly with me, and communicated to me her own affairs,—I was then about fourteen years old, a little more, I think,—I do not believe that I turned away from God in mortal sin, or lost the fear of Him, though I had a greater fear of disgrace. This latter fear had such sway over me, that I never wholly forfeited my good name,—and, as to that, there was nothing in the world for which I would have bartered it, and nobody in the world I liked well enough who could have persuaded me to do it. Thus I might have had the strength never to do any thing against the honour of God, as I had it by nature not to fail in that wherein I thought the honour of the world consisted; and I never observed that I was failing in many other ways. In vainly seeking after it I was extremely care-

Dangerous friendships.

[1] Maria de Cepeda, half-sister of the Saint. She was married to Don Martin de Guzman y Barrientos; and the contract for the dowry was signed Jan. 11, 1531 (*Reforma de los Descalços*, lib. i. ch. vii. § 4).

ful; but in the use of the means necessary for preserving it I was utterly careless. I was anxious only not to be lost altogether.

5. This friendship distressed my father and sister exceedingly. They often blamed me for it; but, as they could not hinder that person from coming into the house, all their efforts were in vain; for I was very adroit in doing any thing that was wrong. Now and then, I am amazed at the evil one bad companion can do,—nor could I believe it, if I did not know it by experience,—especially when we are young: then is it that the evil must be greatest. Oh, that parents would take warning by me, and look carefully to this! So it was; the conversation of this person so changed me, that no trace was left of my soul's natural disposition to virtue, and I became a reflection of her and of another who was given to the same kind of amusements. *The Saint deplores her youthful obstinacy.*

6. I know from this the great advantage of good companions; and I am certain that if at that tender age I had been thrown among good people, I should have persevered in virtue; for if at that time I had found any one to teach me the fear of God, my soul would have grown strong enough not to fall away. Afterwards, when the fear of God had utterly departed from me, the fear of dishonour alone remained, and was a torment to me in all I did. When I thought that nobody would ever know, I ventured upon many things that were neither honourable nor pleasing unto God. *The advantage of good company.*

7. In the beginning, these conversations did me harm—I believe so. The fault was perhaps not hers, but mine; for afterwards my own wickedness was enough to lead me astray, together with the servants about me, whom I found ready enough for all evil. If any one of these had given me good advice, I might perhaps have profited by it; but they were blinded by interest, as I was by passion. Still, I was never inclined to much evil,—for I hated naturally any thing dishonourable,—but only to the amusement of a pleasant conversation. The occasion of sin, however, being present, danger was at hand, and I exposed to it my father and *Her servants helped her astray.*

brothers. God delivered me out of it all, so that I should not be lost, in a manner visibly against my will, yet not so secretly as to allow me to escape without the loss of my good name and the suspicions of my father.

She is sent to the monastery of the Augustinians. 8. I had not spent, I think, three months in these vanities, when they took me to a monastery[1] in the city where I lived, in which children like myself were brought up, though their way of life was not so wicked as mine. This was done with the utmost concealment of the true reason, which was known only to myself and one of my kindred. They waited for an opportunity which would make the change seem nothing out of the way; for, as my sister was married, it was not fitting I should remain alone, without a mother, in the house.

Nothing can be hidden from God. 9. So excessive was my father's love for me, and so deep my dissembling, that he never would believe me to be so wicked as I was; and hence I was never in disgrace with him. Though some remarks were made, yet, as the time had been short, nothing could be positively asserted; and, as I was so much afraid about my good name, I had taken every care to be secret; and yet I never considered that I could conceal nothing from Him who seeth all things. O my God, what evil is done in the world by disregarding this, and thinking that any thing can be kept secret that is done against Thee! I am quite certain that great evils would be avoided if we clearly understood that what we have to do is, not to be on our guard against men, but on our guard against displeasing Thee.

The Saint is reconciled to her lot. 10. For the first eight days, I suffered much; but more from the suspicion that my vanity was known, than from being in the monastery; for I was already weary of myself,—and, though I offended God, I never ceased to have a great fear of Him, and contrived to go to confession as quickly as I could. I was very uncomfortable; but

---

[1] The Augustinian monastery of Our Lady of Grace. It was founded in 1509 by the Venerable Fra Juan of Seville, Vicar-General of the Order (*Reforma de los Descalços*, lib. i. ch. vii. n. 2). There were forty nuns in the house at this time (*De la Fuente*).

within eight days, I think sooner, I was much more contented than I had been in my father's house. All the nuns were pleased with me; for our Lord had given me the grace to please every one, wherever I might be. I was therefore made much of in the monastery. Though at this time I hated to be a nun, yet I was delighted at the sight of nuns so good; for they were very good in that house—very prudent, observant of the rule, and recollected.

11. Yet, for all this, the devil did not cease to tempt me; and people in the world sought means to trouble my rest with messages and presents. As this could not be allowed, it was soon over, and my soul began to return to the good habits of my earlier years; and I recognised the great mercy of God to those whom He places among good people. It seems as if His Majesty had sought and sought again how to convert me to Himself. Blessed be Thou, O Lord, for having borne with me so long! Amen. *Satan tries to disturb her.*

12. Were it not for my many faults, there was some excuse for me, I think, in this: that the conversation I shared in was with one who, I thought, would do well in the estate of matrimony;[1] and I was told by my confessors, and others also, whom in many points I consulted, used to say, that I was not offending God. One of the nuns[2] slept with us who were seculars, and through her it pleased our Lord to give me light, as I shall now explain. *The Saint's confessors admit her innocence.*

[1] Some have said that the Saint at this time intended, or wished, to be married; and F. Bouix translates the passage thus: "une alliance honorable pour moi." But it is more probable that the Saint had listened only to the story of her cousin's intended marriage; for in ch. v. § 12, she says that our Lord had always kept her from seeking to be loved of men.

[2] Doña Maria Brizeño, mistress of the secular children who were educated in the monastery (*Reforma*, lib. i. ch. vii. § 3).

CHAPTER III.

THE BLESSING OF BEING WITH GOOD PEOPLE—HOW CERTAIN ILLUSIONS WERE REMOVED.

The Saint complains of the hardness of her heart. 1. I BEGAN gradually to like the good and holy conversation of this nun. How well she used to speak of God! for she was a person of great discretion and sanctity. I listened to her with delight. I think there never was a time when I was not glad to listen to her. She began by telling me how she came to be a nun through the mere reading of the words of the Gospel: "Many are called, and few are chosen."[1] She would speak of the reward which our Lord gives to those who forsake all things for His sake. This good companionship began to root out the habits which bad companionship had formed, and to bring my thoughts back to the desire of eternal things, as well as to banish in some measure the great dislike I had to be a nun, which had been very great; and if I saw any one weep in prayer, or devout in any other way, I envied her very much; for my heart was now so hard, that I could not shed a tear, even if I read the Passion through. This was a grief to me.

She becomes more fervent. 2. I remained in the monastery a year and a half, and was very much the better for it. I began to say many vocal prayers, and to ask all the nuns to pray for me, that God would place me in that state wherein I was to serve Him; but, for all this, I wished not to be a nun, and that God would not be pleased I should be one, though at the same time I was afraid of marriage. At the end of my stay there, I had a greater inclination to be a nun, yet not in that house, on account of certain devotional practices which I understood prevailed there, and which I thought overstrained. Some of the younger ones encouraged me in this my wish; and if all had been of one mind, I might have profited by

---

[1] S. Matt. xx. 16: "Multi enim sunt vocati, pauci vero electi."

it. I had also a great friend[1] in another monastery; and this made me resolve, if I was to be a nun, not to be one in any other house than where she was. I looked more to the pleasure of sense and vanity than to the good of my soul. These good thoughts of being a nun came to me from time to time. They left me very soon; and I could not persuade myself to become one.

3. At this time, though I was not careless about my own good, our Lord was much more careful to dispose me for that state of life which was best for me. He sent me a serious illness, so that I was obliged to return to my father's house. *An illness.*

4. When I became well again, they took me to see my sister[2] in her house in the country village where she dwelt. Her love for me was so great, that, if she had had her will, I should never have left her. Her husband also had a great affection for me,—at least, he showed me all kindness. This too I owe rather to our Lord, for I have received kindness every where; and all my service in return is, that I am what I am. *Visits her sister,*

5. On the road lived a brother of my father[3]—a prudent and most excellent man, then a widower. Him too our Lord was preparing for Himself. In his old age, he left all his possessions and became a religious. He so finished his course, that I believe him to have the vision of God. He would have me stay with him some days. His practice was to read good books in Spanish; and his ordinary conversation was about God and the vanity of the world. These books he made me read to him; and, though I did not much like them, I appeared as if I did; for in giving pleasure *And an uncle on the way.*

---

[1] Juana Suarez, in the monastery of the Incarnation, Avila (*Reforma*, lib. i. ch. vii. § 7).

[2] Maria de Cepeda, married to Don Martin Guzman y Barrientos. They lived in Castellanos de la Cañada, where they had considerable property; but in the later years of their lives they were in straitened circumstances (*De la Fuente*). See below, ch. xxxiv. § 23.

[3] Don Pedro Sanchez de Cepeda. He lived in Hortigosa, four leagues from Avila (*De la Fuente*).

to others I have been most particular, though it might be painful to myself,—so much so, that what in others might have been a virtue was in me a great fault, because I was often extremely indiscreet. O my God, in how many ways did His Majesty prepare me for the state wherein it was His will I should serve Him!—how, against my own will, He constrained me to do violence to myself! May He be blessed for ever! Amen.

Her vocation. 6. Though I remained here but a few days, yet, through the impression made on my heart by the words of God both heard and read, and by the good conversation of my uncle, I came to understand the truth I had heard in my childhood, that all things are as nothing, the world vanity, and passing rapidly away. I also began to be afraid that, if I were then to die, I should go down to hell. Though I could not bend my will to be a nun, I saw that the religious state was the best and the safest. And thus, by little and little, I resolved to force myself into it.

Interior struggles. 7. The struggle lasted three months. I used to press this reason against myself: The trials and sufferings of living as a nun cannot be greater than those of purgatory, and I have well deserved to be in hell. It is not much to spend the rest of my life as if I were in purgatory, and then go straight to heaven—which was what I desired. I was more influenced by servile fear, I think, than by love, to enter religion.

Satan tempts her. 8. The devil put before me that I could not endure the trials of the religious life, because of my delicate nurture. I defended myself against him by alleging the trials which Christ endured, and that it was not much for me to suffer something for His sake; besides, He would help me to bear it. I must have thought so, but I do not remember this last consideration. I endured many temptations during these days. I was subject to fainting-fits, attended with fever,—for my health was always weak. I had become by this time fond of good books, and that gave me life. I read the Epistles of S. Jerome, which filled me with so much courage, that I resolved to tell my father of my purpose,—which was almost like taking the habit; for I was so jealous of my word, that I would never, for any consideration, recede from a promise when once my word had been given.

9. My father's love for me was so great, that I could never obtain his consent; nor could the prayers of others, whom I persuaded to speak to him, be of any avail. The utmost I could get from him was that I might do as I pleased after his death. I now began to be afraid of myself, and of my own weakness,—for I might go back. So, considering that such waiting was not safe for me, I obtained my end in another way, as I shall now relate. *Her father unwilling to recognise her vocation.*

CHAPTER IV.

OUR LORD HELPS HER TO BECOME A NUN—HER MANY INFIRMITIES.

1. IN those days, when I was thus resolved, I had persuaded one of my brothers,[1] by speaking to him of the vanity of the world, to become a friar; and we agreed together to set out one day very early in the morning for the monastery where that friend of mine lived for whom I had so great an affection:[2] though I would have gone to any other monastery, if I thought I should serve God better in it, or to any one my father liked, so strong was my resolution now to become a nun,—for I thought more of the salvation of my soul now, and made no account whatever of mine own ease. I remember perfectly well, and it is quite true, that the pain I *The Saint quits her father's house by stealth.*

---

[1] Antonio de Ahumada; who, according to the most probable opinion, entered the Dominican monastery of S. Thomas, Avila. It is said that he died before he was professed. Some say he joined the Hieronymites; but this is not so probable (*De la Fuente*). Ribera, however, says that he did enter the noviciate of the Hieronymites, but died before he was out of it (lib. i. ch. vi.).

[2] Juana Suarez, in the monastery of the Incarnation, Avila.

felt when I left my father's house was so great, that I do not believe the pain of dying will be greater,—for it seemed to me as if every bone in my body were wrenched asunder;[1] for, as I had no love of God to destroy my love of father and of kindred, this latter love came upon me with a violence so great that, if our Lord had not been my keeper, my own resolution to go on would have failed me. But He gave me courage to fight against myself, so that I executed my purpose.[2]

First fervours in religion. 2. When I took the habit,[3] our Lord at once made me understand how He helps those who do violence to themselves in order to serve Him. No one observed this violence in me; they saw nothing but the greatest good will. At that moment, because I was entering on that state, I was filled with a joy so great, that it has never failed me to this day; and God converted the aridity of my soul into the greatest tenderness. Every thing in religion was a delight unto me; and it is true that now and then I used to sweep the house during those hours of the day which I had formerly spent on my amusements and my dress; and, calling to mind that I was delivered from such follies, I was filled with a new joy that surprised me, nor could I understand whence it came.

Our own exertions blessed. 3. Whenever I remember this, there is nothing in the world, however hard it may be, that, if it were proposed to me, I would not undertake without any hesitation whatever; for I know now, by experience in many things, that if from the first I resolutely persevere in my purpose, even in this life His Majesty rewards it in a way which

---

[1] See *Relation*, vi. § 3.

[2] The nuns sent word to the father of his child's escape, and of her desire to become a nun, but without any expectation of obtaining his consent. He came to the monastery forthwith, and "offered up his Isaac on Mount Carmel" (*Reforma*, lib. i. ch. viii. § 5).

[3] The Saint entered the monastery of the Incarnation Nov. 2, 1533, and made her profession Nov. 3, 1534 (*Bollandists* and *Bouix*). Ribera says she entered Nov. 2, 1535; and the chronicler of the Order, relying on the contract by which her father bound himself to the monastery, says that she took the habit Nov. 2, 1536, and that Ribera had made a mistake.

he only understands who has tried it. When the act is done for God only, it is His will before we begin it that the soul, in order to the increase of its merits, should be afraid; and the greater the fear, if we do but succeed, the greater the reward, and the sweetness thence afterwards resulting. I know this by experience, as I have just said, in many serious affairs; and so, if I were a person who had to advise any body, I would never counsel any one, to whom good inspirations from time to time may come, to resist them through fear of the difficulty of carrying them into effect; for if a person lives detached for the love of God only, that is no reason for being afraid of failure, for He is omnipotent. May He be blessed for ever! Amen.

4. O supreme Good, and my Rest, those graces ought to have been enough which Thou hadst given me hitherto, seeing that Thy compassion and greatness had drawn me through so many windings to a state so secure, to a house where there are so many servants of God, from whom I might learn how I may advance in Thy service. I know not how to go on, when I call to mind the circumstances of my profession, the great resolution and joy with which I made it, and my betrothal unto Thee. I cannot speak of it without tears; and my tears ought to be tears of blood, my heart ought to break, and that would not be much to suffer because of the many offences against Thee which I have committed since that day. It seems to me now that I had good reasons for not wishing for this dignity, seeing that I have made so sad a use of it. But Thou, O my Lord, hast been willing to bear with me for almost twenty years of my evil using of Thy graces, till I might become better. It seems to me, O my God, that I did nothing but promise never to keep any of the promises then made to Thee. Yet such was not my intention: but I see that what I have done since is of such a nature, that I know not what my intention was. So it was and so it happened, that it may be the better known, O my Bridegroom, who Thou art and what I am.

The Saint's profession.

5. It is certainly true that very frequently the joy I have in that the multitude of Thy mercies is made known in me, softens the bitter sense of my

She bewails her shortcomings.

great faults. In whom, O Lord, can they shine forth as they do in me, who by my evil deeds have shrouded in darkness Thy great graces, which Thou hadst begun to work in me? Woe is me, O my Maker! If I would make an excuse, I have none to offer; and I only am to blame. For if I could return to Thee any portion of that love which Thou hadst begun to show unto me, I would give it only unto Thee, and then every thing would have been safe. But, as I have not deserved this, nor been so happy as to have done it, let Thy mercy, O Lord, rest upon me.

Her health fails.
6. The change in the habits of my life, and in my food, proved hurtful to my health; and though my happiness was great, that was not enough. The fainting-fits began to be more frequent; and my heart was so seriously affected, that every one who saw it was alarmed; and I had also many other ailments. And thus it was I spent the first year, having very bad health, though I do not think I offended God in it much. And as my illness was so serious,— I was almost insensible at all times, and frequently wholly so,—my father took great pains to find some relief; and as the physicians who attended me had none to give, he had me taken to a place which had a great reputation for the cure of other infirmities. They said I should find relief there.[1] That friend of whom I have spoken as being in the house went with me. She was one of the elder nuns. In the house where I was a nun, there was no vow of enclosure.[2]

She could not be cured.
7. I remained there nearly a year, for three months of it suffering most cruel tortures—effects of the violent remedies which they applied. I know not how I endured them; and indeed, though I submitted my-

---

[1] Her father took her from the monastery in the autumn of 1535, according to the Bollandists, but of 1538, according to the Chronicler, who adds, that she was taken to her uncle's house,—Pedro Sanchez de Cepeda, —in Hortigosa, and then to Castellanos de la Cañada, to the house of her sister, Doña Maria, where she remained till the spring, when she went to Bezadas for her cure (*Reforma*, lib. i. ch. xi. § 2).

[2] It was in 1563 that all nuns were compelled to observe enclosure (*Fuente*).

self to them, they were, as I shall relate,[1] more than my constitution could bear.

8. I was to begin the treatment in the spring, and went thither when winter commenced. The intervening time I spent with my sister, of whom I spoke before,[2] in her house in the country, waiting for the month of April, which was drawing near, that I might not have to go and return. The uncle of whom I have made mention before,[3] and whose house was on our road, gave me a book called *Tercer Abecedario*,[4] which treats of the prayer of recollection. Though in the first year I had read good books,—for I would read no others, because I understood now the harm they had done me,—I did not know how to make my prayer, nor how to recollect myself. I was therefore much pleased with the book, and resolved to follow the way of prayer it described with all my might. And as our Lord had already bestowed upon me the gift of tears, and I found pleasure in reading, I began to spend a certain time in solitude, to go frequently to confession, and make a beginning of that way of prayer, with this book for my guide; for I had no master—I mean, no confessor—who understood me, though I sought for such a one for twenty years afterwards: which did me much harm, in that I frequently went backwards, and might have been even utterly lost; for, anyhow, a director would have helped me to escape the risks I ran of sinning against God.

Stays at her sister's house.

9. From the very beginning, God was most gracious unto me. Though I was not so free from sin as the book required, I passed that by; such watchfulness seemed to me almost impossible. I was on my guard against mortal sin—and would to God I had always been so!—but I was careless about venial sins, and that was my ruin. Yet, for all this, at the end of my stay there,—I spent nearly nine months in the practice of solitude,—our Lord began to comfort me so much in this way of prayer, as in His mercy to raise me to the prayer of quiet, and now and then to that of union,

The prayer of quiet.

---

[1] Ch. v. § 15. [2] Ch. iii. § 4. [3] Ch. iii. § 5.
[4] By Fray Francisco de Osuna, of the Order of S. Francis (*Reforma*, lib. i. ch. xi. § 2).

though I understood not what either the one or the other was, nor the great esteem I ought to have had of them. I believe it would have been a great blessing to me if I had understood the matter. It is true that the prayer of union lasted but a short time: I know not if it continued for the space of an *Ave Maria;* but the fruits of it remained; and they were such that, though I was then not twenty years of age, I seemed to despise the world utterly; and so I remember how sorry I was for those who followed its ways, though only in things lawful.

<small>Her way of prayer.</small> 10. I used to labour with all my might to imagine Jesus Christ, our Good and our Lord, present within me. And this was the way I prayed. If I meditated on any mystery of His life, I represented it to myself as within me, though the greater part of my time I spent in reading good books, which was all my comfort; for God never endowed me with the gift of making reflections with the understanding, or with that of using the imagination to any good purpose: my imagination is so sluggish,[1] that even if I would think of, or picture to myself, as I used to labour to picture, our Lord's Humanity, I never could do it.

<small>Advantages of meditation.</small> 11. And though men may attain more quickly to the state of contemplation, if they persevere, by this way of inability to exert the intellect, yet is the process more laborious and painful; for if the will have nothing to occupy it, and if love have no present object to rest on, the soul is without support and without employment—its isolation and dryness occasion great pain, and the thoughts assail it most grievously. Persons in this condition must have greater purity of conscience than those who can make use of their understanding; for he who can use his intellect in the way of meditation on what the world is, on what he owes to God, on the great sufferings of God for him, his own scanty service in return, and on the reward God reserves for those who love Him, learns how to defend himself against his own thoughts, and against the occasions and perils of sin. On the other hand, he who has not that power is in greater danger, and ought to occupy him-

[1] See ch. ix. §§ 4, 7.

self much in reading, seeing that he is not in the slightest degree able to help himself.

12. This way of proceeding is so exceedingly pain- *Of reading.* ful, that if the master who teaches it insists on cutting off the succours which reading gives, and requires the spending of much time in prayer, then, I say, it will be impossible to persevere long in it; and if he persists in his plan, health will be ruined, because it is a most painful process. Reading is of great service towards procuring recollection in any one who proceeds in this way; and it is even necessary for him, however little it may be that he reads, if only as a substitute for the mental prayer which is beyond his reach.

13. Now I seem to understand that it was the *The Saint glad that she* good providence of our Lord over me that found no *could not find* one to teach me. If I had, it would have been im- *a director at this time.* possible for me to persevere during the eighteen years of my trial and of those great aridities, because of my inability to meditate. During all this time, it was only after Communion that I ever ventured to begin my prayer without a book,—my soul was as much afraid to pray without one, as if it had to fight against a host. With a book to help me,—it was like a companion, and a shield whereon to receive the blows of many thoughts,—I found comfort; for it was not usual with me to be in aridity; but I always was so when I had no book; for my soul was disturbed, and my thoughts wandered at once. With one, I began to collect my thoughts, and, using it as a decoy, kept my soul in peace, very frequently by merely opening a book—there was no necessity for more. Sometimes, I read but little; at other times, much—according as our Lord had pity on me.

14. It seemed to me, in these beginnings of which *She recounts* I am speaking, that there could be no danger capable *the mercies of God to her.* of withdrawing me from so great a blessing, if I had but books, and could have remained alone; and I believe that, by the grace of God, it would have been so, if I had had a master or any one to warn me against those occasions of sin in the beginning, and, if I fell, to bring me quickly out of them. If the devil had assailed me openly then, I believe

I should never have fallen into any grievous sin; but he was so subtle, and I so weak, that all my good resolutions were of little service,—though, in those days in which I served God, they were very profitable in enabling me, with that patience which His Majesty gave me, to endure the alarming illnesses which I had to bear. I have often thought with wonder of the great goodness of God; and my soul has rejoiced in the contemplation of His great magnificence and mercy. May He be blessed for ever!—for I see clearly that He has not omitted to reward me, even in this life, for every one of my good desires. My good works, however wretched and imperfect, have been made better and perfected by Him who is my Lord: He has rendered them meritorious. As to my evil deeds and my sins, He hid them at once. The eyes of those who saw them, He made even blind; and He has blotted them out of their memory. He gilds my faults, makes virtue to shine forth, giving it to me Himself, and compelling me to possess it, as it were, by force.

15. I must now return to that which has been enjoined me. I say, that if I had to describe minutely how our Lord dealt with me in the beginning, it would be necessary for me to have another understanding than that I have: so that I might be able to appreciate what I owe to Him, together with my own ingratitude and wickedness; for I have forgotten it all.

May He be blessed for ever who has borne with me so long! Amen.

CHAPTER V.

ILLNESS AND PATIENCE OF THE SAINT—THE STORY OF A PRIEST WHOM SHE RESCUED FROM A LIFE OF SIN.

Her noviciate. 1. I FORGOT to say how, in the year of my noviciate, I suffered much uneasiness about things in themselves of no importance; but I was found fault with very often when I was blameless. I bore it painfully and with imperfection; however, I went through it all, because of the joy I had in being a nun. When they saw me seeking to be alone, and even weeping over my sins at times, they thought I was discontented, and said so.

2. All religious observances had an attraction for me, but I could not endure any which seemed to make me contemptible. I delighted in being thought well of by others, and was very exact in every thing I had to do. All this I thought was a virtue, though it will not serve as any excuse for me, because I knew what it was to procure my own satisfaction in every thing, and so ignorance does not blot out the blame. There may be some excuse in the fact that the monastery was not founded in great perfection. I, wicked as I was, followed after that which I saw was wrong, and neglected that which was good. *Self-accusation.*

3. There was then in the house a nun labouring under a most grievous and painful disorder, for there were open ulcers in her body, caused by certain obstructions, through which her food was rejected. Of this sickness she soon died. All the sisters, I saw, were afraid of her malady. I envied her patience very much; I prayed to God that He would give me a like patience; and then, whatever sickness it might be His pleasure to send, I do not think I was afraid of any, for I was resolved on gaining eternal good, and determined to gain it by any and by every means. *Sick nun in the house, whose patience the Saint envies.*

4. I am surprised at myself because then I had not, as I believe, that love of God which I think I had after I began to pray. Then, I had only light to see that all things that pass away are to be lightly esteemed, and that the good things to be gained by despising them are of great price, because they are for ever. His Majesty heard me also in this, for in less than two years I was so afflicted myself that the illness which I had, though of a different kind from that of the sister, was, I really believe, not less painful and trying for the three years it lasted, as I shall now relate. *God sends her an illness.*

5. When the time had come for which I was waiting in the place I spoke of before[1]—I was in my sister's house, for the purpose of undergoing the *She leaves her convent for a time.*

[1] Ch. iv. § 6. The person to whom she was taken was a woman

medical treatment—they took me away with the utmost care of my comfort; that is, my father, my sister, and the nun, my friend, who had come from the monastery with me,—for her love for me was very great. At that moment, Satan began to trouble my soul; God, however, brought forth a great blessing out of that trouble.

6. In the place to which I had gone for my cure *Of unlearned confessors.* lived a priest of good birth and understanding, with some learning, but not much. I went to confession to him, for I was always fond of learned men, although confessors indifferently learned did my soul much harm; for I did not always find confessors whose learning was as good as I could wish it was. I know by experience that it is better, if the confessors are good men and of holy lives, that they should have no learning at all, than a little; for such confessors never trust themselves without consulting those who are learned— nor would I trust them myself: and a really learned confessor never deceived me.[1] Neither did the others willingly deceive me, only they knew no better; I thought they were learned, and that I was not under any other obligation than that of believing them, as their instructions to me were lax, and left me more at liberty—for if they had been strict with me, I am so wicked, I should have sought for others. That which was a venial sin, they told me was no sin at all; of that which was most grievously mortal, they said it was venial.[2]

7. This did me so much harm, that it is no wonder *The Saint excuses her confessors, and blames herself.* I should speak of it here as a warning to others, that they may avoid an evil so great; for I see clearly that in the eyes of God I was without excuse, that

famous for certain cures she had wrought, but whose skill proved worse than useless to the Saint (*Reforma*, lib. i. ch. ii. § 2).

[1] Schram, *Theolog. Mystic.*, § 483. "Magni doctores scholastici, si non sint spirituales, vel omni rerum spiritualium experientia careant, non solent esse magistri spirituales idonei,—nam theologia scholastica est perfectio intellectus; mystica, perfectio intellectus et voluntatis: unde bonus theologus scholasticus potest esse malus theologus mysticus. In rebus tamen difficilibus, dubiis, spiritualibus, præstat mediocriter spiritualem theologum consulere quam spiritualem idiotam."

[2] See *Way of Perfection*, ch. viii. § 2; but ch. v. ed. Doblado.

the things I did being in themselves not good, this should have been enough to keep me from them. I believe that God, by reason of my sins, allowed those confessors to deceive themselves and to deceive me. I myself deceived many others by saying to them what had been said to me.

8. I continued in this blindness, I believe, more than seventeen years, till a most learned Dominican father[1] undeceived me in part, and those of the Company of Jesus made me altogether so afraid, by insisting on the erroneousness of these principles, as I shall hereafter show.[2] *Her delusions removed.*

9. I began, then, by going to confession to that priest of whom I spoke before.[3] He took an extreme liking to me, because I had then but little to confess in comparison with what I had afterwards; and I had never much to say since I became a nun. There was no harm in the liking he had for me, but it ceased to be good, because it was in excess. He clearly understood that I was determined on no account whatever to do any thing whereby God might be seriously offended. He, too, gave me a like assurance about himself, and accordingly our conferences were many. But at that time, through the knowledge and fear of God which filled my soul, what gave me most pleasure in all my conversations with others was to speak of God; and, as I was so young, this made him ashamed; and then, out of that great good will he bore me, he began to tell me of his wretched state. It was very sad, for he had been nearly seven years in a most perilous condition, because of his affection for, and conversation with, a woman of that place; and yet he used to say Mass. The matter was so public, that his honour and good name were lost, and no one ventured to speak to him about it. I was extremely sorry for him, because I liked him much. I was then so imprudent and so blind as to think it a virtue to be grateful and loyal to one who liked me. Cursed be that loyalty which reaches so far as to go against the law of God. It is a madness common in the world, and it makes me mad to see it. We are indebted to God for all the *The conversion of a careless priest.*

[1] F. Vicente Barron (*Bouix*). [2] See ch. xxiii. [3] § 6.

good that men do to us, and yet we hold it to be an act of virtue not to break a friendship of this kind, though it lead us to go against Him. Oh, blindness of the world! Let me, O Lord, be most ungrateful to the world; never at all unto Thee. But I have been altogether otherwise through my sins.

Sorcery.
10. I procured further information about the matter from members of his household; I learned more of his ruinous state, and saw that the poor man's fault was not so grave, because the miserable woman had had recourse to enchantments, by giving him a little image made of copper, which she had begged him to wear for love of her around his neck; and this no one had influence enough to persuade him to throw away. As to this matter of enchantments, I do not believe it to be altogether true; but I will relate what I saw, by way of warning to men to be on their guard against women who will do things of this kind. And let them be assured of this, that women,—for they are more bound to purity than men,—if once they have lost all shame before God, are in nothing whatever to be trusted; and that in exchange for the gratification of their will, and of that affection which the devil suggests, they will hesitate at nothing.

11. Though I have been so wicked myself, I never *Self-upbraidings.* fell into any thing of this kind, nor did I ever attempt to do evil; nor, if I had the power, would I have ever constrained any one to like me, for our Lord kept me from this. But if He had abandoned me, I should have done wrong in this, as I did in other things,—for there is nothing in me whereon any one may rely.

She prepares the way for awakening the priest.
12. When I knew this, I began to show him greater affection; my intention was good, but the act was wrong, for I ought not to do the least wrong for the sake of any good, how great soever it may be. I spoke to him most frequently of God; and this must have done him good—though I believe that what touched him most was his great affection for me, because, to do me a pleasure, he gave me that little image of copper, and I had it at once thrown into a river. When he had given it up, like a man roused from deep sleep, he began to consider all that he had done in those

years; and then, amazed at himself, lamenting his ruinous state, that woman came to be hateful in his eyes. Our Lady must have helped him greatly, for he had a very great devotion to her Conception, and used to keep the feast thereof with great solemnity. In short, he broke off all relations with that woman utterly, and was never weary of giving God thanks for the light He had given him; and at the end of the year from the day I first saw him, he died.

13. He had been most diligent in the service of God; and as for that great affection he had for me, Spiritual friendships. I never observed any thing wrong in it, though it might have been of greater purity. There were also occasions wherein he might have most grievously offended, if he had not kept himself in the near presence of God. As I said before,[1] I would not then have done any thing I knew was a mortal sin. And I think that observing this resolution in me helped him to have that affection for me; for I believe that all men must have a greater affection for those women whom they see disposed to be good: and even for the attainment of earthly ends, women must have more power over men because they are good, as I shall show hereafter. I am convinced that the priest is in the way of salvation. He died most piously, and completely withdrawn from that occasion of sin. It seems that it was the will of our Lord he should be saved by these means.

14. I remained three months in that place, in the most grievous sufferings; for the treatment was too The Saint's sufferings. severe for my constitution. In two months—so strong were the medicines—my life was nearly worn out; and the severity of the pain in the heart,[2] for the cure of which I was there, was much more keen: it seemed to me, now and then, as if it had been seized by sharp teeth. So great was the torment, that it was feared it might end in madness. There was a great loss of strength, for I could eat nothing whatever, only drink. I had a great loathing for food, and a fever that never left me. I was so reduced, for they had given me purgatives daily for nearly a month, and so parched up, that my sinews began to shrink. The pains I had were unendurable, and I

[1] § 9. [2] Ch. iv. § 6.

was overwhelmed in a most deep sadness, so that I had no rest either night or day.

The physicians despair of her.
15. This was the result; and thereupon my father took me back. Then the physicians visited me again. All gave me up; they said I was also consumptive. This gave me little or no concern; what distressed me were the pains I had—for I was in pain from my head down to my feet. Now, nervous pains, according to the physicians, are intolerable; and all my nerves were shrunk. Certainly, if I had not brought this upon myself by my sins, the torture would have been unendurable.

The Saint's patience.
16. I was not more than three months in this cruel distress, for it seemed impossible that so many ills could be borne together. I now am astonished at myself; and the patience His Majesty gave me—for it clearly came from Him—I look upon as a great mercy of our Lord. It was a great help to me to be patient, that I had read the story of Job, in the *Morals of S. Gregory* (our Lord seems to have prepared me thereby); and that I had begun the practice of prayer, so that I might bear it all, conforming my will to the will of God. All my conversation was with God. I had continually these words of Job in my thoughts and in my mouth: "If we have received good things of the hand of our Lord, why should we not receive evil things?"[1] This seemed to give me courage.

Her death apprehended.
17. The feast of our Lady, in August, came round; from April until then I had been in great pain, but more especially during the last three months. I made haste to go to confession, for I had always been very fond of frequent confession. They thought I was driven by the fear of death; and so my father, in order to quiet me, would not suffer me to go. Oh, the unreasonable love of flesh and blood! Though it was that of a father so Catholic and so wise—he was very much so, and this act of his could not be the effect of any ignorance on his part—what evil it might have done me!

[1] Job ii. 10: "Si bona suscepimus de manu Domini, mala quare non suscipiamus?"

18. That very night my sickness became so acute, that for about four days I remained insensible. They administered the Sacrament of the last Anointing, and every hour, or rather every moment, thought I was dying; they did nothing but repeat the *Credo*, as if I could have understood any thing they said. They must have regarded me as dead more than once, for I found afterwards drops of wax on my eyelids. My father, because he had not allowed me to go to confession, was grievously distressed. Loud cries and many prayers were made to God: blessed be He who heard them.

Receives the last Sacrament.

19. For a day and a half the grave was open in my monastery, waiting for my body;[1] and the friars of our Order, in a house at some distance from this place, performed funeral solemnities. But it pleased our Lord I should come to myself. I wished to go to confession at once. I communicated with many tears; but I do not think those tears had their source in that pain and sorrow only for having offended God, which might have sufficed for my salvation—unless, indeed, the delusion which I laboured under were some excuse for me, and into which I had been led by those who had told me that some things were not mortal sins which afterwards I found were so certainly.

She recovers.

20. Though my sufferings were unendurable, and my perceptions dull, yet my confession, I believe, was complete as to all matters wherein I understood myself to have offended God. This grace, among others, did His Majesty bestow on me, that ever since my first Communion never in confession have I failed to confess any thing I thought to be a sin, though it might be only a venial sin. But I think that undoubtedly my salvation was in great peril, if I had died at that time—partly because my confessors were so unlearned, and partly because I was so very wicked. It is certainly true that when I think of it, and consider how our Lord seems

Integrity of her confession.

---

[1] Some of the nuns of the Incarnation were in the house, sent thither from the monastery; and, but for the father's disbelief in her death, would have taken her home for burial (*Ribera*, lib. i. ch. vii.).

to have raised me up from the dead, I am so filled with wonder, that I almost tremble with fear.[1]

Thanksgiving. 21. And now, O my soul, it were well for thee to look that danger in the face from which our Lord delivered thee; and if thou dost not cease to offend Him out of love, thou shouldst do so out of fear. He might have slain thee a thousand times, and in a far more perilous state. I believe I exaggerate nothing if I say a thousand times again, though he may rebuke me who has commanded me to restrain myself in recounting my sins; and they are glossed over enough. I pray him, for the love of God, not to suppress one of my faults, because herein shines forth the magnificence of God, as well as His long-suffering towards souls. May He be blessed for evermore, and destroy me utterly, rather than let me cease to love Him any more!

CHAPTER VI.

THE GREAT DEBT SHE OWED TO OUR LORD FOR HIS MERCY TO HER—SHE TAKES S. JOSEPH FOR HER PATRON.

Bodily sufferings of the Saint. 1. AFTER those four days, during which I was insensible, so great was my distress, that our Lord alone knoweth the intolerable sufferings I endured. My tongue was bitten to pieces; there was a choking in my throat because I had taken nothing, and because of my weakness, so that I could not swallow even a drop of water; all my bones seemed to be out of joint, and the disorder of my head was extreme. I was bent together like a coil of ropes—for to this was I brought by the torture of those days—unable to move either arm, or foot, or hand, or head, any more than if I had been dead, unless others moved me; I could move, however, I think, one finger of my right hand. Then, as to touching me, that was impossible, for I was so bruised that I could not

---

[1] Ribera, lib. i. ch. vii., says he heard Fra Bañes, in a sermon, say that the Saint told him she had, during these four days, seen hell in a vision. And the Chronicler says that though there was bodily illness, yet it was a trance of the soul at the same time (vol. i. lib. i. ch. xii. § 3).

endure it. They used to move me in a sheet, one holding one end, and another the other. This lasted till Palm Sunday.[1]

2. The only comfort I had was this,—if no one came near me, my pains frequently ceased; and then, because I had a little rest, I considered myself well, for I was afraid my patience would fail: and thus I was exceedingly happy when I saw myself free from those pains which were so sharp and constant, though in the cold fits of an intermittent fever, which were most violent, they were still unendurable. My dislike of food was very great. *Her patience.*

3. I was now so anxious to return to my monastery, that I had myself conveyed thither in the state I was in. There they received alive one whom they had waited for as dead; but her body was worse than dead: the sight of it could only give pain. It is impossible to describe my extreme weakness, for I was nothing but bones. I remained in this state, as I have already said,[2] more than eight months; and was paralytic, though getting better, for about three years. I praised God when I began to crawl on my hands and knees. I bore all this with great resignation, and, if I except the beginning of my illness, with great joy; for all this was as nothing in comparison with the pains and tortures I had to bear at first. I was resigned to the will of God, even if He left me in this state for ever. My anxiety about the recovery of my health seemed to be grounded on my desire to pray in solitude, as I had been taught; for there were no means of doing so in the infirmary. I went to confession most frequently, spoke much about God, and in such a way as to edify every one; and they all marvelled at the patience which our Lord gave me—for if it had not come from the hand of His Majesty, *Severity of her sufferings.*

---

[1] March 25, 1537.

[2] Ch. v. § 17. The Saint left her monastery in 1535; and in the spring of 1536 went from her sister's house to Bezadas; and in July of that year was brought back to her father's house in Avila, wherein she remained till Palm Sunday 1537, when she returned to the monastery of the Incarnation. She had been seized with paralysis there, and laboured under it nearly three years, from 1536 to 1539, when she was miraculously healed through the intercession of S. Joseph (*Bolland.* n. 100, 101). The dates of the Chronicler are different from these.

it seemed impossible to endure so great an affliction with so great a joy.

The gift of prayer. Government of the tongue. 4. It was a great thing for me to have had the grace of prayer which God had wrought in me; it made me understand what it is to love Him. In a little while, I saw these virtues renewed within me; still they were not strong, for they were not sufficient to sustain me in justice. I never spoke ill in the slightest degree whatever of any one, and my ordinary practice was to avoid all detraction; for I used to keep most carefully in mind that I ought not to assent to, nor say of another, anything I should not like to have said of myself. I was extremely careful to keep this resolution on all occasions; though not so perfectly, upon some great occasions that presented themselves, as not to break it sometimes. But my ordinary practice was this: and thus those who were about me, and those with whom I conversed, became so convinced it was right, that they adopted it as a habit. It came to be understood that where I was, absent persons were safe; so they were also with my friends and kindred, and with those whom I instructed. Still, for all this, I have a strict account to give unto God for the bad example I gave in other respects. May it please His Majesty to forgive me, for I have been the cause of much evil; though not with intentions as perverse as were the acts that followed.

5. The longing for solitude remained, and I loved *Her love of solitude.* to discourse and speak of God; for if I found any one with whom I could do so, it was a greater joy and satisfaction to me than all the refinements—or rather, to speak more correctly, the real rudeness—of the world's conversation. I communicated and confessed more frequently still, and desired to do so; I was extremely fond of reading good books. I was most deeply penitent for having offended God; and I remember that very often I did not dare to pray, because I was afraid of that most bitter anguish which I felt for having offended God, dreading it as a great chastisement. This grew upon me afterwards to so great a degree, that I know of no torment wherewith to compare it; and yet it was neither more nor less because of any fear I had at any time, for it came

upon me only when I remembered the consolations of our Lord which He gave me in prayer, the great debt I owed Him, the evil return I made: I could not bear it. I was also extremely angry with myself on account of the many tears I shed for my faults, when I saw how little I improved, seeing that neither my good resolutions, nor the pains I took, were sufficient to keep me from falling whenever I had the opportunity. I looked on my tears as a delusion; and my faults, therefore, I regarded as the more grievous, because I saw the great goodness of our Lord to me in the shedding of those tears, and together with them such deep compunction.

6. I took care to go to confession as soon as I could; and, as I think, did all that was possible on my part to return to a state of grace. But the whole evil lay in my not thoroughly avoiding the occasions of sin, and in my confessors, who helped me so little. If they had told me that I was travelling on a dangerous road, and that I was bound to abstain from those conversations, I believe, without any doubt, that the matter would have been remedied, because I could not bear to remain even for one day in mortal sin, if I knew it. *Her watchfulness over herself.*

7. All these tokens of the fear of God came to me through prayer; and the greatest of them was this, that fear was swallowed up of love,—for I never thought of chastisement. All the time I was so ill, my strict watch over my conscience reached to all that is mortal sin.

8. O my God! I wished for health, that I might serve Thee better; that was the cause of all my ruin. For when I saw how helpless I was through paralysis, being still so young, and how the physicians of this world had dealt with me, I determined to ask those of heaven to heal me —for I wished, nevertheless, to be well, though I bore my illness with great joy. Sometimes, too, I used to think that if I recovered my health, and yet were lost for ever, I was better as I was. But, for all that, I thought I might serve God much better if I were well This is our delusion: we do not resign ourselves absolutely to the disposition of our Lord, who knows best what is for our good. *In perplexity about her health.*

D

9. I began by having Masses and prayers said for my intention—prayers that were highly sanctioned; for I never liked those other devotions which some people, especially women, make use of with a ceremoniousness to me intolerable, but which move them to be devout. I have been given to understand since that they were unseemly and superstitious; and I took for my patron and lord the glorious S. Joseph, and recommended myself earnestly to him. I saw clearly that both out of this my present trouble, and out of others of greater importance, relating to my honour and the loss of my soul, this my father and lord delivered me, and rendered me greater services than I knew how to ask for. I cannot call to mind that I have ever asked him at any time for any thing which he has not granted; and I am filled with amazement when I consider the great favours which God hath given me through this blessed Saint; the dangers from which he hath delivered me, both of body and of soul. To other Saints, our Lord seems to have given grace to succour men in some special necessity; but to this glorious Saint, I know by experience, to help us in all: and our Lord would have us understand that, as He was Himself subject to him upon earth,—for S. Joseph having the title of father, and being His guardian, could command Him,—so now in heaven He performs all his petitions. I have asked others to recommend themselves to S. Joseph, and they too know this by experience; and there are many who are now of late devout to him,[1] having had experience of this truth.

Her devotion to S. Joseph.

10. I used to keep his feast with all the solemnity I could, but with more vanity than spirituality, seeking rather too much splendour and effect, and yet with good intentions. I had this evil in me, that if our

Keeps his feast.

---

[1] Of the devotion to S. Joseph, F. Faber (*The Blessed Sacrament*, bk. ii. p. 199, 3d ed.) says that it took its rise in the west, in a confraternity in Avignon. "Then it spread over the Church. Gerson was raised up to be its doctor and theologian, and S. Teresa to be its Saint, and S. Francis of Sales to be its popular teacher and missionary. The houses of Carmel were like the holy house of Nazareth to it; and the colleges of the Jesuits, its peaceful sojourns in dark Egypt."

Lord gave me grace to do any good, that good became full of imperfections and of many faults; but as for doing wrong, the indulgence of curiosity and vanity, I was very skilful and active therein. Our Lord forgive me!

11. Would that I could persuade all men to be devout to this glorious Saint; for I know by long experience what blessings he can obtain for us from God. I have never known any one who was really devout to him, and who honoured him by particular services, who did not visibly grow more and more in virtue; for he helps in a special way those souls who commend themselves to him. It is now some years since I have always on his feast asked him for something, and I always have it. If the petition be in any way amiss, he directs it aright for my greater good. *Wishes to spread devotion to him.*

12. If I were a person who had authority to write, it would be a pleasure to me to be diffusive in speaking most minutely of the graces which this glorious Saint has obtained for me and for others. But that I may not go beyond the commandment that is laid upon me, I must in many things be more brief than I could wish, and more diffusive than is necessary in others; for, in short, I am a person who, in all that is good, has but little discretion. But I ask, for the love of God, that he who does not believe me will make the trial for himself,—when he will see by experience the great good that results from commending oneself to this glorious patriarch, and being devout to him. Those who give themselves to prayer should in a special manner have always a devotion to S. Joseph; for I know not how any man can think of the Queen of the angels, during the time that she suffered so much with the Infant Jesus, without giving thanks to S. Joseph for the services he rendered them then. He who cannot find any one to teach him how to pray, let him take this glorious Saint for his master, and he will not wander out of the way. *She recommends those who would pray to invoke S. Joseph. S. Joseph and the sacred Infancy.*

13. May it please our Lord that I have not done amiss in venturing to speak about S. Joseph; for, though I publicly profess my devotion to him, I have *Her gratitude to S. Joseph.*

always failed in my service to him and imitation of him. He was like himself when he made me able to rise and walk, no longer a paralytic; and I, too, am like myself when I make so bad a use of this grace.

Self-reproaches of the Saint.

14. Who could have said that I was so soon to fall, after such great consolations from God—after His Majesty had implanted virtues in me which of themselves made me serve Him—after I had been, as it were, dead, and in such extreme peril of eternal damnation—after He had raised me up, soul and body, so that all who saw me marvelled to see me alive? What can it mean, O my Lord? The life we live is so full of danger! While I am writing this,—and it seems to me, too, by Thy grace and mercy,—I may say with S. Paul, though not so truly as he did: "It is not I who live now; but Thou, my Creator, livest in me."[1] For some years past—so it seems to me—Thou hast held me by the hand; and I see in myself desires and resolutions—in some measure tested by experience in many ways during that time—never to do any thing, however slight it may be, contrary to Thy will, though I must have frequently offended Thy Divine Majesty without being aware of it; and I also think that nothing can be proposed to me that I should not with great resolution undertake for Thy love. In some things, Thou hast Thyself helped me to succeed therein. I love neither the world nor the things of the world; nor do I believe that any thing that does not come from Thee can give me pleasure; every thing else seems to me a heavy cross.

The Saint's detachment and distrust of self.

15. Still, I may easily deceive myself, and it may be that I am not what I say I am; but Thou knowest, O my Lord, that, to the best of my knowledge, I lie not. I am afraid, and with good reason, lest Thou shouldst abandon me; for I know now how far my strength and little virtue can reach, if Thou be not ever at hand to supply them, and to help me never to forsake Thee. May His Majesty grant that I be not forsaken of Thee even now, when I am thinking all this of myself!

[1] Galat. ii. 20 : "Vivo autem, jam non ego ; vivit vero in me Christus."

16. I know not how we can wish to live, seeing that every thing is so uncertain. Once, O Lord, I thought it impossible to forsake Thee so utterly; and now that I have forsaken Thee so often, I cannot help being afraid; for when Thou didst withdraw but a little from me, I fell down to the ground at once. Blessed for ever be Thou! Though I have forsaken Thee, Thou hast not forsaken me so utterly but that Thou hast come again and raised me up, giving me Thy hand always. Very often, O Lord, I would not take it: very often I would not listen when Thou wert calling me again, as I am going to show.

Self-reproach.

CHAPTER VII.

LUKEWARMNESS—THE LOSS OF GRACE—INCONVENIENCE OF LAXITY IN RELIGIOUS HOUSES.

1. So, then, going on from pastime to pastime, from vanity to vanity, from one occasion of sin to another, I began to expose myself exceedingly to the very greatest dangers: my soul was so distracted by many vanities, that I was ashamed to draw near unto God in an act of such special friendship as that of prayer.[1] As my sins multiplied, I began to lose the pleasure and comfort I had in virtuous things: and that loss contributed to the abandonment of prayer. I see now most clearly, O my Lord, that this comfort departed from me because I had departed from Thee.

A.D. 1541. The Saint becomes lukewarm,

2. It was the most fearful delusion into which Satan could plunge me—to give up prayer under the pretence of humility. I began to be afraid of giving myself to prayer, because I saw myself so lost. I thought it would be better for me, seeing that in my wickedness I was one of the most wicked, to live like the multitude—to say the prayers which I was bound to say, and that vocally, not to practise mental prayer, nor com-

And neglects prayer, through false humility.

[1] See *Way of Perfection*, ch. xl.; but ch. xxv. of the former editions.

mune with God so much; for I deserved to be with the devils, and was deceiving those who were about me, because I made an outward show of goodness; and therefore the community in which I dwelt is not to be blamed; for with my cunning I so managed matters, that all had a good opinion of me; and yet I did not seek this deliberately by simulating devotion; for in all that relates to hypocrisy and ostentation—glory be to God!—I do not remember that I ever offended Him,[1] so far as I know. The very first movements herein gave me such pain, that the devil would depart from me with loss, and the gain remained with me; and thus, accordingly, he never tempted me much in this way. Perhaps, however, if God had permitted Satan to tempt me as sharply herein as he tempted me in other things, I should have fallen also into this; but His Majesty has preserved me until now. May He be blessed for evermore! It was rather a heavy affliction to me that I should be thought so well of; for I knew my own secret.

Thought well of in her convent, 3. The reason why they thought I was not so wicked was this: they saw that I, who was so young, and exposed to so many occasions of sin, withdrew myself so often into solitude for prayer, read much, spoke of God, that I liked to have His image painted in many places, to have an oratory of my own, and furnish it with objects of devotion, that I spoke ill of no one, and other things of the same kind in me which have the appearance of virtue. Yet all the while I was so vain—I knew how to procure respect for myself by doing those things which in the world are usually regarded with respect.

And treated with great respect. 4. In consequence of this, they gave me as much liberty as they did to the oldest nuns,—and even more,—and had great confidence in me; for as to taking any liberty for myself, or doing any thing without leave,—such as conversing through the door, or in secret, or by night,—I do not think I could have brought myself to speak with any body in the monastery in that way, and I never did it; for our Lord held me back. It seemed

[1] See *Relation*, i. § 18.

to me—for I considered many things carefully and of set purpose—that it would be a very evil deed on my part, wicked as I was, to risk the credit of so many nuns, who were all good,—as if every thing else I did was well done! In truth, the evil I did was not the result of deliberation,—as this would have been, if I had done it,—although it was too much so.

5. Therefore, I think that it did me much harm to be in a monastery not enclosed. The liberty which those who were good might have with advantage— they not being obliged to do more than they do, because they had not bound themselves to enclosure—would certainly have led me, who am wicked, straight to hell, if our Lord, by so many remedies and means of His most singular mercy, had not delivered me out of that danger,—and it is, I believe, the very greatest danger,—namely, a monastery of women unenclosed,—yea, more, I think it is, for those who will be wicked, a road to hell, rather than a help to their weakness. This is not to be understood of my monastery; for there are so many there who in the utmost sincerity, and in great perfection, serve our Lord, so that His Majesty, according to His goodness, cannot but be gracious unto them; neither is it one of those which are most open; for all religious observances are kept in it: and I am speaking only of others which I have seen and known. *Received harm from being in a monastery where enclosure was not kept.*

6. I am exceedingly sorry for these houses, because our Lord must of necessity send His special inspirations not merely once, but many times, if the nuns therein are to be saved,—seeing that the honours and amusements of the world are allowed among them, and the obligations of their state are so ill-understood. God grant they may not count that to be virtue which is sin, as I did so often! It is very difficult to make people understand this; it is necessary our Lord Himself should take the matter seriously into His own hands. *Dangers of lax religious houses.*

7. If parents would take my advice, now that they are at no pains to place their daughters where they may walk in the way of salvation without incurring a greater risk than they would do if they *Parents should be careful about their children's souls.*

were left in the world, let them look at least at that which concerns their good name. Let them marry them to persons of a much lower degree, rather than place them in monasteries of this kind, unless they be of extremely good inclinations,—and God grant that these inclinations may come to good!—or let them keep them at home. If they will be wicked at home, their evil life can be hidden only for a short time; but in monasteries it can be hidden long, and, in the end, it is our Lord that discovers it. They injure not only themselves, but all the nuns also. And all the while the poor things are not in fault; for they walk in the way that is shown them. Many of them are to be pitied; for they wished to withdraw from the world,—and, thinking to escape from the dangers of it, and that they were going to serve our Lord, have found themselves in ten worlds at once, without knowing what to do, or how to help themselves. Youth and sensuality and the devil invite them and incline them to follow certain ways which are of the essence of worldliness. They see these ways, so to speak, considered as safe there.

Heretics self-condemned.
8. Now, these seem to me to be in some degree like those wretched heretics who will make themselves blind, and who will consider that which they do to be good, and so believe, but without really believing; for they have within themselves something that tells them it is wrong.

Dangers of laxity.
9. Oh, what utter ruin! utter ruin of religious persons—I am not speaking now more of women than of men—where the rules of the Order are not kept; where the same monastery offers two roads: one of virtue and observance, the other of inobservance, and both equally frequented! I have spoken incorrectly: they are not equally frequented; for, on account of our sins, the way of the greatest imperfection is the most frequented; and because it is the broadest, it is also the most in favour. The way of religious observance is so little used, that the friar and the nun who would really begin to follow their vocation thoroughly have reason to fear the members of their communities more than all the devils together. They must be more cautious, and

dissemble more, when they would speak of that friendship with God which they desire to have, than when they would speak of those friendships and affections which the devil arranges in monasteries. I know not why we are astonished that the Church is in so much trouble, when we see those, who ought to be an example of every virtue to others, so disfigure the work which the spirit of the Saints departed wrought in their Orders. May it please His Divine Majesty to apply a remedy to this, as He sees it to be needful! Amen.

10. So, then, when I began to indulge in these conversations, I did not think, seeing they were customary, that my soul must be injured and dissipated, as I afterwards found it must be, by such conversations. I thought that, as receiving visits was so common in many monasteries, no more harm would befall me thereby than befell others, whom I knew to be good. I did not observe that they were much better than I was, and that an act which was perilous for me was not so perilous for them; and yet I have no doubt there was some danger in it, were it nothing else but a waste of time. *Converse with seculars.*

11. I was once with a person,—it was at the very beginning of my acquaintance with her,—when our Lord was pleased to show me that these friendships were not good for me: to warn me, also, and in my blindness, which was so great, to give me light. Christ stood before me, stern and grave, giving me to understand what in my conduct was offensive to Him. I saw Him with the eyes of the soul more distinctly than I could have seen Him with the eyes of the body. The vision made so deep an impression upon me, that, though it is more than twenty-six years ago,[1] I seem to see Him present even now. I was greatly astonished and disturbed, and I resolved not to see that person again. *An intellectual vision.*

12. It did me much harm that I did not then know it was possible to see any thing otherwise *Her perplexity about the vision.*

[1] A.D. 1537, when the Saint was twenty-two years old (*Bouix*). This passage, therefore, must be one of the additions to the second Life; for the first was written in 1562, twenty-five years only after the vision.

than with the eyes of the body;[1] so did Satan too, in that he helped me to think so: he made me understand it to be impossible, and suggested that I had imagined the vision— that it might be Satan himself—and other suppositions of that kind. For all this, the impression remained with me that the vision was from God, and not an imagination; but, as it was not to my liking, I forced myself to lie to myself; and as I did not dare to discuss the matter with any one, and as great importunity was used, I went back to my former conversation with the same person, and with others also, at different times; for I was assured that there was no harm in seeing such a person, and that I gained, instead of losing, reputation by doing so. I spent many years in this pestilent amusement; for it never appeared to me, when I was engaged in it, to be so bad as it really was,—though at times I saw clearly it was not good. But no one caused me the same distraction which that person did of whom I am speaking; and that was because I had a great affection for her.

Another vision. 13. At another time, when I was with that person, we saw, both of us, and others who were present also saw, something like a great toad crawling towards us, more rapidly than such a creature is in the habit of crawling. I cannot understand how a reptile of that kind could, in the middle of the day, have come forth from that place; it never had done so before;[2] but the impression it made on me was such, that I think it must have had a meaning; neither have I ever forgotten it. Oh, the greatness of God! with what care and tenderness didst Thou warn me in every way! and how little I profited by those warnings!

A good religious warns the Saint. 14. There was in that house a nun, who was related to me, now grown old, a great servant of God, and a strict observer of the rule. She too warned me from time to time; but I not only did not listen to her, but was even offended, thinking she was scandalised without

[1] See ch. xxvii. § 3.
[2] In the parlour of the monastery of the Incarnation, Avila, a painting of this is preserved to this day (*De la Fuente*).

cause. I have mentioned this in order that my wickedness and the great goodness of God might be understood, and to show how much I deserved hell for ingratitude so great, and, moreover, if it should be our Lord's will and pleasure that any nun at any time should read this, that she might take warning by me. I beseech them all, for the love of our Lord, to flee from such recreations as these.

15. May His Majesty grant I may undeceive some one of the many I led astray when I told them there was no harm in these things, and assured them there was no such great danger therein. I did so because I was blind myself; for I would not deliberately lead them astray. By the bad example I set before them,—I spoke of this before,[1]—I was the occasion of much evil, not thinking I was doing so much harm. <small>*The Saint regrets her follies.*</small>

16. In those early days, when I was ill, and before I knew how to be of use to myself, I had a very strong desire to further the progress of others:[2] a most common temptation of beginners. With me, however, it had good results. Loving my father so much, I longed to see him in the possession of that good which I seemed to derive myself from prayer. I thought that in this life there could not be a greater good than prayer; and so, by roundabout ways, as well as I could, I contrived to make him enter upon it; I gave him books for that end. As he was so good,—I said so before,[3]—this exercise took such a hold upon him, that in five or six years, I think it was, he made so great a progress that I used to praise our Lord for it. It was a very great consolation to me. He had most grievous trials of diverse kinds; and he bore them all with the greatest resignation. He came often to see me; for it was a comfort to him to speak of the things of God. <small>*Persuades her father to practise mental prayer.*</small>

17. And now that I had become so dissipated, and had ceased to pray, and yet saw that he still thought I was what I used to be, I could not endure it, and so undeceived him. I had been a year and more without praying, thinking it an act of greater humility to abstain. <small>*She gives up the practice of mental prayer,*</small>

[1] Ch. vi. § 4.   [2] See *Inner Fortress*, v. iii. § 1.   [3] Ch. i. § 1.

This—I shall speak of it again[1]—was the greatest temptation I ever had, because it very nearly wrought my utter ruin;[2] for, when I used to pray, if I offended God one day, on the following days I would recollect myself, and withdraw farther from the occasions of sin.

And tells her father of her neglect. 18. When that blessed man, having that good opinion of me, came to visit me, it pained me to see him so deceived as to think that I used to pray to God as before. So I told him that I did not pray; but I did not tell him why. I put my infirmities forward as an excuse; for though I had recovered from that which was so troublesome, I have always been weak, even very much so; and though my infirmities are somewhat less troublesome now than they were, they still afflict me in many ways: specially, I have been suffering for twenty years from sickness every morning,[3] so that I could not take any food till past midday, and even occasionally not till later; and now, since my Communions have become more frequent, it is at night, before I lie down to rest, that the sickness occurs, and with greater pain; for I have to bring it on with a feather, or other means. If I do not bring it on, I suffer more; and thus I am never, I believe, free from great pain, which is sometimes very acute, especially about the heart; though the fainting-fits are now but of rare occurrence. I am also, these eight years past, free from the paralysis, and from other infirmities of fever, which I had so often. These afflictions I now regard so lightly, that I am even glad of them, believing that our Lord in some degree takes His pleasure in them.

Her excuses. 19. My father believed me when I gave him that for a reason, as he never told a lie himself; neither should I have done so, considering the relation we were in. I told him, in order to be the more easily believed, that it was much for me to be able to attend in choir, though I saw clearly that this was no excuse whatever; neither, however, was it a sufficient reason for giving up a practice which does not require, of necessity, bodily strength, but only love and a habit thereof;

---

[1] Ch. xix. §§ 9, 17.   [2] See § 2, above.
[3] See ch. xi. § 26; *Inner Fortress*, vi. i. § 8.

yet our Lord always furnishes an opportunity for it, if we but seek it. I say always; for though there may be times, as in illness, and from other causes, when we cannot be much alone, yet it never can be but there must be opportunities when our strength is sufficient for the purpose; and in sickness itself, and amidst other hindrances, true prayer consists, when the soul loves, in offering up its burden, and in thinking of Him for whom it suffers, and in the resignation of the will, and in a thousand ways which then present themselves. It is under these circumstances that love exerts itself; for it is not necessarily prayer when we are alone; and neither is it not prayer when we are not.

20. With a little care, we may find great blessings on those occasions when our Lord, by means of afflictions, deprives us of time for prayer; and so I found it when I had a good conscience. But my father, having that opinion of me which he had, and because of the love he bore me, believed all I told him; moreover, he was sorry for me; and as he had now risen to great heights of prayer himself, he never remained with me long; for when he had seen me, he went his way, saying that he was wasting his time. As I was wasting it in other vanities, I cared little about this. *Her father's progress.*

21. My father was not the only person whom I prevailed upon to practise prayer, though I was walking in vanity myself. When I saw persons fond of reciting their prayers, I showed them how to make a meditation, and helped them and gave them books; for from the time I began myself to pray, as I said before,[1] I always had a desire that others should serve God. I thought now that I did not myself serve our Lord according to the light I had, that the knowledge His Majesty had given me ought not to be lost, and that others should serve Him for me.[2] I say this in order to explain the great blindness I was in: going to ruin myself, and labouring to save others. *She teaches others also.*

22. At this time, that illness befell my father of which he died;[3] it lasted some days. I went to *Her father's illness.*

[1] § 16.   [2] See *Inner Fortress*, v. iii. § 1.
[3] In 1541, when the Saint was twenty-five years of age (*Bouix*).

nurse him, being more sick in spirit than he was in body, owing to my many vanities,—though not, so far as I know, to the extent of being in mortal sin,—through the whole of that wretched time of which I am speaking; for, if I knew myself to be in mortal sin, I would not have continued in it on any account. I suffered much myself during his illness. I believe I rendered him some service in return for what he had suffered in mine. Though I was very ill, I did violence to myself; and though in losing him I was to lose all the comfort and good of my life,—he was all this to me,—I was so courageous, that I never betrayed my sorrows, concealing them till he was dead, as if I felt none at all. It seemed as if my very soul were wrenched when I saw him at the point of death—my love for him was so deep.

He receives the last Sacraments.
23. It was a matter for which we ought to praise our Lord—the death that he died, and the desire he had to die; so also was the advice he gave us after the last anointing, how he charged us to recommend him to God, and to pray for mercy for him, how he bade us serve God always, and consider how all things come to an end. He told us with tears how sorry he was that he had not served Him himself; for he wished he was a friar—I mean, that he had been one in the strictest Order that is. I have a most assured conviction that our Lord, some fifteen days before, had revealed to him he was not to live; for up to that time, though very ill, he did not think so; but now, though he was somewhat better, and the physicians said so, he gave no heed to them, but employed himself in the ordering of his soul.

Is consoled by his daughter.
24. His chief suffering consisted in a most acute pain of the shoulders, which never left him: it was so sharp at times, that it put him into great torture. I said to him, that as he had so great a devotion to our Lord carrying His cross on His shoulders, he should now think that His Majesty wished him to feel somewhat of that pain which He then suffered Himself. This so comforted him, that I do not think I heard him complain afterwards.

His death.
25. He remained three days without consciousness; but on the day he died, our Lord restored him

so completely, that we were astonished: he preserved his understanding to the last; for in the middle of the creed, which he repeated himself, he died. He lay there like an angel,—such he seemed to me, if I may say so, both in soul and disposition: he was very good.

26. I know not why I have said this, unless it be for the purpose of showing how much the more I am to be blamed for my wickedness; for after seeing such a death, and knowing what his life had been, I, in order to be in any wise like unto such a father, ought to have grown better. His confessor, a most learned Dominican,[1] used to say that he had no doubt he went straight to heaven.[2] He had heard his confession for some years, and spoke with praise of the purity of his conscience. *The purity of his life.*

27. This Dominican father, who was a very good man, fearing God, did me a very great service; for I confessed to him. He took upon himself the task of helping my soul in earnest, and of making me see the perilous state I was in.[3] He sent me to Communion once a fortnight;[4] and I, by degrees beginning to speak to him, told him about my prayer. He charged me never to omit it: that, anyhow, it could not do me any thing but good. I began to return to it,—though I did not cut off the occasions of sin,—and never afterwards gave it up. My life became most wretched, because I learned in prayer more and more of my faults. On one side, God was calling me; on the other, I was following the world. All the things of God gave me great pleasure; and I was a prisoner to the things of the world. It seemed as if I wished to reconcile two contradictions, so much at variance one with another as are the life of the spirit and the joys and pleasures and amusements of sense.[5] *The Saint resumes the practice of prayer.*

[1] F. Vicente Barron (*Reforma*, lib. i. ch. xv.).
[2] See ch. xxxviii. § 1.
[3] See ch. xix. § 20.
[4] The Spanish editor calls attention to this as a proof of great laxity in those days—that a nun like S. Teresa should be urged to communicate as often as once in a fortnight.
[5] See ch. xiii § 7, 8.

28. I suffered much in prayer; for the spirit was slave, and not master; and so I was not able to shut myself up within myself—that was my whole method of prayer—without shutting up with me a thousand vanities at the same time. I spent many years in this way; and I am now astonished that any one could have borne it without abandoning either the one or the other. I know well that it was not in my power then to give up prayer, because He held me in His hand who sought me that He might show me greater mercies.

Prayer proves difficult.

29. O my God! if I might, I would speak of the occasions from which God delivered me, and how I threw myself into them again; and of the risks I ran of losing utterly my good name, from which He delivered me. I did things to show what I was; and our Lord hid the evil, and revealed some little virtue—if so be I had any—and made it great in the eyes of all, so that they always held me in much honour. For although my follies came occasionally into light, people would not believe it when they saw other things, which they thought good. The reason is, that He who knoweth all things saw it was necessary it should be so, in order that I might have some credit given me by those to whom in after years I was to speak of His service. His supreme munificence regarded not my great sins, but rather the desires I frequently had to please Him, and the pain I felt because I had not the strength to bring those desires to good effect.

The Saint accuses herself.

30. O Lord of my soul! how shall I be able to magnify the graces which Thou, in those years, didst bestow upon me? Oh, how, at the very time that I offended Thee most, Thou didst prepare me in a moment, by a most profound compunction, to taste of the sweetness of Thy consolations and mercies! In truth, O my King, Thou didst administer to me the most delicate and painful chastisement it was possible for me to bear; for Thou knewest well what would have given me the most pain. Thou didst chastise my sins with great consolations. I do not believe I am saying foolish things, though it may well be that I am beside

How God prepared her.

myself whenever I call to mind my ingratitude and my wickedness.

31. It was more painful for me, in the state I was in, to receive graces, when I had fallen into grievous faults, than it would have been to receive chastisement; for one of those faults, I am sure, used to bring me low, shame and distress me, more than many diseases, together with many heavy trials, could have done. For, as to the latter, I saw that I deserved them; and it seemed to me that by them I was making some reparation for my sins, though it was but slight,—for my sins are so many. But when I see myself receive graces anew, after being so ungrateful for those already received, that is to me—and, I believe, to all who have any knowledge or love of God—a fearful kind of torment. We may see how true this is by considering what a virtuous mind must be. Hence my tears and vexation when I reflected on what I felt, seeing myself in a condition to fall at every moment, though my resolutions and desires then—I am speaking of that time—were strong. *The multitude of God's graces distresses her.*

32. It is a great evil for a soul to be alone in the midst of such great dangers; it seems to me that if I had had any one with whom I could have spoken of all this, it might have helped me not to fall. I might, at least, have been ashamed before him—and yet I was not ashamed before God. *Advantage of a director,*

33. For this reason, I would advise those who give themselves to prayer, particularly at first, to form friendships, and converse familiarly, with others who are doing the same thing. It is a matter of the last importance, even if it lead only to helping one another by prayer: how much more, seeing that it has led to much greater gain! Now, if in their intercourse one with another, and in the indulgence of human affections even not of the best kind, men seek friends with whom they may refresh themselves, and for the purpose of having greater satisfaction in speaking of their empty joys, I know no reason why it should not be lawful for him who is beginning to love and serve God in earnest to confide to another his joys and sorrows; for *And of communicating to others our joys and trials.*

they who are given to prayer are thoroughly accustomed to both.

34. For if that friendship with God which he desires be real, let him not be afraid of vain-glory; and if the first movements thereof assail him, he will escape from it with merit; and I believe that he who will discuss the matter with this intention will profit both himself and those who hear him, and thus will derive more light for his own understanding, as well as for the instruction of his friends. He who in discussing his method of prayer falls into vain-glory will do so also when he hears Mass devoutly, if he is seen of men, and in doing other good works, which must be done under pain of being no Christian; and yet these things must not be omitted through fear of vain-glory.

Vain-glory.

35. Moreover, it is a most important matter for those souls who are not strong in virtue; for they have so many people, enemies as well as friends, to urge them the wrong way, that I do not see how this point is capable of exaggeration. It seems to me that Satan has employed this artifice,—and it is of the greatest service to him,— namely, that men who really wish to love and please God should hide the fact, while others, at his suggestion, make open show of their malicious dispositions; and this is so common, that it seems a matter of boasting now, and the offences committed against God are thus published abroad.

An artifice of Satan.

36. I do not know whether the things I am saying are foolish or not. If they be so, your reverence will strike them out. I entreat you to help my simplicity by adding a good deal to this, because the things that relate to the service of God are so feebly managed, that it is necessary for those who would serve Him to join shoulder to shoulder, if they are to advance at all; for it is considered safe to live amidst the vanities and pleasures of the world, and few there be who regard them with unfavourable eyes. But if any one begins to give himself up to the service of God, there are so many to find fault with him, that it becomes necessary for him to seek companions, in order that he may find protection among them till he grows strong enough

The friends of God should be more courageous.

not to feel what he may be made to suffer. If he does not, he will find himself in great straits.

37. This, I believe, must have been the reason why some of the Saints withdrew into the desert. And it is a kind of humility in man not to trust to himself, but to believe that God will help him in his relations with those with whom he converses; and charity grows by being diffused; and there are a thousand blessings herein which I would not dare to speak of, if I had not known by experience the great importance of it. It is very true that I am the most wicked and the basest of all who are born of women; but I believe that he who, humbling himself, though strong, yet trusteth not in himself, and believeth another who in this matter has had experience, will lose nothing. Of myself I may say that, if our Lord had not revealed to me this truth, and given me the opportunity of speaking very frequently to persons given to prayer, I should have gone on falling and rising till I tumbled into hell. I had many friends to help me to fall; but as to rising again, I was so much left to myself, that I wonder now I was not always on the ground. I praise God for His mercy; for it was He only who stretched out His hand to me. May He be blessed for ever! Amen. *[marginal note: How much her confessors helped the Saint.]*

CHAPTER VIII.

THE SAINT CEASES NOT TO PRAY—PRAYER THE WAY TO RECOVER WHAT IS LOST—ALL EXHORTED TO PRAY—THE GREAT ADVANTAGE OF PRAYER, EVEN TO THOSE WHO MAY HAVE CEASED FROM IT.

1. IT is not without reason that I have dwelt so long on this portion of my life. I see clearly that it will give no one pleasure to see any thing so base; and certainly I wish those who may read this to have me in abhorrence, as a soul so obstinate and so ungrateful to Him who did so much for me. I could wish, too, I had permission to say how often at this time I failed in my duty to God, because *[marginal note: The Saint deplores her past life.]*

I was not leaning on the strong pillar of prayer. I passed nearly twenty years on this stormy sea, falling and rising, but rising to no good purpose, seeing that I went and fell again. My life was one of perfection; but it was so mean, that I scarcely made any account whatever of venial sins; and though of mortal sins I was afraid, I was not so afraid of them as I ought to have been, because I did not avoid the perilous occasions of them. I may say that it was the most painful life that can be imagined, because I had no sweetness in God, and no pleasure in the world.

The Saint perseveres in prayer.
2. When I was in the midst of the pleasures of the world, the remembrance of what I owed to God made me sad; and when I was praying to God, my worldly affections disturbed me. This is so painful a struggle, that I know not how I could have borne it for a month, let alone for so many years. Nevertheless, I can trace distinctly the great mercy of our Lord to me, while thus immersed in the world, in that I had still the courage to pray. I say courage, because I know of nothing in the whole world which requires greater courage than plotting treason against the King, knowing that He knows it, and yet never withdrawing from His presence; for, granting that we are always in the presence of God, yet it seems to me that those who pray are in His presence in a very different sense: for they, as it were, see that He is looking upon them; while others may be for days together without even once recollecting that God sees them.

Watches over herself.
3. It is true, indeed, that during these years there were many months, and, I believe, occasionally a whole year, in which I so kept guard over myself that I did not offend our Lord, gave myself much to prayer, and took some pains, and that successfully, not to offend Him. I speak of this now, because all I am saying is strictly true; but I remember very little of those good days, and so they must have been few; while my evil days were many. Still, the days that passed over without my spending a great part of them in prayer were few, unless I was very ill, or very much occupied.

4. When I was ill, I was well with God. I contrived that those about me should be so too, and I made supplications to our Lord for this grace, and spoke frequently of Him. Thus, with the exception of that year of which I have been speaking, during eight-and-twenty years of prayer I spent more than eighteen in that strife and contention which arose out of my attempts to reconcile God and the world. As to the other years, of which I have now to speak, in them the grounds of the warfare, though it was not slight, were changed; but inasmuch as I was—at least, I think so—serving God, and aware of the vanity of the world, all has been pleasant, as I shall show hereafter.[1]

Her struggles.

5. The reason, then, of my telling this at so great a length is that, as I have just said,[2] the mercy of God and my ingratitude, on the one hand, may become known; and, on the other, that men may understand how great is the good which God works in a soul when He gives it a disposition to pray in earnest, though it may not be so well prepared as it ought to be. If that soul perseveres in spite of sins, temptations, and relapses, brought about in a thousand ways by Satan, our Lord will bring it at last—I am certain of it—to the harbour of salvation, as He has brought me myself; for so it seems to me now. May His Majesty grant I may never go back and be lost! He who gives himself to prayer is in possession of a great blessing, of which many saintly and good men have written,—I am speaking of mental prayer,—glory be to God for it; and, if they had not done so, I am not proud enough, though I have but little humility, to presume to discuss it.

The advantages of mental prayer.

6. I may speak of that which I know by experience; and so I say, let him never cease from prayer who has once begun it, be his life ever so wicked; for prayer is the way to amend it, and without prayer such amendment will be much more difficult. Let him not be tempted by Satan, as I was, to give it up, on the pretence of humility;[3] let him rather believe that His words are true who says that, if we truly repent, and resolve never to offend Him,

Let him not grow weary of prayer who has once begun it.

[1] Ch. ix. § 10. [2] § 1, above. [3] Ch. vii. § 17; ch. xix. § 9.

He will take us into His favour again,[1] give us the graces He gave us before, and occasionally even greater, if our repentance deserve it. And as to him who has not begun to pray, I implore him by the love of our Lord not to deprive himself of so great a good.

Mental prayer.

7. Herein there is nothing to be afraid of, but every thing to hope for. Granting that such a one does not advance, nor make an effort to become perfect, so as to merit the joys and consolations which the perfect receive from God, yet he will by little and little attain to a knowledge of the road which leads to heaven. And if he perseveres, I hope in the mercy of God for him, seeing that no one ever took Him for his friend that was not amply rewarded; for mental prayer is nothing else, in my opinion, but being on terms of friendship with God, frequently conversing in secret with Him who, we know, loves us. Now, true love and lasting friendship require certain dispositions: those of our Lord, we know, are absolutely perfect; ours, vicious, sensual, and thankless; and you cannot, therefore, bring yourselves to love Him as He loves you, because you have not the disposition to do so; and if you do not love Him, yet, seeing how much it concerns you to have His friendship, and how great is His love for you, rise above that pain you feel at being much with Him who is so different from you.

Patience of God.

8. O infinite goodness of my God! I seem to see Thee and myself in this relation to one another. O Joy of the angels! when I consider it, I wish I could wholly die of love! How true it is that Thou endurest those who will not endure Thee! Oh, how good a friend art Thou, O my Lord! how Thou comfortest and endurest, and also waitest for them to make themselves like unto Thee, and yet, in the mean while, art Thyself so patient of the state they are in! Thou takest into account the occasions during which they seek Thee, and for a moment of penitence forgettest their offences against Thyself.

[1] Ezech. xviii. 21: "Si autem impius egerit pœnitentiam, ... vita vivet, et non morietur. Omnium iniquitatum ejus . . . non recordabor."

9. I have seen this distinctly in my own case, and I cannot tell why the whole world does not labour to draw near to Thee in this particular friendship. The wicked, who do not resemble Thee, ought to do so, in order that Thou mayest make them good, and for that purpose should permit Thee to remain with them at least for two hours daily, even though they may not remain with Thee but, as I used to do, with a thousand distractions, and with worldly thoughts. In return for this violence which they offer to themselves for the purpose of remaining in a company so good as Thine,—for at first they can do no more, and even afterwards at times,— Thou, O Lord, defendest them against the assaults of evil spirits, whose power Thou restrainest, and even lessenest daily, giving to them the victory over these their enemies. So it is, O Life of all lives, Thou slayest none that put their trust in Thee, and seek Thy friendship; yea, rather, Thou sustainest their bodily life in greater vigour, and makest their soul to live.

God helps those who try to pray.

10. I do not understand what there can be to make them afraid who are afraid to begin mental prayer, nor do I know what it is they dread. The devil does well to bring this fear upon us, that he may really hurt us; if, by putting me in fear, he can make me cease from thinking of my offences against God, of the great debt I owe Him, of the existence of heaven and hell, and of the great sorrows and trials He underwent for me. That was all my prayer, and had been, when I was in this dangerous state, and it was on those subjects I dwelt whenever I could; and very often, for some years, I was more occupied with the wish to see the end of the time I had appointed for myself to spend in prayer, and in watching the hour-glass, than with other thoughts that were good. If a sharp penance had been laid upon me, I know of none that I would not very often have willingly undertaken, rather than prepare myself for prayer by self-recollection. And certainly the violence with which Satan assailed me was so irresistible, or my evil habits were so strong, that I did not betake myself to prayer; and the sadness I felt on entering the oratory was so great, that it required all the courage I had to

The Saint's prayer.

force myself in. They say of me that my courage is not slight, and it is known that God has given me a courage beyond that of a woman; but I have made a bad use of it. In the end, our Lord came to my help; and then, when I had done this violence to myself, I found greater peace and joy than I sometimes had when I had a desire to pray.

Prayer victorious in the end.

11. If, then, our Lord bore so long with me, who was so wicked,—and it is plain that it was by prayer all my evil was corrected,—why should any one, how wicked soever he may be, have any fear ? Let him be ever so wicked, he will not remain in his wickedness so many years as I did, after receiving so many graces from our Lord. Is there any one who can despair, when He bore so long with me, only because I desired and contrived to find some place and some opportunities for Him to be alone with me,—and that very often against my will ? for I did violence to myself, or rather our Lord Himself did violence to me.

The blessings of prayer.

12. If, then, to those who do not serve God, but rather offend Him, prayer be all this, and so necessary, and if no one can really find out any harm it can do him, and if the omission of it be not a still greater harm, why, then, should they abstain from it who serve and desire to serve God? Certainly I cannot comprehend it, unless it be that men have a mind to go through the troubles of this life in greater misery, and to shut the door in the face of God, so that He shall give them no comfort in it. I am most truly sorry for them, because they serve God at their own cost; for of those who pray, God Himself defrays the charges, seeing that for a little trouble He gives sweetness, in order that, by the help it supplies, they may bear their trials.

Prayer the door by which God enters the soul.

13. But because I have much to say hereafter of this sweetness, which our Lord gives to those who persevere in prayer,[1] I do not speak of it here; only this will I say : prayer is the door to those great graces which our Lord bestowed upon me. If this door be shut, I do not see how He can bestow them ; for even if He entered into a soul to take His delight therein, and to make that soul

[1] See ch. x. § 2, and ch. xi. § 22.

also delight in Him, there is no way by which He can do so; for His will is, that such a soul should be lonely and pure, with a great desire to receive His graces. If we put many hindrances in the way, and take no pains whatever to remove them, how can He come to us, and how can we have any desire that He should show us His great mercies?

14. I will speak now—for it is very important to understand it—of the assaults which Satan directs against a soul for the purpose of taking it, and of the contrivances and compassion wherewith our Lord labours to convert it to Himself, in order that men may behold His mercy, and the great good it was for me that I did not give up prayer and spiritual reading, and that they may be on their guard against the dangers against which I was not on my guard myself. And, above all, I implore them for the love of our Lord, and for the great love with which He goeth about seeking our conversion to Himself, to beware of the occasions of sin; for once placed therein, we have no ground to rest on,— so many enemies then assail us, and our own weakness is such, that we cannot defend ourselves. *Necessity of avoiding occasions of sin.*

15. Oh, that I knew how to describe the captivity of my soul in those days! I understood perfectly that I was in captivity, but I could not understand the nature of it; neither could I entirely believe that those things which my confessors did not make so much of were so wrong as I in my soul felt them to be. One of them— I had gone to him with a scruple—told me that, even if I were raised to high contemplation, those occasions and conversations were not unfitting for me. This was towards the end, when, by the grace of God, I was withdrawing more and more from those great dangers, but not wholly from the occasions of them. *The interior struggles of the Saint. Ignorant confessors.*

16. When they saw my good desires, and how I occupied myself in prayer, I seemed to them to have done much; but my soul knew that this was not doing what I was bound to do for Him to whom I owed so much. I am sorry for my poor soul even now, because of its great sufferings, and the little help it had from any one except God, and for the wide door that man opened for it, that it might go forth to *Her regrets.*

its pastimes and pleasures, when they said that these things were lawful.

17. Then there was the torture of sermons, and <small>Her delight in sermons.</small> that not a slight one; for I was very fond of them. If I heard any one preach well and with unction, I felt, without my seeking it, a particular affection for him, neither do I know whence it came. Thus, no sermon ever seemed to me so bad, but that I listened to it with pleasure; though, according to others who heard it, the preaching was not good. If it was a good sermon, it was to me a most special refreshment. To speak of God, or to hear Him spoken of, never wearied me. I am speaking of the time after I gave myself to prayer. At one time I had great comfort in sermons, at another they distressed me, because they made me feel that I was very far from being what I ought to have been.

18. I used to pray to our Lord for help; but, as <small>The Saint's lamentation over her early life of prayer.</small> it now seems to me, I must have committed the fault of not putting my whole trust in His Majesty, and of not thoroughly distrusting myself. I sought for help, took great pains; but it must be that I did not understand how all is of little profit if we do not root out all confidence in ourselves, and place it wholly in God. I wished to live, but I saw clearly that I was not living, but rather wrestling with the shadow of death; there was no one to give me life, and I was not able to take it. He who could have given it me had good reasons for not coming to my aid, seeing that He had brought me back to Himself so many times, and I as often had left Him.

CHAPTER IX.

THE MEANS WHEREBY OUR LORD QUICKENED HER SOUL, GAVE HER LIGHT IN HER DARKNESS, AND MADE HER STRONG IN GOODNESS.

1. My soul was now grown weary; and the <small>A picture of the Crucifixion.</small> miserable habits it had contracted would not suffer it to rest, though it was desirous of doing so. It came to pass one day, when I went into the oratory, that I

saw a picture which they had put by there, and which had been procured for a certain feast observed in the house. It was a representation of Christ most grievously wounded; and so devotional, that the very sight of it, when I saw it, moved me,—so well did it show forth that which He suffered for us. So keenly did I feel the evil return I had made for those wounds, that I thought my heart was breaking. I threw myself on the ground beside it, my tears flowing plenteously, and implored Him to strengthen me once for all, so that I might never offend Him any more.

2. I had a very great devotion to the glorious Magdalene, and very frequently used to think of her conversion—especially when I went to Communion. As I knew for certain that our Lord was then within me, I used to place myself at His feet, thinking that my tears would not be despised. I did not know what I was saying; only He did great things for me, in that He was pleased I should shed those tears, seeing that I so soon forgot that impression. I used to recommend myself to that glorious Saint, that she might obtain my pardon. *The Saint's devotion to S. Mary Magdalene.*

3. But this last time, before that picture of which I am speaking, I seem to have made greater progress; for I was now very distrustful of myself, placing all my confidence in God. It seems to me that I said to Him then that I would not rise up till He granted my petition. I do certainly believe that this was of great service to me, because I have grown better ever since.[1] *Her fervent prayer.*

4. This was my method of prayer: as I could not make reflections with my understanding, I contrived to picture Christ as within me;[2] and I used to find myself the better for thinking of those mysteries of His life during which He was most lonely. It seemed to me that the being alone and afflicted, like a person in trouble, must needs permit me to come near unto Him. *Her inability to make a meditation.*

5. I did many simple things of this kind; and in particular I used to find myself most at home in the prayer in the Garden, whither I went in His *Her meditation on the Passion.*

---
[1] In the year 1555 (*Bouix*).   [2] See ch. iv. § 11; ch. x. § 1.

company. I thought of the bloody sweat, and of the affliction He endured there; I wished, if it had been possible, to wipe away that painful sweat from His face; but I remember that I never dared to form such a resolution,—my sins stood before me so grievously. I used to remain with Him there as long as my thoughts allowed me, and I had many thoughts to torment me. For many years, nearly every night before I fell asleep, when I recommended myself to God, that I might sleep in peace, I used always to think a little of this mystery of the prayer in the Garden—yea, even before I was a nun, because I had been told that many indulgences were to be gained thereby. For my part, I believe that my soul gained very much in this way, because I began to practise prayer without knowing what it was; and now that it had become my constant habit, I was saved from omitting it, as I was from omitting to bless myself with the sign of the cross before I slept.

<small>Benefits of the method of prayer which the Saint now had.</small> 6. And now to go back to what I was saying of the torture which my thoughts inflicted upon me. This method of praying, in which the understanding makes no reflections, hath this property: the soul must gain much, or lose. I mean, that those who advance without meditation make great progress, because it is done by love. But to attain to this involves great labour, except to those persons whom it is our Lord's good pleasure to lead quickly to the prayer of quiet. I know of some. For those who walk in this way, a book is profitable, that by the help thereof they may the more quickly recollect themselves. It was a help to me also to look on fields, water, and flowers.[1] In them I saw traces of the Creator—I mean, that the sight of these things was as a book unto me; it roused me, made me recollected, and reminded me of my ingratitude and of my sins. My understanding was so dull, that I could never represent in the imagination either heavenly or high things in any form whatever until our Lord placed them before me in another way.[2]

<small>Of the good of images.</small> 7. I was so little able to put things before me by the help of my understanding, that, unless I saw a thing with my eyes, my imagination was of no use

---

[1] See *Relation*, i. § 12. [2] See ch. iv. § 11.

whatever. I could not do as others do, who can put matters before themselves so as to become thereby recollected. I was able to think of Christ only as man. But so it was; and I never could form any image of Him to myself, though I read much of His beauty, and looked at pictures of Him. I was like one who is blind, or in the dark, who, though speaking to a person present, and feeling his presence, because he knows for certain that he is present,—I mean, that he understands him to be present, and believes it,—yet does not see him. It was thus with me when I used to think of our Lord. This is why I was so fond of images. Wretched are they who, through their own fault, have lost this blessing; it is clear enough that they do not love our Lord—for if they loved Him, they would rejoice at the sight of His picture, just as men find pleasure when they see the portrait of one they love.

8. At this time, the *Confessions* of S. Augustine were given me. Our Lord seems to have so ordained it, for I did not seek them myself, neither had I ever seen them before. I have a very great devotion to S. Augustine, because the monastery in which I lived when I was yet in the world was of his Order;[1] and also because he had been a sinner—for I used to find great comfort in those Saints whom, after they had sinned, our Lord converted to Himself. I thought they would help me, and that, as our Lord had forgiven them, so also He would forgive me. One thing, however, there was that troubled me—I have spoken of it before[2]— our Lord had called them but once, and they never relapsed; while my relapses were now so many. This it was that vexed me. But calling to mind the love that He bore me, I took courage again. Of His mercy I never doubted once, but I did very often of myself.

The Saint's trust in God.

9. O my God, I am amazed at the hardness of my heart amidst so many succours from Thee. I am filled with dread when I see how little I could do with myself, and how I was clogged, so that I could not resolve to give myself entirely to God. When I began to read the *Confessions*, I thought I saw myself there described, and began

Reads the Confessions of S. Augustine.

[1] Ch. ii. § 8.   [2] In the Prologue.

to recommend myself greatly to this glorious Saint. When I came to his conversion, and read how he heard that voice in the garden, it seemed to me nothing less than that our Lord had uttered it for me: I felt so in my heart. I remained for some time lost in tears, in great inward affliction and distress. O my God, what a soul has to suffer because it has lost the liberty it had of being mistress over itself! and what torments it has to endure! I wonder now how I could live in torments so great: God be praised who gave me life, so that I might escape from so fatal a death! I believe that my soul obtained great strength from His Divine Majesty, and that He must have heard my cry, and had compassion upon so many tears.

<small>And seeks to love God.</small> 10. A desire to spend more time with Him began to grow within me, and also to withdraw from the occasions of sin: for as soon as I had done so, I turned lovingly to His Majesty at once. I understood clearly, as I thought, that I loved Him; but I did not understand, as I ought to have understood it, wherein the true love of God consists. I do not think I had yet perfectly disposed myself to seek His service when His Majesty turned towards me with His consolations. What others strive after with great labour, our Lord seems to have looked out for a way to make me willing to accept—that is, in these later years to give me joy and comfort. But as for asking our Lord to give me either these things or sweetness in devotion, I never dared to do it; the only thing I prayed Him to give me was the grace never to offend Him, together with the forgiveness of my great sins. When I saw that my sins were so great, I never ventured deliberately to ask either for consolation or for sweetness. He had compassion enough upon me, I think,—and, in truth, He dealt with me according to His great mercy,—when He allowed me to stand before Him, and when He drew me into His presence; for I saw that, if He had not drawn me, I should not have come at all.

<small>She once prayed for sweetness.</small> 11. Once only in my life do I remember asking for consolation, being at the time in great aridities. When I considered what I had done, I was so confounded, that the very distress I suffered from seeing how little

humility I had, brought me that which I had been so bold as to ask for. I knew well that it was lawful to pray for it; but it seemed to me that it is lawful only for those who are in good dispositions, who have sought with all their might to attain to true devotion—that is, not to offend God, and to be disposed and resolved for all goodness. I looked upon those tears of mine as womanish and weak, seeing that I did not obtain my desires by them; nevertheless, I believe that they did me some service; for, specially after those two occasions of great compunction and sorrow of heart,[1] accompanied by tears, of which I am speaking, I began in an especial way to give myself more to prayer, and to occupy myself less with those things which did me harm—though I did not give them up altogether. But God Himself, as I have just said, came to my aid, and helped me to turn away from them. As His Majesty was only waiting for some preparation on my part, the spiritual graces grew in me as I shall now explain. It is not the custom of our Lord to give these graces to any but to those who keep their consciences in greater pureness.[2]

CHAPTER X.

THE GRACES SHE RECEIVED IN PRAYER—WHAT WE CAN DO OURSELVES—THE GREAT IMPORTANCE OF UNDERSTANDING WHAT OUR LORD IS DOING FOR US—SHE DESIRES HER CONFESSORS TO KEEP HER WRITINGS SECRET, BECAUSE OF THE SPECIAL GRACES OF OUR LORD TO HER, WHICH THEY HAD COMMANDED HER TO DESCRIBE.

1. I USED to have at times, as I have said,[3]—though it used to pass quickly away,—certain commencements of that which I am going now to describe. When I formed those pictures within myself of throw- *Mystical theology.*

---

[1] § 1.   [2] Ch. iv. § 10.
[3] The Saint interrupts her history here to enter on the difficult questions of mystical theology, and resumes it in ch. xxiii.

ing myself at the feet of Christ, as I said before,[1] and sometimes even when I was reading, a feeling of the presence of God would come over me unexpectedly, so that I could in no wise doubt either that He was within me, or that I was wholly absorbed in Him. It was not by way of vision; I believe it was what is called mystical theology. The soul is suspended in such a way that it seems to be utterly beside itself. The will loves; the memory, so it seems to me, is as it were lost; and the understanding, so I think, makes no reflections—yet is not lost: as I have just said, it is not at work, but it stands as if amazed at the greatness of the things it understands; for God wills it to understand that it understands nothing whatever of that which His Majesty places before it.

What our own efforts may do spiritually. 2. Before this, I had a certain tenderness of soul which was very abiding, partially attainable, I believe, in some measure, by our own efforts: a consolation which is not wholly in the senses, nor yet altogether in the spirit, but is all of it the gift of God. However, I think we can contribute much towards the attaining of it by considering our vileness and our ingratitude towards God —the great things He has done for us—His Passion, with its grievous pains—and His life, so full of sorrows; also, by rejoicing in the contemplation of His works, of His greatness, and of the love that He bears us. Many other considerations there are which he who really desires to make progress will often stumble on, though he may not be very much on the watch for them. If with this there be a little love, the soul is comforted, the heart is softened, and tears flow. Sometimes it seems that we do violence to ourselves and weep; at other times, our Lord seems to do so, so that we have no power to resist Him. His Majesty seems to reward this slight carefulness of ours with so grand a gift as is this consolation which He ministers to the soul of seeing itself weeping for so great a Lord. I am not surprised; for the soul has reason enough, and more than enough, for its joy. Here it comforts itself—here it rejoices.

[1] Ch. ix. § 4.

3. The comparison which now presents itself seems to me to be good. These joys in prayer are like what those of heaven must be. As the vision of the Saints, which is measured by their merits there, reaches no further than our Lord wills, and as the blessed see how little merit they had, every one of them is satisfied with the place assigned him: there being the very greatest difference between one joy and another in heaven, and much greater than between one spiritual joy and another on earth—which is, however, very great. And in truth, in the beginning, a soul in whom God works this grace thinks that now it has scarcely any thing more to desire, and counts itself abundantly rewarded for all the service it has rendered Him. And there is reason for this; for one of those tears—which, as I have just said, are almost in our own power, though without God nothing can be done—cannot, in my opinion, be purchased with all the labours of the world, because of the great gain it brings us. And what greater gain can we have than some testimony of our having pleased God? Let him, then, who shall have attained to this, give praise unto God—acknowledge himself to be one of His greatest debtors; because it seems to be His will to take him into His house, having chosen him for His kingdom, if he does not turn back. *The joys of heaven.*

4. Let him not regard certain kinds of humility which exist, and of which I mean to speak.[1] Some think it humility not to believe that God is bestowing His gifts upon them. Let us clearly understand this, and that it is perfectly clear God bestows His gifts without any merit whatever on our part; and let us be grateful to His Majesty for them; for if we do not recognise the gifts received at His hands, we shall never be moved to love Him. It is a most certain truth, that the richer we see ourselves to be, confessing at the same time our poverty, the greater will be our progress, and the more real our humility. *Importance of discerning the gifts of God.*

5. An opposite course tends to take away all courage; for we shall think ourselves incapable of great blessings, if we begin to frighten ourselves with *Danger of false humility.*

[1] Ch. xxx. § 10.

the dread of vain-glory when our Lord begins to show His mercy upon us.[1] Let us believe that He who gives these gifts will also, when the devil begins to tempt us herein, give us the grace to detect him, and the strength to resist him,— that is, He will do so if we walk in simplicity before God, aiming at pleasing Him only, and not men. It is a most evident truth, that our love for a person is greater, the more distinctly we remember the good he has done us.

<small>Reasons for acknowledging the gifts of God.</small> 6. If, then, it is lawful, and so meritorious, always to remember that we have our being from God, that He has created us out of nothing, that He preserves us, and also to remember all the benefits of His death and Passion, which He suffered long before He made us for every one of us now alive,—why should it not be lawful for me to discern, confess, and consider often that I was once accustomed to speak of vanities, and that now our Lord has given me the grace to speak only of Himself?

<small>And confessing them.</small> 7. Here, then, is a precious pearl, which, when we remember that it is given us, and that we have it in possession, powerfully invites us to love. All this is the fruit of prayer founded on humility. What, then, will it be when we shall find ourselves in possession of other pearls of greater price, such as contempt of the world and of self, which some servants of God have already received? It is clear that such souls must consider themselves greater debtors—under greater obligations to serve Him: we must acknowledge that we have nothing of ourselves, and confess the munificence of our Lord, who, on a soul so wretched and poor, and so utterly undeserving, as mine is,—for whom the first of these pearls was enough, and more than enough,— would bestow greater riches than I could desire.

<small>We must be grateful for God's gifts.</small> 8. We must renew our strength to serve Him, and strive not to be ungrateful, because it is on this condition that our Lord dispenses His treasures; for if we do not make a good use of them, and of the high estate to which He raises us, He will return and take them from us, and we shall be poorer than ever. His Majesty will

---

[1] See ch. xiii. § 5.

give the pearls to him who shall bring them forth and employ them usefully for himself and others. For how shall he be useful, and how shall he spend liberally, who does not know that he is rich? It is not possible, I think, our nature being what it is, that he can have the courage necessary for great things who does not know that God is on his side; for so miserable are we, so inclined to the things of this world, that he can hardly have any real abhorrence of, with great detachment from, all earthly things who does not see that he holds some pledges for those things that are above. It is by these gifts that our Lord gives us that strength which we through our sins have lost.

9. A man will hardly wish to be held in contempt and abhorrence, nor will he seek after the other great virtues to which the perfect attain, if he has not some pledges of the love which God bears him, together with a living faith. Our nature is so dead, that we go after that which we see immediately before us; and it is these graces, therefore, that quicken and strengthen our faith. It may well be that I, who am so wicked, measure others by myself, and that others require nothing more than the verities of the faith, in order to render their works most perfect; while I, wretched that I am! have need of every thing. *The Saint's self-depreciation.*

10. Others will explain this. I speak from my own experience, as I have been commanded; and if what I say be not correct, let him[1] to whom I send it destroy it; for he knows better than I do what is wrong in it. I entreat him, for the love of our Lord, to publish abroad what I have thus far said of my wretched life, and of my sins. I give him leave to do so; and to all my confessors, also,—of whom he is one,—to whom this is to be sent, if it be their pleasure, even during my life, so that I may no longer deceive people who think there must be some good in me.[2] Certainly, I speak in all sincerity, so far as I understand myself. Such publication will give me great comfort. *The Saint is willing that all the world may know her sins.*

[1] F. Pedro Ybañez, of the Order of S. Dominic.
[2] See ch. xxxi. § 19.

But is not willing that it should be known how it was that she received the graces she is about to speak of.

11. But as to that which I am now going to say, I give no such leave; nor, if it be shown to any one, do I consent to its being said who the person is whose experience it describes, nor who wrote it. This is why I mention neither my own name, nor that of any other person whatever. I have written it in the best way I could, in order not to be known; and this I beg of them for the love of God. Persons so learned and grave as they are[1] have authority enough to approve of whatever right things I may say, should our Lord give me the grace to do so; and if I should say any thing of the kind, it will be His, and not mine,—because I am neither learned nor of good life, and I have no person of learning or any other to teach me; for they only who ordered me to write know that I am writing, and at this moment they are not here. I have, as it were, to steal the time, and that with difficulty, because my writing hinders me from spinning. I am living in a house that is poor, and have many things to do.[2] If, indeed, our Lord had given me greater abilities and a better memory, I might then profit by what I have seen and read; but my abilities are very slight. If, then, I should say any thing that is right, our Lord will have it said for some good purpose; that which may be wrong will be mine, and your reverence will strike it out.

Nothing to be gained by publishing her name.

12. In neither case will it be of any use to publish my name: during my life, it is clear that no good I may have done ought to be told; after death, there is no reason against it, except that it will lose all authority and credit, because related of a person so vile and so wicked as I am. And because I think your reverence and the others who may see this writing will do this that I ask of you, for the love of our Lord, I write with freedom. If it were not so, I should have great scruples, except in declaring my sins: and in that matter I should have none at all. For the rest, it is enough that I am a woman to make my sails droop: how much more, then, when I am a woman, and a wicked one?

---

[1] See ch. xv. § 15.   [2] See ch. xiv. § 12.

13. So, then, every thing here beyond the simple story of my life your reverence must take upon yourself,—since you have so pressed me to give some account of the graces which our Lord bestowed upon me in prayer,—if it be consistent with the truths of our holy Catholic faith; if it be not, your reverence must burn it at once,—for I give my consent. I will recount my experience, in order that, if it be consistent with those truths, your reverence may make some use of it; if not, you will deliver my soul from delusion, so that Satan may gain nothing there where I seemed to be gaining myself. Our Lord knows well that I—as I shall show hereafter[1]—have always laboured to find out those who could give me light.

The Saint always sought for those who could give her light.

14. How clear soever I may wish to make my account of that which relates to prayer, it will be obscure enough for those who are without experience. I shall speak of certain hindrances, which, as I understand it, keep men from advancing on this road,—and of other things which are dangerous, as our Lord has taught me by experience. I have also discussed the matter with men of great learning, with persons who for many years had lived spiritual lives, who admit that, in the twenty-seven years only during which I have given myself to prayer,—though I walked so ill, and stumbled so often on the road,—His Majesty granted me that experience which others attain to in seven-and-thirty, or seven-and-forty, years; and they, too, being persons who ever advanced in the way of penance and of virtue.

The progress of the Saint in prayer.

15. Blessed be God for all, and may His infinite Majesty make use of me! Our Lord knoweth well that I have no other end in this than that He may be praised and magnified a little, when men shall see that on a dunghill so foul and rank He has made a garden of flowers so sweet. May it please His Majesty that I may not by my own fault root them out, and become again what I was before. And I entreat your reverence, for the love of our Lord, to beg this of Him for me, seeing that you have a clearer knowledge of what I am than you have allowed me to give of myself here.

[1] See ch. xxiv. § 16.

CHAPTER XI.

WHY MEN DO NOT ATTAIN QUICKLY TO THE PERFECT LOVE OF GOD—OF FOUR DEGREES OF PRAYER—OF THE FIRST DEGREE—THE DOCTRINE PROFITABLE FOR BEGINNERS, AND FOR THOSE WHO HAVE NO SENSIBLE SWEETNESS.

It is our own fault that we do not love God perfectly.

1. I SPEAK now of those who begin to be the servants of love; that seems to me to be nothing else but to resolve to follow Him in the way of prayer who has loved us so much. It is a dignity so great, that I have a strange joy in thinking of it; for servile fear vanishes at once, if we are, as we ought to be, in the first degree. O Lord of my soul, and my Good, how is it that, when a soul is determined to love Thee,—doing all it can, by forsaking all things, in order that it may the better occupy itself with the love of God,—it is not Thy will it should have the joy of ascending at once to the possession of perfect love? I have spoken amiss; I ought to have said, and my complaint should have been, why is it we do not? for the fault is wholly our own that we do not rejoice at once in a dignity so great, seeing that the attaining to the perfect possession of this true love brings all blessings with it.

What the fault is.

2. We think so much of ourselves, and are so dilatory in giving ourselves wholly to God, that, as His Majesty will not let us have the fruition of that which is so precious but at a great cost, so neither do we perfectly prepare ourselves for it. I see plainly that there is nothing by which so great a good can be procured in this world. If, however, we did what we could, not clinging to any thing upon earth, but having all our thoughts and conversation in heaven, I believe that this blessing would quickly be given us, provided we perfectly prepared ourselves for it at once, as some of the Saints have done. We think we are giving all to God; but, in fact, we are offering only the revenue or the produce, while we retain the fee-simple of the land in our own possession.

3. We resolve to become poor, and it is a resolution of great merit; but we very often take great care not to be in want, not simply of what is necessary, but of what is superfluous: yea, and to make for ourselves friends who may supply us; and in this way we take more pains, and perhaps expose ourselves to greater danger, in order that we may want nothing, than we did formerly, when we had our own possessions in our own power. *Defective poverty.*

4. We thought, also, that we gave up all desire of honour when we became religious, or when we began the spiritual life, and followed after perfection; and yet, when we are touched on the point of honour, we do not then remember that we had given it up to God. We would seize it again, and take it, as they say, out of His hands, even after we had made Him, to all appearance, the Lord of our own will. So is it in every thing else. *Sensitiveness.*

5. A pleasant way this of seeking the love of God! we retain our own affections, and yet will have that love, as they say, by handfuls. We make no efforts to bring our desires to good effect, or to raise them resolutely above the earth; and yet, with all this, we must have many spiritual consolations. This is not well, and we are seeking things that are incompatible one with the other. So, because we do not give ourselves up wholly and at once, this treasure is not given wholly and at once to us. May it be the good pleasure of our Lord to give it us drop by drop, though it may cost us all the trials in the world. *Inconsistency.*

6. He showeth great mercy unto him to whom He gives the grace and resolution to strive for this blessing with all his might; for God withholds Himself from no one who perseveres. He will by little and little strengthen that soul, so that it may come forth victorious. I say resolution, because of the multitude of those things which Satan puts before it at first, to keep it back from beginning to travel on this road; for he knoweth what harm will befall him thereby—he will lose not only that soul, but many others also. If he who enters on this road does violence to himself, with the help of God, so as to reach the summit of perfection, such a one, *Perseverance in prayer.*

I believe, will never go alone to heaven; he will always take many with him : God gives to him, as to a good captain, those who shall be of his company.

Great courage necessary. 7. Thus, then, the dangers and difficulties which Satan puts before them are so many, that they have need, not of a little, but of a very great, resolution, and great grace from God, to save them from falling away.

The beginning difficult. 8. Speaking, then, of their beginnings who are determined to follow after this good, and to succeed in their enterprise,—what I began to say[1] of mystical theology—I believe they call it by that name—I shall proceed with hereafter,—I have to say that the labour is greatest at first; for it is they who toil, our Lord, indeed, giving them strength. In the other degrees of prayer, there is more of fruition ; although they who are in the beginning, the middle, and the end, have their crosses to carry : the crosses, however, are different. They who would follow Christ, if they do not wish to be lost, must walk in the way He walked Himself. Blessed labours ! even here, in this life, so superabundantly rewarded !

The Saint finds it difficult to explain herself. 9. I shall have to make use of a comparison ; I should like to avoid it, because I am a woman, and write simply what I have been commanded. But this language of spirituality is so difficult of utterance for those who are not learned, and such am I. I have therefore to seek for some means to make the matter plain. It may be that the comparison will very rarely be to the purpose, —your reverence will be amused when you see my stupidity. I think, now, I have either read or heard of this comparison ; but as my memory is bad, I know not where, nor on what occasion; however, I am satisfied with it for my present purpose.[2]

The soul compared to a garden. 10. A beginner must look upon himself as making a garden, wherein our Lord may take His delight, but in a soil unfruitful, and abounding in weeds. His Majesty roots up the weeds, and has to plant good herbs. Let us, then, take for granted that this is already done when a soul is determined to give itself to prayer, and has begun the

---

[1] Ch. x. § 1.
[2] *Vide* S. Bernard, *in Cantic.* Serm. 30, n. 7, ed. Ben.

practice of it. We have, then, as good gardeners, by the help of God, to see that the plants grow, to water them carefully, that they may not die, but produce blossoms, which shall send forth much fragrance, refreshing to our Lord, so that He may come often for His pleasure into this garden, and delight Himself in the midst of these virtues.

11. Let us now see how this garden is to be watered, that we may understand what we have to do: how much trouble it will cost us, whether the gain be greater than the trouble, or how long a time it will take us. It seems to me that the garden may be watered in four ways: by water taken out of a well, which is very laborious; or with water raised by means of an engine and buckets, drawn by a windlass,—I have drawn it this way sometimes,—it is a less troublesome way than the first, and gives more water; or by a stream or brook, whereby the garden is watered in a much better way,—for the soil is more thoroughly saturated, and there is no necessity to water it so often, and the labour of the gardener is much less; or by showers of rain, when our Lord Himself waters it, without labour on our part,—and this way is incomparably better than all the others of which I have spoken. *Four ways of watering the garden.*

12. Now, then, for the application of these four ways of irrigation by which the garden is to be maintained; for without water it must fail. The comparison is to my purpose, and it seems to me that by the help of it I shall be able to explain, in some measure, the four degrees of prayer to which our Lord, of His goodness, has occasionally raised my soul. May He graciously grant that I may so speak as to be of some service to one of those who has commanded me to write, whom our Lord has raised in four months to a greater height than I have reached in seventeen years! He prepared himself better than I did, and therefore is his garden, without labour on his part, irrigated by these four waters,—though the last of them is only drop by drop; but it is growing in such a way, that soon, by the help of our Lord, he will be swallowed up therein, and it will be a pleasure to me, if he finds my explanation absurd, that he should laugh at it. *Corresponding with four degrees of prayer.*

13. Of those who are beginners in prayer, we may say, that they are those who draw the water up out of the well,—a process which, as I have said, is very laborious; for they must be wearied in keeping the senses recollected, and this is a great labour, because the senses have been hitherto accustomed to distractions. It is necessary for beginners to accustom themselves to disregard what they hear or see, and to put it away from them during the time of prayer; they must be alone, and in retirement think over their past life. Though all must do this many times, beginners as well as those more advanced; all, however, must not do so equally, as I shall show hereafter.[1] Beginners at first suffer much, because they are not convinced that they are penitent for their sins; and yet they are, because they are so sincerely resolved on serving God. They must strive to meditate on the life of Christ, and the understanding is wearied thereby. Thus far we can advance of ourselves,—that is, by the grace of God,—for without that, as every one knows, we never can have one good thought.

Beginners must toil.

14. This is beginning to draw water up out of the well. God grant there may be water in it! That, however, does not depend on us; we are drawing it, and doing what we can towards watering the flowers. So good is God, that when, for reasons known to His Majesty,—perhaps for our greater good,—it is His will the well should be dry, He Himself preserves the flowers without water,—we, like good gardeners, doing what lies in our power,—and makes our virtues grow. By water here I mean tears, and if there be none, then tenderness and an inward feeling of devotion.

The increase from God.

15. What, then, will he do here who sees that, for many days, he is conscious only of aridity, disgust, dislike, and so great an unwillingness to go to the well for water, that he would give it up altogether, if he did not remember that he has to please and serve the Lord of the garden; if he did not trust that his service was not in vain, and did not hope for some gain by a labour so great as that of lowering the bucket into the well so often, and drawing it up without water in it? It will happen that he is often unable to

Discouragements.

[1] Ch. xiii. § 23.

move his arms for that purpose, or to have one good thought: working with the understanding is drawing water out of the well.

16. What, then, once more, will the gardener do now? He must rejoice and take comfort, and consider it as the greatest favour to labour in the garden of so great an Emperor; and as he knows that he is pleasing Him in the matter,—and his purpose must be not to please himself, but Him,—let him praise Him greatly for the trust He has in him,—for He sees that, without any recompense, he is taking so much care of that which has been confided to him; let him help Him to carry the cross, and let him think how He carried it all His life long; let him not seek his kingdom here, nor ever intermit his prayer; and so let him resolve, if this aridity should last even his whole life long, never to let Christ fall down beneath the cross.[1]

Striving.

17. The time will come when he shall be paid once for all. Let him have no fear that his labour is in vain: he serves a good Master, whose eyes are upon him. Let him make no account of evil thoughts, but remember that Satan suggested them to St. Jerome also in the desert.[2] These labours have their reward, I know it; for I am one who underwent them for many years. When I drew but one drop of water out of this blessed well, I considered it was a mercy of God. I know these labours are very great, and require, I think, greater courage than many others in this world; but I have seen clearly that God does not leave them without a great recompense, even in this life; for it is very certain that in one hour, during which our Lord gave me to taste His sweetness, all the anxieties which I had to bear when persevering in prayer seem to me ever afterwards perfectly rewarded.

The reward certain.

[1] See ch. xv. § 17.
[2] Epist. 22, *ad Eustochium:* "O quoties ego ipse in eremo constitutus, et in illa vasta solitudine quæ exusta solis ardoribus horridum monachis præstat habitaculum putabam me Romanis interesse deliciis. Sedebam solus. . . . . Horrebant sacco membra deformia. . . . Ille igitur ego, qui ob Gehennæ metum tali me carcere damnaveram, scorpionum tantum

18. I believe that it is our Lord's good pleasure *Trials before great graces.* frequently in the beginning, and at times in the end, to send these torments, and many other incidental temptations, to try those who love Him, and to ascertain if they will drink the chalice,[1] and help Him to carry the cross, before He intrusts them with His great treasures. I believe it to be for our good that His Majesty should lead us by this way, so that we may perfectly understand how worthless we are; for the graces which He gives afterwards are of a dignity so great, that He will have us by experience know our wretchedness before He grants them, that it may not be with us as it was with Lucifer.

God never abandons those who love Him. 19. What canst thou do, O my Lord, that is not for the greater good of that soul which Thou knowest to be already Thine, and which gives itself up to Thee to follow Thee whithersoever Thou goest, even to the death of the cross; and which is determined to help Thee to carry that cross, and not to leave Thee alone with it? He who shall discern this resolution in himself has nothing to fear: no, no; spiritual people have nothing to fear. There is no reason why he should be distressed who is already raised to so high a degree as this is of wishing to converse in solitude with God, and to abandon the amusements of the world. The greater part of the work is done; give praise to His Majesty for it, and trust in His goodness who has never failed those who love Him. Close the eyes of your imagination, and do not ask why He gives devotion to this person in so short a time, and none to me after so many years. Let us believe that all is for our greater good; let His Majesty guide us whithersoever He will: we are not our own, but His. He shows us mercy enough when it is His pleasure we should be willing to dig in His garden, and to be so near the Lord of it: He certainly is near to us. If it be His will that these plants and flowers should grow,—some of them when He gives water we may

socius et ferarum, sæpe choris intereram puellarum, pallebant ora jejuniis, et mens desideriis æstuabat in frigido corpore, et ante hominem sua jam carne præmortuum sola libidinum incendia bulliebant."
[1] S. Matt. xx. 22: "Potestis bibere calicem?"

draw from the well, others when He gives none,—what is that to me? Do Thou, O Lord, accomplish Thy will; let me never offend Thee, nor let my virtues perish; if Thou hast given me any, it is out of Thy mere goodness. I wish to suffer, because Thou, O Lord, hast suffered; do Thou in every way fulfil Thy will in me, and may it never be the pleasure of Thy Majesty that a gift of so high a price, as that of Thy love, be given to people who serve Thee only because of the sweetness they find thereby.

20. It is much to be observed, and I say so because I know by experience, that the soul which begins to walk in the way of mental prayer with resolution, and is determined not to care much, neither to rejoice nor to be greatly afflicted, whether sweetness and tenderness fail it, or our Lord grants them, has already travelled a great part of the road. Let that soul, then, have no fear that it is going back, though it may frequently stumble; for the building is begun on a firm foundation. It is certain that the love of God does not consist in tears, nor in this sweetness and tenderness which we for the most part desire, and with which we console ourselves; but rather in serving Him in justice, fortitude, and humility. That seems to me to be a receiving rather than a giving of any thing on our part. *Mental prayer.*

21. As for poor women, such as I am, weak and infirm of purpose, it seems to me to be necessary that I should be led on through consolations, as God is doing now, so that I might be able to endure certain afflictions which it has pleased His Majesty I should have. But when the servants of God, who are men of weight, learning, and sense, make so much account, as I see they do, whether God gives them sweetness in devotion or not, I am disgusted when I listen to them. I do not say that they ought not to accept it, and make much of it, when God gives it,—because, when He gives it, His Majesty sees it to be necessary for them,—but I do say that they ought not to grow weary when they have it not. They should then understand that they have no need of it, and be masters of themselves, when His Majesty does not give it. Let them be convinced of this, there is a fault here; *Consolations for the weak, not for the strong.*

I have had experience of it, and know it to be so. Let them believe it is an imperfection; they are not advancing in liberty of spirit, but shrinking like cowards from the assault.

Of certain beginners who never end. 22. It is not so much to beginners that I say this—though I do insist upon it, because it is of great importance to them that they should begin with this liberty and resolution—as to others, of whom there are many, who make a beginning, but never come to the end; and that is owing, I believe, in great measure, to their not having embraced the cross from the first. They are distressed, thinking they are doing nothing; the understanding ceases from its acts, and they cannot bear it. Yet perhaps, at that very time, the will is feeding and gathering strength, and they know it not.

Bodily health influences the spiritual life. 23. We must suppose that our Lord does not regard these things; for though they seem to us to be faults, yet they are not. His Majesty knoweth our misery and natural vileness better than we do ourselves. He knoweth that these souls long to be always thinking of Him and loving Him. It is this resolution that He seeks in us; the other anxieties which we inflict upon ourselves serve to no other end but to disquiet the soul—which, if it be unable to derive any profit in one hour, will by them be disabled for four. This comes most frequently from bodily indisposition,—I have had very great experience in the matter, and I know it is true; for I have carefully observed it and discussed it afterwards with spiritual persons,—for we are so wretched, that this poor prisoner of a soul shares in the miseries of the body. The changes of the seasons, and the alterations of the humours, very often compel it, without fault of its own, not to do what it would, but rather to suffer in every way. Meanwhile, the more we force the soul on these occasions, the greater the mischief, and the longer it lasts. Some discretion must be used, in order to ascertain whether ill-health be the occasion or not. The poor soul must not be stifled. Let those who thus suffer understand that they are ill; a change should be made in the hour of prayer, and oftentimes that change should be continued for some days. Let souls pass out of this desert as they can, for it is very often the misery of one that loves God to see itself living in such wretchedness, unable to do what it would, because it has to keep so evil a guest as the body.

24. I spoke of discretion, because sometimes the devil will do the same work; and so it is not always right to omit prayer when the understanding is greatly distracted and disturbed, nor to torment the soul to the doing of that which is out of its power. There are other things then to be done—exterior works, as of charity and spiritual reading—though at times the soul will not be able to do them. Take care, then, of the body, for the love of God, because at many other times the body must serve the soul; and let recourse be had to some recreations,—holy ones,—such as conversation, or going out into the fields, as the confessor shall advise. Altogether, experience is a great matter, and it makes us understand what is convenient for us. Let God be served in all things—His yoke is sweet;[1] and it is of great importance that the soul should not be dragged, as they say, but carried gently, that it may make greater progress. *Satan imitates the effects of bodily ill-health.*

25. So, then, I come back to what I advised before,[2]—and though I repeat it often, it matters not; it is of great importance that no one should distress himself on account of aridities, or because his thoughts are restless and distracted; neither should he be afflicted thereat, if he would attain to liberty of spirit, and not be always in trouble. Let him begin by not being afraid of the cross, and he will see how our Lord will help him to carry it, how joyfully he will advance, and what profit he will derive from it all. It is now clear, if there is no water in the well, that we at least can put none into it. It is true we must not be careless about drawing it when there is any in it, because at that time it is the will of God to multiply our virtues by means thereof. *The soul is not to trouble itself because of difficulties.*

[1] S. Matt. xi. 30 : "Jugum enim meum suave est." [2] § 18.

CHAPTER XII.

WHAT WE CAN OURSELVES DO — THE EVIL OF DESIRING TO ATTAIN TO SUPERNATURAL STATES BEFORE OUR LORD CALLS US.

What our own efforts may do.
1. MY aim in the foregoing chapter—though I digressed to many other matters, because they seemed to me very necessary—was to explain how much we may attain to of ourselves; and how, in these beginnings of devotion, we are able in some degree to help ourselves : because thinking of, and pondering on, the sufferings of our Lord for our sake moves us to compassion, and the sorrow and tears which result therefrom are sweet. The thought of the blessedness we hope for, of the love our Lord bore us, and of His resurrection, kindle within us a joy which is neither wholly spiritual nor wholly sensual; but the joy is virtuous, and the sorrow is most meritorious.

Beginners must be content.
2. Of this kind are all those things which produce a devotion acquired in part by means of the understanding, though it can neither be merited nor had, if God grants it not. It is best for a soul which God has not raised to a higher state than this not to try to rise of itself. Let this be well considered, because all the soul will gain in that way will be a loss. In this state it can make many acts of good resolutions to do much for God, and enkindle its love; other acts also, which may help the growth of virtues, according to that which is written in a book called *The Art of Serving God*;[1] a most excellent work, and profitable for those who are in this state, because the understanding is active now.

The presence of God.
3. The soul may also place itself in the presence of Christ, and accustom itself to many acts of love directed to His sacred Humanity, and remain in His presence continually, and speak to Him, pray to Him in its

---

[1] *Arte de servir a Dios,* by Rodrigue de Solis, friar of the Augustinian Order (*Bouix*). *Arte para servir a Dios,* by Fra Alonso de Madrid (*De la Fuente*).

necessities, and complain to Him of its troubles; be merry with Him in its joys, and yet not forget Him because of its joys. All this it may do without set prayers, but rather with words befitting its desires and its needs.

4. This is an excellent way whereby to advance, and that very quickly. He that will strive to have this precious companionship, and will make much of it, and will sincerely love our Lord, to whom we owe so much, is one, in my opinion, who has made some progress. There is therefore no reason why we should trouble ourselves because we have no sensible devotion, as I said before.[1] But let us rather give thanks to our Lord, who allows us to have a desire to please Him, though our works be poor. This practice of the presence of Christ is profitable in all states of prayer, and is a most safe way of advancing in the first state, and of attaining quickly to the second; and as for the last states, it secures us against those risks which the devil may occasion. *Progress of beginners.*

5. This, then, is what we can do. He who would pass out of this state, and upraise his spirit, in order to taste consolations denied him, will, in my opinion, lose both the one and the other.[2] Those consolations being supernatural, and the understanding inactive, the soul is then left desolate and in great aridity. As the foundation of the whole building is humility, the nearer we draw unto God, the more this virtue should grow; if it does not, every thing is lost. It seems to be a kind of pride when we seek to ascend higher, seeing that God descends so low, when He allows us, being what we are, to draw near unto Him. *Necessity of humility.*

6. It must not be supposed that I am now speaking of raising our thoughts to the consideration of the high things of heaven and of its glory, or unto God and His great wisdom. I never did this myself, because *The Saint's humility.*

---

[1] Ch. xi. §§ 20, 25.
[2] That is, he will lose the prayer of acquired quiet, because he voluntarily abandons it before the time; and will not attain to the prayer of infused quiet, because he attempts to rise into it before he is called (Francis. de Santo Thomas, *Medula Mystic.* tr. iv. ch. xi. n. 69).

I had not the capacity for it—as I said before;[1] and I was so worthless, that, as to thinking even of the things of earth, God gave me grace to understand this truth : that in me it was no slight boldness to do so. How much more, then, the thinking of heavenly things ? Others, however, will profit in that way, particularly those who are learned; for learning, in my opinion, is a great treasury in the matter of this exercise, if it be accompanied with humility. I observed this a few days ago in some learned men who had shortly before made a beginning, and had made great progress. This is the reason why I am so very anxious that many learned men may become spiritual. I shall speak of this by and by.[2]

Beginners must wait on God. 7. What I am saying—namely, let them not rise if God does not raise them—is the language of spirituality. He will understand me who has had any experience; and I know not how to explain it, if what I have said does not make it plain.

Mystical theology. 8. In mystical theology,—of which I spoke before,[3] —the understanding ceases from its acts, because God suspends it—as I shall explain by and by, if I can ; and God give me the grace to do so. We must neither imagine nor think that we can of ourselves bring about this suspension. That is what I say must not be done ; nor must we allow the understanding to cease from its acts ; for in that case we shall be stupid and cold, and the result will be neither the one nor the other. For when our Lord suspends the understanding, and makes it cease from its acts, He puts before it that which astonishes and occupies it: so that, without making any reflections, it shall comprehend in a moment[4] more than we could comprehend in many years with all the efforts in the world.

Humility the ground of progress. 9. To have the powers of the mind occupied, and to think that you can keep them at the same time quiet, is folly. I repeat it, though it be not so understood, there is no great humility in this; and, if it be blameless, it is not left unpunished—it is labour thrown away, and the

[1] Ch. iv. § 10.   [2] Ch. xxxiv. § 9.
[3] Ch. x. § 1.   [4] "En un credo."

soul is a little disgusted: it feels like a man about to take a leap, and is held back. Such a one seems to have used up his strength already, and finds himself unable to do that which he wished to have done: so here, in the scanty gain that remains, he who will consider the matter will trace that slight want of humility of which I have spoken;[1] for that virtue has this excellence: there is no good work attended by humility that leaves the soul disgusted. It seems to me that I have made this clear enough; yet, after all, perhaps only for myself. May our Lord open their eyes who read this, by giving them experience; and then, however slight that experience may be, they will immediately understand it.

10. For many years I read much, and understood nothing; and for a long time, too, though God gave me understanding herein, I never could utter a word by which I might explain it to others. This was no little trouble to me. When His Majesty pleases, He teaches every thing in a moment, so that I am lost in wonder. One thing I can truly say: though I conversed with many spiritual persons, who sought to make me understand what our Lord was giving me, in order that I might be able to speak of it, the fact is, that my dulness was so great, that I derived no advantage whatever, much or little, from their teaching. *The Saint once unable to describe her interior life.*

11. Or it may be, as His Majesty has always been my Master,—may He be blessed for ever! for I am ashamed of myself that I can say so with truth,—that it was His good pleasure I should meet with no one to whom I should be indebted in this matter. So, without my wishing or asking it,—I never was careful about this, for that would have been a virtue in me, but only about vanity,—God gave me to understand with all distinctness in a moment, and also enabled me to express myself, so that my confessors were astonished; but I more than they, because I knew my own dulness better. It is not long since this happened. And so that which our Lord has not taught me, I seek not to know it, unless it be a matter that touches my conscience. *Why.*

[1] § 5.

12. Again I repeat my advice: it is of great moment not to raise our spirit ourselves, if our Lord does not raise it for us; and if He does, there can be no mistaking it. For women, it is specially wrong, because the devil can delude them,—though I am certain our Lord will never allow him to hurt any one who labours to draw near unto God in humility. On the contrary, such a one will derive more profit and advantage out of that attack by which Satan intended to hurt him.

The soul must wait upon God.

13. I have dwelt so long upon this matter because this way of prayer is the most common with beginners, and because the advice I have given is very important. It will be found much better given elsewhere: that I admit; and I admit, also, that in writing it I am ashamed of myself, and covered with confusion—though not so much so as I ought to be. Blessed for ever be our Lord, of whose will and pleasure it is that I am allowed, being what I am, to speak of things which are His, of such a nature, and so deep!

CHAPTER XIII.

OF CERTAIN TEMPTATIONS OF SATAN—INSTRUCTIONS RELATING THERETO.

1. I HAVE thought it right to speak of certain temptations I have observed to which beginners are liable,—some of them I have had myself,—and to give some advice about certain things which to me seem necessary. In the beginning, then, we should strive to be cheerful and unconstrained; for there are people who think it is all over with devotion if they relax themselves ever so little. It is right to be afraid of self: so that, having no confidence in ourselves, much or little, we may not place ourselves in those circumstances wherein men usually sin against God; for it is a most necessary fear, till we become very perfect in virtue. And there are not many who are so perfect as to be able to relax themselves on those occasions

Occasions of sin to be avoided by beginners.

which offer temptations to their natural temper; for always while we live, were it only to preserve humility, it is well we should know our own miserable nature; but there are many occasions on which it is permitted us—as I said just now[1]—to take some recreation, in order that we may with more vigour resume our prayer.

2. Discretion is necessary throughout. We must have great confidence; because it is very necessary for us not to contract our desires, but put our trust in God; for, if we do violence to ourselves by little and little, we shall, though not at once, reach that height which many Saints by His grace have reached. If they had never resolved to desire, and had never by little and little acted upon that resolve, they never could have ascended to so high a state. *Discretion.*

3. His Majesty seeks and loves courageous souls; but they must be humble in their ways, and have no confidence in themselves. I never saw one of these lag behind on the road; and never a cowardly soul, though aided by humility, make that progress in many years which the former makes in a few. I am astonished at the great things done on this road by encouraging oneself to undertake great things, though we may not have the strength for them at once: the soul takes a flight upwards and ascends high, though, like a little bird whose wings are weak, it grows weary and rests. *Great courage necessary,*

4. At one time, I used often to think of those words of S. Paul: "That all things are possible in God."[2] I saw clearly that of myself I could do nothing. This was of great service to me. So also was the saying of S. Augustine: "Give me, O Lord, what Thou commandest, and command what Thou wilt."[3] I was often thinking how S. Peter lost nothing by throwing himself into the sea, though he was afterwards afraid.[4] These first resolutions are a great matter,—although it is necessary in the beginning that we should be very reserved, controlled by the discretion and authority of a director; but we must take care *And great confidence in God.*

[1] Ch. xi. § 24.   [2] Philipp. iv. 13 : "Omnia possum in Eo."
[3] *Confess.* x. ch. 29 : "Da quod jubes, et jube quod vis."
[4] S. Matt. xiv. 30 : "Videns vero ventum validum, timuit."

that he be one who does not teach us to crawl like toads, nor one who may be satisfied when the soul shows itself fit only to catch lizards. Humility must always go before: so that we may know that this strength can come out of no strength of our own.

Of true humility. 5. But it is necessary we should understand what manner of humility this should be, because Satan, I believe, does great harm; for he hinders those who begin to pray from going onwards, by suggesting to them false notions of humility. He makes them think it is pride to have large desires, to wish to imitate the Saints, and to long for martyrdom. He tells us forthwith, or he makes us think, that the actions of the Saints are to be admired, not to be imitated, by us who are sinners. I, too, say the same thing; but we must see what those actions are which we are to admire, and what those are which we are to imitate; for it would be wrong in a person who is weak and sickly to undertake much fasting and sharp penances—to retire into the desert, where he could not sleep, nor find any thing to eat; or, indeed, to undertake any austerities of this kind.

What we must labour after. 6. But we ought to think that we can force ourselves, by the grace of God, to hold the world in profound contempt—to make light of honour, and be detached from our possessions. Our hearts, however, are so mean, that we think the earth would fail us under our feet, if we were to cease to care even for a moment for the body, and give ourselves up to spirituality. Then we think that to have all we require contributes to recollection, because anxieties disturb prayer. It is painful to me that our confidence in God is so scanty, and our self-love so strong, as that any anxiety about our own necessities should disturb us. But so it is; for when our spiritual progress is so slight, a mere nothing will give us as much trouble as great and important matters will give to others. And we think ourselves spiritual!

Religious and married persons must live differently. 7. Now, to me, this way of going on seems to betray a disposition to reconcile soul and body together, in order that we may not miss our ease in this world, and yet have the fruition of God in the next; and so it will be if we walk according to justice, clinging to virtue; but it is the pace of a hen—it will never bring us to liberty of spirit. It is a course of proceeding, as it seems to me, most excellent for those who are in the married state, and who must live according to their vocation; but for the other state, I by no means wish for such a method of progress, neither can I be made to believe it to be sound; for I have tried it, and I should have remained in that way, if our Lord in His goodness had not taught me another and a shorter road.

8. Though, in the matter of desires, I always had generous ones; but I laboured, as I said before,[1] to make my prayer, and, at the same time, to live at my ease. If there had been any one to rouse me to a higher flight, he might have brought me, so I think, to a state in which these desires might have had their effects; but, for our sins, so few and so rare are they whose discretion in that matter is not excessive. That, I believe, is reason enough why those who begin do not attain more quickly to great perfection; for our Lord never fails us, and it is not His fault; the fault and the wretchedness of this being all our own. *Excessive discretion hurtful,*

9. We may also imitate the Saints by striving after solitude and silence, and many other virtues that will not kill these wretched bodies of ours, which insist on being treated so orderly, that they may disorder the soul; and Satan, too, helps much to make them unmanageable. When he sees us a little anxious about them, he wants nothing more to convince us that our way of life must kill us, and destroy our health; even if we weep, he makes us afraid of blindness. I have passed through this, and therefore I know it; but I know of no better sight or better health that we can desire, than the loss of both in such a cause. Being myself so sickly, I was always under constraint, and good for nothing, till I resolved to make no account of my body nor of my health; even now I am worthless enough. *And helps Satan to tempt.*

10. But when it pleased God to let me find out this device of Satan, I used to say to the latter, when he suggested to me that I was ruining my health, that my death was of no consequence; when *How the Saint's health became better when she ceased to care for it.*

[1] Ch. vii. §§ 27, 30.

he suggested rest, I replied that I did not want rest, but the cross. His other suggestions I treated in the same way. I saw clearly that in most things, though I was really very sickly, it was either a temptation of Satan, or a weakness on my part. My health has been much better since I have ceased to look after my ease and comforts. It is of great importance not to let our own thoughts frighten us in the beginning, when we set ourselves to pray. Believe me in this, for I know it by experience. As a warning to others, it may be that this story of my failures may be useful.

Another temptation of beginners. 11. There is another temptation, which is very common: when people begin to have pleasure in the rest and the fruit of prayer, they will have every body else be very spiritual also. Now, to desire this is not wrong, but to try to bring it about may not be right, except with great discretion and with much reserve, without any appearance of teaching. He who would do any good in this matter ought to be endowed with solid virtues, that he may not put temptation in the way of others. It happened to me—that is how I know it—when, as I said before,[1] I made others apply themselves to prayer, to be a source of temptation and disorder; for, on the one hand, they heard me say great things of the blessedness of prayer, and, on the other, saw how poor I was in virtue, notwithstanding my prayer. They had good reasons on their side, and afterwards they told me of it; for they knew not how these things could be compatible one with the other. This it was that made them not to regard that as evil which was really so in itself, namely, that they saw me do it myself, now and then, during the time that they thought well of me in some measure.

A trick of Satan. 12. This is Satan's work: he seems to take advantage of the virtues we may have, for the purpose of giving a sanction, so far as he can, to the evil he aims at; how slight soever that evil may be, his gain must be great, if it prevail in a religious house. How much, then, must his gain have been, when the evil I did was so very great! And thus, during many years, only three persons were the better

[1] Ch. vii. § 16.

for what I said to them; but now that our Lord has made me stronger in virtue, in the course of two or three years many persons have profited, as I shall show hereafter.[1]

13. There is another great inconvenience in addition to this: the loss to our own soul; for the utmost we have to do in the beginning is to take care of our own soul only, and consider that in the whole world there is only God and our soul. This is a point of great importance. *Charity begins at home.*

14. There is another temptation,—we ought to be aware of it, and be cautious in our conduct: persons are carried away by a zeal for virtue, through the pain which the sight of the sins and failings of others occasions them. Satan tells them that this pain arises only out of their desire that God may not be offended, and out of their anxiety about His honour; so they immediately seek to remedy the evil. This so disturbs them, that they cannot pray. The greatest evil of all is their thinking this an act of virtue, of perfection, and of a great zeal for God. I am not speaking of the pain which public sins occasion, if they be habitual in any community, nor of wrongs done to the Church, nor of heresies by which so many souls are visibly lost; for this pain is most wholesome, and being wholesome is no source of disquiet. The security, therefore, of that soul which would apply itself to prayer lies in casting away from itself all anxiety about persons and things, in taking care of itself, and in pleasing God. This is the most profitable course. *The sins of others a source of temptation to beginners.*

15. If I were to speak of the mistakes which I have seen people make, in reliance on their own good intentions, I should never come to an end. Let us labour, therefore, always to consider the virtues and the good qualities which we discern in others, and with our own great sins cover our eyes, so that we may see none of their failings. This is one way of doing our work; and though we may not be perfect in it at once, we shall acquire one great virtue,—we shall look upon all men as better than ourselves; and we begin to acquire that virtue in this way, by the grace of God, which is necessary in all things—for when we have it *Who ought to think others better than themselves.*

[1] See ch. xxxi. § 7, and ch. xxxix. § 14.

not, all our endeavours are in vain—and by imploring Him to give us this virtue; for He never fails us, if we do what we can.

Advice to those who meditate. 16. This advice, also, they must take into their consideration who make much use of their understanding, eliciting from one subject many thoughts and conceptions. As to those who, like myself, cannot do it, I have no advice to give, except that they are to have patience, until our Lord shall send them both matter and light; for they can do so little of themselves, that their understanding is a hindrance to them rather than a help.

They are not to spend the whole time of prayer in making reflections. 17. To those, then, who can make use of their understanding, I say that they are not to spend the whole time in that way; for though it be most meritorious, yet they must not, when prayer is sweet, suppose that there never will be a Sunday or a time when no work ought to be done. They think it lost time to do otherwise; but I think that loss their greatest gain. Let them rather, as I have said,[1] place themselves in the presence of Christ, and, without fatiguing the understanding, converse with Him, and in Him rejoice, without wearying themselves in searching out reasons; but let them rather lay their necessities before Him, and the just reasons there are why He should not suffer us in His presence: at one time this, at another time that, lest the soul should be wearied by always eating of the same food. These meats are most savoury and wholesome, if the palate be accustomed to them; they will furnish a great support for the life of the soul, and they have many other advantages also.

The doctrine of prayer difficult. 18. I will explain myself further; for the doctrine of prayer is difficult, and, without a director, very hard to understand. Though I would willingly be concise, and though a mere hint is enough for his clear intellect who has commanded me to write on the subject of prayer, yet so it is, my dulness does not allow me to say or explain in a few words that which it is so important to explain well. I, who have gone through so much, am sorry for those

[1] Ch. xii. § 3.

who begin only with books; for there is a strange difference between that which we learn by reading, and that which we learn by experience.

19. Going back, then, to what I was saying. We set ourselves to meditate upon some mystery of the Passion: let us say, our Lord at the pillar. The understanding goeth about seeking for the sources out of which came the great dolors and the bitter anguish which His Majesty endured in that desolation. It considers that mystery in many lights, which the intellect, if it be skilled in its work, or furnished with learning, may there obtain. This is a method of prayer which should be to every one the beginning, the middle, and the end; a most excellent and safe way, until our Lord shall guide them to other supernatural ways. *Example of a meditation.*

20. I say to all, because there are many souls who make greater progress by meditation on other subjects than on the Sacred Passion; for as there are many mansions in heaven, so are there also many roads leading thither. Some persons advance by considering themselves in hell, others in heaven,—and these are distressed by meditations on hell. Others meditate on death; some persons, if tender-hearted, are greatly fatigued by continual meditations on the Passion; but are consoled and make progress when they meditate on the power and greatness of God in His creatures, and on His love visible in all things. This is an admirable method,—not omitting, however, from time to time the Passion and Life of Christ, the Source of all good that ever came, and that ever shall come. *Different subjects of meditation for different people.*

21. He who begins is in need of instruction, whereby he may ascertain what profits him most. For this end it is very necessary he should have a director, who ought to be a person of experience; for if he be not, he will make many mistakes, and direct a soul without understanding its ways, or suffering it to understand them itself; for such a soul, knowing that obedience to a director is highly meritorious, dares not transgress the commandments it receives. I have met with souls cramped and tormented, because he who directed them had no experience: that made me sorry for them. *Directors necessary for beginners.*

Some of them knew not what to do with themselves; for directors who do not understand the spirit of their penitents afflict them soul and body, and hinder their progress.[1]

The Saint helps a person misdirected. 22. One person I had to do with had been kept by her director for eight years, as it were, in prison: he would not allow her to quit the subject of self-knowledge; and yet our Lord had already raised her to the prayer of quiet; so she had much to suffer.

Self-knowledge necessary for all. 23. Although this matter of self-knowledge must never be put aside,—for there is no soul so great a giant on this road but has frequent need to turn back, and be again an infant at the breast; and this must never be forgotten. I shall repeat it,[2] perhaps, many times, because of its great importance—for among all the states of prayer, however high they may be, there is not one in which it is not often necessary to go back to the beginning. The knowledge of our sins, and of our own selves, is the bread which we have to eat with all the meats, however delicate they may be, in the way of prayer; without this bread, life cannot be sustained, though it must be taken by measure. When a soul beholds itself resigned, and clearly understands that there is no goodness in it,—when it feels itself abashed in the presence of so great a King, and sees how little it pays of the great debt it owes Him,—why should it be necessary for it to waste its time on this subject? Why should it not rather proceed to other matters which our Lord places before it, and for neglecting which there is no reason? His Majesty surely knows better than we do what kind of food is proper for us.

Directors must be prudent men. 24. So, then, it is of great consequence that the director should be prudent—I mean, of sound understanding—and a man of experience. If, in addition to this, he is a learned man, it is a very great matter. But if these three qualities cannot be had together, the first two are the most important, because learned men may be found with whom we can communicate when it is necessary. I mean, that

---

[1] See S. John of the Cross, *Living Flame*, pp. 267, 278-284, Engl. trans.

[2] See ch. xv. § 20.

for beginners learned men are of little use, if they are not men of prayer. I do not say that they are to have nothing to do with learned men, because a spirituality, the foundations of which are not resting on the truth, I would rather were not accompanied with prayer. Learning is a great thing, for it teaches us who know so little, and enlightens us; so when we have come to the knowledge of the truths contained in the holy writings, we do what we ought to do. From silly devotions, God deliver us!

25. I will explain myself further; for I am meddling, I believe, with too many matters. It has always been my failing that I could never make myself understood,—as I said before,[1]—but at the cost of many words. A nun begins to practise prayer; if her director be silly, and if he should take it into his head, he will make her feel that it is better for her to obey him than her own superior. He will do all this without any evil purpose, thinking that he is doing right. For if he be not a religious himself, he will think this right enough. If his penitent be a married woman, he will tell her that it is better for her to give herself unto prayer, when she ought to attend to her house, although she may thereby displease her husband. And so it is he knows not how to make arrangements for time and business, so that every thing may be done as it ought to be done; he has no light himself, and can therefore give none to others, however much he may wish to do so. *Example of a wrong direction.*

26. Though learning does not seem necessary for direction, my opinion has always been, and will be, that every Christian should continue to be guided by a learned director if he can, and the more learned the better. They who walk in the way of prayer have the greater need of learning; and the more spiritual they are, the greater is that need. Let them not say that learned men not given to prayer are not fit counsellors for those who pray: that is a delusion. I have conversed with many; and now for some years I have sought them the more, because of my greater need of them. I have always been fond of them; for though some of them have *Directors should be learned men,*

[1] § 18.

no experience, they do not dislike spirituality, neither are they ignorant of what it is, because in the sacred writings with which they are familiar they always find the truth about spirituality. I am certain myself that a person given to prayer, who treats of these matters with learned men, unless he is deceived with his own consent, will never be carried away by any illusions of the devil. I believe that the evil spirits are exceedingly afraid of learned men who are humble and virtuous, knowing that they will be found out and defeated by them.

<small>Even if not spiritual.</small> 27. I have said this because there are opinions held to the effect that learned men, if they are not spiritual, are not suited for persons given to prayer. I have just said that a spiritual director is necessary; but if he be not a learned man, he is a great hindrance. It will help us much if we consult those who are learned, provided they be virtuous; even if they be not spiritual, they will be of service to me, and God will enable them to understand what they should teach; He will even make them spiritual, in order that they may help us on. I do not say this without having had experience of it; and I have met with more than two.

<small>The dangers of choosing an unfit director.</small> 28. I say, then, that a person who shall resign his soul to be wholly subject to one director will make a great mistake, if he is in religion, unless he finds a director of this kind, because of the obedience due to his own superior. His director may be deficient in the three requisites I speak of,[1] and that will be no slight cross, without voluntarily subjecting the understanding to one whose understanding is none of the best. At least, I have never been able to bring myself to do it, neither does it seem to me to be right.

<small>Directors to be chosen freely.</small> 29. But if he be a person living in the world, let him praise God for the power he has of choosing whom he will obey, and let him not lose so excellent a liberty; yea, rather let him be without a director till he finds him,—for our Lord will give him one, if he is really humble, and has a desire to meet with the right person. I praise God greatly—we women, and those who are unlearned, ought always to render Him unceasing thanks—because there are persons

---

[1] Prudence, experience, and learning; see § 24.

who, by labours so great, have attained to the truth, of which we unlearned people are ignorant. I often wonder at learned men—particularly those who are in religion—when I think of the trouble they have had in acquiring that which they communicate to me for my good, and that without any more trouble to me than the asking for it. And yet there are people who will not take advantage of their learning: God grant it may not be so!

30. I see them undergo the poverty of the religious life, which is great, together with its penances, *Religious directors.* its meagre food, the yoke of obedience, which makes me ashamed of myself at times; and with all this, interrupted sleep, trials every where, every where the Cross. I think it would be a great evil for any one to lose so great a good by his own fault. It may be that some of us, who are exempted from these burdens,—who have our food put into our mouths, as they say, and live at our ease,—may think, because we give ourselves a little more to prayer, that we are raised above the necessity of such great hardships. Blessed be Thou, O Lord, who hast made me so incapable and so useless; but I bless Thee still more for this—that Thou quickenest so many to quicken us. Our prayer must therefore be very earnest for those who give us light. What should we be without them in the midst of these violent storms which now disturb the Church? If some have fallen, the good will shine more and more.[1] May it please our Lord to hold them in His hand, and help them, that they may help us.

31. I have gone far away from the subject I began to speak of; but all is to the purpose for those *She returns to the subject.* who are beginners, that they may begin a journey which is so high in such a way as that they shall go on by the right road. Coming back, then, to what I spoke of before,[2] the meditation on Christ bound to the pillar, it is well we should make reflections for a time, and consider the sufferings He there endured, for whom He endured them, who He is who

[1] Dan. xii. 3: "Qui autem docti fuerint, fulgebunt quasi splendor firmamenti."
[2] § 19.

endured them, and the love with which He bore them. But a person should not always fatigue himself in making these reflections, but rather let him remain there with Christ, in the silence of the understanding.

<small>Another method much praised by the Saint.</small> 32. If he is able, let him employ himself in looking upon Christ, who is looking upon him; let him accompany Him, and make his petitions to Him; let him humble himself, and delight himself in Christ, and keep in mind that He never deserved to be there. When he shall be able to do this, though it may be in the beginning of his prayer, he will find great advantage; and this way of prayer brings great advantages with it—at least, so my soul has found it. I do not know whether I am describing it aright; you, my father, will see to it. May our Lord grant me to please Him rightly for ever! Amen.

CHAPTER XIV.

THE SECOND STATE OF PRAYER—ITS SUPERNATURAL CHARACTER.

<small>The second degree of prayer</small> 1. HAVING spoken of the toilsome efforts and of the strength required for watering the garden when we have to draw the water out of the well, let us now speak of the second manner of drawing the water, which the Lord of the vineyard has ordained; of the machine of wheel and buckets whereby the gardener may draw more water with less labour, and be able to take some rest without being continually at work. This, then, is what I am now going to describe; and I apply it to the prayer called the prayer of quiet.

2. Herein the soul begins to be recollected; it <small>Is less laborious.</small> is now touching on the supernatural,—for it never could by any efforts of its own attain to this. True, it seems at times to have been wearied at the wheel, labouring with the understanding, and filling the buckets; but in this second degree the water is higher, and accordingly the labour

is much less than it was when the water had to be drawn up out of the well; I mean, that the water is nearer to it, for grace reveals itself more distinctly to the soul.

3. This is a gathering together of the faculties of the soul within itself, in order that it may have the fruition of that contentment in greater sweetness; but the faculties are not lost, neither are they asleep: the will alone is occupied in such a way that, without knowing how it has become a captive, it gives a simple consent to become the prisoner of God; for it knows well what it is to be the captive of Him it loves. O my Jesus and my Lord, how pressing now is Thy love![1] It binds our love in bonds so straitly, that it is not in its power at this moment to love any thing else but Thee. *The constraining force of God's grace.*

4. The other two faculties help the will, that it may render itself capable of the fruition of so great a good; nevertheless, it occasionally happens, even when the will is in union, that they hinder it very much: but then it should never heed them at all, simply abiding in its fruition and quiet.[2] For if it tried to make them recollected, it would miss its way together with them, because they are at this time like doves which are not satisfied with the food the master of the dovecot gives them without any labouring for it on their part, and which go forth in quest of it elsewhere, and so hardly find it that they come back. And so the memory and the understanding come and go, seeking whether the will is going to give them that into the fruition of which it has entered itself. *The will must be at rest.*

5. If it be our Lord's pleasure to throw them any food, they stop; if not, they go again to seek it. They must be thinking that they are of some service to the will; and now and then the memory or the imagination, seeking to represent to it that of which it has the fruition, does it harm. The will, therefore, should be careful to deal with them as I shall explain. Every thing that takes *The memory and the understanding hurt the will at times.*

[1] 2 Cor. v. 14: "Charitas enim Christi urget nos."
[2] See ch. xvii. § 12; *Way of Perfection*, ch. liii., but xxxi. of the old editions.

place now in this state brings the very greatest consolation; and the labour is so slight, that prayer, even if persevered in for some time, is never wearisome. The reason is, that the understanding is now working very gently, and is drawing very much more water than it drew out of the well. The tears, which God now sends, flow with joy; though we feel them, they are not the result of any efforts of our own.

Virtues grow in the second state. 6. This water of grand blessings and graces, which our Lord now supplies, makes the virtues thrive much more, beyond all comparison, than they did in the previous state of prayer; for the soul is already ascending out of its wretched state, and some little knowledge of the blissfulness of glory is communicated to it. This, I believe, is it that makes the virtues grow the more, and also to draw nearer to essential virtue, God Himself, from whom all virtues proceed; for His Majesty has begun to communicate Himself to this soul, and will have it feel how He is communicating Himself.

Supernatural joys of prayer. 7. As soon as the soul has arrived thus far, it begins to lose the desire of earthly things:[1] and no wonder; for it sees clearly that, even for a moment, this joy is not to be had on earth; that there are no riches, no dominion, no honours, no delights, that can for one instant, even for the twinkling of an eye, minister such a joy; for it is a true satisfaction, and the soul sees that it really does satisfy. Now, we who are on earth, as it seems to me, scarcely ever understand wherein our satisfaction lies, for it is always liable to disappointment; but in this, at that time, there is none: the disappointment cometh afterwards, when the soul sees that all is over, and that it has no power to recover it, neither does it know how; for if it cut itself in pieces by penance and prayer, and every other kind of austerities, all would be of little use, if our Lord did not grant it. God, in His great mercy, will have the soul comprehend that His Majesty is so near to it, that it need not send messengers to Him, but may speak to Him itself, and not with a loud crying, because so near is He already, that He understands even the movements of its lips.

[1] See *Relation*, i. § 12.

8. It seems absurd to say this, seeing that we know that God understands us always, and is present with us. It is so, and there can be no doubt of it; but our Emperor and Lord will have us now understand that He understands us; and also have us understand what His presence bringeth about, and that He means in a special way to begin a work in the soul, which is manifested in the great joy, inward and outward, which He communicates, and in the difference there is, as I said just now, between this joy and delight and all the joys of earth; for He seems to be filling up the void in our souls occasioned by our sins. *God will have the soul know that He is working in it.*

9. This satisfaction lies in the innermost part of the soul, and the soul knows not whence, nor how, it came; very often it knows not what to do, or wish, or pray for. It seems to find all this at once, and knoweth not what it hath found; nor do I know how to explain it, because learning is necessary for many things. Here, indeed, learning would be very much to the purpose, in order to explain the general and particular helps of grace; for there are many who know nothing about them. Learning would serve to show how our Lord now will have the soul to see, as it were, with the naked eye, as men speak, this particular help of grace, and be also useful in many other ways wherein I am likely to go astray. But as what I write is to be seen by those who have the learning to discover whether I make mistakes or not, I go on without anxiety; for I know I need have none whatever about either the letter or the spirit, because it is in their power to whom it is to be sent to do with it as they will: they will understand it, and blot out whatever may be amiss. *The Saint wishes she had more learning.*

10. I should like them to explain this, because it is a principal point, and because a soul, when our Lord begins to bestow these graces upon it, does not understand them, and does not know what to do with itself; for if God leads it by the way of fear, as He led me, its trial will be heavy, if there be no one who understands the state it is in; and to see itself as in a picture is a great comfort; and then it sees clearly that it is travelling on *Experience more valuable than books.*

that road. The knowledge of what it has to do is a great blessing for it, so that it may advance forwards in every one of these degrees of prayer; for I have suffered greatly, and lost much time, because I did not know what to do; and I am very sorry for those souls who find themselves alone when they come to this state; for though I read many spiritual books, wherein this very matter is discussed, they threw very little light upon it. And if it be not a soul much exercised in prayer, it will find it enough to understand its state, be the books ever so clear.

Experience a safeguard against delusion. 11. I wish much that our Lord would help me to describe the effects on the soul of these things, now that they begin to be supernatural, so that men might know by these effects whether they come from the Spirit of God. I mean, known as things are known here below,—though it is always well to live in fear, and on our guard; for even if they do come from God, now and then the devil will be able to transform himself into an angel of light;[1] and the soul, if not experienced herein, will not understand the matter; and it must have so much experience for the understanding thereof, that it is necessary it should have attained to the highest perfection of prayer.

The Saint writes under difficulties. 12. The little time I have helps me but little, and it is therefore necessary His Majesty should undertake it Himself; for I have to live in community, and have very many things to employ me, as I am in a house which is newly founded,—as will appear hereafter;[2] and so I am writing, with very many interruptions, by little and little at a time. I wish I had leisure; for when our Lord gives the spirit, it is more easily and better done; it is then as with a person working embroidery with the

[1] 2 Cor. xi. 14: "Ipse enim Satanas transfigurat se in angelum lucis."
[2] See ch. x. § 11. As that passage refers probably to the monastery of the Incarnation, this must refer to that of S. Joseph, newly founded in Avila; for that of the Incarnation was founded a short time before the Saint was born; and she could hardly say of it, now that she was at least in her forty-seventh year, that it was newly founded. The house, however, was poor; for she says, ch. xxxii. § 12, that the nuns occasionally quitted the monastery for a time, because of its poverty.

pattern before her; but if the spirit be wanting, there is no more meaning in the words than in gibberish, so to speak, though many years may have been spent in prayer. And thus I think it a very great advantage to be in this state of prayer when I am writing this; for I see clearly that it is not I who speak, nor is it I who with her understanding has arranged it; and afterwards I do not know how I came to speak so accurately.[1] It has often happened to me thus.

13. Let us now return to our orchard, or flower-garden, and behold now how the trees begin to fill with sap for the bringing forth of the blossoms, and then of the fruit,—the flowers and the plants, also, their fragrance. This illustration pleases me; for very often, when I was beginning,—and our Lord grant that I have really begun to serve His Majesty—I mean, begun in relation to what I have to say of my life,—it was to me a great joy to consider my soul as a garden, and our Lord as walking in it. I used to beseech Him to increase the fragrance of the little flowers of virtues,—which were beginning, as it seemed, to bud,—and preserve them, that they might be to His glory; for I desired nothing for myself. I prayed Him to cut those He liked, because I already knew that they would grow the better. *The soul likened to a garden.*

14. I say cut; for there are times in which the soul has no recollection of this garden,—every thing seems parched, and there is no water to be had for preserving it,—and in which it seems as if the soul had never possessed any virtue at all. This is the season of heavy trials; for our Lord will have the poor gardener suppose all the trouble he took in maintaining and watering the garden to have been taken to no purpose. Then is the time really for *Rooting up of imperfections.*

---

[1] See ch. xviii. § 12. In the second Report of the Rota, p. 477,—quoted by Benedict XIV., *De Canoniz.* iii. 26, n. 12, and by the Bollandists in the *Acta*, 1315,—we have these words, and they throw great light on the text: "Sunt et alii testes de visu affirmantes quod quando beata Teresa scribebat libros, facies ejus resplendebat." In the information taken in Granada, the Mother Anne of the Incarnation says she saw the Saint one night, while writing the *Fortress of the Soul*, with her face shining; and Mary of S. Francis deposes to the same effect in the informations taken in Medina (*De la Fuente*, vol. ii. pp. 389, 392).

weeding and rooting out every plant, however small it may be, that is worthless, in the knowledge that no efforts of ours are sufficient, if God withholds from us the waters of His grace; and in despising ourselves as being nothing, and even less than nothing. In this way we gain great humility—the flowers grow afresh.

The soul's delight in God. 15. O my Lord and my Good! I cannot utter these words without tears, and rejoicing in my soul; for Thou wilt be thus with us, and art with us, in the Sacrament. We may believe so most truly; for so it is, and the comparison I make is a great truth; and, if our sins stand not in the way, we may rejoice in Thee, because Thou rejoicest in us; for Thou hast told us that Thy delight is to be with the children of men.[1] O my Lord, what does it mean? Whenever I hear these words, they always give me great consolation, and did so even when I was most wicked.

16. Is it possible, O Lord, that there can be a soul which, after attaining to this state wherein Thou bestowest upon it the like graces and consolations, and wherein it understands that Thou delightest to be with it, can yet fall back and offend Thee after so many favours, and such great demonstrations of the love Thou bearest it, and of which there cannot be any doubt, because the effect of it is so visible? Such a soul there certainly is; for I have done so, not once, but often. May it please Thy goodness, O Lord, that I may be alone in my ingratitude—the only one who has committed so great an iniquity, and whose ingratitude has been so immeasurable! But even out of my ingratitude Thine infinite goodness has brought forth some good; and the greater my wickedness, the greater the splendour of the great mercy of Thy compassions. Oh, what reasons have I to magnify them for ever!

She prays for final perseverance. 17. May it be so, I beseech Thee, O my God, and may I sing of them for ever, now that Thou hast been pleased to show mercies so great unto me that they who see them are astonished, mercies which draw me out of myself continually, that I may praise Thee more and more! for, remaining in myself, without Thee, I could do

[1] Prov. viii. 31: "Deliciæ meæ esse cum filiis hominum."

nothing, O my Lord, but be as the withered flowers of the garden; so that this miserable earth of mine becomes a heap of refuse, as it was before. Let it not be so, O Lord!—let not a soul which Thou hast purchased with so many labours be lost, one which Thou hast so often ransomed anew, and delivered from between the teeth of the hideous dragon!

18. You, my father, must forgive me for wandering from the subject; and, as I am speaking to the purpose I have in view, you must not be surprised. What I write is what my soul has understood; and it is very often hard enough to abstain from the praises of God when, in the course of writing, the great debt I owe Him presents itself before me. Nor do I think that it can be disagreeable to you; because both of us, I believe, may sing the same song, though in a different way; for my debt is much the greater, seeing that God has forgiven me more, as you, my father, know.

CHAPTER XV.

INSTRUCTIONS FOR THOSE WHO HAVE ATTAINED TO THE PRAYER OF QUIET—MANY ADVANCE SO FAR, BUT FEW GO FARTHER.

1. LET us now go back to the subject. This quiet and recollection of the soul makes itself in great measure felt in the satisfaction and peace, attended with very great joy and repose of the faculties, and most sweet delight, wherein the soul is established.[1] It thinks, because it has not gone beyond it, that there is nothing further to wish for, but that its abode might be there, and it would willingly say so with S. Peter.[2] It dares not move nor stir, because it thinks that this blessing it has received must then escape out of its hands; now and then, it could wish it did not even breathe.[3] The poor little soul is not aware that, as of itself it could do nothing to draw down this blessing on itself, it is still less able to retain it a moment longer than our Lord wills it should remain.

The prayer of quiet in its effects.

[1] See *Way of Perfection*, ch. liii., but ch. xxxi. of the old edition.
[2] S. Matt. xvii. 4 : " Bonum est nos hic esse."   [3] See ch. xvii. § 8.

2. I have already said that, in the prior recollection and quiet,[1] there is no failure of the powers of the soul; but the soul is so satisfied in God that, although two of its powers be distracted, yet, while the recollection lasts, as the will abides in union with God, so its peace and quiet are not disturbed; on the contrary, the will by degrees brings the understanding and the memory back again; for though the will is not yet altogether absorbed, it continues still occupied without knowing how, so that, notwithstanding all the efforts of the memory and the understanding, they cannot rob it of its delight and joy,[2]—yea, rather, it helps without any labour at all to keep this little spark of the love of God from being quenched.

In itself.

3. Oh, that his Majesty would be gracious unto me, and enable me to give a clear account of the matter; for many are the souls who attain to this state, and few are they who go farther: and I know not who is in fault; most certainly it is not God; for when His Majesty shows mercy unto a soul, so that it advances so far, I believe that He will not fail to be more merciful still, if there be no shortcomings on our part.

Few souls advance beyond the prayer of quiet.

4. And it is of great importance for the soul that has advanced so far as this to understand the great dignity of its state, the great grace given it by our Lord, and how in all reason it should not belong to earth; because He, of His goodness, seems to make it here a denizen of heaven, unless it be itself in fault. And miserable will that soul be, if it turns back; it will go down—I think so—even to the abyss, as I was going myself, if the mercy of our Lord had not brought me back; because, for the most part, it must be the effect of grave faults—that is my opinion: nor is it possible to forsake so great a good otherwise than through the blindness occasioned by much evil.

The soul ought to be aware of the state it is in,

5. Therefore, for the love of our Lord, I implore those souls to whom His Majesty has given so great a grace—the attainment of this state—to know and make much of themselves, with a humble and holy presumption,

And watch against sin.

---

[1] Ch. x. § 1.   [2] Ch. xiv. §§ 3, 4.

in order that they may never return to the flesh-pots of Egypt. And if through weakness and wickedness, and a mean and wretched nature, they should fall, as I did, let them always keep in mind the good they have lost; let them suspect and fear—they have reason to do so—that, if they do not resume their prayer, they may go on from bad to worse. I call that a real fall which makes us hate the way by which so great a good was obtained. I address myself to those souls; but I am not saying that they will never offend God, nor fall into sin,—though there are good reasons why those who have received these graces should keep themselves carefully from sin; but we are miserable creatures. What I earnestly advise is this: let there be no giving up of prayer; it is by prayer they will understand what they are doing, and obtain from our Lord the grace to repent, and strength to rise again; they must believe and believe again that, if they cease from praying, they run—so I think—into danger. I know not if I understand what I am saying; for, as I said before, I measure others by myself.[1]

6. The prayer of quiet, then, is a little spark of the true love of Himself, which our Lord begins to enkindle in the soul; and His will is, that the soul should understand what this love is by the joy it brings. *Great fruits of the prayer of quiet.* This quiet and recollection and little spark, if it is the work of the Spirit of God, and not a sweetness supplied by Satan, or brought about by ourselves, produces great results. A person of experience, however, cannot possibly fail to understand at once that it is not a thing that can be acquired, were it not that our nature is so greedy of sweetness, that it seeks for it in every way. But it becomes cold very soon; for, however much we try to make the fire burn, in order to obtain this sweetness, it does not appear that we do any thing else but throw water on it, to put it out. This spark, then, given of God, however slight it may be, causes a great crackling; and if men do not quench it by their faults, it is the beginning of the great fire, which sends forth—I shall speak of it in the proper place[2]—the flames of that most vehement love of God which His Majesty will have perfect souls to possess.

[1] Ch. x. § 11. [2] Ch. xviii. § 5, and ch. xxi. § 9.

7. This little spark is a sign or pledge which God gives to a soul, in token of His having chosen it for great things, if it will prepare to receive them. It is a great gift, much too great for me to be able to speak of it. It is a great sorrow to me; because, as I said before,[1] I know that many souls come thus far, and that those who go farther, as they ought to go, are so few, that I am ashamed to say it. I do not mean that they are absolutely few: there must be many, because God is patient with us, for some reasons; I speak of what I have seen.

Few souls go on to perfection.

8. I should like much to recommend these souls to take care that they do not hide their talent; for it may be that God has chosen them to be the edification of many others, especially in these days, when the friends of God should be strong, in order that they may support the weak. Those who discern in themselves this grace, must look upon themselves as such friends, if they would fulfil the law which even the honourable friendship of the world respects; if not, as I said just now,[2] let them fear and tremble, lest they should be doing mischief to themselves—and God grant it be to themselves only!

Friends of God.

9. What the soul has to do at those seasons wherein it is raised to the prayer of quiet is nothing more than to be gentle and without noise. By noise, I mean going about with the understanding in search of words and reflections whereby to give God thanks for this grace, and heaping up its sins and imperfections together to show that it does not deserve it. All this commotion takes place now, and the understanding comes forward, and the memory is restless, and certainly to me these powers bring much weariness at times; for though my memory is not strong, I cannot control it. Let the will quietly and wisely understand that it is not by dint of labour on our part that we can converse to any good purpose with God, and that our own efforts are only great logs of wood, laid on without discretion to quench this little spark; and let it confess this, and in humility say, O Lord, what can I do here? what has the servant to do with her Lord, and earth with heaven? or words of love that sug-

How the soul is to order itself in the prayer of quiet.

[1] § 3.   [2] § 5.

gest themselves now, firmly grounded in the conviction that what it says is truth; and let it make no account of the understanding, which is simply tiresome.

10. And if the will wishes to communicate to the understanding any portion of that the fruition of which itself has entered on, or if it labours to make the understanding recollected, it shall not succeed; for it will often happen that the will is in union and at rest, while the understanding is in extreme disorder. It is better for it to leave it alone, and not to run after it—I am speaking of the will; for the will should abide in the fruition of that grace, recollected itself, like the prudent bee; for if no bees entered the hive, and each of them wandered abroad in search of the rest, the honey would hardly be made. In the same way, the soul will lose much if it be not careful now, especially if the understanding be acute; for when it begins to make reflections and search for reasons, it will think at once that it is doing something if its reasons and reflections are good. *Distractions of the understanding.*

11. The only reason that ought to be admitted now is to understand clearly that there is no reason whatever, except His mere goodness, why God should grant us so great a grace, and to be aware that we are so near Him, and to pray to His Majesty for mercies, to make intercession for the Church, for those who have been recommended to us, and for the souls in purgatory,—not, however, with noise of words, but with a heartfelt desire to be heard. This is a prayer that contains much, and by it more is obtained than by many reflections of the understanding. Let the will stir up some of those reasons, which proceed from reason itself, to quicken its love, such as the fact of its being in a better state, and let it make certain acts of love, as what it will do for Him to whom it owes so much,—and that, as I said just now, without any noise of the understanding, in the search after profound reflections. A little straw,—and it will be less than straw, if we bring it ourselves,—laid on with humility, will be more effectual here, and will help to kindle the fire more than many fagots of most learned reasons, which, in my opinion, will put it out in a moment. *Earnest prayer.*

Learning of no great use during prayer.

12. This is good for those learned men who have commanded me to write,[1] and who all, by the goodness of God, have come to this state; for it may be that they spend the time in making applications of passages of the Scriptures. And though learning could not fail to be of great use to them, both before and after prayer, still, in the very time of prayer itself, there is little necessity for it, in my opinion, unless it be for the purpose of making the will tepid; for the understanding then, because of its nearness to the light, is itself illuminated; so that even I, who am what I am, seem to be a different person. And so it is; for it has happened to me, who scarcely understand a word of what I read in Latin, and specially in the Psalms, when in the prayer of quiet, not only to understand the Latin as if it were Spanish, but, still more, to take a delight in dwelling on the meaning of that I knew through the Spanish. We must make an exception: if these learned men have to preach or to teach, they will do well to take advantage of their learning, that they may help poor people of little learning, of whom I am one. Charity is a great thing; and so always is ministering unto souls, when done simply for God.

The use of learning for men of prayer.

13. So, then, when the soul is in the prayer of quiet, let it repose in its rest—let learning be put on one side. The time will come when they may make use of it in the service of our Lord—when they that possess it will appreciate it so highly as to be glad that they had not neglected it even for all the treasures of the world, simply because it enables them to serve His Majesty; for it is a great help. But in the eyes of Infinite Wisdom, believe me, a little striving after humility, and a single act thereof, are worth more than all the science in the world. This is not the time for discussing, but for understanding plainly what we are, and presenting ourselves in simplicity before God, who will have the soul make itself as a fool—as, indeed, it is—in His presence, seeing that His Majesty so humbles Himself as to suffer it to be near Him, we being what we are.

[1] Ch. x. § 12.

14. Moreover, the understanding bestirs itself to make its thanksgiving in phrases well arranged; but the will, in peace, not daring to lift up its eyes with the publican,[1] makes perhaps a better act of thanksgiving than the understanding, with all the tropes of its rhetoric. In a word, mental prayer is not to be abandoned altogether now, nor even vocal prayer, if at any time we wish, or can, to make use of either of them; for if the state of quiet be profound, it becomes difficult to speak, and it can be done only with great pain.

Vocal prayer may be had recourse to at times.

15. I believe myself that we know whether this proceeds from the Spirit of God, or is brought about by endeavours of our own, in the commencement of devotion which God gives; and we seek of ourselves, as I said before,[2] to pass onwards to this quiet of the will. Then, no effect whatever is produced; it is quickly over, and aridity is the result. If it comes from Satan, the practised soul, in my opinion, will detect it, because it leaves trouble behind, and scant humility and poor dispositions for those effects which are wrought if it comes from God; it leaves neither light in the understanding nor steadiness in the truth.[3]

False and true quiet.

16. Here Satan can do little or no harm, if the soul directs unto God the joy and sweetness it then feels; and if it fixes the thoughts and desires on Him, according to the advice already given, the devil can gain nothing whatever—on the contrary, by the permission of God, he will lose much by that very joy which he causes in the soul, because that joy will help the soul, inasmuch as it thinks the joy comes from God, to betake itself often to prayer in its desire for it. And if the soul is humble,

How the soul may profit by the attempts of Satan to deceive.

[1] S. Luke xviii. 13: "Nolebat nec oculos ad cœlum levare."
[2] Ch. xii. § 5.
[3] "Firmeza en la verdad." Francisco de S. Thomas, in his *Medula Mystica*, p. 204, quoting this passage, has, "firmeza en la voluntad." Philip. a SS. Trinitate, *Theolog. Mystic.* p. 354, and his Abbreviator, Anton. a Sp. Sancto, *Direct. Mystic.* tr. iv. disp. i. § 11, n. 94, seem also to have preferred " voluntad" to " verdad ;" for the words they use are, " nec intellectui lux nec voluntati firmitas;" and, " defectus lucis in intellectu, et firmitatis in voluntate."

indifferent to, and detached from, all joy, however spiritual, and if it loves the cross, it will make no account of the sweetness which Satan sends. But it cannot so deal with that which comes from the Spirit of God; of that it will make much. Now, when Satan sends it, as he is nothing but a lie, and when he sees that the soul humbles itself through that joy and sweetness,— and here, in all things relating to prayer and sweetness, we must be very careful to endeavour to make ourselves humble,—Satan will not often repeat his work, when he sees that he loses by it.

17. For this and for many other reasons, when *Detachment necessary.* I was speaking of the first degree of prayer, and of the first method of drawing the water,[1] I insisted upon it that the great affair of souls is, when they begin to pray, to begin also to detach themselves from every kind of joy, and to enter on it resolved only on helping to carry the cross of Christ like good soldiers, willing to serve their King without present pay, because they are sure of it at last, having their eyes directed to the true and everlasting kingdom at the conquest of which we are aiming.

18. It is a very great matter to have this always *Beginning and perfection compared.* before our eyes, especially in the beginning; afterwards, it becomes so clear, that it is rather a matter of necessity to forget it, in order to live on. Now, labouring to keep in mind that all things here below are of short duration, that they are all nothing, that the rest we have here is to be accounted as none,—all this, I say, seems to be exceedingly low; and so, indeed, it is,—because those who have gone on to greater perfection would look upon it as a reproach, and be ashamed of themselves, if they thought that they were giving up the goods of this world because they are perishable, or that they would not be glad to give them up for God—even if they were to last for ever. The greater the perfection of these persons, the greater their joy, and the greater also would that joy be if the duration of these worldly goods were greater.

19. In these persons, thus far advanced, love is *Beginners must begin humbly.* already grown, and love is that which does this work. But as to beginners, to them it is of the utmost im-

[1] Ch. xi. § 16.

portance, and they must not regard this consideration as unbecoming, for the blessings to be gained are great,—and that is why I recommend it so much to them; for they will have need of it—even those who have attained to great heights of prayer—at certain times, when God will try them, and when His Majesty seems to have forsaken them.

20. I have said as much already, and I would not have it forgotten,[1] in this our life on earth, the growth of the soul is not like that of the body. We, however, so speak of it—and, in truth, it does grow. A youth that is grown up, whose body is formed, and who is become a man, does not ungrow, nor does his body lessen in size; but as to the soul, it so is by our Lord's will, so far as I have seen it in my own experience,—but I know nothing of it in any other way. It must be in order to humble us for our greater good, and to keep us from being careless during our exile; seeing that he who has ascended the higher has the more reason to be afraid, and to be less confident in himself. A time may come when they whose will is so wrapt up in the will of God—and who, rather than fall into a single imperfection, would undergo torture and suffer a thousand deaths—will find it necessary, if they would be delivered from offending God, and from the commission of sin, to make use of the first armour of prayer, to call to mind how every thing is coming to an end, that there is a heaven and a hell, and to make use of other reflections of that nature, when they find themselves assailed by temptations and persecutions.

The soul's growth and ungrowth.

21. Let us go back to what I was saying. The great source of our deliverance from the cunning devices and the sweetness which Satan sends is to begin with a resolution to walk in the way of the Cross from the very first, and not to desire any sweetness at all, seeing that our Lord Himself has pointed out to us the way of perfection, saying, "Take up thy cross and follow Me."[2] He is our example; and whosoever follows His counsels only to please Him has nothing to fear. In the improvement which they detect in

How the work of Satan may be detected.

[1] Ch. xiii. § 23.
[2] S. Matt. xvi. 24: "Tollat crucem suam et sequatur Me."

themselves, they who do so will see that this is no work of Satan; and if they fall, they have a sign of the presence of our Lord in their rising again at once. They have other signs, also, of which I am going to speak.

22. When it is the work of the Spirit of God, <small>Effects of the Spirit of God.</small> there is no necessity for going about searching for reasons, on the strength of which we may elicit acts of humility and of shame, because our Lord Himself supplies them in a way very different from that by which we could acquire them by our own poor reflections, which are as nothing in comparison with that real humility arising out of the light which our Lord here gives us, and which begets a confusion of face that undoes us. The knowledge with which God supplies us, in order that we may know that of ourselves we have no good in us, is perfectly apprehended—and the more perfectly, the greater the graces. It fills us with a great desire of advancing in prayer, and of never giving it up, whatever troubles may arise. The soul offers to suffer every thing. A certain security, joined with humility and fear concerning our salvation, casts out servile fear at once from the soul, and in its place plants a loyal fear[1] of more perfect growth.[2] There is a visible beginning of a love of God, utterly divested of all self-interest, together with a longing after seasons of solitude, in order to obtain a greater fruition of this good.

<small>The effects of certain natural dispositions.</small> 23. In short, not to weary myself, it is the beginning of all good; the flowers have so thriven, that they are on the point of budding. And this the soul sees most clearly, and it is impossible to persuade it now that God was not with it, till it turns back upon itself, and beholds its own failings and imperfections. Then it fears for every thing; and it is well it should do so—though there are souls whom the certain conviction that God is with them benefits more than all the fear they may ever have. If a soul love greatly, and is thankful naturally, the remembrance of the mercies of God makes it turn towards Him more effectually than all the chastisements of hell it can ever picture to itself—at least, it was so with me, though I am so wicked.

[1] "Fiel temor." In the previous editions it was *filial*. [2] Ch. xi. § 1.

24. As I shall speak at greater length of the signs of a good spirit[1]—it has cost me much labour to be clear about them—I do not treat of them here. I believe, too, that, with the help of God, I shall be able to speak somewhat to the point, because—setting aside the experience I have had, and by which I learned much—I have had the help of some most learned men and persons of great holiness, whom we may reasonably believe in the matter. Souls, therefore, are not to weary themselves so much as I did, when, by the goodness of our Lord, they may have come to this state.

CHAPTER XVI.

THE THIRD STATE OF PRAYER — DEEP MATTERS — WHAT THE SOUL CAN DO THAT HAS REACHED IT — EFFECTS OF THE GREAT GRACES OF OUR LORD.

1. LET us now speak of the third water wherewith this garden is watered,—water running from a river or from a brook,—whereby the garden is watered with very much less trouble, although there is some in directing the water.[2] In this state our Lord will help the gardener, and in such a way as to be, as it were, the Gardener Himself, doing all the work. It is a sleep of the powers of the soul, which are not wholly lost, nor yet understanding how they are at work. The pleasure, sweetness, and delight are incomparably greater than in the former state of prayer; and the reason is, that the waters of grace have risen up to the neck of the soul, so that it can neither advance nor retreat—nor does it know how to do so;

---

[1] See ch. xxv.
[2] "The third degree, or third water, of the Saint must begin, I think, with the prayer of infused recollection, include that of infused quiet, and end in that of inebriation; because it is not in our power to draw this water—all we can do is to direct the stream" (Francis. de S. Thomas, *Medula Mystica*, tr. iv. ch. xii. p. 208).

it seeks only the fruition of exceeding bliss. It is like a dying man with the candle in his hand, on the point of dying the death desired. It is rejoicing in this agony with unutterable joy; to me it seems to be nothing else but a death, as it were, to all the things of this world, and a fruition of God. I know of no other words whereby to describe it or to explain it; neither does the soul then know what to do,—for it knows not whether it should speak or be silent, whether it should laugh or weep. It is a glorious folly, a heavenly madness, wherein true wisdom is acquired; and to the soul a kind of fruition most full of delight.[1]

The Saint raised to this degree of prayer without knowing what it was. 2. It is now some five or six years, I believe, since our Lord raised me to this state of prayer, in its fulness, and that more than once,—and I never understood it, and never could explain it; and so I was resolved, when I should come thus far in my story, to say very little or nothing at all. I knew well enough that it was not altogether the union of all the faculties, and yet most certainly it was higher than the previous state of prayer; but I confess that I could not determine and understand the difference.

3. The humility of your reverence, willing to be *Spiritual inebriation.* helped by a simplicity so great as mine, has been the cause, I believe, why our Lord, to-day, after Communion, admitted me to this state of prayer, without the power of going further, and suggested to me these comparisons, and taught me how to speak of it, and of what the soul must do therein. Certainly, I was amazed, and in a moment understood it all. I have often been thus, as it were, beside myself, drunk with love, and yet never could understand how it was. I knew well that it was the work of God, but I never was able to understand the manner of His working here; for, in fact, the faculties are almost all completely in union, yet not so absorbed that they do not act. I have been singularly delighted in that I have been able to comprehend the matter at last. Blessed be our Lord, who has thus consoled me!

[1] See S. John of the Cross *Spirit. Canticle*, stanza xvii. vol. ii. p. 98, Engl. trans.

4. The faculties of the soul now retain only the power of occupying themselves wholly with God; not one of them ventures to stir, neither can we move one of them without making great efforts to distract ourselves—and, indeed, I do not think we can do it at all at this time. Many words are then uttered in praise of God— but disorderly, unless it be that our Lord orders them Himself. At least, the understanding is utterly powerless here; the soul longs to send forth words of praise, but it has no control over itself,—it is in a state of sweet restlessness. The flowers are already opening; they are beginning to send forth their fragrance.

The faculties of the soul rendered powerless.

5. The soul in this state would have all men behold it, and know of its bliss, to the praise of God, and help it to praise Him. It would have them to be partakers of its joy; for its joy is greater than it can bear. It seems to me that it is like the woman in the Gospel, who would, or used to, call in her neighbours.[1] The admirable spirit of David, the royal prophet, must have felt in the same way, so it seems to me, when he played on the harp, singing the praises of God. I have a very great devotion to this glorious king;[2] and I wish all had it, particularly those who are sinners like myself.

The soul beside itself,

6. O my God, what must that soul be when it is in this state? It wishes it were all tongue, in order that it may praise our Lord. It utters a thousand holy follies, striving continually to please Him by whom it is thus possessed. I know one[3] who, though she was no poet, yet composed, without any preparation, certain stanzas, full of feeling, most expressive of her pain: they were not the work of her own understanding; but, in order to have a greater fruition of that bliss which so sweet a pain occasioned her, she complained of it in that way to God. She was willing to be cut in pieces, soul and body, to show the delight she felt in that pain. To what torments could she be then exposed, that

In the greatness of its love.

---

[1] S. Luke xv. 9 : "Convocat amicas et vicinas."
[2] *Foundations,* ch. xxvii. § 16.
[3] The Saint herself (*De la Fuente*).

would not be delicious to endure for her Lord? She sees clearly that the martyrs did little or nothing, so far as they were concerned, when they endured their tortures, because the soul is well aware that its strength is derived from another source.

The pain of returning to consciousness. 7. But what will be its sufferings when it returns to the use of the senses, to live in the world, and go back to the anxieties and the fashions thereof? I do not think that I have exaggerated in any way, but rather have fallen short, in speaking of that joy which our Lord, of His good pleasure, gives to the soul in this its exile. Blessed for ever be Thou, O Lord! and may all created things praise Thee for ever!

Spiritual madness. 8. O my King, seeing that I am now, while writing this, still under the power of this heavenly madness, an effect of Thy mercy and goodness,—and it is a mercy I never deserved,—grant, I beseech Thee, that all those with whom I may have to converse may become mad through Thy love, or let me converse with none, or so order it that I may have nothing to do in the world, or take me away from it. This Thy servant, O my God, is no longer able to endure sufferings so great as those are which she must bear when she sees herself without Thee: if she must live, she seeks no repose in this life,—and do Thou give her none. This my soul longs to be free—eating is killing it, and sleep is wearisome; it sees itself wasting the time of this life in comforts, and that there is no comfort for it now but in Thee; it seems to be living contrary to nature—for now, it desires to live not in itself, but in Thee.

The cross light and heavy. 9. O my true Lord and my happiness! what a cross hast Thou prepared for those who attain to this state!—light and most heavy at the same time: light, because sweet; heavy, because now and then there is no patience left to endure it,—and yet the soul never wishes to be delivered from it, unless it be that it may come to Thee. When the soul remembers that it has never served Thee at all, and that by living on it may do Thee some service, it longs for a still heavier cross, and never to die before the end of the world. Its own repose it counts as nothing in comparison with doing a slight service to Thee. It knows not what to desire; but it clearly understands that it desires nothing else but Thee.

10. O my son,[1]—so humble is he to whom this writing is directed, and who has commanded me to write, that he suffers himself to be thus addressed, —you, my father, only must see these things, in which I seem to have transgressed all bounds; for no reason can keep me reasonable when our Lord draws me out of myself. Since my communion this morning,[2] I do not believe that I am the person who is speaking; I seem to be dreaming the things I see, and I wish I might never see any but people ill, as I am now. I beseech you, my father, let us all be mad, for the love of Him who for our sakes suffered men to say of Him that He was mad.[3] *Exuberance of love.*

11. You, my father, say that you wish me well. I wish you would prove it by disposing yourself so that God may bestow this grace upon you; for I see very few people who have not too much sense for every thing they have to do: and it may be that I have more than any body else. Your reverence must not allow it; you are my father, for you are my confessor, and the person to whom I have trusted my soul; disperse my delusions by telling the truth; for truths of this sort are very rarely told. *Truth rarely told.*

12. I wish we five, who now love one another in our Lord, had made some such arrangement as this: as others in these times have met together in secret[4] to plot wickedness and heresies against His Majesty, so we might contrive to meet together now and then, in order to undeceive one *The Saint's desire for sincerity.*

---

[1] This was either F. Ibañez or the Inquisitor Soto, if the expression did not occur in the first Life. F. Dom. Bañes struck out "son," and wrote "father" in its place, omitting the words, "so humble is he" (*De la Fuente*).
[2] See § 3, above.
[3] S. John x. 20: "Dæmonium habet et insanit."
[4] The Saint refers to the secret meetings of heretics in Valladolid, under the direction of a fallen priest, the Doctor Agostino Cazalla, whose vanity led him to imitate Luther. Some nuns in Valladolid were imprisoned, Cazalla strangled, and his body burnt, in 1559 (*De la Fuente*).

another, to tell each other wherein we might improve ourselves, and be more pleasing unto God; for there is no one that knows himself as well as he is known of others who see him, if it be with eyes of love and the wish to do him good. I say, in secret; for language of this kind is no longer in use; even preachers go about arranging their sermons so as to displease no one.[1] They have a good intention, and their work is good; yet still few amend their lives. But how is it that they are not many who, in consequence of these sermons, abstain from public sins? Well, I think it is because the preachers are highly sensible men. They are not burning with the great fire of the love of God, as the Apostles were, casting worldly prudence aside; and so their fire throws out but little heat. I do not say that their fire ought to burn like that of the Apostles, but I do wish it were a stronger fire than I see it is. Do you, my father, know wherein much of this fire consists? In the hatred of this life, in the desertion of its honours, in being utterly indifferent whether we lose or gain any thing or every thing, provided the truth be told and maintained for the glory of God; for he who is courageously in earnest for God, looks upon loss or gain indifferently. I do not say that I am a person of this kind, but I wish I was.

13. Oh, grand freedom, to regard it as a captivity to be obliged to live and converse with men according to the laws of the world! It is the gift of our Lord; there is not a slave who would not imperil every thing that he might escape and return to his country; and as this is the true road, there is no reason why we should linger; for we shall never effectually gain a treasure so great, so long as this life is not ended. May our Lord give us His grace for that end! You, my father, if it shall seem good to you, will tear up what I have written, and consider it as a letter for yourself alone, and forgive me that I have been very bold.

Freedom of detachment.

---

[1] Father Bañes wrote here on the margin of the Saint's MS.: "Legant prædicatores" (*De la Fuente*).

CHAPTER XVII.

THE THIRD STATE OF PRAYER—THE EFFECTS THEREOF—THE HINDRANCE CAUSED BY THE IMAGINATION AND THE MEMORY.

1. ENOUGH has been said of this manner of prayer, and of what the soul has to do, or rather, to speak more correctly, of what God is doing within it; for it is He who now takes upon Himself the gardener's work, and who will have the soul take its ease; except that the will is consenting to the graces, the fruition of which it has, and that it must resign itself to all that the True Wisdom would accomplish in it—for which it is certain it has need of courage; because the joy is so great, that the soul seems now and then to be on the very point of going forth out of the body: and what a blessed death that would be! Now, I think it is for the soul's good—as you, my father, have been told—to abandon itself into the arms of God altogether; if He will take it to heaven, let it go; if to hell, no matter, as it is going thither with its sovereign Good. If life is to come to an end for ever, so it wills; if it is to last a thousand years, it wills that also: His Majesty may do with it as with His own property, —the soul no longer belongs to itself, it has been given wholly to our Lord; let it cast all care utterly away. *The soul is passive in this state.*

2. My meaning is that, in a state of prayer so high as this, the soul understands that God is doing His work without any fatiguing of the understanding, except that, as it seems to me, it is as if amazed in beholding our Lord taking upon Himself the work of the good gardener, refusing to let the soul undergo any labour whatever, but that of taking its pleasure in the flowers beginning to send forth their fragrance; for when God raises a soul up to this state, it can do all this, and much more,—for these are the effects of it. *Because God Himself is working.*

3. In one of these visits, how brief soever it may be, the Gardener, being who He is,—in a word, the Creator of the water,—pours the water without stint; and what the poor soul, with the labour, perhaps, of twenty *Rapidity of the divine work.*

years in fatiguing the understanding, could not bring about, that the heavenly Gardener accomplishes in an instant, causing the fruit both to grow and ripen ; so that the soul, such being the will of our Lord, may derive its sustenance from its garden. But He allows it not to divide the fruit with others, until by eating thereof it is strong enough not to waste it in the mere tasting of it,—giving to Him none of the produce, nor making any compensation for it to Him who supplies it,—lest it should be maintaining others, feeding them at its own cost, and itself perhaps dying of hunger.[1] The meaning of this is perfectly clear for those who have understanding enough to apply it— much more clear than I can make it ; and I am tired.

The virtues stronger. Humility deeper.
4. Finally, the virtues are now stronger than they were during the preceding prayer of quiet ; for the soul sees itself to be other than it was, and it knows not how it is beginning to do great things in the odour which the flowers send forth ; it being our Lord's will that the flowers should open, in order that the soul may believe itself to be in possession of virtue; though it sees most clearly that it cannot, and never could, acquire them in many years, and that the heavenly Gardener has given them to it in that instant. Now, too, the humility of the soul is much greater and deeper than it was before ; because it sees more clearly that it did neither much nor little, beyond giving its consent that our Lord might work those graces in it, and then accepting them willingly.

The third state of prayer.
5. This state of prayer seems to me to be a most distinct union of the whole soul with God, but for this, that His Majesty appears to give the faculties leave to be intent upon, and have the fruition of, the great work He is doing then. It happens at times, and indeed very often, that, the will being in union, the soul should be aware of it, and see that the will is a captive and in joy, that the will alone is abiding in great peace,—while, on the other hand, the understanding and the memory are so free, that they can be employed in affairs and be occupied in works of charity. I say this, that you, my father, may see it is so, and understand the

[1] See ch. xix. § 5.

matter when it shall happen to yourself; at least, it carried me out of myself, and that is the reason why I speak of it here.

6. It differs from the prayer of quiet, of which I have spoken,[1] though it does seem as if it were all one with it. In that prayer, the soul, which would willingly neither stir nor move, is delighting in the holy repose of Mary; but in this prayer it can be like Martha also.[2] Accordingly, the soul is, as it were, living the active and contemplative life at once, and is able to apply itself to works of charity and the affairs of its state, and to spiritual reading. Still, those who arrive at this state are not wholly masters of themselves, and are well aware that the better part of the soul is elsewhere. It is as if we were speaking to one person, and another speaking to us at the same time, while we ourselves are not perfectly attentive either to the one or the other. It is a state that is most easily ascertained, and one, when attained to, that ministers great joy and contentment, and that prepares the soul in the highest degree, by observing times of solitude, or of freedom from business, for the attainment of the most tranquil quietude. It is like the life of a man who is full, requiring no food, with his appetite satisfied, so that he will not eat of every thing set before him, yet not so full either as to refuse to eat if he saw any desirable food. So the soul has no satisfaction in the world, and seeks no pleasure in it then; because it has in itself that which gives it a greater satisfaction, greater joys in God, longings for the satisfaction of its longing to have a deeper joy in being with Him—this is what the soul seeks.

How it differs from the prayer of quiet.

7. There is another kind of union, which, though not a perfect union, is yet more so than the one of which I have just spoken; but not so much so as this spoken of as the third water. You, my father, will be delighted greatly if our Lord should bestow them all upon you, if you have them not already, to find an account of the matter in writing, and to understand it; for it is one grace

The great advantage of understanding the graces given us.

[1] Ch. xv. § 1.
[2] See *Relation*, viii. § 6; and *Way of Perfection*, ch. liii., but ch. xxxi. of former editions. See also *Concept. of the Love of God*, ch. vii.

that our Lord gives grace; and it is another grace to understand what grace and what gift it is; and it is another and further grace to have the power to describe and explain it to others. Though it does not seem that more than the first of these—the giving of the grace—is necessary to enable the soul to advance without confusion and fear, and to walk with the greater courage in the way of our Lord, trampling under foot all the things of this world, it is a great advantage and a great grace to understand it; for every one who has it has great reason to praise our Lord; and so, also, has he who has it not: because His Majesty has bestowed it upon some person living who is to make us profit by it.

The prayer of imperfect union. 8. This union, of which I would now speak, frequently occurs, particularly to myself. God has very often bestowed such a grace upon me, whereby He constrains the will, and even the understanding, as it seems to me, seeing that it makes no reflections, but is occupied in the fruition of God: like a person who looks on, and sees so many things, that he knows not where to look—one object puts another out of sight, and none of them leaves any impression behind.

Disturbed by the memory. 9. The memory remains free, and it must be so, together with the imagination; and so, when it finds itself alone, it is marvellous to behold what war it makes on the soul, and how it labours to throw every thing into disorder. As for me, I am wearied by it, and I hate it; and very often do I implore our Lord to deprive me of it on these occasions, if I am to be so much troubled by it. Now and then, I say to Him: O my God, when shall my soul praise Thee without distraction, not dissipated in this way, unable to control itself! I understand now the mischief that sin has done, in that it has rendered us unable to do what we desire—to be always occupied in God.[1]

The Saint's experience of this degree of prayer. 10. I say that it happens to me from time to time,—it has done so this very day, and so I remember it well,—to see my soul tear itself, in order to find itself there where the greater part of it is, and

---

[1] See *Relation*, viii. § 17.

to see, at the same time, that it is impossible: because the memory and the imagination assail it with such force, that it cannot prevail against them; yet, as the other faculties give them no assistance, they are not able to do it any harm—none whatever; they do enough when they trouble its rest. When I say they do no harm, my meaning is, that they cannot really hurt it, because they have not strength enough, and because they are too discursive. As the understanding gives no help, neither much nor little, in the matters put before the soul, they never rest any where, but hurry to and fro, like nothing else but gnats at night, troublesome and unquiet: and so they go about from one subject to another.

11. This comparison seems to me to be singularly to the purpose; for the memory and the imagination, though they have no power to do any harm, are very troublesome. I know of no remedy for it; and, hitherto, God has told me of none. If He had, most gladly would I make use of it; for I am, as I say, tormented very often. This shows our wretchedness, and brings out most distinctly the great power of God, seeing that the faculty which is free hurts and wearies us so much; while the others, occupied with His Majesty, give us rest. *No help against the importunities of the memory*

12. The only remedy I have found, after many years of weariness, is that I spoke of when I was describing the prayer of quiet:[1] to make no more account of it than of a madman, but let it go with its subject; for God alone can take it from it,—in short, it is a slave here. We must bear patiently with it, as Jacob bore with Lia; for our Lord showeth us mercy enough when we are allowed to have Rachel with us. *But that of neglecting it.*

13. I say that it remains a slave; for, after all, let it do what it will, it cannot drag the other faculties in its train; on the contrary, they, without taking any trouble, compel it to follow after them. Sometimes God is pleased to take pity upon it, when He sees it so lost and so unquiet, through the longing it has to be *God sends help at times.*

[1] Ch. xiv. § 4. See also *Way of Perfection*, ch. liii., but ch. xxxi. of the old editions.

united with the other faculties, and His Majesty consents to its burning itself in the flame of that divine candle by which the others are already reduced to ashes, and their nature lost, being, as it were, supernaturally in the fruition of blessings so great.

The explanation of the Saint as clear as any that can be given. 14. In all these states of prayer of which I have spoken, while explaining this last method of drawing the water out of the well, so great is the bliss and repose of the soul, that even the body most distinctly shares in its joy and delight,—and this is most plain; and the virtues continue to grow, as I said before.[1] It seems to have been the good pleasure of our Lord to explain these states of prayer, wherein the soul finds itself, with the utmost clearness possible, I think, here on earth.

15. Do you, my father, discuss it with any spiritual person who has arrived at this state, and is learned. If he says of it, it is well, you may believe that God has spoken it, and you will give thanks to His Majesty; for, as I said just now,[2] in the course of time you will rejoice greatly in that you have understood it. Meanwhile, if He does not allow you to understand what it is, though He does give you the possession of it, yet, with your intellect and learning, seeing that His Majesty has given you the first, you will know what it is, by the help of what I have written here. Unto Him be praise for ever and ever! Amen.

CHAPTER XVIII.

THE FOURTH STATE OF PRAYER—THE GREAT DIGNITY OF THE SOUL RAISED TO IT BY OUR LORD—ATTAINABLE ON EARTH, NOT BY OUR MERIT, BUT BY THE GOODNESS OF OUR LORD.

The fourth water. 1. MAY our Lord teach me words whereby I may in some measure describe the fourth water.[3] I have great need of His help—even more than I had while speaking of the last; for in that the soul still feels that it is not dead altogether. We may thus speak, seeing that to the world it

[1] Ch. xiv. § 6. [2] § 7. [3] See ch. xi. § 4.

is really dead. But, as I have said,[1] it retains the sense to see that it is in the world, and to feel its own loneliness; and it makes use of that which is outward for the purpose of manifesting its feelings, at least by signs. In the whole of the prayer already spoken of, and in all the states of it, the gardener undergoes some labour; though in the later states the labour is attended with so much bliss and comfort of the soul, that the soul would never willingly pass out of it,—and thus the labour is not felt as labour, but as bliss.

2. In this the fourth state there is no sense of any thing, only fruition, without understanding what that is the fruition of which is granted. It is understood that the fruition is of a certain good containing in itself all good together at once; but this good is not comprehended. The senses are all occupied in this fruition in such a way that not one of them is at liberty, so as to be able to attend to any thing else, whether outward or inward. *Effects of the prayer of passive union.*

3. The senses were permitted before, as I have said,[2] to give some signs of the great joy they feel; but now, in this state, the joy of the soul is incomparably greater, and the power of showing it is still less; for there is no power in the body, and the soul has none, whereby this fruition can be made known. Every thing of that kind would be a great hindrance, a torment, and a disturbance of its rest. And I say, if it really be a union of all the faculties, that the soul, even if it wished,—I mean, when it is in union,—cannot make it known; and if it can, then it is not union at all. *The senses wholly absorbed.*

4. How this, which we call union, is effected, and what it is, I cannot tell. Mystical theology explains it, and I do not know the terms of that science; nor can I understand what the mind is, nor how it differs from the soul or the spirit either: all three seem to me but one; though I do know that the soul sometimes leaps forth out of itself, like a fire that is burning and is become a flame; and occasionally this fire increases violently—the flame ascends high above the fire; but it is not therefore a different thing: *Mystical theology.*

[1] Ch. xvi. §§ 5, 6.   [2] Ch. xvii. § 5.

it is still the same flame of the same fire. Your learning, my fathers, will enable you to understand the matter; I can go no further.

All souls unworthy of the divine munificence. 5. What I undertake to explain is that which the soul feels when it is in the divine union. It is plain enough what union is—two distinct things becoming one. O my Lord, how good Thou art! Blessed be Thou for ever, O my God! Let all creatures praise Thee, who hast so loved us that we can truly speak of this communication which Thou hast with souls in this our exile! Yea, even if they be good souls, it is on Thy part great munificence and magnanimity,—in a word, it is Thy munificence, O my Lord, seeing that Thou givest like Thyself. O infinite Munificence! —how magnificent are Thy works! Even he whose understanding is not occupied with the things of earth is amazed that he is unable to understand these truths. Why, then, give graces so high to souls who have been such great sinners? Truly, this passeth my understanding; and when I come to think of it, I can get no further. Is there any way at all for me to go on which is not a going back? For, as to giving Thee thanks for mercies so great, I know not how to do it. Sometimes I relieve myself by giving utterance to follies. It often happens to me, either when I receive these graces, or when God is about to bestow them,—for, in the midst of them, I have already said,[1] I was able to do nothing,—that I would break out into words like these:

Prayer of the Saint. 6. O Lord, consider what Thou art doing; forget not so soon the great evils that I have done. To forgive me, Thou must already have forgotten them; yet, in order that there may be some limit to Thy graces, I beseech Thee remember them. O my Creator, pour not a liquor so precious into a vessel so broken; for Thou hast already seen how on other occasions I allowed it to run waste. Lay not up treasure like this, where the longing after the consolations of this life is not so mortified as it ought to be; for it will be utterly lost. How canst Thou commit the defence of the city and the keys of its fortress to a commander so

[1] § 4.

cowardly, who at the first assault will let the enemy enter within? Oh, let not Thy love be so great, O King Eternal, as to imperil jewels so precious! O my Lord, to me it seems that it becomes a ground for undervaluing them, when Thou puttest them in the power of one so wretched, so vile, so frail, so miserable, and so worthless as I am, who, though she may labour not to lose them, by the help of Thy grace,—and I have need of no little grace for that end, being what I am,—is not able to win over any one to Thee,—in short, I am a woman, not good, but wicked. It seems to me that the talents are not only hidden, but buried, when they are committed to earth so vile. It is not Thy wont, O Lord, to bestow graces and mercies like these upon a soul, unless it be that it may edify many.

7. Thou, O my God, knowest already that I beg this of Thee with my whole will, from the bottom of my heart, and that I have done so more than once, and I account it a blessing to lose the greatest blessings which may be had on earth, if Thou wouldst but bestow these graces upon him who will make a better use of them to the increase of Thy glory. These, and expressions like these, it has happened to me often to utter. I saw afterwards my own foolishness and want of humility; for our Lord knoweth well what is expedient, and that there is no strength in my soul to be saved, if His Majesty did not give it with graces so great.

8. I purpose also to speak of the graces and effects which abide in the soul, and of that which the soul itself can do, or rather, if it can do any thing of itself towards attaining to a state so high. The elevation of the spirit, or union, comes together with heavenly love; but, as I understand it, union is a different thing from elevation in union itself. To him who may not have had any experience of the latter, it must seem that it is not; and, according to my view of it, even if they are both one, the operations of our Lord therein are different: there is a growth of the soul's detachment from creatures more abundantly still in the flights of the spirit.[1] I have clearly seen that this is a particular grace,—though, as I say, it may be the same, or seem to be so, with the

Union and elevation.

[1] See ch. xx. § 10; and *Relation*, viii. § 11.

other; but a little fire, also, is as much fire as a great fire, and yet there is a visible difference between them. Before a small piece of iron is made red-hot in a little fire, some time must pass; but if the fire be great, the iron very quickly, though bulky, loses its nature altogether in appearance.

The Saint makes excuses for teaching mystical theology. 9. So, it seems to me, is it with these two kinds of graces which our Lord bestows. He who has had raptures will, I am sure, understand it well; to him who has not had that experience, it must appear folly. And, indeed, it may well be so; for if a person like myself should speak of a matter of this kind, and give any explanation at all of that for the description of which no words even can possibly be found, it is not to be wondered at that I may be speaking foolishly.

The Saint's reasons for writing. 10. But I have this confidence in our Lord, that He will help me here; for His Majesty knoweth that my object in writing—the first is to obey—is to inspire souls with a longing after so high a good. I will speak of nothing that I do not know by great experience: and so, when I began to describe the last kind of water, I thought it more impossible for me to speak of it at all than to speak Greek. It is a very difficult matter; so I left it, and went to Communion. Blessed be our Lord, who is merciful to the ignorant! Oh, virtue of obedience! it can do every thing! God enlightened my understanding—at one time suggesting the words, at another showing me how to use them; for, as in the preceding state of prayer, so also now, His Majesty seems to utter what I can neither speak nor understand.[1]

11. What I am saying is the simple truth; and *The teaching from God.* therefore whatever is good herein is His teaching; what is erroneous, clearly comes out of that sea of evil—myself. If there be any—and there must be many—who, having attained to these states of prayer whereunto our Lord in His mercy has brought me—wretch that I am!—and who, thinking they have missed their way, desire to treat of these matters with me, I am sure that our Lord will help His servant to declare the truth more plainly.

[1] See ch. xiv. § 12.

12. I am now speaking of the water which cometh down from heaven to fill and saturate in its abundance the whole of this garden with water. If our Lord never ceased to pour it down whenever it was necessary, the gardener certainly would have plenty of rest; and if there were no winter, but an ever temperate season, fruits and flowers would never fail. The gardener would have his delight therein; but in this life that is impossible. We must always be careful, when one water fails, to obtain another. This water from heaven comes down very often when the gardener least expects it. *The fourth water.*

13. The truth is that, in the beginning, this almost always happens after much mental prayer. Our Lord advances step by step to lay hold of the little bird, and to lay it in the nest where it may repose. He observed it fluttering for a long time, striving with the understanding and the will, and with all its might, to seek God and to please Him; so now it is His pleasure to reward it even in this life. And what a reward!—one moment is enough to repay all the possible trials of this life. *Perseverance in prayer rewarded.*

14. The soul, while thus seeking after God, is conscious, with a joy excessive and sweet, that it is, as it were, utterly fainting away in a kind of trance: breathing, and all the bodily strength, fail it, so that it cannot even move the hands without great pain; the eyes close involuntarily, and if they are open, they are as if they saw nothing; nor is reading possible,—the very letters seem strange, and cannot be distinguished,—the letters, indeed, are visible, but, as the understanding furnishes no help, all reading is impracticable, although seriously attempted. The ear hears; but what is heard is not comprehended. The senses are of no use whatever, except to hinder the soul's fruition; and so they rather hurt it. It is useless to try to speak, because it is not possible to conceive a word; nor, if it were conceived, is there strength sufficient to utter it; for all bodily strength vanishes, and that of the soul increases, to enable it the better to have the fruition of its joy. Great and most perceptible, also, is the outward joy now felt. *The prayer of passive union.*

K

15. This prayer, however long it may last, does no harm—at least, it has never done any to me; nor do I remember, however ill I might have been when our Lord had mercy upon me in this way, that I ever felt the worse for it—on the contrary, I was always better afterwards. But so great a blessing, what harm can it do? The outward effects are so plain as to leave no doubt possible that there must have been some great cause, seeing that it thus robs us of our bodily powers with so much joy, in order to leave them greater.

Not followed by any bodily suffering.

16. The truth is, it passes away so quickly in the beginning—at least, so it was with me—that neither by the outward signs, nor by the failure of the senses, can it be perceived when it passes so quickly away. But it is plain, from the overflowing abundance of grace, that the brightness of the sun which had shone there must have been great, seeing that it has thus made the soul to melt away. And this is to be considered; for, as it seems to me, the period of time, however long it may have been, during which the faculties of the soul were entranced, is very short: if half an hour, that would be a long time. I do not think that I have ever been so long.[1] The truth of the matter is this: it is extremely difficult to know how long, because the senses are in suspense; but I think that at any time it cannot be very long before some one of the faculties recovers itself. It is the will that persists in the work; the other two faculties quickly begin to molest it. As the will is calm, it entrances them again; they are quiet for another moment, and then they recover themselves once more.

Passes quickly away.

17. In this way, some hours may be, and are, passed in prayer; for when the two faculties begin to drink deep, and to perceive the taste of this divine wine, they give themselves up with great readiness, in order to be the more absorbed: they follow the will, and the three rejoice together. But this state of complete absorption, together with the utter rest of the imagination,—for I believe that even the imagination is then wholly at rest,—lasts only for a short

Short duration of a trance.

[1] See Anton. a Sp. Sancto, *Director. Mystic.* tr. iv. § 9, n. 72.

time; though the faculties do not so completely recover themselves as not to be for some hours afterwards as if in disorder: God, from time to time, drawing them to Himself.

18. Let us now come to that which the soul feels interiorly. Let him describe it who knows it; for as it is impossible to understand it, much more is it so to describe it. When I purposed to write this, I had just communicated, and had risen from the very prayer of which I am speaking. I was thinking of what the soul was then doing. Our Lord said to me: It undoes itself utterly, My daughter, in order that it may give itself more and more to Me: it is not itself that then lives, it is I. As it cannot comprehend what it understands, it understands by not understanding.[1] *What occurs in a trance.*

19. He who has had experience of this will understand it in some measure, for it cannot be more clearly described, because what then takes place is so obscure. *Suspension of all the senses.* All I am able to say is, that the soul is represented as being close to God; and that there abides a conviction thereof so certain and strong, that it cannot possibly help believing so. All the faculties fail now, and are suspended in such a way that, as I said before,[2] their operations cannot be traced. If the soul is making a meditation on any subject, the memory of it is lost at once, just as if it had never been thought of. If it reads, what is read is not remembered nor dwelt upon; neither is it otherwise with vocal prayer. Accordingly, the restless little butterfly of the memory has its wings burnt now, and

[1] Thomas à Jesu, *De Contemplatione Divina*, lib. v. c. xiii.: " Quasi dicat: Cum intellectus non possit Dei immensam illam claritatem et incomprehensibilem plenitudinem comprehendere, hoc ipsum est illam conspicere ac intelligere, intelligere se non posse intellectu cognoscere: quod quidem nihil aliud est quam Deum sub ratione incomprehensibilitatis videre ac cognoscere."

Philip. a SS. Trinitate, *Theolog. Mystic. Disc. Proem.* art. iv. p. 6: "Cum ipsa [S. Teresa] scire vellet, quid in illa mystica unione operaretur intellectus, respondit [Christus] illi, cum non possit comprehendere quod intelligit, est non intelligere intelligendo: tum quia præ claritate nimia quodammodo offuscatur intellectus, unde præ altissima et supereminentissima Dei cognitione videtur anima potius Deum ignorare quam cognoscere."

[2] Ch. x. § 1, and ch. xviii. § 16.

it cannot fly. The will must be fully occupied in loving, but it understands not how it loves; the understanding, if it understands, does not understand how it understands—at least, it can comprehend nothing of that it understands: it does not understand, as it seems to me, because, as I said just now, this cannot be understood. I do not understand it at all myself.

Ignorance of theology disturbed her prayer. 20. In the beginning, it happened to me that I was ignorant of one thing—I did not know that God is in all things:[1] and when He seemed to me to be so near, I thought it impossible. Not to believe that He was present, was not in my power; for it seemed to me, as it were, evident that I felt there His very presence. Some unlearned men used to say to me, that He was present only by His grace. I could not believe that, because, as I am saying, He seemed to me to be present Himself: so I was distressed. A most learned man, of the Order of the glorious Patriarch S. Dominic, delivered me from this doubt; for he told me that He was present, and how He communed with us: this was a great comfort to me.

21. It is to be observed and understood that this water from heaven,—this greatest grace of our Lord,—always leaves in the soul the greatest fruits, as I shall now show.

CHAPTER XIX.

THE EFFECTS OF THIS FOURTH STATE OF PRAYER—EARNEST EXHORTATIONS TO THOSE WHO HAVE ATTAINED TO IT NOT TO GO BACK, NOR TO CEASE FROM PRAYER, EVEN IF THEY FALL—THE GREAT CALAMITY OF GOING BACK.

Effects of the passive union. Tenderness of the soul. 1. THERE remains in the soul, when the prayer of union is over, an exceedingly great tenderness; so much so, that it would undo itself—not from pain, but through tears of joy: it finds itself bathed therein, without being aware of it, and it knows not how or

[1] See *Inner Fortress*, v. ch. i. § 11.

when it wept them. But to behold the violence of the fire subdued by the water, which yet makes it burn the more, gives it great delight. It seems as if I were speaking an unknown language. So it is, however.

2. It has happened to me occasionally, when this prayer was over, to be so beside myself as not to know whether I had been dreaming, or whether the bliss I felt had really been mine; and, on finding myself in a flood of tears—which had painlessly flowed, with such violence and rapidity that it seemed as if a cloud from heaven[1] had shed them—to perceive that it was no dream. Thus it was with me in the beginning, when it passed quickly away. The soul remains possessed of so much courage, that if it were now hewn in pieces for God, it would be a great consolation to it. This is the time of resolutions, of heroic determinations, of the living energy of good desires, of the beginning of hatred of the world, and of the most clear perception of its vanity. The soul makes greater and higher progress than it ever made before in the previous states of prayer; and grows in humility more and more, because it sees clearly that neither for obtaining nor for retaining this grace, great beyond all measure, has it ever done, or ever been able to do, any thing of itself. It looks upon itself as most unworthy—for in a room into which the sunlight enters strongly, not a cobweb can be hid; it sees its own misery; self-conceit is so far away, that it seems as if it never could have had any— for now its own eyes behold how very little it could ever do, or rather, that it never did any thing, that it hardly gave even its own consent, but that it rather seemed as if the doors of the senses were closed against its will, in order that it might have more abundantly the fruition of our Lord. It is abiding alone with Him: what has it to do but to love Him? It neither sees nor hears, unless on compulsion: no thanks to it. Its past life stands before it then, together with the great mercy of God, in great distinctness; and it is not necessary for it to go forth to hunt with the understanding, because what it has to eat and ruminate upon, it sees now ready prepared. It sees,

Generous resolutions.

[1] See ch. xx. § 2.

so far as itself is concerned, that it has deserved hell, and that its punishment is bliss. It undoes itself in the praises of God, and I would gladly undo myself now.

3. Blessed be Thou, O my Lord, who, out of a pool so filthy as I am, bringest forth water so clean as to be meet for Thy table! Praised be Thou, O Joy of the Angels, who hast been thus pleased to exalt so vile a worm!

Fruits of the prayer of union. 4. The good effects of this prayer abide in the soul for some time. Now that it clearly apprehends that the fruit is not its own, the soul can begin to share it with others, and that without any loss to itself. It begins to show signs of its being a soul that is guarding the treasures of heaven, and to be desirous of communicating them to others,[1] and to pray to God that itself may not be the only soul that is rich in them. It begins to benefit its neighbours, as it were, without being aware of it, or doing any thing consciously: its neighbours understand the matter, because the odour of the flowers has grown so strong as to make them eager to approach them. They understand that this soul is full of virtue: they see the fruit, how delicious it is, and they wish to help that soul to eat it.

Necessity of watching over the soul, 5. If this ground be well dug by troubles, by persecutions, detractions, and infirmities,—they are few who ascend so high without this,—if it be well broken up by great detachment from all self-interest, it will drink in so much water that it can hardly ever be parched again. But if it be ground which is mere waste, and covered with thorns (as I was when I began); if the occasions of sin be not avoided; if it be an ungrateful soil, unfitted for so great a grace,—it will be parched up again. If the gardener become careless,—and if our Lord, out of His mere goodness, will not send down rain upon it,—the garden is ruined. Thus has it been with me more than once, so that I am amazed at it; and if I had not found it so by experience, I could not have believed it.

And of courage to persevere. 6. I write this for the comfort of souls which are weak, as I am, that they may never despair, nor cease to trust in the power of God; even if they

[1] See ch. xvii. § 4.

should fall after our Lord has raised them to so high a degree of prayer as this is, they must not be discouraged, unless they would lose themselves utterly. Tears gain every thing, and one drop of water attracts another.

7. One of the reasons that move me, who am what I am, under obedience to write this, and give an account of my wretched life, and of the graces our Lord has wrought in me,—though I never served Him, but offended Him rather,—is what I have just given: and, certainly, I wish I was a person of great authority, that people might believe what I say. I pray to our Lord that His Majesty would be pleased to grant me this grace. I repeat it, let no one who has begun to give himself to prayer be discouraged, and say: If I fall into sin, it will be worse for me if I go on now with the practice of prayer. I think so too, if he gives up prayer, and does not correct his evil ways; but if he does not give up prayer, let him be assured of this—prayer will bring him to the haven of light. *One of the Saint's reasons for writing.*

8. In this the devil turned his batteries against me, and I suffered so much because I thought it showed but little humility if I persevered in prayer when I was so wicked, that—as I have already said[1]—I gave it up for a year and a half—at least, for a year, but I do not remember distinctly the other six months. This could not have been, neither was it, any thing else but to throw myself down into hell; there was no need of any devils to drag me thither. O my God, was there ever blindness so great as this? How well Satan prepares his measures for his purpose, when he pursues us in this way! The traitor knows that he has already lost that soul which perseveres in prayer, and that every fall which he can bring about helps it, by the goodness of God, to make greater progress in His service. Satan has some interest in this. *Temptation of Satan to omit prayer.*

9. O my Jesus, what a sight that must be—a soul so highly exalted falling into sin, and raised up again by Thee; who, in Thy mercy, stretchest forth Thine hand to save! How such a soul confesses Thy greatness *The soul praises God.*

[1] Ch. vii. § 17, and ch. viii. § 6.

and compassion, and its own wretchedness! It really looks on itself as nothingness, and confesses Thy power. It dares not lift up its eyes; it raises them, indeed, but it is to acknowledge how much it oweth unto Thee. It becomes devout to the Queen of Heaven, that she may propitiate Thee; it invokes the Saints, who fell after Thou hadst called them, for succour. Thou seemest now to be too bountiful in Thy gifts, because it feels itself to be unworthy of the earth it treads on. It has recourse to the Sacraments, to a quickened faith, which abides in it at the contemplation of the power which Thou hast lodged in them. It praises Thee because Thou hast left us such medicines and ointment for our wounds, which not only heal them on the surface, but remove all traces whatever of them.

10. The soul is amazed at it. Who is there, O Lord of my soul, that is not amazed at compassion so great and mercy so surpassing, after treason so foul and so hateful? I know not how it is that my heart does not break when I write this, for I am wicked. With these scanty tears which I am now weeping, but yet Thy gift,—water out of a well, so far as it is mine, so impure,—I seem to make Thee some recompense for treachery so great as mine, in that I was always doing evil, labouring to make void the graces Thou hast given me. Do Thou, O Lord, make my tears available; purify the water which is so muddy; at least, let me not be to others a temptation to rash judgments, as I have been to myself, when I used to think such thoughts as these. Why, O Lord, dost Thou pass by most holy persons, who have always served Thee, and who have been tried; who have been brought up in religion, and are really religious—not such as I am, having only the name—so as to make it plain that they are not recipients of those graces which Thou hast bestowed upon me?

The Saint makes excuses for her detractors. 11. I see clearly now, O Thou my Good, Thou hast kept the reward to give it them all at once: my weakness has need of these succours. They, being strong, serve Thee without them, and Thou dealest with them as with a strong race, free from all self-interest. But yet Thou knowest, O my Lord, that I have often cried unto Thee, making excuses for those who murmured against me; for I thought they had reason on their side. This I did then when Thou of Thy goodness hadst kept me back from offending Thee so much, and when I was departing from every thing which I thought displeasing unto Thee. It was when I did this that Thou, O Lord, didst begin to lay open Thy treasures for Thy servant. It seemed as if Thou wert looking for nothing else but that I should be willing and ready to receive them; accordingly, Thou didst begin at once, not only to give them, but also to make others know that Thou wert giving them.

12. When this was known, there began to prevail a good opinion of her, of whom all had not yet clearly understood how wicked she was, though much of that wickedness was plain enough. Calumny and persecution began at once, and, as I think, with good reason; so I looked on none of them as an enemy, but made my supplications to Thee, imploring Thee to consider the grounds they had. They said that I wished to be a saint, and that I invented novelties; but I had not then attained in many things even to the observance of my rule; nor had I come near those excellent and holy nuns who were in the house,—and I do not believe I ever shall, if God of His goodness will not do that for me Himself; on the contrary, I was there only to do away with what was good, and introduce customs which were not good; at least, I did what I could to bring them in, and I was very powerful for evil. Thus it was that they were blameless, when they blamed me. I do not mean the nuns only, but the others as well: they told me truths; for it was Thy will.

S. Teresa evil spoken of.

13. I was once saying the Office,—I had had this temptation for some time,—and when I came to these words, "Justus es, Domine, et rectum judicium tuum,"[1] I began to think what a deep truth it was. Satan never was strong enough to tempt me in any way to doubt of Thy goodness, or of any article of the faith: on the contrary, it seems to me that the more these truths were above nature, the more firmly I held them, and my devotion grew; when I

The ways of God. Divine locution.

[1] Ps. cxviii. 137: "Thou art just, O Lord, and Thy judgment is right."

thought of Thy omnipotence, I accepted all Thy wonderful works, and, I say it again, I never had a doubt. Then, as I was thinking how it could be just in Thee to allow so many, who, as I said, are Thy most faithful servants, to remain without those consolations and graces which Thou hast given to me, who am what I am, Thou, O my Lord, didst answer me : Serve thou Me, and meddle not with this.

Effects of the divine locution. 14. This was the first word which I ever heard Thee speak to me, and it made me greatly afraid. But as I shall speak hereafter[1] of this way of hearing, and of other matters, I say nothing here; for to do so would be to digress from my subject, and I have already made digressions enough. I scarcely know what I have said, nor can it be otherwise; but you, my father, must bear with these interruptions; for when I consider what God must have borne with from me, and when I see the state I am in, it is not strange that I should wander in what I am saying, and what I have still to say.

Dangers of false humility. 15. May it please our Lord that my wanderings may be of this kind, and may His Majesty never suffer me to have strength to resist Him even in the least; yea, rather than that, may He destroy me this moment. It is evidence enough of His great compassions, that He has forgiven so much ingratitude, not once, but often. He forgave S. Peter once; but I have been forgiven many times. Satan had good reasons for tempting me : I ought never to have pretended to a strict friendship with One, my hatred of whom I made so public. Was there ever blindness so great as mine ? Where could I think I should find help but in Thee ? What folly to run away from the light, to be for ever stumbling! What a proud humility was that which Satan devised for me, when I ceased to lean upon the pillar, and threw the staff away which supported me, in order that my fall might not be great !²

16. I make the sign of the cross this moment. *The risks the Saint ran* I do not think I ever escaped so great a danger as this device of Satan, which he would have imposed

¹ See ch. xxv. ² See ch. viii. § 1.

upon me in the disguise of humility.[1] He filled me with such thoughts as these: How could I make my prayer, who was so wicked, and yet had received so many mercies? It was enough for me to recite the Office, as all others did; but as I did not that much well, how could I desire to do more? I was not reverential enough, and made too little of the mercies of God. There was no harm in these thoughts and feelings in themselves; but to act upon them, that was an exceedingly great wickedness. Blessed be Thou, O Lord; for Thou camest to my help. This seems to me to be in principle the temptation of Judas, only that Satan did not dare to tempt me so openly. But he might have led me by little and little, as he led Judas, to the same pit of destruction.

17. Let all those who give themselves to prayer, for the love of God, look well to this. They should know that when I was neglecting it, my life was much worse than it had ever been; let them reflect on the excellent help and the pleasant humility which Satan provided for me: it was a grave interior disquietude. But how could my spirit be quiet? It was going away in its misery from its true rest. I remembered the graces and mercies I had received, and felt that the joys of this world were loathsome. I am astonished that I was able to bear it. It must have been the hope I had; for, as well as I can remember now, it is more than twenty-one years ago. I do not think I ever gave up my purpose of resuming my prayer; but I was waiting to be very free from sin first. *During the year she did not practise mental prayer.*

18. Oh, how deluded I was in this expectation! The devil would have held it out before me till the day of judgment, that he might then take me with him to hell. Then, when I applied myself to prayer and to spiritual reading,—whereby I might perceive these truths, and the evil nature of the way I was walking in, and was often importunate with our Lord in tears,—I was so wicked, that it availed me nothing; when I gave that up, and wasted my time in amusing myself, in great danger of falling into sin, and with scanty helps,—and I may venture to say no help at all, unless it *The Saint's self-accusations.*

[1] Ch. vii. § 17.

was a help to my ruin,—what could I expect but that of which I have spoken?

19. I believe that a certain Dominican friar, a most learned man, has greatly merited in the eyes of God; for it was he who roused me from this slumber. He made me—I think I said so before[1]—go to Communion once a fortnight, and be less given to evil; I began to be converted, though I did not cease to offend our Lord all at once: however, as I had not lost my way, I walked on in it, though slowly, falling and rising again; and he who does not cease to walk and press onwards, arrives at last, even if late. To lose one's way is—so it seems to me—nothing else but the giving up of prayer. God, of His mercy, keep us from this!

<small>Fr. Vicente Baron.</small>

20. It is clear from this,—and, for the love of God, consider it well,—that a soul, though it may receive great graces from God in prayer, must never rely on itself, because it may fall, nor expose itself in any way whatever to any risks of sin. This should be well considered, because much depends on it; for the delusion here, wherein Satan is able to entangle us afterwards, though the grace be really from God, lies in the traitor's making use of that very grace, so far as he can, for his own purpose, and particularly against persons not grown strong in virtues, who are neither mortified nor detached; for these are not at present strong enough—as I shall explain hereafter[2]—to expose themselves to dangerous occasions, notwithstanding the noble desires and resolutions they may have.

<small>Necessity of distrust of self.</small>

21. This doctrine is excellent, and not mine, but the teaching of God, and accordingly I wish ignorant people like myself knew it; for even if a soul were in this state, it must not rely so much upon itself as to go forth to the battle, because it will have enough to do in defending itself. Defensive armour is the present necessity; the soul is not yet strong enough to assail Satan, and to trample him under foot, as those are who are in the state of which I shall speak further on.[3]

<small>This doctrine from God.</small>

[1] Ch. vii. § 27.   [2] Ch. xxxi. § 21.
[3] Ch. xx. § 33, and ch. xxv. § 24.

22. This is the delusion by which Satan prevails: when a soul sees itself so near unto God, when it sees the difference there is between the things of heaven and those of earth, and when it sees the love which our Lord bears it, there grows out of that love a certain trust and confidence that there is to be no falling away from that the fruition of which it then possesses. It seems to see the reward distinctly, as if it were impossible for it to abandon that which, even in this life, is so delicious and sweet, for any thing so mean and impure as worldly joy. Through this confidence, Satan robs it of that distrust which it ought to have in itself; and so, as I have just said,[1] the soul exposes itself to dangers, and begins, in the fulness of its zeal, to give away without discretion the fruit of its garden, thinking that now it has no reason to be afraid for itself. Yet this does not come out of pride; for the soul clearly understands that of itself it can do no good thing; but rather out of an excessive confidence in God, without discretion: because the soul does not see itself to be unfledged. It can go forth out of its nest, and God Himself may take it out, but still it cannot fly, because the virtues are not strong, and itself has no experience wherewith to discern the dangers; nor is it aware of the evil which trusting to itself may do it.

Dangers of self-confidence.

23. This it was that ruined me. Now, to understand this, and every thing else in the spiritual life, we have great need of a director, and of conference with spiritual persons. I fully believe, with respect to that soul which God raises to this state, that He will not cease to be gracious to it, nor suffer it to be lost, if it does not utterly forsake His Majesty. But when that soul—as I said—falls, let it look to it again and again, for the love of our Lord, that Satan deceive it not by tempting it to give up prayer, as he tempted me, through that false humility of which I have spoken before,[2] and would gladly speak of again and again. Let it rely on the goodness of God, which is greater than all the evil we can do. When we, acknowledging our own vileness, desire to return into His grace, He remembers our ingratitude no

Necessity of perseverance in prayer.

[1] Ch. xvii. § 4.   [2] See § 16.

more,—no, not even the graces He has given us, for the purpose of chastising us, because of our misuse of them; yea, rather, they help to procure our pardon the sooner, as of persons who have been members of His household, and who, as they say, have eaten of His bread.

24. Let them remember His words, and behold what He hath done unto me, who grew weary of sinning before He grew weary of forgiving. He is never weary of giving, nor can His compassion be exhausted. Let us not grow weary ourselves of receiving. May He be blessed for ever, amen; and may all created things praise Him!

Mercies of God.

CHAPTER XX.

THE DIFFERENCE BETWEEN UNION AND RAPTURE—WHAT RAPTURE IS—THE BLESSING IT IS TO THE SOUL—THE EFFECTS OF IT.

1. I WISH I could explain, with the help of God, wherein union differs from rapture, or from transport, or from flight of the spirit, as they speak, or from a trance, which are all one.[1] I mean, that all these are only different names for that one and the same thing, which is also called ecstasy.[2] It is more excellent than union, the fruits

Raptures.

---

[1] See *Inner Fortress*, vi. ch. v.; Philippus a SS. Trinitate, *Theolog. Mystic.* par. iii tr. 1, art. 3: "Hæc oratio raptûs superior est præcedentibus orationis gradibus, etiam orationis unionis ordinariæ, et habet effectus multo excellentiores et multas alias operationes."

[2] "She says that rapture is more excellent than union; that is, that the soul in a rapture has a greater fruition of God, and that God takes it then more into His own hands. That is evidently so; because in a rapture the soul loses the use of its exterior and interior faculties. When she says that union is the beginning, middle, and end, she means that pure union is almost always uniform; but that there are degrees in rapture, of which some are, as it were, the beginning, some the middle, others the end. That is the reason why it is called by different names; some of which denote the least, others the most, perfect form of it, as it will appear hereafter."—Note in the Spanish edition of Lopez (*De la Fuente*).

of it are much greater, and its other operations more manifold; for union is uniform in the beginning, the middle, and the end, and is so also interiorly. But as raptures have ends of a much higher kind, they produce effects both within and without.[1] As our Lord has explained the other matters, so also may He explain this; for certainly, if He had not shown me in what way and by what means this explanation was in some measure possible, I should never have been able to do it.

2. Consider we now that this last water, of which I am speaking, is so abundant that, were it not that the ground refuses to receive it, we might suppose *How effected.* that the cloud of His great Majesty is here raining down upon us on earth. And when we are giving Him thanks for this great mercy, drawing near to Him in earnest, with all our might, then it is our Lord draws up the soul, as the clouds, so to speak, gather the mists from the face of the earth, and carries it away out of itself,—I have heard it said that the clouds, or the sun, draw the mists together,[2]—and as a cloud, rising up to heaven, takes the soul with Him, and begins to show it the treasures of the kingdom which He has prepared for it. I know not whether the comparison be accurate or not; but the fact is, that is the way in which it is brought about. During rapture, the soul does not seem to animate the body, the natural heat of which is perceptibly lessened; the coldness increases, though accompanied with exceeding joy and sweetness.[3]

[1] Anton. a Spirit. Sancto, *Direct. Mystic.* tr. 4, d. i. n. 95: "Licet oratio raptûs idem sit apud mysticos ac oratio volatûs, seu elevationis spiritus seu extasis: reipsa tamen raptus aliquid addit super extasim: nam extasis importat simplicem excessum mentis in seipso secundum quem aliquis extra suam cognitionem ponitur. Raptus vero super hoc addit violentiam quandam ab aliquo extrinseco."

[2] The words between the dashes are in the handwriting of the Saint —not, however, in the text, but on the margin (*De la Fuente*).

[3] See *Inner Fortress*, vi. ch. x: "Primus effectus orationis ecstaticæ est in corpore, quod ita remanet, ac si per animam non informaretur, infrigidatur enim calore naturali deficiente, clauduntur suaviter oculi, et alii sensus amittuntur: contingit tamen quod corpus infirmum in hac oratione sanitatem recuperat." Anton. a Spirit. Sancto, *Direct. Mystic.* tr. iv. d. 2, § 6, n. 150.

3. A rapture is absolutely irresistible; whilst union, inasmuch as we are then on our own ground, may be hindered, though that resistance be painful and violent; it is, however, almost always possible. But rapture, for the most part, is irresistible. It comes, in general, as a shock, quick and sharp, before you can collect your thoughts, or help yourself in any way, and you see and feel it as a cloud, or a strong eagle rising upwards, and carrying you away on its wings.

Union may be hindered.

4. I repeat it : you feel and see yourself carried away, you know not whither. For though we feel how delicious it is, yet the weakness of our nature makes us afraid at first, and we require a much more resolute and courageous spirit than in the previous states, in order to risk every thing, come what may, and to abandon ourselves into the hands of God, and go willingly whither we are carried, seeing that we must be carried away, however painful it may be; and so trying is it, that I would very often resist, and exert all my strength, particularly at those times when the rapture was coming on me in public. I did so, too, very often when I was alone, because I was afraid of delusions. Occasionally I was able, by great efforts, to make a slight resistance; but afterwards I was worn out, like a person who had been contending with a strong giant; at other times it was impossible to resist at all : my soul was carried away, and almost always my head with it,—I had no power over it,—and now and then the whole body as well, so that it was lifted up from the ground.

But rapture is irresistible.

5. This has not happened to me often : once, however, it took place when we were all together in choir, and I, on my knees, on the point of communicating. It was a very sore distress to me; for I thought it a most extraordinary thing, and was afraid it would occasion much talk; so I commanded the nuns—for it happened after I was made Prioress—never to speak of it. But at other times, the moment I felt that our Lord was about to repeat the act, and once, in particular, during a sermon,—it was the feast of our house, some great ladies being present,—I threw myself on

S. Teresa in raptures.

the ground; then the nuns came around me to hold me; but still the rapture was observed.

6. I made many supplications to our Lord, that He would be pleased to give me no more of those graces which were outwardly visible; for I was weary of living under such great restraint, and because His Majesty could not bestow such graces on me without their becoming known. It seems that, of His goodness, He has been pleased to hear my prayer; for I have never been enraptured since. It is true that it was not long ago.[1] *Prays to be delivered from them.*

7. It seemed to me, when I tried to make some resistance, as if a great force beneath my feet lifted me up. I know of nothing with which to compare it; but it was much more violent than the other spiritual visitations, and I was therefore as one ground to pieces; for it is a great struggle, and, in short, of little use, whenever our Lord so wills it. There is no power against His power. *How raptures took place.*

8. At other times He is pleased to be satisfied when He makes us see that He is ready to give us this grace, and that it is not He that withholds it. Then, when we resist it out of humility, He produces those very effects which would have resulted if we had fully consented to it. *Their effects produced without them.*

9. The effects of rapture are great: one is that the mighty power of our Lord is manifested; and as we are not strong enough, when His Majesty wills it, to control either soul or body, so neither have we any power over it; but, whether we like it or not, we see that there is one mightier than we are, that these graces are His gifts, and that of ourselves we can do nothing whatever; and humility is deeply imprinted in us. And further, I confess that it threw me into great fear, very great indeed at first; for when I saw my body thus lifted up from the earth, how could I help it? Though the spirit draws it upwards after itself, and that with great sweetness, if unresisted, the senses are not lost; at least, I was so much myself as to be able to see that I was being *Effects of raptures.*

[1] This passage could not have been in the first Life; for that was written before she had ever been Prioress.

lifted up. The majesty of Him who can effect this so manifests itself, that the hairs of my head stand upright,[1] and a great fear comes upon me of offending God, who is so mighty. This fear is bound up in exceedingly great love, which is acquired anew, and directed to Him, who, we see, bears so great a love to a worm so vile, and who seems not to be satisfied with attracting the soul to Himself in so real a way, but who will have the body also, though it be mortal and of earth so foul, such as it is through our sins, which are so great.

10. Rapture leaves behind a certain strange detachment also, which I shall never be able to describe;

Detachment.

I think I can say that it is in some respects different from—yea, higher than—the other graces, which are simply spiritual; for though these effect a complete detachment in spirit from all things, it seems that in this of rapture our Lord would have the body itself be detached also; and thus a certain singular estrangement from the things of earth is wrought, which makes life much more distressing. Afterwards it causes a pain, which we can never inflict of ourselves, nor remove when once it has come.

11. I should like very much to explain this great pain, and I believe I shall not be able; however, I

Pains of rapture

will say something if I can. And it is to be observed that this is my present state, and one to which I have been brought very lately, after all the visions and revelations of which I shall speak, and after that time, wherein I gave myself to prayer, in which our Lord gave me so much sweetness and delight.[2] Even now I have that sweetness occasionally; but it is the pain of which I speak that is the most frequent and the most common. It varies in its intensity. I will now speak of it when it is sharpest; for I shall speak later on[3] of the great shocks I used to feel when our Lord would throw me into those trances, and which are, in my opinion, as different from this pain as the most corporeal thing is from the most spiritual; and I believe that I am not exaggerating much.

---

[1] Job iv. 15: "Inhorruerunt pili carnis meæ." (See S. John of the Cross, *Spiritual Canticle*, sts. 14, 15, vol. ii. p. 83, Engl. trans.)
[2] See ch. xxix.   [3] See ch. xxi. § 8.

For though the soul feels that pain, it is in company with the body;[1] both soul and body apparently share it, and it is not attended with that extremity of abandonment which belongs to this.

12. As I said before,[2] we have no part in causing this pain; but very often there springs up a desire unexpectedly,—I know not how it comes,—and because of this desire, which pierces the soul in a moment, the soul begins to be wearied, so much so that it rises upwards above itself, and above all created things. God then so strips it of every thing, that, do what it may, there is nothing on earth that can be its companion. Neither, indeed, would it wish to have any; it would rather die in that loneliness. If people spoke to it, and if itself made every effort possible to speak, it would be of little use: the spirit, notwithstanding all it may do, cannot be withdrawn from that loneliness; and though God seems, as it were, far away from the soul at that moment, yet He reveals His grandeurs at times in the strangest way conceivable. That way is indescribable; I do not think any one can believe or comprehend it who has not previously had experience of it. It is a communication made, not to console, but to show the reason why the soul must be weary: because it is far away from the Good which in itself comprehends all good. *Beyond our power.*

13. In this communication the desire grows, so also does the bitterness of that loneliness wherein the soul beholds itself, suffering a pain so sharp and piercing that, in that very loneliness in which it dwells, it may literally say of itself,—and perhaps the royal prophet said so, being in that very loneliness himself, except that our Lord may have granted to him, being a saint, to feel it more deeply,— "Vigilavi, et factus sum sicut passer solitarius in tecto."[3] These words presented themselves to me in such a way that I thought I saw them fulfilled in myself. It was a comfort to know that others had felt this extreme loneliness; how much greater my *Loneliness of the soul.*

---

[1] § 10, *supra.* [2] § 4.
[3] Ps. ci. 8: "I have watched, and become as a sparrow alone on the house-top."

comfort, when these persons were such as David was! The soul is then—so I think—not in itself, but on the house-top, or on the roof, above itself, and above all created things; for it seems to me to have its dwelling higher than even in the highest part of itself.

The soul in rapture is as it were on the cross. 14. On other occasions, the soul seems to be, as it were, in the utmost extremity of need, asking itself, and saying, "Where is thy God?"[1] And it is to be remembered, that I did not know how to express in Spanish the meaning of those words. Afterwards, when I understood what it was, I used to console myself with the thought, that our Lord, without any effort of mine, had made me remember them. At other times, I used to recollect a saying of S. Paul's, to the effect that he was crucified to the world.[2] I do not mean that this is true of me: I know it is not; but I think it is the state of the enraptured soul. No consolation reaches it from heaven, and it is not there itself; it wishes for none from earth, and it is not there either; but it is, as it were, crucified between heaven and earth, enduring its passion: receiving no succour from either.

Interior sufferings. 15. Now, the succour it receives from heaven—which, as I have said,[3] is a most marvellous knowledge of God, above all that we can desire—brings with it greater pain; for the desire then so grows, that, in my opinion, its intense painfulness now and then robs the soul of all sensation; only, it lasts but for a short time after the senses are suspended. It seems as if it were the point of death; only, the agony carries with it so great a joy, that I know of nothing wherewith to compare it. It is a sharp martyrdom, full of sweetness; for if any earthly thing be then offered to the soul, even though it may be that which it habitually found most sweet, the soul will have none of it; yea, it seems to throw it away at once. The soul sees distinctly that it seeks nothing but God; yet its love dwells not on any

---

[1] Ps. xli. 4: "Ubi est Deus tuus?"
[2] Galat. vi. 14: "In cruce Jesu Christi: per quem mihi mundus crucifixus est, et ego mundo."
[3] §§ 9 and 12.

attribute of Him in particular; it seeks Him as He is, and knows not what it seeks. I say that it knows not, because the imagination forms no representation whatever; and, indeed, as I think, during much of that time the faculties are at rest. Pain suspends them then, as joy suspends them in union and in a trance.

16. O Jesus! oh, that some one would clearly explain this to you, my father, were it only that you may tell me what it means, because this is the habitual state of my soul! *Physical sufferings after raptures.* Generally, when I am not particularly occupied, I fall into these agonies of death, and I tremble when I feel them coming on, because they are not unto death. But when I am in them, I then wish to spend therein all the rest of my life, though the pain be so very great, that I can scarcely endure it. Sometimes my pulse ceases, as it were, to beat at all,—so the sisters say, who sometimes approach me, and who now understand the matter better,—my bones are racked, and my hands become so rigid, that I cannot always join them. Even on the following day I have a pain in my wrists, and over my whole body, as if my bones were out of joint.[1] Well, I think sometimes, if it continues as at present, that it will end, in the good pleasure of our Lord, by putting an end to my life; for the pain seems to me sharp enough to cause death; only, I do not deserve it.

17. All my anxiety at these times is that I should die: I do not think of purgatory, nor of the great sins I have committed, and by which I have deserved hell. *The Saint's anxiety to die.* I forget every thing in my eagerness to see God; and this abandonment and loneliness seem preferable to any company in the world. If any thing can be a consolation in this state, it is to speak to one who has passed through this trial, seeing that, though the soul may complain of it, no one seems disposed to believe in it.

18. The soul is tormented also because the pain has increased so much, that it seeks solitude no longer, as it did before, nor companionship, unless it *Nearness to death.*

[1] Daniel x. 16: "In visione tua dissolutæ sunt compages meæ." See S. John of the Cross, *Spiritual Canticle*, st. 14, vol. ii. p. 84, Engl. trans.; and also *Relation*, viii. § 8, where this is repeated.

be that of those to whom it may make its complaint. It is now like a person who, having a rope around his neck, and being strangled, tries to breathe. This desire of companionship seems to me to proceed from our weakness; for, as pain brings with it the risk of death,—which it certainly does ; for I have been occasionally in danger of death, in my great sickness and infirmities, as I have said before,[1] and I think I may say that this pain is as great as any,—so the desire not to be parted, which possesses soul and body, is that which raises the cry for succour in order to breathe, and by speaking of it, by complaining, and distracting itself, causes the soul to seek means of living very much against the will of the spirit, or the higher part of the soul, which would not wish to be delivered from this pain.

Sweetness of the soul's sufferings, 19. I am not sure that I am correct in what I say, nor do I know how to express myself, but to the best of my knowledge it comes to pass in this way. See, my father, what rest I can have in this life, now that what I once had in prayer and loneliness—therein our Lord used to comfort me—has become in general a torment of this kind ; while, at the same time, it is so full of sweetness, that the soul, discerning its inestimable worth, prefers it to all those consolations which it formerly had. It seems, also, to be a safer state, because it is the way of the cross ; and involves, in my opinion, a joy of exceeding worth, because the state of the body in it is only pain. It is the soul that suffers and exults alone in that joy and contentment which suffering supplies.

And its exultation in them. 20. I know not how this can be, but so it is ; it comes from the hand of our Lord, and, as I said before,[2] is not any thing that I have acquired myself, because it is exceedingly supernatural, and I think I would not barter it for all the graces of which I shall speak further on : I do not say for all of them together, but for any one of them separately. And it must not be forgotten that, as I have just said, these impetuosities came upon me after I had received those graces[3] from our Lord which I am speaking of now, and

[1] Ch. v. § 18.   [2] § 12.
[3] The words from "I have just said" to "graces" are in the margin of the text, but in the handwriting of the Saint (*De la Fuente*).

all those described in this book, and it is in that state our Lord keeps me at this moment.¹

21. In the beginning I was afraid,—it happens to me to be almost always so when our Lord leads me by a new way, until His Majesty reassures me as I proceed,—and so our Lord bade me not to fear, but to esteem this grace more than all the others He had given me; for the soul was purified by this pain—burnished, or refined as gold in the crucible, so that it might be the better enamelled with His gifts, and the dross burnt away in this life, which would have to be burnt away in purgatory. *Anticipation of purgatory.*

22. I understood perfectly that this pain was a great grace; but I was much more certain of it now: and my confessor tells me I did well. And though I was afraid, because I was so wicked, I never could believe it was any thing wrong: on the other hand, the exceeding greatness of the blessing made me afraid, when I called to mind how little I had deserved it. Blessed be our Lord, who is so good! Amen. *Pain of the ecstatic union.*

23. I have, it seems, wandered from my subject; for I began by speaking of raptures, and that of which I have been speaking is even more than a rapture, and the effects of it are what I have described. Now let us return to raptures, and speak of their ordinary characteristics. I have to say that, when the rapture was over, my body seemed frequently to be buoyant, as if all weight had departed from it; so much so, that now and then I scarcely knew that my feet touched the ground. But during the rapture itself the body is very often as if it were dead, perfectly powerless. It continues in the position it was in when the rapture came upon it,—if sitting, sitting; if the hands were open, or if they were shut, they will remain open or shut.² For though the senses fail but rarely, it has happened to me occasionally to lose them wholly—seldom, however, and then only for a short time. But in general they are in disorder; and though they have no power whatever to deal with outward things, there remains the power of hearing and seeing; but it is *Physical effects of raptures.*

¹ See § 11.   ² See *Relation*, viii. § 8.

as if the things heard and seen were at a great distance, far away.

Suspension of the senses. 24. I do not say that the soul sees and hears when the rapture is at the highest,—I mean by at the highest, when the faculties are lost, because profoundly united with God,—for then it neither sees, nor hears, nor perceives, as I believe; but, as I said of the previous prayer of union,[1] this utter transformation of the soul in God continues only for an instant; yet while it continues no faculty of the soul is aware of it, or knows what is passing there. Nor can it be understood while we are living on the earth—at least, God will not have us understand it, because we must be incapable of understanding it. I know it by experience.

The memory and the understanding not always at rest. 25. You, my father, will ask me: How comes it, then, that a rapture occasionally lasts so many hours? What has often happened to me is this,—I spoke of it before, when writing of the previous state of prayer,[2] —the rapture is not continuous, the soul is frequently absorbed, or, to speak more correctly, our Lord absorbs it in Himself; and when He has held it thus for a moment, the will alone remains in union with Him. The movements of the two other faculties seem to me to be like those of the needle of sun-dials, which is never at rest; yet when the Sun of Justice will have it so, he can hold it still.

Supremacy of the will. 26. This I speak of lasts but a moment;[3] yet, as the impulse and the upraising of the spirit were vehement, and though the other faculties bestir themselves again, the will continues absorbed, and causes this operation in the body, as if it were the absolute mistress; for now that the two other faculties are restless, and attempt to disturb it, it takes care—for if it is to have enemies, the fewer the better—that the senses also shall not trouble it: and thus it comes to pass that the senses are suspended; for so our Lord wills it. And for the most part the eyes are closed, though we may not wish to close them; and if occasionally they remain open, as I said just now, the soul neither discerns nor considers what it sees.

[1] Ch. xviii. § 16.   [2] Ch. xviii. § 17.   [3] See ch. xl. § 12.

27. What the body then can do here is still less, *The awaking of the faculties.* in order that, when the faculties come together again, there may not be so much to do. Let him, therefore, to whom our Lord has granted this grace, be not discouraged when he finds himself in this state—the body under constraint for many hours, the understanding and the memory occasionally astray. The truth is that, in general, they are inebriated with the praises of God, or with searching to comprehend or understand that which has passed over them. And yet even for this they are not thoroughly awake, but are rather like one who has slept long, and dreamed, and is hardly yet awake.

28. I dwell so long on this point because I know that there are persons now, even in this place,[1] to whom our Lord is granting these graces; and if their *Why the Saint speaks so much of this.* directors have had no experience in the matter, they will think, perhaps, that they must be as dead persons during the trance,— and they will think so the more if they have no learning. It is piteous to see what those confessors who do not understand this make people suffer. I shall speak of it by and by.[2] Perhaps I do not know what I am saying. You, my father, will understand it, if I am at all correct; for our Lord has admitted you to the experience of it: yet, because that experience is not very great, it may be, perhaps, that you have not considered the matter so much as I have done.

29. So, then, though I do all I can, my body has no strength to move for some time; the soul took it *Weakness of the body after raptures.* all away. Very often, too, he who was before sickly and full of pain remains healthy, and even stronger; for it is something great that is given to the soul in rapture; and sometimes, as I have said already,[3] our Lord will have the body rejoice, because it is obedient in that which the soul requires of it. When we recover our consciousness, the faculties may remain, if the rapture has been deep, for a day or two, and even for three days, so absorbed, or as if stunned,—so much so, as to be in appearance no longer themselves.

[1] Avila.   [2] Ch. xxv. § 18.   [3] § 11.

30. Here comes the pain of returning to this life; here it is the wings of the soul grew, to enable it to fly so high: the weak feathers are fallen off. Now the standard of Christ is raised up aloft, which seems to be nothing else but the going up, or the carrying up, of the Captain of the fort to the highest tower of it, there to raise up the standard of God. The soul, as in a place of safety, looks down on those below; it fears no dangers now—yea, rather, it courts them, as one assured beforehand of victory. It sees most clearly how lightly are the things of this world to be esteemed, and the nothingness thereof. The soul now seeks not, and possesses not, any other will but that of doing our Lord's will,[1] and so it prays Him to let it be so; it gives to Him the keys of its own will. Lo, the gardener is now become the commander of a fortress! The soul will do nothing but the will of our Lord; it will not act as the owner even of itself, nor of any thing, not even of a single apple in the orchard; only, if there be any good thing in the garden, it is at His Majesty's disposal; for from henceforth the soul will have nothing of its own,—all it seeks is to do every thing for His glory, and according to His will.

True and false raptures.

31. This is really the way in which these things come to pass; if the raptures be true raptures, the fruits and advantages spoken of abide in the soul; but if they did not, I should have great doubts about their being from God—yea, rather, I should be afraid they were those frenzies of which S. Vincent speaks.[2] I have seen it myself, and I know it by experience, that the soul in rapture is mistress of every thing, and acquires such freedom in one hour, and even

[1] "Other will . . . Lord's will." These words—in Spanish, "Otra voluntad, sino hacer la de nuestro Señor"—are not in the handwriting of the Saint; perhaps it was Father Bañes who wrote them. The MS. is blurred, and the original text seems to have been, "libre alvedrio nin guerra" (*De la Fuente*).

[2] S. Vincent. Ferrer, *Instruct. de Vit. Spirit.* c. xii. p. 14: "Si dicerent tibi aliquid quod sit contra fidem, et contra Scripturam Sacram, aut contra bonos mores, abhorreas eorum visionem et judicia, tanquam stultas dementias, et eorum raptus, sicut rabiamenta"—which word the Saint translates by "rabiamientos."

in less, as to be unable to recognise itself. It sees distinctly that all this does not belong to it, neither knows it how it came to possess so great a good; but it clearly perceives the very great blessing which every one of these raptures always brings. No one will believe this who has not had experience of it, and so they do not believe the poor soul: they saw it lately so wicked, and now they see it pretend to things of so high an order; for it is not satisfied with serving our Lord in the common way,—it must do so forthwith in the highest way it can. They consider this a temptation and a folly; yet they would not be astonished, if they knew that it comes not from the soul, but from our Lord, to whom it has given up the keys of its will.

32. For my part, I believe that a soul which has reached this state neither speaks nor acts of itself, but rather that the supreme King takes care of all it has to do. O my God, how clear is the meaning of those words, and what good reason the Psalmist had, and all the world will ever have, to pray for the wings of a dove![1] It is plain that this is the flight of the spirit rising upwards above all created things, and chiefly above itself: but it is a sweet flight, a delicious flight—a flight without noise. *Supernatural state of enraptured souls.*

33. Oh, what power that soul possesses which our Lord raises to this state! how it looks down upon every thing, entangled by nothing! how ashamed it is of the time when it was entangled! how it is amazed at its own blindness! how it pities those who are still in darkness, especially if they are men of prayer, and have received consolations from God! It would like to cry out to them, that they might be made to see the delusions they are in: and, indeed, it does so now and then; and then a thousand persecutions fall upon it as a shower. People consider it wanting in humility, and think it means to teach those from whom it should learn, particularly if it be a woman. Hence its condemnation; and not without reason; because they know not how strong the influence is that moves it. The soul at times cannot help itself; nor can it refrain from undeceiving those it *Their anxiety for others.*

[1] Ps. liv. 7: "Quis dabit mihi pennas sicut columbæ?"

loves, and whom it longs to see delivered out of the prison of this life; for that state in which the soul itself had been before neither is, nor seems to be, any thing else but a prison.

<small>Undeceiving of the soul.</small> 34. The soul is weary of the days during which it respected points of honour, and the delusion which led it to believe that to be honour which the world calls by that name; now it sees it to be the greatest lie, and that we are all walking therein. It understands that true honour is not delusive, but real, esteeming that which is worthy of esteem, and despising that which is despicable; for every thing is nothing, and less than nothing, whatever passeth away, and is not pleasing unto God. The soul laughs at itself when it thinks of the time in which it regarded money, and desired to possess it,—though, as to this, I verily believe that I never had to confess such a fault; it was fault enough to have regarded money at all. If I could purchase with money the blessings which I possess, I should make much of it; but it is plain that these blessings are gained by abandoning all things.

<small>Vanity of possessions.</small> 35. What is there that is procurable by this money which we desire? Is it any thing of worth, any thing lasting? Why, then, do we desire it? A dismal resting-place it provides, which costs so dear! Very often it obtains for us hell itself, fire everlasting, and torments without end. Oh, if all men would but regard it as profitless dross, how peaceful the world would be! how free from bargaining! How friendly all men would be one with another, if no regard were paid to honour and money! I believe it would be a remedy for every thing.

<small>Enlightenment of the soul in rapture.</small> 36. The soul sees how blind men are to the nature of pleasure—how by means of it they provide for themselves trouble and disquietude even in this life. What restlessness! how little satisfaction! what labour in vain! It sees, too, not only the cobwebs that cover it, and its great faults, but also the specks of dirt, however slight they may be; for the sun shines most clearly; and thus, however much the soul may have laboured at its own perfection, it sees itself to be very unclean, if the rays of the sun fall really upon

it. The soul is like water in a vessel, which appears pellucid when the sun does not shine through it; but if it does, the water then is found to be full of motes.

37. This comparison is literally correct. Before the soul fell into the trance, it thought itself to be careful about not offending God, and that it did what it could in proportion to its strength; but now that it has attained to this state, in which the Sun of Justice shines upon it, and makes it open its eyes, it beholds so many motes, that it would gladly close them again. It is not so truly the child of the noble eagle, that it can gaze upon the sun; but, for the few instants it can keep them open, it beholds itself wholly unclean. It remembers the words: "Who shall be just in Thy presence?"[1] When it looks on this divine Sun, the brightness thereof dazzles it,—when it looks on itself, its eyes are blinded by the dust: the little dove is blind. So it happens very often: the soul is utterly blinded, absorbed, amazed, dizzy at the vision of so much grandeur. Clear vision of its defects.

38. It is in rapture that true humility is acquired —humility that will never say any good of self, nor suffer others to do so. The Lord of the garden, not the soul, distributes the fruit thereof, and so none remains in its hands; all the good it has, it refers to God; if it says any thing about itself, it is for His glory. It knows that it possesses nothing here; and even if it wished, it cannot continue ignorant of that. It sees this, as it were, with the naked eye; for, whether it will or not, its eyes are shut against the things of this world, and open to see the truth. True humility.

[1] Job iv. 17: "Numquid homo Dei comparatione justificabitur?"

CHAPTER XXI.

CONCLUSION OF THE SUBJECT—PAIN OF THE AWAKENING—
LIGHT AGAINST DELUSIONS.

1. To bring this matter to an end, I say that it
Deceitfulness of the world. is not necessary for the soul to give its consent here;
it is already given : the soul knows that it has given
up its will into His hands,[1] and that it cannot deceive Him,
because He knoweth all things. It is not here as it is in the
world, where all life is full of deceit and double-dealing. When
you think you have gained one man's good will, because of the
outward show he makes, you afterwards learn that all was a
lie. No one can live in the midst of so much scheming, particularly if there be any interests at stake.

2. Blessed, then, is that soul which our Lord
Blessedness of this state of prayer. draws on to the understanding of the truth! Oh,
what a state for kings! How much better it would
be for them if they strove for this, rather than for great dominions! How justice would prevail under their rule! What
evils would be prevented, and might have been prevented already! Here no man fears to lose life or honour for the love
of God. What a grand thing this would be in him who is
more bound than those beneath him to regard the honour of
our Lord!—for it is kings whom the crowd must follow. To
make one step in the propagation of the faith, and to give one
ray of light to heretics, I would forfeit a thousand kingdoms.
And with good reason: for it is another thing altogether to
gain a kingdom that shall never end, because one drop of the
water of that kingdom, if the soul but tastes it, renders the
things of this world utterly loathsome.

3. If, then, the soul should be wholly engulfed,
Incredulity of the world. what then? O Lord, if Thou wert to give me the
right to publish this abroad, people would not believe
me—as they do not believe many who are able to speak of it
in a way very different from mine: but I should satisfy myself,

---

[1] Ch. xx. § 30.

at least. I believe I should count my life as nothing, if I might make others understand but one of these truths. I know not what I should do afterwards, for I cannot trust myself; though I am what I am, I have a violent desire, which is wasting me, to say this to those who are in authority. And now that I can do no more, I betake myself to Thee, O my Lord, to implore a remedy for all. Thou knowest well that I would gladly divest myself of all the graces which Thou hast given me,—provided I remained in a condition never to offend Thee,—and give them up to those who are kings; for I know it would then be impossible for them to allow what they allow now, or fail to receive the very greatest blessings.

4. O my God, make kings to understand how far their obligations reach! Thou hast been pleased to distinguish them on earth in such a way that—so I have heard—Thou showest signs in the heavens when Thou takest any of them away. Certainly, when I think of this, my devotion is stirred, because Thou wilt have them learn, O my King, even from this, that they must imitate Thee in their lives, seeing that, when they die, signs are visible in the heavens, as it was when Thou wert dying Thyself. *Duties of kings.*

5. I am very bold; if it be wrong, you, my father, will tear this out: only believe that I should speak much more to the purpose in the presence of kings,—if I might, or thought they would listen to me,—for I recommend them greatly to God, and I wish I might be of service to them. All this makes one risk life; for I long frequently to lose mine,—and that would be to lose a little for the chance of gaining much; for surely it is not possible to live, when we see with our eyes the great delusion wherein we are walking, and the blindness in which we are living. *Supernatural courage of the Saint.*

6. A soul that has attained to this is not limited to the desires it has to serve God; for His Majesty gives it strength to bring those desires to good effect. Nothing can be put before it into which it will not throw itself, if only it thinks that God may be served thereby: and yet it is doing nothing, because, as I said before,[1] it sees clearly *Desires to serve God.*

[1] Ch. xx. § 34.

that all is nothing, except pleasing God. The trial is, that those who are so worthless as I am, have no trial of the kind. May it be Thy good pleasure, O my Good, that the time may come in which I may be able to pay one farthing, at least, of the heavy debt I owe Thee! Do Thou, O Lord, so dispose matters according to Thy will, that this Thy servant may do Thee some service. Other women there have been who did heroic deeds for Thee; I am good only to talk; and so it has not been Thy pleasure, O my God, that I should do any thing: all ends in talk and desires—that is all my service. And yet even in this I am not free, because it is possible I might fail altogether.

7. Strengthen Thou my soul, and prepare it, O Good of all good; and, my Jesus, then ordain Thou the means whereby I may do something for Thee, so that there may be not even one who can bear to receive so much, and make no payment in return. Cost what it may, O Lord, let me not come before Thee with hands so empty,[1] seeing that the reward of every one will be according to his works.[2] Behold my life, behold my good name and my will; I have given them all to Thee; I am Thine: dispose of me according to Thy will. I see well enough, O Lord, how little I can do; but now, having drawn near to Thee,—having ascended to this watch-tower, from which the truth may be seen,—and while Thou departest not from me, I can do all things; but if Thou departest from me, were it but for a moment, I shall go thither where I was once—that is, to hell.[3]

Prayer for strength.

8. Oh, what it is for a soul in this state to have to return to the commerce of the world, to see and look on the farce of this life,[4] so ill-ordered; to waste its time in attending to the body by sleeping and eating![5] All is wearisome; it cannot run away,—it sees itself chained and imprisoned; it feels then most keenly the captivity into which

Miseries of this life.

[1] Exod. xxiii. 15: "Non apparebis in conspectu meo vacuus."
[2] Apoc. ii. 23: "Dabo unicuique vestrum secundum opera sua."
[3] See ch. xxxii. § 1.
[4] "Farsa desta vida tan mal concertada."
[5] *Inner Fortress*, iv. ch. i. § 11.

the body has brought us, and the wretchedness of this life. It understands the reason why S. Paul prayed God to deliver him from it.[1] The soul cries with the Apostle, and calls upon God to deliver it, as I said on another occasion.[2] But here it often cries with so much violence, that it seems as if it would go out of the body in search of its freedom, now that they do not take it away. It is as a slave sold into a strange land; and what distresses it most is, that it cannot find many who make the same complaint and the same prayer: the desire of life is more common.

9. Oh, if we were utterly detached,—if we never placed our happiness in any thing of this world,— how the pain, caused by living always away from God, would temper the fear of death with the desire of enjoying the true life! Sometimes I consider, if a person like myself—because our Lord has given this light to me, whose love is so cold, and whose true rest is so uncertain, for I have not deserved it by my works—frequently feels her banishment so much, what the feelings of the Saints must have been. What must S. Paul and the Magdalene, and others like them, have suffered, in whom the fire of the love of God had grown so strong? Their life must have been a continual martyrdom. It seems to me that they who bring me any comfort, and whose conversation is any relief, are those persons in whom I find these desires—I mean, desires with acts. I say with acts, for there are people who think themselves detached, and who say so of themselves,—and it must be so, for their vocation demands it, as well as the many years that are past since some of them began to walk in the way of perfection,—but my soul distinguishes clearly, and afar off, between those who are detached in words, and those who make good those words by deeds. The little progress of the former, and the great progress of the latter, make it plain. This is a matter which a person of any experience can see into most clearly.

The desire of God lessens the fear of death.

10. So far, then, of the effects of those raptures which come from the Spirit of God. The truth is, that these are greater or less. I say less, because in

Effects of raptures

[1] Rom. vii. 24: "Quis me liberabit de corpore mortis hujus?"
[2] Ch. xvi. § 12.

the beginning, though the effects are wrought, they are not tested by works, and so it cannot be clear that a person has them: and perfection, too, is a thing of growth, and of labouring after freedom from the cobwebs of memory; and this requires some time. Meanwhile, the greater the growth of love and humility in the soul, the stronger the perfume of the flowers of virtues is for itself and for others. The truth is, that our Lord can so work in the soul in an instant during these raptures, that but little remains for the soul to do in order to attain to perfection. No one, who has not had experience of it, will ever be able to believe what our Lord now bestows on the soul. No efforts of ours—so I think—can ever reach so far.

Wrought immediately by God. 11. However, I do not mean to say that those persons who during many years make use of the methods prescribed by writers on prayer,—who discuss the principles thereof, and the means whereby it may be acquired,—will not, by the help of our Lord, attain to perfection and great detachment, with much labour; but they will not attain to it so rapidly as by the way of raptures, in which our Lord works independently of us, draws the soul utterly away from earth, and gives it dominion over all things here below, though the merits of that soul may not be greater than mine were: I cannot use stronger language, for my merits are as nothing. Why His Majesty doeth this is, because it is His pleasure, and He doeth it according to His pleasure: even if the soul be without the fitting disposition, He disposes it for the reception of that blessing which He is giving to it. Although it be most certain that He never fails to comfort those who do well, and strive to be detached, still He does not always give these effects because they have deserved them at His hands by cultivating the garden, but because it is His will to show His greatness at times in soil which is most worthless, as I have just said, and to prepare it for all good: and all this in such a way that it seems as if the soul was now, in a manner, unable to go back and live in sin against God, as it did before.

Moral effects of prayer. 12. The mind is now so inured to the comprehension of that which is truth indeed, that every thing else seems to it to be but child's play. It laughs to itself, at times, when it sees grave men — men given to prayer, men of religion — make much of points of honour, which itself is trampling beneath its feet. They say that discretion, and the dignity of their callings, require it of them as a means to do more good; but that soul knows perfectly well that they would do more good in one day by preferring the love of God to this their dignity, than they will do in ten years by considering it.

13. The life of this soul is a life of trouble: the cross is always there, but the progress it makes is great. *Progress of the soul.* When those who have to do with it think it has arrived at the summit of perfection, within a little while they see it much more advanced; for God is ever giving it grace upon grace. God is the Soul of that soul now; it is He who has the charge of it: and so He enlightens it; for He seems to be watching over it, always attentive to it, that it may not offend Him,—giving it grace, and stirring it up in His service. When my soul reached this state, in which God showed me mercy so great, my wretchedness came to an end, and our Lord gave me strength to rise above it. The former occasions of sin, as well as the persons with whom I was accustomed to distract myself, did me no more harm than if they had never existed; on the contrary, that which ordinarily did me harm, helped me on. Every thing contributed to make me know God more, and to love Him; to make me see how much I owed Him, as well as to be sorry for being what I had been.

14. I saw clearly that this did not come from myself, that I had not brought it about by any efforts of my own, and that there was not time *Raptures strengthen the soul.* enough for it. His Majesty, of His mere goodness, had given me strength for it. From the time our Lord began to give me the grace of raptures, until now, this strength has gone on increasing. He, of His goodness, hath held me by the hand, that I might not go back. I do not think that I am doing any thing myself—certainly I do not; for I see distinctly that all this is the work of our Lord. For this reason, it seems to me that the soul in which our Lord worketh these graces,—if

it walks in humility and fear, always acknowledging the work of our Lord, and that we ourselves can do, as it were, nothing, —may be thrown among any companions, and, however distracted and wicked these may be, will neither be hurt nor disturbed in any way; on the contrary, as I have just said, that will help it on, and be a means unto it whereby it may derive much greater profit.

<small>God communicates with the soul in raptures.</small> 15. Those souls are strong which are chosen by our Lord to do good to others; still, this their strength is not their own. When our Lord brings a soul on to this state, He communicates to it of His greatest secrets by degrees. True revelations—the great gifts and visions—come by ecstasies, all tending to make the soul humble and strong, to make it despise the things of this world, and have a clearer knowledge of the greatness of the reward which our Lord has prepared for those who serve Him.[1]

16. May it please His Majesty that the great munificence with which He hath dealt with me, miserable sinner that I am, may have some weight with those who shall read this, so that they may be strong and courageous enough to give up every thing utterly for God. If His Majesty repays us so abundantly, that even in this life the reward and gain of those who serve Him become visible, what will it be in the next?

CHAPTER XXII.

THE SECURITY OF CONTEMPLATIVES LIES IN THEIR NOT ASCENDING TO HIGH THINGS IF OUR LORD DOES NOT RAISE THEM—THE SACRED HUMANITY MUST BE THE ROAD TO THE HIGHEST CONTEMPLATION—A DELUSION IN WHICH THE SAINT WAS ONCE ENTANGLED.

<small>Certain delusions to which contemplatives are liable.</small> 1. THERE is one thing I should like to say—I think it important: and if you, my father, approve, it will serve for a lesson that possibly may be necessary; for in some books on prayer the writers say that

[1] 1 Cor. ii. 9 : " Quæ præparavit Deus iis qui diligunt Illum."

the soul, though it cannot in its own strength attain to this state,—because it is altogether a supernatural work wrought in it by our Lord,—may nevertheless succeed, by lifting up the spirit above all created things, and raising it upwards in humility, after some years spent in the purgative life, and advancing in the illuminative. I do not very well know what they mean by illuminative: I understand it to mean the life of those who are making progress. And they advise us much to withdraw from all bodily imagination, and draw near to the contemplation of the Divinity; for they say that those who have advanced so far would be embarrassed or hindered in their way to the highest contemplation, if they regarded even the Sacred Humanity itself.[1] They defend their opinion[2] by bringing forward the words[3] of our Lord to the Apostles, concerning the coming of the Holy Ghost; I mean that coming which was after the Ascension. If the Apostles had believed, as they believed after the coming of the Holy Ghost, that He is both God and Man, His bodily Presence would, in my opinion, have been no hindrance; for those words were not said to the Mother of God, though she loved Him more than all.[4] They think that, as this work of contemplation is wholly spiritual, any bodily object whatever can disturb or hinder it. They say that the contemplative should regard himself as being within a definite space, God every where around, and himself absorbed in Him. This is what he should aim at.

[1] See *Inner Fortress*, vi. 7, § 4.
[2] This opinion is supposed to be justified by the words of S. Thomas, 3 Sent. dist. 22, qu. 3, art. 1, *ad quintum:* " Corporalis præsentia Christi in duobus poterat esse nociva. Primo, quantum ad fidem, quia videntes Eum in forma in qua erat minor Patre, non ita de facili crederent Eum æqualem Patri, ut dicit glossa super Joannem. Secundo, quantum ad dilectionem, quia Eum non solum spiritualiter, sed etiam carnaliter diligeremus, conversantes cum Ipso corporaliter, et hoc est de imperfectione dilectionis."
[3] S. John xvi. 7 : "Expedit vobis ut Ego vadam ; si enim non abiero, Paracletus non veniet ad vos."
[4] This sentence is in the margin of the original MS., not in the text, but in the handwriting of the Saint (*De la Fuente*).

2. This seems to me right enough now and then; but to withdraw altogether from Christ, and to compare His divine Body with our miseries or with any created thing whatever, is what I cannot endure. May God help me to explain myself! I am not contradicting them on this point, for they are learned and spiritual persons, understanding what they say: God, too, is guiding souls by many ways and methods, as He has guided mine. It is of my own soul that I wish to speak now,—I do not intermeddle with others,—and of the danger I was in because I would comply with the directions I was reading. I can well believe that he who has attained to union, and advances no further,—that is, to raptures, visions, and other graces of God given to souls,—will consider that opinion to be best, as I did myself: and if I had continued in it, I believe I should never have reached the state I am in now. I hold it to be a delusion: still, it may be that it is I who am deluded. But I will tell you what happened to me.

Answer to the foregoing difficulty.

3. As I had no director, I used to read these books, where, by little and little, I thought I might understand something. I found out afterwards that, if our Lord had not shown me the way, I should have learned but little from books; for I understood really nothing till His Majesty made me learn by experience: neither did I know what I was doing. So, in the beginning, when I attained to some degree of supernatural prayer,—I speak of the prayer of quiet,—I laboured to remove from myself every thought of bodily objects; but I did not dare to lift up my soul, for that I saw would be presumption in me, who was always so wicked. I thought, however, that I had a sense of the presence of God: this was true, and I contrived to be in a state of recollection before Him. This method of prayer is full of sweetness, if God help us in it, and the joy of it is great. And so, because I was conscious of the profit and delight which this way furnished me, no one could have brought me back to the contemplation of the Sacred Humanity; for that seemed to me to be a real hindrance to prayer.

Spiritual books dangerous without a director.

4. O Lord of my soul, and my Good! Jesus Christ crucified! I never think of this opinion, which I then held, without pain; I believe it was an act of high treason, though done in ignorance. Hitherto, I had been all my life long so devout to the Sacred Humanity—for this happened but lately; I mean by lately, that it was before our Lord gave me the grace of raptures and visions. I did not continue long of this opinion,[1] and so I returned to my habit of delighting in our Lord, particularly at Communion. I wish I could have His picture and image always before my eyes, since I cannot have Him graven in my soul as deeply as I wish. *The Saint's sorrow for her delusion.*

5. Is it possible, O my Lord, that I could have had the thought, if only for an hour, that Thou couldst be a hindrance to my greatest good? Whence are all my blessings? are they not from Thee? I will not think that I was blamable, for I was very sorry for it, and it was certainly done in ignorance. And so it pleased Thee, in Thy goodness, to succour me, by sending me one who delivered me from this delusion; and afterwards by showing Thyself to me so many times, as I shall relate hereafter,[2] that I might clearly perceive how great my delusion was, and also tell it to many persons; which I have done, as well as describe it as I am doing now. I believe myself that this is the reason why so many souls, after advancing to the prayer of union, make no further progress, and do not attain to very great liberty of spirit. *The danger of it.*

6. It seems to me that there are two considerations on which I may ground this opinion. Perhaps I am saying nothing to the purpose, yet what I say is the result of experience; for my soul was in a very evil plight, till our Lord enlightened it: all its joys were but sips; and when it had come forth therefrom, it never found itself in that company which afterwards it had in trials and temptations. *Why so few make progress.*

[1] "I mean by lately ... and visions" is in the margin of the MS., but in the handwriting of the Saint (*De la Fuente*).

[2] Ch. xxviii. § 4.

7. The first consideration is this: there is a little absence of humility—so secret and so hidden, that we do not observe it. Who is there so proud and wretched as I, that, even after labouring all his life in penances and prayers and persecutions, can possibly imagine himself not to be exceedingly rich, most abundantly rewarded, when our Lord permits him to stand with S. John at the foot of the cross? I know not into whose head it could have entered to be not satisfied with this, unless it be mine, which has gone wrong in every way where it should have gone right onwards.

First consideration.

8. Then, if our constitution—or perhaps sickness —will not permit us always to think of His Passion, because it is so painful, who is to hinder us from thinking of Him risen from the grave, seeing that we have Him so near us in the Sacrament, where He is glorified, and where we shall not see Him in His great weariness— scourged, streaming with blood, faint by the way, persecuted by those to whom He had done good, and not believed in by the Apostles? Certainly, it is not always that one can bear to meditate on sufferings so great as were those He underwent. Behold Him here, before His ascension into heaven, without pain, all-glorious, giving strength to some and courage to others. In the most Holy Sacrament, He is our companion, as if it was not in His power to withdraw Himself for a moment from us. And yet it was in my power to withdraw from Thee, O my Lord, that I might serve Thee better! It may be that I knew Thee not when I sinned against Thee; but how could I, having once known Thee, ever think I should gain more in this way? O Lord, what an evil way I took! and I was going out of the way, if Thou hadst not brought me back to it. When I see Thee near me, I see all good things together. No trial befalls me that is not easy to bear, when I think of Thee standing before those who judged Thee.

Those who are unable to meditate on the Passion may meditate on the resurrection.

9. With so good a Friend and Captain ever present, Himself the first to suffer, every thing can be borne. He helps, He strengthens, He never fails, He is the true Friend. I see clearly, and since then have always seen, that if we are to please God, and if He is to

All blessings come through the Sacred Humanity.

give us His great graces, every thing must pass through the hands of His most Sacred Humanity, in whom His Majesty said that He is well pleased.[1] I know this by repeated experience: our Lord has told it me. I have seen clearly that this is the door[2] by which we are to enter, if we would have His supreme Majesty reveal to us His great secrets.

10. So, then, I would have your reverence seek no other way, even if you were arrived at the highest contemplation. This way is safe. Our Lord is He by whom all good things come to us; He will teach you. Consider His life; that is the best example. What more can we want than so good a Friend at our side, who will not forsake us when we are in trouble and distress, as they do who belong to this world! Blessed is he who truly loves Him, and who always has Him near him! Let us consider the glorious S. Paul, who seems as if Jesus was never absent from his lips, as if he had Him deep down in his heart. After I had heard this of some great Saints given to contemplation, I considered the matter carefully; and I see that they walked in no other way. S. Francis with the stigmata proves it, S. Antony of Padua with the Infant Jesus; S. Bernard rejoiced in the Sacred Humanity; so did S. Catherine of Siena, and many others, as your reverence knows better than I do. *Shown from the history of the Saints.*

11. This withdrawing from bodily objects must no doubt be good, seeing that it is recommended by persons who are so spiritual; but, in my opinion, it ought to be done only when the soul has made very great progress; for until then it is clear that the Creator must be sought for through His creatures. All this depends on the grace which our Lord distributes to every soul. I do not intermeddle here. What I would say is, that the most Sacred Humanity of Christ is not to be counted among the objects from which we have to withdraw. Let this be clearly understood. I wish I knew how to explain it.[3] *She excuses those who taught her wrong.*

[1] S. Matt. iii. 17: "Hic est Filius Meus dilectus, in quo Mihi complacui."
[2] S. John x. 7, 9: "Ego sum ostium."
[3] See S. John of the Cross, *Mount Carmel*, b. iii. ch. i.

12. When God suspends all the powers of the soul,—as we see He does in the states of prayer already described,—it is clear that, whether we wish it or not, this presence is withdrawn. Be it so, then. The loss is a blessed one, because it takes place in order that we may have a deeper fruition of what we seem to have lost; for at that moment the whole soul is occupied in loving Him whom the understanding has toiled to know; and it loves what it has not comprehended, and rejoices in what it could not have rejoiced in so well, if it had not lost itself, in order, as I am saying, to gain itself the more. But that we should carefully and laboriously accustom ourselves not to strive with all our might to have always—and please God it be always!—the most Sacred Humanity before our eyes,—this, I say, is what seems to me not to be right: it is making the soul, as they say, to walk in the air; for it has nothing to rest on, how full soever of God it may think itself to be.

Supernatural withdrawal of the presence of the Sacred Humanity.

13. It is a great matter for us to have our Lord before us as Man while we are living and in the flesh. This is that other inconvenience which I say must be met with. The first—I have already begun to describe it—is a little failure in humility, in that the soul desires to rise of itself before our Lord raises it, and is not satisfied with meditation on so excellent a subject,—seeking to be Mary before it has laboured with Martha. If our Lord will have a soul to be Mary, even on the first day, there is nothing to be afraid of; but we must not be self-invited guests, as I think I said on another occasion.[1] This little mote of want of humility, though in appearance a mere nothing, does a great deal of harm to those who wish to advance in contemplation.

Mary and Martha.

14. I now come back to the second consideration. We are not angels, for we have a body; to seek to make ourselves angels while we are on the earth, and so much on the earth as I was, is an act of folly. In general, our thoughts must have something to rest on, though the soul may go forth out of itself now and then, or it may be

The second consideration.

[1] Ch. xii. §§ 8, 9.

very often so full of God as to be in need of no created thing by the help of which it may recollect itself. But this is not so common a case; for when we have many things to do, when we are persecuted and in trouble, when we cannot have much rest, and when we have our seasons of dryness, Christ is our best Friend; for we regard Him as Man, and behold Him faint and in trouble, and He is our Companion; and when we shall have accustomed ourselves in this way, it is very easy to find Him near us, although there will be occasions from time to time when we can do neither the one nor the other.

15. For this end, that is useful which I spoke of before:[1] we must not show ourselves as labouring after spiritual consolations; come what may, to embrace the cross is the great thing. The Lord of all consolation was Himself forsaken: they left Him alone in His sorrows. Do not let us forsake Him; for His hand will help us to rise more than any efforts we can make; and He will withdraw Himself when He sees it to be expedient for us, and when He pleaseth will also draw the soul forth out of itself, as I said before.[2]

16. God is greatly pleased when He beholds a soul in its humility making His Son a Mediator between itself and Him, and yet loving Him so much as to confess its own unworthiness, even when He would raise it up to the highest contemplation, and saying with S. Peter:[3] "Go Thou away from me, O Lord, for I am a sinful man." I know this by experience: it was thus that God directed my soul. Others may walk, as I said before,[4] by another and a shorter road. What I have understood of the matter is this: that the whole foundation of prayer must be laid in humility, and that the more a soul humbles itself in prayer, the more God lifts it up. I do not remember that He ever showed me any of those most marvellous mercies, of which I shall speak hereafter,[5] at any other time than when I was as one brought to nothing[6] by seeing how wicked I was,

Prayer must be grounded on humility.

---

[1] Ch. xv. § 21.   [2] Ch. xx. § 2.
[3] S. Luke v. 8: "Exi a me, quia homo peccator sum, Domine."
[4] Ch. xii. § 6.   [5] Ch. xxviii.
[6] Ps. lxxii. 22: "Et ego ad nihilum redactus sum, et nescivi."

Moreover, His Majesty contrived to make me understand matters that helped me to know myself, but which I could never have even imagined of myself.

The soul must be calm,

17. I believe myself that if a soul makes any efforts of its own in order to further itself in the way of the prayer of union, and though it may seem to make immediate progress, it will quickly fall back, because the foundations were not duly laid. I fear, too, that such a soul will never attain to true poverty of spirit, which consists in seeking consolation or sweetness, not in prayer,—the consolations of the earth are already abandoned,—but rather in sorrows, for the love of Him who always lived in sorrows Himself;[1] and in being calm in the midst of sorrows and aridities. Though the soul may feel it in some measure, there is no disquiet, nor any of that pain which some persons suffer, who, if they are not always labouring with the understanding and with a sense of devotion, think every thing lost,—as if their efforts merited so great a blessing!

And wait upon God.

18. I am not saying that men should not seek to be devout, nor that they should not stand with great reverence in the presence of God, but only that they are not to vex themselves if they cannot find even one good thought, as I said in another place;[2] for we are unprofitable servants.[3] What do we think we can do? Our Lord grant that we understand this, and that we may be those little asses who drive the windlass I spoke of:[4] these, though their eyes are bandaged, and they do not understand what they are doing, yet draw up more water than the gardener can draw with all his efforts. We must walk in liberty on this road, committing ourselves into the hands of God. If it be His Majesty's good pleasure to raise us and place us among His chamberlains and secret counsellors, we must go willingly; if not, we must serve Him in the lower offices of His house, and not sit

---

[1] Isai. liii. 3 : "Virum dolorum, et scientem infirmitatem."
[2] Ch. xi. § 13.
[3] S. Luke xvii. 10 : "Servi inutiles sumus."
[4] Ch. xi. § 11.

down on the upper seats.¹ As I have sometimes said,² God is more careful of us than we are ourselves, and knows what each one of us is fit for.

19. What use is there in governing oneself by oneself, when the whole will has been given up to God? *All progress from God,* I think this less endurable now than in the first state of prayer, and it does much greater harm; for these blessings are supernatural. If a man has a bad voice, let him force himself ever so much to sing, he will never improve it; but if God gives him a good voice, he has no need to try it twice. Let us, then, pray Him always to show His mercy upon us, with a submissive spirit, yet trusting in the goodness of God. And now that the soul is permitted to sit at the feet of Christ, let it contrive not to quit its place, but keep it anyhow. Let it follow the example of the Magdalene; and when it shall be strong enough, God will lead it into the wilderness.³

20. You, then, my father, must be content with this until you meet with some one of more experience *And supernatural.* and better knowledge than I am. If you see people who are beginning to taste of God, do not trust them if they think that they advance more, and have a deeper fruition of God, when they make efforts of their own. Oh, when God wills it, how He discovers Himself without these little efforts of ours! We may do what we like, but He throws the spirit into a trance as easily as a giant takes up a straw; no resistance is possible. What a thing to believe, that God will wait till the toad shall fly of itself, when He has already willed it should do so! Well, it seems to me still more difficult and hard for our spirit to rise upwards, if God does not raise it, seeing that it is burdened with earth, and hindered in a thousand ways. Its willingness to rise is of no service to it; for, though an aptness for flying be more natural to it than to a toad, yet is it so sunk in the mire as to have lost it by its own fault.

---

[1] S. Luke xiv. 8: "Non discumbas in primo loco." See *Way of Perfection*, ch. xxvi. § 1; but ch. xvii. of the old editions.

[2] Ch. xii. § 12, ch. xix. § 23.

[3] Os. ii. 14: "Ducam eam in solitudinem."

21. I come, then, to this conclusion : whenever we think of Christ, we should remind ourselves of the love that made Him bestow so many graces upon us, and also how great that love is which our Lord God has shown us, in giving us such a pledge of the love He bears us ; for love draws forth love. And though we are only at the very beginning, and exceedingly wicked, yet let us always labour to keep this in view, and stir ourselves up to love ; for if once our Lord grant us this grace, of having this love imprinted in our hearts, every thing will be easy, and we shall do great things in a very short time, and with very little labour. May His Majesty give us that love,—He knows the great need we have of it,—for the sake of that love which He bore us, and of His glorious Son, to whom it cost so much to make it known to us ! Amen.

Effects of divine love.

22. There is one thing I should like to ask you, my father. How is it that, when our Lord begins to bestow upon a soul a grace so great as this of perfect contemplation, it is not, as it ought to be, perfect at once ? Certainly, it seems it should be so ; for he who receives a grace so great ought never more to seek consolations on earth. How is it, I ask, that a soul which has ecstasies, and so far is more accustomed to receive graces, should yet seem to bring forth fruits still higher and higher,—and the more so, the more it is detached,—when our Lord might have sanctified it at once, the moment He came near it ? How is it, I ask again, that the same Lord brings it to the perfection of virtue only in the course of time ? I should be glad to learn the reason, for I know it not. I do know, however, that in the beginning, when a trance lasts only the twinkling of an eye, and is almost imperceptible but for the effects it produces, the degree of strength which God then gives is very different from that which He gives when this grace is a trance of longer duration.

Why a soul subject to ecstasies grows in grace by degrees.

23. Very often, when thinking of this, have I imagined the reason might be, that the soul does not despise itself all at once, till our Lord instructs it by degrees, and makes it resolute, and gives it the strength of manhood, so that it may trample utterly upon every thing. He

The Saint's solution.

gave this strength to the Magdalene in a moment. He gives the same grace to others, according to the measure of their abandonment of themselves into the hands of His Majesty, that He may do with them as He will. We never thoroughly believe that God rewards a hundredfold even in this life.[1]

24. I also thought of this comparison : supposing the grace given to those who are far advanced to be the same with that given to those who are but beginners, we may then liken it to a certain food of which many persons partake : they who eat a little retain the savour of it for a moment, they who eat more are nourished by it, but those who eat much receive life and strength. Now, the soul may eat so frequently and so abundantly of this food of life as to have no pleasure in eating any other food, because it sees how much good it derives from it. Its taste is now so formed upon it, that it would rather not live than have to eat any other food ; for all food but this has no other effect than to take away the sweet savour which this good food leaves behind. *Another solution.*

25. Further, the conversation of good people does not profit us in one day as much as it does in many; and we may converse with them long enough to become like them, by the grace of God. In short, the whole matter is as His Majesty wills. He gives His grace to whom He pleases; but much depends on this: he who begins to receive this grace must make a firm resolution to detach himself from all things, and esteem this grace according to reason. *A third solution.*

26. It seems also to me as if His Majesty were going about to try those who love Him,—now one, now another,—revealing Himself in supreme joy, so as to quicken our belief, if it should be dead, in what He will give us, saying, Behold ! this is but a drop of the immense sea of blessings ; for He leaves nothing undone for those He loves ; and as He sees them receive it, so He gives, and He gives Himself. He loves those who love Him. Oh, how dear He is !—how good a Friend ! O my soul's Lord, who can *The munificence of God.*

[1] S. Matt. xix. 29 : "Qui reliquerit domum, ... centuplum accipiet."

find words to describe what Thou givest to those who trust in Thee, and what they lose who come to this state, and yet dwell in themselves! Oh, let not this be so, O my Lord! for Thou doest more than this when Thou comest to a lodging so mean as mine. Blessed be Thou for ever and ever!

The Saint's comment on certain forms of spirituality.
27. I now humbly ask you, my father, if you mean to discuss what I have written on prayer with spiritual persons, to see that they are so really; for if they be persons who know only one way, or who have stood still midway, they will not be able to understand the matter. There are also some whom God leads at once by the highest way; these think that others might advance in the same manner—quiet the understanding, and make bodily objects none of their means; but these people will remain dry as a stick. Others, also, there are who, having for a moment attained to the prayer of quiet, think forthwith that, as they have had the one, so they may have the other. These, instead of advancing, go back, as I said before.[1] So, throughout, experience and discretion are necessary. May our Lord, of His goodness, bestow them on us!

CHAPTER XXIII.

THE SAINT RESUMES THE HISTORY OF HER LIFE—AIMING AT PERFECTION — MEANS WHEREBY IT MAY BE GAINED — INSTRUCTIONS FOR CONFESSORS.

The Saint resumes her story.
1. I SHALL now return to that point in my life where I broke off,[2] having made, I believe, a longer digression than I need have made, in order that what is still to come may be more clearly understood. Henceforth, it is another and a new book,—I mean, another and a new life. Hitherto, my life was my own; my life, since I began to explain these methods of prayer, is the life which

[1] Ch. xii. § 8.
[2] At the end of ch. ix. The thirteen chapters interposed between that and this—the twenty-third—are a treatise on mystical theology.

God lived in me,—so it seems to me; for I feel it to be impossible that I should have escaped in so short a time from ways and works that were so wicked. May our Lord be praised, who has delivered me from myself!

2. When, then, I began to avoid the occasions of sin, and to give myself more unto prayer, our Lord also began to bestow His graces upon me, as one who desired, so it seemed, that I too should be willing to receive them. His Majesty began to give me most frequently the grace of the prayer of quiet, and very often that of union, which lasted some time. But as, in these days, women have fallen into great delusions and deceits of Satan,[1] I began to be afraid, because the joy and sweetness which I felt were so great, and very often beyond my power to avoid. On the other hand, I felt in myself a very deep conviction that God was with me, especially when I was in prayer. I saw, too, that I grew better and stronger thereby. *Her fear of delusions.*

3. But if I was a little distracted, I began to be afraid, and to imagine that perhaps it was Satan that suspended my understanding, making me think it to be good, in order to withdraw me from mental prayer, hinder my meditation on the Passion, and debar me the use of my understanding: this seemed to me, who did not comprehend the matter, to be a grievous loss; but, as His Majesty was pleased to give me light to offend Him no more, and to understand how much I owed Him, this fear so grew upon me, that it made me seek out diligently for spiritual persons with whom I might treat of my state. I had already heard of some; for the Fathers of the Society of Jesus had come hither;[2] and I, though I knew none of them, was greatly attracted by them, merely because I had heard of their way of life and of prayer; but I did not think myself fit to speak to them, or strong enough to obey them; and this *Her search after direction.*

---

[1] She refers to Magdalene of the Cross (*Reforma de los Descalços*, vol. i. lib. i. c. xix. § 2).

[2] The college of the Society at Avila was founded in 1555; but some of the Fathers had come thither in 1553 (*De la Fuente*).

made me still more afraid; for to converse with them, and remain what I was, seemed to me somewhat rude.

4. I spent some time in this state, till, after much *Her fear of direction.* inward contention and fear, I determined to confer with some spiritual person, to ask him to tell me what that method of prayer was which I was using, and to show me whether I was in error. I was also resolved to do every thing I could not to offend God; for the want of courage of which I was conscious, as I said before,[1] made me so timid. Was there ever delusion so great as mine, O my God, when I withdrew from good in order to become good! The devil must lay much stress on this in the beginning of a course of virtue; for I could not overcome my repugnance. He knows that the whole relief of the soul consists in conferring with the friends of God. Hence it was that no time was fixed in which I should resolve to do this. I waited to grow better first, as I did before when I ceased to pray,[2]—and perhaps I never should have become better; for I had now sunk so deeply into the petty ways of an evil habit,—I could not convince myself that they were wrong,—that I needed the help of others, who should hold out a hand to raise me up. Blessed be Thou, O Lord!—for the first hand outstretched to me was Thine.

5. When I saw that my fear was going so far, *Expedients to avoid direction.* it struck me—because I was making progress in prayer—that this must be a great blessing, or a very great evil; for I understood perfectly that what had happened was something supernatural, because at times I was unable to withstand it; to have it when I would was also impossible. I thought to myself that there was no help for it, but in keeping my conscience pure, avoiding every occasion even of venial sins; for if it was the work of the Spirit of God, the gain was clear; and if the work of Satan, so long as I strove to please, and did not offend, our Lord, Satan could do me little harm; on the contrary, he must lose in the struggle. Determined on this course, and always praying God to help me, striving also after purity of conscience for

[1] Ch. vii. § 37.   [2] Ch. xix. § 9.

some days, I saw that my soul had not strength to go forth alone to a perfection so great. I had certain attachments to trifles, which, though not very wrong in themselves, were yet enough to ruin all.

6. I was told of a learned ecclesiastic,[1] dwelling in this city, whose goodness and pious life our Lord was beginning to make known to the world. I contrived to make his acquaintance through a saintly nobleman[2] living in the same place. This latter is a married man; but his life is so edifying and virtuous, so given to prayer, and so full of charity, that the goodness and perfection of it shine forth in all he does: and most justly so; for many souls have been greatly blessed through him, because of his great gifts, which, though his condition of a layman be a hindrance to him, never lie idle. He is a man of great sense, and very gentle with all people; his conversation is never wearisome, but so sweet and gracious, as well as upright and holy, that he pleases every body very much with whom he has any relations. He directs it all to the great good of those souls with whom he converses; and he seems to have no other end in view but to do all he may be permitted to do for all men, and make them content. *How the Saint was delivered from her troubles*

7. This blessed and holy man, then, seems to me, by the pains he took, to have been the beginning of salvation to my soul. His humility in his relations with me makes me wonder; for he had spent, I believe, *By the help of Don Francisco de Salcedo.*

---

[1] Gaspar Daza had formed a society of priests in Avila, and was a very laborious and holy man. It was he who said the first Mass in the monastery of S. Joseph, founded by S. Teresa, whom he survived, dying Nov. 24, 1592. He committed the direction of his priests to F. Baltasar Alvarez (*Bouix*). Juan of Avila acted much in the same way when the Jesuits settled in Avila (*De la Fuente*).

[2] Don Francisco de Salcedo. After the death of his wife, he became a priest, and was chaplain and confessor of the Carmelite nuns of S. Joseph. For twenty years of his married life he attended regularly the theological lectures of the Dominicans, in the house of S. Thomas. His death took place Sept. 12, 1580, when he had been a priest for ten years (*S. Teresa's Letters*, vol. iv. letter 43, note 13: letter 368, ed. of De la Fuente).

nearly forty years in prayer,—it may be two or three years less,—and all his life was ordered with that perfection which his state admitted. His wife is so great a servant of God, and so full of charity, that nothing is lost to him on her account,[1]— in short, she was the chosen wife of one who God knew would serve Him so well. Some of their kindred are married to some of mine. Besides, I had also much communication with another great servant of God, married to one of my first cousins.

The Saint discloses her state to Gaspar Daza,

8. It was thus I contrived that the ecclesiastic I speak of, who was so great a servant of God, and his great friend, should come to speak to me, intending to confess to him, and to take him for my director. When he had brought him to speak to me, I, in the greatest confusion at finding myself in the presence of so holy a man, revealed to him the state of my soul, and my way of prayer. He would not be my confessor; he said that he was very much occupied: and so, indeed, he was. He began with a holy resolution to direct me as if I was strong,—I ought to have been strong, according to the method of prayer which he saw I used,—so that I should in nothing offend God. When I saw that he was resolved to make me break off at once with the petty ways I spoke of before,[2] and that I had not the courage to go forth at once in the perfection he required of me, I was distressed; and when I perceived that he ordered the affairs of my soul as if I ought to be perfect at once, I saw that much more care was necessary in my case. In a word, I felt that the means he would have employed were not those by which my soul could be helped onwards; for they were fitted for a soul more perfect than mine; and though the graces I had received from God were very many, I was still at the very beginning in the matter of virtue and of mortification.

Whose direction was not suited for her.

9. I believe certainly, if I had only had this ecclesiastic to confer with, that my soul would have made no progress; for the pain it gave me to see that I was

---

[1] Doña Mencia del Aguila (*De la Fuente*, in a note on letter 10, vol. ii. p. 9, where he corrects himself,—having previously called her Mencia de Avila).

[2] § 4.

not doing—and, as I thought, could not do—what he told me, was enough to destroy all hope, and make me abandon the matter altogether. I wonder at times how it was that he, being one who had a particular grace for the direction of beginners in the way of God, was not permitted to understand my case, or to undertake the care of my soul. I see it was all for my greater good, in order that I might know and converse with persons so holy as the members of the Society of Jesus.

10. After this, I arranged with that saintly nobleman that he should come and see me now and then. *Is directed by a layman.* It shows how deep his humility was; for he consented to converse with a person so wicked as I was. He began his visits, he encouraged me, and told me that I ought not to suppose I could give up every thing in one day; God would bring it about by degrees: he himself had for some years been unable to free himself from some very slight imperfections. O humility! what great blessings thou bringest to those in whom thou dwellest, and to them who draw near to those who possess thee! This holy man—for I think I may justly call him so—told me of weaknesses of his own, in order to help me. He, in his humility, thought them weaknesses; but, if we consider his state, they were neither faults nor imperfections; yet, in my state, it was a very great fault to be subject to them.

11. I am not saying this without a meaning, though I seem to be enlarging on trifles; but these *Effects of that direction.* trifles contribute so much towards the beginning of the soul's progress and its flight upwards, though it has no wings, as they say; and yet no one will believe it who has not had experience of it; but, as I hope in God that your reverence will help many a soul, I speak of it here. My whole salvation depended on his knowing how to treat me, on his humility, on the charity with which he conversed with me, and on his patient endurance of me when he saw that I did not mend my ways at once. He went on discreetly, by degrees showing me how to overcome Satan. My affection for him so grew upon me, that I never was more at ease than on

the day I used to see him. I saw him, however, very rarely. When he was long in coming, I used to be very much distressed, thinking that he would not see me because I was so wicked.

Perplexity of the director, and the fears of the Saint.

12. When he found out my great imperfections, —they might well have been sins, though since I conversed with him I am somewhat improved,—and when I recounted to him, in order to obtain light from him, the great graces which God had bestowed upon me, he told me that these things were inconsistent one with another; that these consolations were given to people who had made great progress, and led mortified lives; that he could not help being very much afraid—he thought that the evil spirit might have something to do in my case; he would not decide that question, however, but he would have me carefully consider my whole method of prayer, and then tell him of it. That was the difficulty: I did not understand it myself, and so I could tell him nothing of my prayer; for the grace to understand it —and, understanding it, to describe it—has only lately been given me of God. This saying of his, together with the fear I was in, distressed me exceedingly, and I cried; for certainly I was anxious to please God, and I could not persuade myself that Satan had any thing to do with it. But I was afraid, on account of my great sins, that God might leave me blind, so that I should understand nothing.

The Saint's obedience and fears. A.D. 1557.

13. Looking into books to see if I could find any thing there by which I might recognise the prayer I practised, I found in one of them, called the *Ascent of the Mount*,[1] and in that part of it which relates to the union of the soul with God, all those marks which I had in myself, in that I could not think of any thing. This is what I most dwelt on—that I could think of nothing when I was in prayer. I marked that passage, and gave him the book, that he, and the ecclesiastic mentioned before,[2] saint and servant of God, might consider it, and tell me what I should do.

[1] *Subida del Monte Sion*, by a Franciscan friar, Bernardino de Laredo (*Reforma*, vol. i. lib i. c. xix. § 7).

[2] § 6.

If they thought it right, I would give up that method of prayer altogether; for why should I expose myself to danger, when, at the end of nearly twenty years, during which I had used it, I had gained nothing, but had fallen into a delusion of the devil? It was better for me to give it up. And yet this seemed to me hard; for I had already discovered what my soul would become without prayer. Every thing seemed full of trouble. I was like a person in the middle of a river, who, in whatever direction he may turn, fears a still greater danger, and is well-nigh drowned. This is a very great trial, and I have gone through many like it, as I shall show hereafter;[1] and though it does not seem to be of any importance, it will perhaps be advantageous to understand how the spirit is to be tried.

14. And certainly the affliction to be borne is great, and caution is necessary, particularly in the case of women,—for our weakness is great,—and much evil may be the result of telling them very distinctly that the devil is busy with them; yea, rather, the matter should be very carefully considered, and they should be removed out of reach of the dangers that may arise. They should be advised to keep things secret; and it is necessary, also, that their secret should be kept. I am speaking of this as one to whom it has been a sore trouble; for some of those with whom I spoke of my prayer did not keep my secret, but, making inquiries one of another, for a good purpose, did me much harm; for they made things known which might well have remained secret, because not intended for every one: and it seemed as if I had made them public myself.[2] *Great caution necessary in the trial of spirits.*

15. I believe that our Lord permitted[3] this to be done without sin on their part, in order that I might suffer. I do not say that they revealed any thing I discussed with them in confession; still, as they were persons to whom, in my fears, I gave a full account of myself, in order that they might give me light, I thought they ought to have been silent. Nevertheless, I never dared to conceal any thing from such persons. My meaning, then, is, that women should be directed with much discretion; their *The Saint suffered from the indiscretion of those she consulted.*

[1] See ch. xxv. § 18.   [2] See ch. xxviii. § 18.   [3] See *Relation*, vii. § 17.

directors should encourage them, and bide the time when our Lord will help them, as He has helped me. If He had not, the greatest harm would have befallen me, for I was in great fear and dread; and as I suffered from disease of the heart,[1] I am astonished that all this did not do me a great deal of harm.

Her two advisers decide against her, and advise her to seek a director among the Jesuits.

16. Then, when I had given him the book, and told the story of my life and of my sins, the best way I could in general,—for I was not in confession, because he was a layman; yet I gave him clearly to understand how wicked I was,—those two servants of God, with great charity and affection, considered what was best for me. When they had made up their minds what to say,—I was waiting for it in great dread, having begged many persons to pray to God for me, and I too had prayed much during those days,—the nobleman came to me in great distress, and said that, in the opinion of both, I was deluded by an evil spirit; that the best thing for me to do was to apply to a certain father of the Society of Jesus, who would come to me if I sent for him, saying I had need of him; that I ought, in a general confession, to give him an account of my whole life, and of the state I was in,—and all with great clearness: God would, in virtue of the Sacrament of Confession, give him more light concerning me; for those fathers were very experienced men in matters of spirituality. Further, I was not to swerve in a single point from the counsels of that father; for I was in great danger, if I had no one to direct me.

The Saint resolves to make a general confession.

17. This answer so alarmed and distressed me, that I knew not what to do—I did nothing but cry. Being in an oratory in great affliction, not knowing what would become of me, I read in a book—it seemed as if our Lord had put it into my hands—that S. Paul said, God is faithful;[2] that He will never permit Satan to deceive those who love Him. This gave me great consolation. I began to prepare for my general confession, and to write out all the evil and all the good: a history of my life, as clearly as

[1] See ch. iv. § 6.
[2] 1 Cor. x. 13: "Fidelis autem Deus est, qui non patietur vos tentari supra id quod potestis."

I understood it, and knew how to make it, omitting nothing whatever. I remember, when I saw I had written so much evil, and scarcely any thing that was good, that I was exceedingly distressed and sorrowful. It pained me, also, that the nuns of the community should see me converse with such holy persons as those of the Society of Jesus; for I was afraid of my own wickedness, and I thought I should be obliged to cease from it, and give up my amusements; and that if I did not do so, I should grow worse: so I persuaded the sacristan and the portress to tell no one of it. This was of little use, after all; for when I was called down there was one at the door, as it happened, who told it to the whole convent. But what difficulties and what terrors Satan troubles them with who would draw near unto God!

18. I communicated the whole state of my soul to that servant of God[1]—and he was a great servant of His, and very prudent. He understood all I told him, explained it to me, and encouraged me greatly. He said that all was very evidently the work of the Spirit of God; only it was necessary for me to go back again to my prayer, because I was not well grounded, and had not begun to understand what mortification meant,—that was true, for I do not think I knew it even by name,—that I was by no means to give up prayer; on the contrary, I was to do violence to myself in order to practise it, because God had bestowed on me such special graces as made it impossible to say whether it was, or was not, the will of our Lord to do good to many through me. He went further, for he seems to have prophesied of that which our Lord afterwards did with me, and said that I should be very much to blame if I did not correspond with the graces which God bestowed upon me. It seems to me that the Holy Ghost was speaking by his mouth in order to heal my soul, so deep was the impression he made. He made me very much ashamed of myself, and directed me by a way which seemed to

Her new director's advice to her.

---

[1] F. Juan de Padranos, whom S. Francis de Borja had sent in 1555, with F. Fernando Alvarez del Aguila, to found the house of the Society in Avila (*De la Fuente*). Ribera, i. 9, says he heard that F. Juan de Padranos gave in part the Exercises of S. Ignatius to the Saint.

change me altogether. What a grand thing it is to understand a soul! He told me to make my prayer every day on some mystery of the Passion, and that I should profit by it, and to fix my thoughts on the Sacred Humanity only, resisting to the utmost of my power those recollections and delights, to which I was not to yield in any way till he gave me further directions in the matter.

Obedience of the Saint to her confessors. 19. He left me consoled and fortified: our Lord came to my succour and to his, so that he might understand the state I was in, and how he was to direct me. I made a firm resolution not to swerve from any thing he might command me, and to this day I have kept it. Our Lord be praised, who has given me grace to be obedient to my confessors,[1] however imperfectly!—and they have almost always been those blessed men of the Society of Jesus; though, as I said, I have but imperfectly obeyed them. My soul began to improve visibly, as I am now going to say.

CHAPTER XXIV.

PROGRESS UNDER OBEDIENCE—HER INABILITY TO RESIST THE GRACES OF GOD—GOD MULTIPLIES HIS GRACES.

Courage of the Saint, and her perfect obedience. 1. AFTER this my confession, my soul was so docile that, as it seems to me, there was nothing in the world I was not prepared to undertake. I began at once to make a change in many things, though my confessor never pressed me—on the contrary, he seemed to make light of it all. I was the more influenced by this, because he led me on by the way of the love of God; he left me free, and did not press me, unless I did so myself, out of love. I continued thus nearly two months, doing all I could to resist the sweetness and graces that God sent. As to my outward life, the change was visible; for our Lord gave me courage to go through with certain things, of which those who knew me—

[1] See *Relation*, i. § 9.

and even those in the community—said that they seemed to them extreme; and, indeed, compared with what I had been accustomed to do, they were extreme: people, therefore, had reason to say so. Yet, in those things which were of obligation, considering the habit I wore, and the profession I had made, I was still deficient. By resisting the sweetness and joys which God sent me, I gained this, that His Majesty taught me Himself; for, previously, I used to think that, in order to obtain sweetness in prayer, it was necessary for me to hide myself in secret places, and so I scarcely dared to stir. Afterwards, I saw how little that was to the purpose; for the more I tried to distract myself, the more our Lord poured over me that sweetness and joy which seemed to me to be flowing around me, so that I could not in any way escape from it: and so it was. I was so careful about this resistance, that it was a pain to me. But our Lord was more careful to show His mercies, and during those two months to reveal Himself more than before, so that I might the better comprehend that it was no longer in my power to resist Him.

2. I began with a renewed love of the most Sacred Humanity; my prayer began to be solid, like a house, the foundations of which are strong; and I was inclined to practise greater penance, having been negligent in this matter hitherto because of my great infirmities. The holy man who heard my confession told me that certain penances would not hurt me, and that God perhaps sent me so much sickness because I did no penance; His Majesty would therefore impose it Himself. He ordered me to practise certain acts of mortification not very pleasant for me.[1] I did so, because I felt that our Lord was enjoining it all, and giving him grace to command me in such a way as to make me obedient unto him. *Gives herself more to penance and watchfulness.*

3. My soul was now sensitive to every offence I committed against God, however slight it might be; so much so, that if I had any superfluity about me, I could not recollect myself in prayer till I had got rid of it. *Sensitiveness of her conscience.*

[1] The Saint now treated her body with extreme severity, disciplining herself even unto blood (*Reforma*, vol. i. lib. i. c. xx. § 4).

I prayed earnestly that our Lord would hold me by the hand, and not suffer me to fall again, now that I was under the direction of His servants. I thought that would be a great evil, and that they would lose their credit through me.

She consults S. Francis Borja. 4. At this time, Father Francis, who was Duke of Gandia,[1] came here; he had left all he possessed some years before, and had entered the Society of Jesus. My confessor, and the nobleman of whom I spoke before,[2] contrived that he should visit me, in order that I might speak to him, and give him an account of my way of prayer; for they knew him to be greatly favoured and comforted of God: he had given up much, and was rewarded for it even in this life. When he had heard me, he said to me that it was the work of the Spirit of God,[3] and that he thought it was not right now to prolong that resistance; that hitherto it had been safe enough,—only, I should always begin my prayer by meditating on some part of the Passion; and that if our Lord should then raise up my spirit, I should make no resistance, but suffer His Majesty to raise it upwards, I myself not seeking it. He gave both medicine and advice, as one who had made great progress himself; for experience is very important in these matters. He said that further resistance would be a mistake. I was exceedingly consoled; so, too, was the nobleman, who rejoiced greatly when he was told that it was the work of God. He always helped me and gave me advice according to his power,—and that power was great.

Juan de Padranos removed from Avila. 5. At this time, they changed my confessor's residence. I felt it very much, for I thought I should go back to my wickedness, and that it was not possible to find another such as he. My soul was, as it were, in a desert, most sorrowful and afraid. I knew not what to do with myself. One of my kinswomen contrived to get me into her house, and I contrived at once to find another

---

[1] S. Francis de Borja came to Avila, where S. Teresa lived, in 1557 (*De la Fuente*). This passage must have been written after the foundation of S. Joseph, for it was not in the first Life, as the Saint says, ch. x. § 11, that she kept secret the names of herself and all others.

[2] Ch. xxiii. § 6.   [3] See *Relation*, viii. § 6.

confessor,[1] in the Society of Jesus. It pleased our Lord that I should commence a friendship with a noble lady,[2] a widow, much given to prayer, who had much to do with the fathers. She made her own confessor[3] hear me, and I remained in her house some days. She lived near, and I delighted in the many conferences I had with the fathers; for merely by observing the holiness of their way of life, I felt that my soul profited exceedingly.

6. This father began by putting me in the way of greater perfection. He used to say to me, that I ought to leave nothing undone that I might be wholly pleasing unto God. He was, however, very prudent and very gentle at the same time; for my soul was not at all strong, but rather very weak, especially as to giving up certain friendships, though I did not offend God by them: there was much natural affection in them, and I thought it would be an act of ingratitude if I broke them off. And so, as I did not offend God, I asked him if I must be ungrateful. He told me to lay the matter before God for a few days, and recite the hymn, "Veni, Creator," that God might enlighten me as to the better course. One day, having prayed for some time, and implored our Lord to help me to please Him in all things, I began the hymn; and as I was saying it, I fell into a trance —so suddenly, that I was, as it were, carried out of myself. I could have no doubt about it, for it was most plain. *She is under the care of Father B. Alvarez.*

7. This was the first time that our Lord bestowed on me the grace of ecstasy. I heard these words: "I will not have thee converse with men, but with *The first ecstasy of the Saint.*

---

[1] Who he was is not certainly known. The Bollandists decline to give an opinion; but F. Bouix thinks it was F. Ferdinand Alvarez, who became her confessor on the removal of F. Juan de Padranos, and that it was to him she confessed till she placed herself under the direction of F. Baltasar Alvarez, the confessor of Doña Guiomar, as it is stated in the next paragraph,—unless the confessor there mentioned was F. Ferdinand.

[2] Doña Guiomar de Ulloa. See below, ch. xxxii. § 13.

[3] If this confessor was F. Baltasar Alvarez, the Saint, F. Bouix observes, passes rapidly over the history of the year 1557, and the greater part, perhaps, of 1558; for F. Baltasar was ordained priest only in the latter year.

angels." This made me wonder very much; for the commotion of my spirit was great, and these words were uttered in the very depth of my soul. They made me afraid,—though, on the other hand, they gave me great comfort, which, when I had lost the fear,—caused, I believe, by the strangeness of the visitation,—remained with me.

Effects of the ecstasy. 8. Those words have been fulfilled; for I have never been able to form friendship with, nor have any comfort in, nor any particular love for, any persons whatever, except those who, as I believe, love God, and who strive to serve Him. It has not been in my power to do it. It is nothing to me that they are my kindred, or my friends, if I do not know them to be lovers of God, or persons given to prayer. It is to me a painful cross to converse with any one. This is the truth, so far as I can judge.[1] From that day forth, I have had courage so great as to leave all things for God, who in one moment—and it seems to me but a moment—was pleased to change His servant into another person. Accordingly, there was no necessity for laying further commands upon me in this matter. When my confessor saw how much I clung to these friendships, he did not venture to bid me distinctly to give them up. He must have waited till our Lord did the work—as He did Himself. Nor did I think myself that I could succeed; for I had tried before, and the pain it gave me was so great that I abandoned the attempt, on the ground that there was nothing unseemly in those attachments. Now our Lord set me at liberty, and gave me strength also to use it.

The Saint freed from her trouble. 9. So I told my confessor of it, and gave up every thing, according to his advice. It did a great deal of good to those with whom I used to converse, to see my determination. God be blessed for ever! who in one moment set me free, while I had been for many years making many efforts, and had never succeeded, very often also doing such violence to myself as injured my health; but, as it was done by Him who is almighty, and the true Lord of all, it gave me no pain whatever.

[1] See *Relation*, i. § 6.

CHAPTER XXV.

DIVINE LOCUTIONS—DELUSIONS ON THAT SUBJECT.

1. It will be as well, I think, to explain these locutions of God, and to describe what the soul feels when it receives them, in order that you, my father, may understand the matter; for ever since that time of which I am speaking, when our Lord granted me that grace, it has been an ordinary occurrence until now, as will appear by what I have yet to say.[1] *Divine locutions.*

2. The words are very distinctly formed; but by the bodily ear they are not heard. They are, however, much more clearly understood than they would be if they were heard by the ear. It is impossible not to understand them, whatever resistance we may offer. When we wish not to hear any thing in this world, we can stop our ears, or give our attention to something else: so that, even if we do hear, at least we can refuse to understand. In this locution of God addressed to the soul there is no escape, for in spite of ourselves we must listen; and the understanding must apply itself so thoroughly to the comprehension of that which God wills we should hear, that it is nothing to the purpose whether we will it or not; for it is His will, who can do all things. We should understand that His will must *Nature of them.*

---

[1] Philip. a SS. Trinitate, *Theolog. Mystic.* par. 2, tr. iii. art. v.: "Tres sunt modi divinæ locutionis; completur enim divina locutio vel verbis successivis, vel verbis formalibus, vel verbis substantialibus. Completur verbis successivis cum anima in semetipsa multum collecta quosdam discursus internos de Deo vel de aliis divina format directione, hujusmodi quippe discursus, quamvis ab ipsa sibi formati, a Deo tamen dirigente procedunt. Completur verbis cum anima vel in se collecta, vel aliis occupata, percipit quædam verba formaliter ac distincte divinitus expressa, ad quorum formationem anima passive penitus se habet. Completur verbis substantialibus cum anima vel in se collecta, vel etiam distracta, percipit quædam verba viva et efficacia, divinitus ad se directa, quæ virtutem aut substantialem effectum per ipsa significatum fortiter ac infallibiliter causant." See also S. John of the Cross, *Ascent of Mount Carmel*, b. ii. ch. xxviii. and the following.

be done; and He reveals Himself as our true Lord, having dominion over us. I know this by much experience; for my resistance lasted nearly two years,[1] because of the great fear I was in; and even now I resist occasionally; but it is of no use.

Of delusions incidental to locutions.
3. I should like to explain the delusions which may happen here, though he who has had much experience will run little or no risk, I think; but the experience must be great. I should like to explain also how those locutions which come from the Good Spirit differ from those which come from an evil spirit; and, further, how they may be but an apprehension of the understanding,—for that is possible,—or even words which the mind addressed to itself. I do not know if it be so; but even this very day I thought it possible. I know by experience in many ways when these locutions come from God. I have been told things two or three years beforehand, which have all come to pass; and in none of them have I been hitherto deceived. There are also other things in which the Spirit of God may be clearly traced, as I shall relate by and by.[2]

Of the difference between the divine and the imaginary locutions.
4. It seems to me that a person commending a matter to God with great love and earnestness may think that he hears in some way or other whether his prayer will be granted or not, and it is most impossible; but he who has heard the divine locution will see clearly enough what this is, because there is a great difference between the two. If it be any thing which the understanding has fashioned, however cunningly it may have done so, he sees that it is the understanding which has arranged that locution, and that it is speaking of itself. This is nothing else but a word uttered by one, and listened to by another: in that case, the understanding will see that it has not been listening only, but also forming the words; and the words it forms are something indistinct, fantastic, and not clear like the divine locutions. It is in our power to turn away our attention from

---

[1] From 1555 to 1557, when the Saint was advised by S. Francis de Borja to make no further resistance (*Bouix*).

[2] Ch. xxvi. § 4.

these locutions of our own, just as we can be silent when we are speaking; but, with respect to the former, that cannot be done.

5. There is another test more decisive still. The words formed by the understanding effect nothing; but, when our Lord speaks, it is at once word and work; and though the words may not be meant to stir up our devotion, but are rather words of reproof, they dispose a soul at once, strengthen it, make it tender, give it light, console and calm it; and if it should be in dryness, or in trouble and uneasiness, all is removed, as if by the action of a hand, and even better; for it seems as if our Lord would have the soul understand that He is all-powerful, and that His words are deeds. *Efficacy of the divine locutions.*

6. It seems to me that there is as much difference between these two locutions as there is between speaking and listening, neither more nor less; for when I speak, as I have just said,[1] I go on with my understanding arranging what I am saying; but if I am spoken to by others, I do nothing else but listen, without any labour. The human locution is as something which we cannot well make out, as if we were half asleep; but the divine locution is a voice so clear that not a syllable of its utterance is lost. It may occur, too, when the understanding and the soul are so troubled and distracted that they cannot form one sentence correctly; and yet grand sentences, perfectly arranged, such as the soul in its most recollected state never could have formed, are uttered, and at the first word, as I said,[2] change it utterly. Still less could it have formed them if they are uttered in an ecstasy, when the faculties of the soul are suspended; for how should the soul then comprehend any thing, when it remembers nothing?—yea, rather, how can it remember them then, when the memory can hardly do any thing at all, and the imagination is, as it were, suspended? *Illustration of the difference.*

7. But it is to be observed, that if we see visions and hear words it never is as at the time when the soul is in union in the very rapture itself,—so it seems to me. At that moment, as I have shown,— *Visions and divine locutions occur not during the complete rapture.*

[1] § 4. [2] § 9.

I think it was when I was speaking of the second water,[1]—all the faculties of the soul are suspended; and, as I think, neither vision, nor understanding, nor hearing, is possible at that time. The soul is then wholly in the power of another; and in that instant—a very brief one, in my opinion—our Lord leaves it free for nothing whatever; but when this instant is passed, the soul continuing still entranced, then is the time of which I am speaking; for the faculties, though not completely suspended, are so disposed that they are scarcely active, being, as it were, absorbed, and incapable of making any reflections.

Difference between the divine and the human locution.

8. There are so many ways of ascertaining the nature of these locutions, that if a person be once deceived, he will not be deceived often. I mean, that a soul accustomed to them, and on its guard, will most clearly see what they are; for, setting other considerations aside which prove what I have said, the human locution produces no effect, neither does the soul accept it,—though it must admit the other, whether we like it or not,—nor does it believe it; on the contrary, it is known to be a delusion of the understanding, and is therefore put away as we would put away the ravings of a lunatic.

Divine locutions cannot be mistaken.

9. But as to the divine locution, we listen to that as we do to a person of great holiness, learning, or authority, whom we know to be incapable of uttering a falsehood. And yet this is an inadequate illustration; for these locutions proceed occasionally in such great majesty that, without our recollecting who it is that utters them, they make us tremble if they be words of reproof, and die of love if words of love. They are also, as I have said,[2] matters of which the memory has not the least recollection; and expressions so full are uttered so rapidly, that much time must have been spent in arranging them, if we formed them our-

---

[1] The doctrine here laid down is not that of the second water,—ch. xiv. and xv.,—but that of the third, ch. xvi. The Saint herself speaks doubtfully; and as she had but little time for writing, she could not correct nor read again what she had written (*De la Fuente*).

[2] § 6.

selves; and so it seems to me that we cannot possibly be ignorant at the time that we have never formed them ourselves at all.

10. There is no reason, therefore, why I should dwell longer on this matter. It is a wonder to me that any experienced person, unless he deliberately chooses to do so, can fall into delusions. It has often happened to me, when I had doubts, to distrust what I heard, and to think that it was all imagination,—but this I did afterwards; for at the moment that is impossible,—and at a later time to see the whole fulfilled; for our Lord makes the words dwell in the memory so that they cannot be forgotten. Now, that which comes forth from our understanding is, as it were, the first movement of thought, which passes away and is forgotten; but the divine locution is a work done; and though some of it may be forgotten, and time have lapsed, yet is it not so wholly forgotten that the memory loses all traces of what was once spoken,—unless, indeed, after a very long time, or unless the locution were words of grace or of instruction. But as to prophetic words, they are never forgotten, in my opinion; at least, I have never forgotten any,—and yet my memory is weak. *The Saint's own experience.*

11. I repeat it, unless a soul be so wicked as to pretend that it has these locutions, which would be a great sin, and say that it hears divine words when it hears nothing of the kind, it cannot possibly fail to see clearly that itself arranges the words, and utters them to itself. That seems to me altogether impossible for any soul that has ever known the Spirit of God. If it has not, it may continue all its life long in this delusion, and imagine that it hears and understands, though I know not how that can be. A soul desires to hear these locutions, or it does not; if it does not, it is distressed because it hears them, and is unwilling to listen to them, because of a thousand fears which they occasion, and for many other reasons it has for being quiet in prayer without these interruptions. How is it that the understanding has time enough to arrange these locutions? They require time. *Delusions exposed.*

12. But, on the other side, the divine locutions instruct us without loss of time, and we understand matters which seem to require a month on our part to arrange. The understanding itself, and the soul, stand amazed at some of the things we understand. So it is; and he who has any experience of it will see that what I am saying is literally true. I give God thanks that I have been able thus to explain it. I end by saying that, in my opinion, we may hear the locutions that proceed from the understanding whenever we like, and think that we hear them whenever we pray. But it is not so with the divine locutions: for many days I may desire to hear them, and I cannot; and at other times, even when I would not, as I said before,[1] hear them, I must. It seems to me that any one disposed to deceive people by saying that he heard from God that which he has invented himself, might as easily say that he heard it with his bodily ears. It is most certainly true that I never imagined there was any other way of hearing or understanding till I had proof of it in myself; and so, as I said before,[2] it gave me trouble enough.

Efficacy of the divine locutions.

13. Locutions that come from Satan not only do not leave any good effects behind, but do leave evil effects. This has happened to me; but not more than two or three times. Our Lord warned me at once that they came from Satan. Over and above the great aridity which remains in the soul after these evil locutions, there is also a certain disquiet, such as I have had on many other occasions, when, by our Lord's permission, I fell into great temptations and travail of soul in diverse ways; and though I am in trouble often enough, as I shall show hereafter,[3] yet this disquiet is such that I know not whence it comes; only the soul seems to resist, is troubled and distressed, without knowing why; for the words of Satan are good, and not evil. I am thinking whether this may not be so because one spirit is conscious of the presence of another.

Diabolic locutions.

14. The sweetness and joy which Satan gives are, in my opinion, of a very different kind. By means of these sweetnesses he may deceive any one

Easily delude those who have not true spiritual tastes.

[1] § 2.   [2] Ch. vii. § 12.   [3] Ch. xxviii. § 7, ch. xxx. § 7.

who does not, or who never did, taste of the sweetness of God,—by which I mean a certain sweet, strong, impressive, delightsome, and calm refreshing. Those little, fervid bursts of tears, and other slight emotions,—for at the first breath of persecution these little flowers wither,—I do not call devotion, though they are a good beginning, and are holy impressions; but they are not a test to determine whether these locutions come from a good or an evil spirit. It is therefore best for us to proceed always with great caution; for those persons who have advanced in prayer only so far as this may most easily fall into delusions, if they have visions or revelations. For myself, I never had a single vision or revelation till God had led me on to the prayer of union,— unless it be on that occasion, of which I have spoken before,[1] now many years ago, when I saw our Lord. Oh, that His Majesty had been pleased to let me then understand that it was a true vision, as I have since understood it was! it would have been no slight blessing to me.

15. After these locutions of the evil one, the soul is never gentle, but is, as it were, terrified, and greatly disgusted.

16. I look upon it as a most certain truth, that the devil will never deceive, and that God will not suffer him to deceive, that soul which has no confidence whatever in itself; which is strong in faith, and resolved to undergo a thousand deaths for any one article of the creed; which in its love of the faith, infused of God once for all,—a faith living and strong,—always labours, seeking for further light on this side and on that, to mould itself on the teaching of the Church, as one already deeply grounded in the truth. No imaginable revelations, not even if it saw the heavens open, could make that soul swerve in any degree from the doctrine of the Church. If, however, it should at any time find itself wavering even in thought on this point, or stopping to say to itself, If God says this to me, it may be true, as well as what He said to the Saints,—the soul must not be sure of it. I do not mean that it so believes, only that Satan has taken

The true faith the soul's safeguard.

[1] Ch. vii. § 11.

the first step towards tempting it; and the giving way to the first movements of a thought like this is evidently most wrong. I believe, however, that these first movements will not take place if the soul is so strong in the matter—as that soul is to whom our Lord sends these graces—that it seems as if it could crush the evil spirits in defence of the very least of the truths which the Church holds.

Test of the diabolic locutions.
17. If the soul does not discern this great strength in itself, and if the particular devotion or vision help it not onwards, then it must not look upon it as safe. For though at first the soul is conscious of no harm, great harm may by degrees ensue; because, so far as I can see, and by experience understand, that which purports to come from God is to be received only in so far as it corresponds with the sacred writings; but if it varies therefrom ever so little, I am incomparably more convinced that it comes from Satan than I am now convinced it comes from God, however deep that conviction may be. In this case, there is no need to ask for signs, nor from what spirit it proceeds, because this varying is so clear a sign of the devil's presence, that if all the world were to assure me that it came from God, I would not believe it. The fact is, that all good seems to be lost out of sight, and to have fled from the soul, when the devil has spoken to it; the soul is thrown into a state of disgust, and is troubled, able to do no good thing whatever—for if it conceives good desires, they are not strong; its humility is fictitious, disturbed, and without sweetness. Any one who has ever tasted of the Spirit of God will, I think, understand it.

The Saint's spirit condemned by those she consulted.
18. Nevertheless, Satan has many devices; and so there is nothing more certain than that it is safer to be afraid, and always on our guard, under a learned director, from whom nothing is concealed. If we do this, no harm can befall us, though much has befallen me through the excessive fears which possessed some people. For instance, it happened so once to me, when many persons in whom I had great confidence, and with good reason, had assembled together,—five or six in number, I think,—and all very great servants of God. It is true, my relations were with one

of them only; but by his orders I made my state known to the others. They had many conferences together about my necessities; for they had a great affection for me, and were afraid I was under a delusion. I, too, was very much afraid whenever I was not occupied in prayer; but when I prayed, and our Lord bestowed His graces upon me, I was instantly reassured. My confessor told me they were all of opinion that I was deceived by Satan; that I must communicate less frequently, and contrive to distract myself in such a way as to be less alone.

19. I was in great fear myself, as I have just said, and my disease of the heart[1] contributed thereto, so that very often I did not dare to remain alone in my cell during the day. When I found so many maintain this, and myself unable to believe them, I had at once a most grievous scruple; for it seemed to me that I had very little humility, especially as they all led lives incomparably better than mine: they were also learned men. Why should I not believe them? I did all I could to believe them. I reflected on my wicked life, and therefore what they said to me must be true. *Her great fear.*

20. In this distress, I quitted the church,[2] and entered an oratory. I had not been to Communion for many days, nor had I been alone, which was all my comfort. I had no one to speak to, for every one was against me. Some, I thought, made a mock of me when I spoke to them of my prayer, as if I were a person under delusions of the imagination; others warned my confessor to be on his guard against me; and some said it was clear the whole was an operation of Satan. My confessor, though he agreed with them for the sake of trying me, as I understood afterwards, always comforted me: and he alone did so. He told me that, if I did not offend God, my prayer, even if it was the work of Satan, could do me no harm; that I should be delivered from it. He bade me pray much to God: he himself, and all his penitents, and many others, did so earnestly; I, too, with all my might, and as many as I knew to be servants of God, *The Saint's distress.*

---

[1] Ch. iv. § 6, ch. v. § 14.
[2] It was the church of the Jesuits (*Bouix*).

prayed that His Majesty would be pleased to lead me by another way. This lasted, I think, about two years; and this was the subject of my continual prayer to our Lord.

<small>Effects of her fear of delusion.</small> 21. But there was no comfort for me when I thought of the possibility that Satan could speak to me so often. Now that I was never alone for prayer, our Lord made me recollected even during conversation: He spoke what He pleased,—I could not avoid it; and, though it distressed me, I was forced to listen. I was by myself, having no one in whom I could find any comfort; unable to pray or read, like a person stunned by heavy trials, and by the dread that the evil one had deluded me; utterly disquieted and wearied, not knowing what would become of me. I have been occasionally—yea, very often—in distress, but never before in distress so great. I was in this state for four or five hours; there was no comfort for me, either from heaven or on earth— only our Lord left me to suffer, afraid of a thousand dangers.

<small>Her instantaneous deliverance.</small> 22. O my Lord, how true a friend art Thou! how powerful! Thou showest Thy power when Thou wilt; and Thou dost will it always, if only we will it also. Let the whole creation praise Thee, O Thou Lord of the world! Oh, that a voice might go forth over all the earth, proclaiming Thy faithfulness to those who love Thee! All things fail; but Thou, Lord of all, never failest! They who love Thee, oh, how little they have to suffer! oh, how gently, how tenderly, how sweetly Thou, O my Lord, dealest with them! Oh, that no one had ever been occupied with any other love than Thine! It seems as if Thou didst subject those who love Thee to a severe trial; but it is in order that they may learn, in the depths of that trial, the depths of Thy love. O my God, oh, that I had understanding and learning, and a new language, in order to magnify Thy works, according to the knowledge of them which my soul possesses! Every thing fails me, O my Lord; but if Thou wilt not abandon me, I will never fail Thee. Let all the learned rise up against me, —let the whole creation persecute me,—let the evil spirits torment me,—but do Thou, O Lord, fail me not; for I know by experience now the blessedness of that deliverance which Thou

dost effect for those who trust only in Thee. In this distress, —for then I had never had a single vision,—these Thy words alone were enough to remove it, and give me perfect peace: " Be not afraid, my daughter : it is I ; and I will not abandon thee. Fear not."[1]

23. It seems to me that, in the state I was in then, many hours would have been necessary to calm me, and that no one could have done it. Yet I found myself, through these words alone, tranquil and strong, courageous and confident, at rest and enlightened; in a moment, my soul seemed changed, and I felt I could maintain against all the world that my prayer was the work of God. Oh, how good is God! how good is our Lord, and how powerful! He gives not counsel only, but relief as well. His words are deeds. O my God! as He strengthens our faith, love grows. So it is, in truth; for I used frequently to recollect how our Lord, when the tempest arose, commanded the winds to be still over the sea.[2] So I said to myself: Who is He, that all my faculties should thus obey Him? Who is He, that gives light in such darkness in a moment; who softens a heart that seemed to be made of stone; who gives the waters of sweet tears, where for a long time great dryness seems to have prevailed; who inspires these desires; who bestows this courage? What have I been thinking of? what am I afraid of? what is it? I desire to serve this my Lord; I aim at nothing else but His pleasure; I seek no joy, no rest, no other good than that of doing His will. I was so confident that I had no other desire, that I could safely assert it.

Effects of the divine locution.

24. Seeing, then, that our Lord is so powerful, —as I see and know He is,—and that the evil spirits are His slaves,—of which there can be no doubt, because it is of faith,—and I a servant of this our Lord and King,—what harm can Satan do unto me? Why have I not strength enough to fight against all hell? I took up the cross in my hand,—I was changed in a moment into another person,

Renewed courage of the Saint.

[1] See *Inner Fortress*, vi. 3, 5.
[2] S. Matt. viii. 26 : " Imperavit ventis et mari, et facta est tranquillitas magna."

and it seemed as if God had really given me courage enough not to be afraid of encountering all the evil spirits. It seemed to me that I could, with the cross, easily defeat them altogether. So I cried out, Come on, all of you; I am the servant of our Lord: I should like to see what you can do against me.

<small>Evil spirits afraid of those who fear them not.</small> 25. And certainly they seemed to be afraid of me, for I was left in peace: I feared them so little, that the terrors, which until now oppressed me, quitted me altogether; and, though I saw them occasionally,—I shall speak of this by and by,[1]—I was never again afraid of them—on the contrary, they seemed to be afraid of me.[2] I found myself endowed with a certain authority over others, given me by the Lord of all, so that I cared no more for them than for flies. They seem to be such cowards; for their strength fails them at the sight of any one who despises them. These enemies have not the courage to assail any but those whom they see ready to give in to them, or when God permits them to do so, for the greater good of His servants, whom they may try and torment.

<small>The assaults of Satan are with our consent.</small> 26. May it please His Majesty that we fear Him whom we ought to fear,[3] and understand that one venial sin can do us more harm than all hell together; for that is the truth. The evil spirits keep us in terror, because we expose ourselves to the assaults of terror by our attachments to honours, possessions, and pleasures. For then the evil spirits, uniting themselves with us,—we become our own enemies when we love and seek what we ought to hate,— do us great harm. We ourselves put weapons into their hands, that they may assail us; those very weapons with which we should defend ourselves. It is a great pity. But if, for the love of God, we hated all this, and embraced the cross, and set about His service in earnest, Satan would fly away before such realities, as from the plague. He is the friend of lies, and a lie himself.[4] He will have nothing to do with those who walk

---

[1] Ch. xxxi. § 1.
[2] S. John of the Cross, *Spiritual Canticle*, st. 24, p. 128, Engl. trans.
[3] S. Matt. x. 26, 28: "Ne ergo timueritis eos, . . . sed potius timete Eum."
[4] S. John viii. 44 : "Mendax est, et pater ejus."

in the truth. When he sees the understanding of any one obscured, he simply helps to pluck out his eyes; if he sees any one already blind, seeking peace in vanities,—for all the things of this world are so utterly vanity, that they seem to be but the playthings of a child,—he sees at once that such a one is a child; he treats him as a child, and ventures to wrestle with him—not once, but often.

27. May it please our Lord that I be not one of these; and may His Majesty give me grace to take that for peace which is really peace, that for honour which is really honour, and that for delight which is really a delight. Let me never mistake one thing for another—and then I snap my fingers at all the devils, for they shall be afraid of me. I do not understand those terrors which make us cry out, Satan, Satan! when we may say, God, God! and make Satan tremble. Do we not know that he cannot stir without the permission of God? What does it mean? I am really much more afraid of those people who have so great a fear of the devil, than I am of the devil himself. Satan can do me no harm whatever, but they can trouble me very much, particularly if they be confessors. I have spent some years of such great anxiety, that even now I am amazed that I was able to bear it. Blessed be our Lord, who has so effectually helped me! *Fears of the devil unreasonable.*

CHAPTER XXVI.

HOW THE FEARS OF THE SAINT VANISHED — HOW SHE WAS ASSURED THAT HER PRAYER WAS THE WORK OF THE HOLY SPIRIT.

1. I LOOK upon the courage which our Lord has implanted in me against evil spirits as one of the greatest mercies which He has bestowed upon me; for a cowardly soul, afraid of any thing but sin against God, is a very unseemly thing, when we have on our side the King omnipotent, our Lord most high, who can do all things, and *If God be with us, that is enough.*

subjects all things to Himself. There is nothing to be afraid of if we walk, as I said before,[1] in the truth, in the sight of His Majesty, with a pure conscience. And for this end, as I said in the same place, I would have myself all fears, that I may not for one instant offend Him who in that instant is able to destroy us. If His Majesty is pleased with us, whoever resists us—be he who he may—will be utterly disappointed.

2. It may be so, you will say; but, then, where *Love of God violent.* is that soul so just as to please Him in every thing? —and that is the reason why we are afraid. Certainly it is not my soul, which is most wretched, unprofitable, and full of misery. God is not like man in His ways; He knows our weakness. But the soul perceives, by the help of certain great signs, whether it loves God of a truth; for the love of those souls who have come to this state is not hidden, as it was at first, but is full of high impulses, and of longings for the visions of God, as I shall show hereafter—or rather, as I have shown already.[2] Every thing wearies, every thing distresses, every thing torments the soul, unless it be suffered with God, or for God. There is no rest which is not a weariness, because the soul knows itself to be away from its true rest; and so love is made most manifest, and, as I have just said, impossible to hide.

Foundation of the convent of S. Joseph, Avila. 3. It happened to me, on another occasion, to be grievously tried, and much spoken against on account of a certain affair,—of which I will speak hereafter,[3] —by almost every body in the place where I am living, and by the members of my Order. When I was in this distress, and afflicted by many occasions of disquiet wherein I was placed, our Lord spoke to me, saying: "What art thou afraid of? knowest thou not that I am almighty? I will do what I have promised thee." And so, afterwards, was it done. I found myself at once so strong, that I could have undertaken any thing, so it seemed, immediately, even if I had to endure greater trials for His service, and had to enter on a new state

[1] Ch. xxv. § 26.   [2] Ch. xv. § 6.
[3] Ch. xxviii.; the foundation of the house of S. Joseph.

of suffering. These locutions are so frequent, that I cannot count them; many of them are reproaches, and He sends them when I fall into imperfections. They are enough to destroy a soul. They correct me, however; for His Majesty —as I said before[1]—gives both counsel and relief. There are others which bring my former sins into remembrance,— particularly when He is about to bestow upon me some special grace,—in such a way that the soul beholds itself as being really judged; for those reproaches of God put the truth before it so distinctly, that it knows not what to do with itself. Some are warnings against certain dangers to myself or others; many of them are prophecies of future things, three or four years beforehand; and all of them have been fulfilled: some of them I could mention. Here, then, are so many reasons for believing that they come from God, as make it impossible, I believe, for any body to mistake them.

4. The safest course in these things is to declare, without fail, the whole state of the soul, together with the graces our Lord gives me, to a confessor who is learned, and obey him. I do so; and if I did not, I should have no peace. Nor is it right that we women, who are unlearned, should have any: there can be no danger in this, but rather great profit. This is what our Lord has often commanded me to do, and it is what I have often done. I had a confessor[2] who mortified me greatly, and now and then distressed me: he tried me heavily, for he disquieted me exceedingly; and yet he was the one who, I believe, did me the most good. Though I had a great affection for him, I was occasionally tempted to leave him; I thought that the pain he inflicted on me disturbed my prayer. Whenever I was resolved on leaving him, I used to feel instantly that I ought not to do so; and one reproach of our Lord would press more heavily upon me than all that my confessor did. Now and then, I was worn

Necessity of openness with a director.

---

[1] Ch. xxv. § 23.

[2] The Bollandists, n. 185, attribute some of the severity with which her confessor treated the Saint to the spirit of desolation with which he was then tried himself; and, in proof of it, refer to the account which F. Baltasar Alvarez gave of his own prayer to the General of the Society.

out—torture on the one hand, reproaches on the other. I required it all, for my will was but little subdued. Our Lord said to me once, that there was no obedience where there was no resolution to suffer; that I was to think of His sufferings, and then every thing would be easy.

<small>Erroneous direction of one of the Saint's confessors.</small>
5. One of my confessors, to whom I went in the beginning, advised me once, now that my spiritual state was known to be the work of God, to keep silence, and not speak of these things to any one, on the ground that it was safer to keep these graces secret. To me, the advice seemed good, because I felt it so much whenever I had to speak of them to my confessor;[1] I was also so ashamed of myself, that I felt it more keenly at times to speak of them than I should have done in confessing grave sins, particularly when the graces I had to reveal were great. I thought they did not believe me, and that they were laughing at me. I felt it so much,—for I look on this as an irreverent treatment of the marvels of God,—that I was glad to be silent. I learned then that I had been ill-advised by that confessor, because I ought never to hide any thing from my confessor; for I should find great security if I told every thing; and if I did otherwise, I might at any time fall into delusions.[2]

<small>The Saint's perfect obedience.</small>
6. Whenever our Lord commanded me to do one thing in prayer, and if my confessor forbade it, our Lord Himself told me to obey my confessor. His Majesty afterwards would change the mind of that confessor, so that he would have me do what he had forbidden before. When we were deprived of many books written in Spanish, and forbidden to read them,—I felt it deeply, for some of these books were a great comfort to me, and I could not read them in Latin,—our Lord said to me, "Be not troubled; I will give thee a living book." I could not understand why this was said to me, for at that time I had never had a vision.[3] But, a very few days afterwards, I understood it well enough; for I had so

[1] See *Relation*, vii. § 7.
[2] S. John of the Cross, *Mount Carmel*, bk. ii. ch. 22.
[3] The visions of the Saint began in 1558 (*De la Fuente*); or, according to Father Bouix, in 1559.

much to think of, and such reasons for self-recollection in what I saw before me, and our Lord dealt so lovingly with me, in teaching me in so many ways, that I had little or no need whatever of books. His Majesty has been to me a veritable Book, in which I saw all truth. Blessed be such a Book, which leaves behind an impression of what is read therein, and in such a way that it cannot be forgotten!

7. Who can look upon our Lord, covered with wounds, and bowed down under persecutions, without accepting, loving, and longing for them? Who can behold but a part of that glory which He will give to those who serve Him without confessing that all he may do, and all he may suffer, are altogether as nothing, when we may hope for such a reward? Who can look at the torments of lost souls without acknowledging the torments of this life to be joyous delights in comparison, and confessing how much they owe to our Lord in having saved them so often from the place of torments?[1] But as, by the help of God, I shall speak more at large of certain things, I wish now to go on with the story of my life. Our Lord grant that I have been clear enough in what I have hitherto said! I feel assured that He will understand me who has had experience herein, and that he will see I have partially succeeded; but as to him who has had no such experience, I should not be surprised if he regarded it all as folly. It is enough for him that it is I who say it, in order to be free from blame; neither will I blame any one who shall so speak of it. Our Lord grant that I may never fail to do His will! Amen.

The sufferings of our Lord.

[1] S. Luke xvi. 28: "Ne et ipsi veniant in hunc locum tormentorum."

CHAPTER XXVII.

THE SAINT PRAYS TO BE DIRECTED BY A DIFFERENT WAY—
INTELLECTUAL VISIONS.

The Saint's perplexities.
1. I NOW resume the story of my life. I was in great pain and distress; and many prayers, as I said,[1] were made on my behalf, that our Lord would lead me by another and a safer way; for this, they told me, was so suspicious. The truth is, that though I was praying to God for this, and wished I had a desire for another way, yet, when I saw the progress I was making, I was unable really to desire a change,—though I always prayed for it,—excepting on those occasions when I was extremely cast down by what people said to me, and by the fears with which they filled me.

Her earnest prayers.
2. I felt that I was wholly changed; I could do nothing but put myself in the hands of God: He knew what was expedient for me; let Him do with me according to His will in all things. I saw that by this way I was directed heavenwards, and that formerly I was going down to hell. I could not force myself to desire a change, nor believe that I was under the influence of Satan. Though I was doing all I could to believe the one and to desire the other, it was not in my power to do so. I offered up all my actions, if there should be any good in them, for this end; I had recourse to the Saints for whom I had a devotion, that they might deliver me from the evil one; I made novenas; I commended myself to S. Hilarion, to the angel S. Michael, to whom I had recently become devout, for this purpose; and many other Saints I importuned, that our Lord might show me the way,—I mean, that they might obtain this for me from His Majesty.

Intellectual visions.
3. At the end of two years spent in prayer by myself and others for this end, namely, that our Lord would either lead me by another way, or show the truth of this,—for now the locutions of our Lord were ex-

[1] Ch. xxv. § 20.

tremely frequent,—this happened to me. I was in prayer one day,—it was the feast of the glorious S. Peter,[1]—when I saw Christ close by me, or, to speak more correctly, felt Him; for I saw nothing with the eyes of the body, nothing with the eyes of the soul. He seemed to me to be close beside me; and I saw, too, as I believe, that it was He who was speaking to me. As I was utterly ignorant that such a vision was possible,[2] I was extremely afraid at first, and did nothing but weep; however, when He spoke to me but one word to reassure me, I recovered myself, and was, as usual, calm and comforted, without any fear whatever. Jesus Christ seemed to be by my side continually; and, as the vision was not imaginary, I saw no form; but I had a most distinct feeling that He was always on my right hand, a witness of all I did; and never at any time, if I was but slightly recollected, or not too much distracted, could I be ignorant of His near presence.[3]

4. I went at once to my confessor,[4] in great distress, to tell him of it. He asked in what form I saw our Lord. I told him I saw no form. He then said: "How did you know that it was Christ?" I replied, that I did not know how I knew it; but I could not help knowing that He was close beside me,—that I saw Him distinctly, and felt His presence,—that the recollectedness of my soul was deeper in the prayer of quiet, and more continuous,—that the effects thereof were very different from what I had hitherto experienced,—and that it was most certain. I could only make comparisons in order to explain myself; and certainly there are no comparisons, in my opinion, by which visions of this kind can be described. Afterwards I learnt from Friar Peter of Alcantara, a holy man of great spirituality,—of whom I shall speak by and by,[5]—and from others of great learning, that this vision was of the highest order, and one with

Intellectual visions hard to explain.

---

[1] See ch. xxviii. § 4, and ch. xxix. § 4. The vision took place, it seems, on the 29th of June. See ch. xxix. § 6.
[2] See ch. vii. § 12.
[3] See Anton. a Spiritu Sancto, *Direct. Mystic.* tr. iii. disp. v. § 3.
[4] See *Inner Fortress*, vi. 8, 3.
[5] § 17, *infra*.

P

which Satan can least interfere ; and therefore there are no words whereby to explain,—at least, none for us women, who know so little: learned men can explain it better.

<small>Certainty of the vision.</small> 5. For if I say that I see Him neither with the eyes of the body, nor with those of the soul,— because it was not an imaginary vision,—how is it that I can understand and maintain that He stands beside me, and be more certain of it than if I saw Him ? If it be supposed that it is as if a person were blind, or in the dark, and therefore unable to see another who is close to him, the comparison is not exact. There is a certain likelihood about it, however, but not much, because the other senses tell him who is blind of that presence : he hears the other speak or move, or he touches him ; but in these visions there is nothing like this. The darkness is not felt ; only He renders himself present to the soul by a certain knowledge of Himself which is more clear than the sun.[1] I do not mean that we now see either a sun or any brightness, only that there is a light not seen, which illumines the understanding so that the soul may have the fruition of so great a good. This vision brings with it great blessings.

<small>Intellectual visions different from the presence of God.</small> 6. It is not like that presence of God which is frequently felt, particularly by those who have attained to the prayer of union and of quiet, when we seem, at the very commencement of our prayer, to find Him with whom we would converse, and when we seem to feel that He hears us by the effects and the spiritual impressions of great love and faith of which we are then conscious, as well as by the good resolutions, accompanied by sweetness, which we then make. This is a great grace from God ; and let him to whom He has given it esteem it much, because it is a very high degree of prayer ; but it is not vision. God is understood to be present there by the effects He works in the soul : that is the way His Majesty makes His presence felt; but here, in this vision, it is seen clearly that Jesus Christ is present, the Son of the Virgin. In the prayer of union and of quiet, certain inflowings of the Godhead are present ; but in the vision, the

[1] See *Relation*, vii. § 26.

Sacred Humanity also, together with them, is pleased to be our visible companion, and to do us good.

7. My confessor next asked me, who told me it was Jesus Christ.[1] I replied, that He often told me so Himself; but, even before He told me so, there was an impression on my understanding that it was He; and before this He used to tell me so, and I saw Him not. If a person whom I had never seen, but of whom I had heard, came to speak to me, and I were blind or in the dark, and told me who he was, I should believe him; but I could not so confidently affirm that he was that person, as I might do if I had seen him. But in this vision I could do so, because so clear a knowledge is impressed on the soul that all doubt seems impossible, though He is not seen. Our Lord wills that this knowledge be so graven on the understanding, that we can no more question His presence than we can question that which we see with our eyes: not so much even; for very often there arises a suspicion that we have imagined things we think we see; but here, though there may be a suspicion in the first instant, there remains a certainty so great, that the doubt has no force whatever. So also is it when God teaches the soul in another way, and speaks to it without speaking, in the way I have described. *Certainty of vision.*

8. There is so much of heaven in this language, that it cannot well be understood on earth, though we may desire ever so much to explain it, if our Lord will not teach it experimentally. Our Lord impresses in the innermost soul that which He wills that soul to understand; and He manifests it there without images or formal words, after the manner of the vision I am speaking of. Consider well this way in which God works, in order that the soul may understand what He means—His great truths and mysteries; for very often what I understand, when our Lord explains to me the vision, which it is His Majesty's pleasure to set before me, is after this manner; and it seems to me that this is a state with which the devil can least interfere, for these reasons; but if these reasons are not good, *God speaks to the soul without words.*

[1] *Inner Fortress*, vi. 8, § 3.

I must be under a delusion. The vision and the language are matters of such pure spirituality, that there is no turmoil of the faculties, or of the senses, out of which—so it seems to me —the devil can derive any advantage.

The senses not always suspended.
9. It is only at intervals, and for an instant, that this occurs; for generally—so I think—the senses are not taken away, and the faculties are not suspended: they preserve their ordinary state. It is not always so in contemplation; on the contrary, it is very rarely so; but when it is so, I say that we do nothing whatever ourselves: no work of ours is then possible; all that is done is apparently the work of our Lord. It is as if food had been received into the stomach which had not first been eaten, and without our knowing how it entered; but we do know well that it is there, though we know not its nature, nor who it was that placed it there. In this vision, I know who placed it; but I do not know how He did it. I neither saw it, nor felt it; I never had any inclination to desire it, and I never knew before that such a thing was possible.

Compulsory attention of the understanding to the divine locutions.
10. In the locutions of which I spoke before,[1] God makes the understanding attentive, though it may be painful to understand what is said; then the soul seems to have other ears wherewith it hears; and He forces it to listen, and will not let it be distracted. The soul is like a person whose hearing was good, and who is not suffered to stop his ears, while people standing close beside him speak to him with a loud voice. He may be unwilling to hear, yet hear he must. Such a person contributes something of his own; for he attends to what is said to him; but here there is nothing of the kind: even that little, which is nothing more than the bare act of listening, which is granted to it in the other case, is now out of its power. It finds its food prepared and eaten; it has nothing more to do but to enjoy it. It is as if one without ever learning, without taking the pains even to learn to read, and without studying any subject whatever, should find himself in possession of all knowledge, not knowing how or whence

[1] Ch. xxv. § 1.

it came to him, seeing that he had never taken the trouble even to learn the alphabet. This last comparison seems to me to throw some light on this heavenly gift; for the soul finds itself learned in a moment, and the mystery of the most Holy Trinity so clearly revealed to it, together with other most deep doctrines, that there is no theologian in the world with whom it would hesitate to dispute for the truth of these matters.

11. It is impossible to describe the surprise of the soul when it finds that one of these graces is enough to change it utterly, and make it love nothing but Him who, without waiting for any thing itself might do, renders it fit for blessings so high, communicates to it His secrets, and treats it with so much affection and love. Some of the graces He bestows are liable to suspicion because they are so marvellous, and given to one who has deserved them so little—incredible, too, without a most lively faith. I intend, therefore, to mention very few of those graces which our Lord has wrought in me, if I should not be ordered otherwise; but there are certain visions of which I shall speak, an account of which may be of some service. In doing so, I shall either dispel his fears to whom our Lord sends them, and who, as I used to do, thinks them impossible, or I shall explain the way, or the road, by which our Lord has led me; and that is what I have been commanded to describe. Some effects of vision.

12. Now, going back to speak of this way of understanding, what it is seems to me to be this: it is our Lord's will in every way that the soul should have some knowledge of what passes in heaven; and I think that, as the blessed there without speech understand one another,—I never knew this for certain till our Lord of His goodness made me see it ; He showed it to me in a trance,—so is it here: God and the soul understand one another, merely because His Majesty so wills it, without the help of other means, to express the love there is between them both. In the same way on earth, two persons of sound sense, if they love each other much, can even, without any signs, understand one another only by their looks. It must be so here, though we do not see Love, to make itself known, requires no words.

how, as these two lovers earnestly regard each the other: the bridegroom says so to the bride in the Canticle, so I believe, and I have heard that it is spoken of there.[1]

Inestimable worth of this supernatural grace. 13. Oh, marvellous goodness of God, in that Thou permittest eyes which have looked upon so much evil as those of my soul to look upon Thee! May they never accustom themselves, after looking on Thee, to look upon vile things again! and may they have pleasure in nothing but in Thee, O Lord! Oh, ingratitude of men, how far will it go! I know by experience that what I am saying is true, and that all we can say is exceedingly little, when we consider what Thou doest to the soul which Thou hast led to such a state as this. O souls, you who have begun to pray, and you who possess the true faith, what can you be in search of even in this life, let alone that which is for ever, that is comparable to the least of these graces? Consider, and it is true, that God gives Himself to those who give up every thing for Him. God is not an accepter of persons.[2] He loves all; there is no excuse for any one, however wicked he may be, seeing that He hath thus dealt with me, raising me to the state I am in. Consider that what I am saying is not even an iota of what may be said; I say only that which is necessary to show the kind of the vision and of the grace which God bestows on the soul; for that cannot be told which it feels when our Lord admits it to the understanding of His secrets and of His mighty works. The joy of this is so far above all conceivable joys, that it may well make us loathe all the joys of earth; for they are all but dross; and it is an odious thing to make them enter into the comparison, even if we might have them for ever. Those which our Lord gives, what are they? One drop only of the waters of the overflowing river which He is reserving for us.

14. It is a shame! And, in truth, I am ashamed *Necessity of penance.* of myself; if shame could have a place in heaven, I should certainly be the most ashamed there. Why

[1] Cant. vi. 4: "Averte oculos tuos a me, quia ipsi me avolare fecerunt." S. John of the Cross, *Mount Carmel*, bk. ii. ch. xxix, p. 192, Engl. trans.

[2] Acts x. 35: "Non est personarum acceptor Deus."

do we seek blessings and joys so great, bliss without end, and all at the cost of our good Jesus ? Shall we not at least weep with the daughters of Jerusalem,[1] if we do not help to carry His cross with the Cyrenean ?[2] Is it by pleasure and idle amusements that we can attain to the fruition of what He purchased with so much blood? It is impossible. Can we think that we can, by preserving our honour, which is vanity, recompense Him for the sufferings He endured, that we might reign with Him for ever ? This is not the way; we are going by the wrong road utterly, and we shall never arrive there. You, my father, must lift up your voice, and utter these truths aloud, seeing that God has taken from me the power of doing it. I should like to utter them to myself for ever. I listened to them myself, and came to the knowledge of God so late, as will appear by what I have written, that I am ashamed of myself when I speak of this ; and so I should like to be silent.

15. Of one thing, however, I will speak, and I think of it now and then,—may it be the good pleasure of our Lord to bring me on, so that I may have the fruition of it !—what will be the accidental glory *Joy of late, but faithful, penitents in heaven.* and the joy of the blessed who have entered on it, when they see that, though they were late, yet they left nothing undone which it was possible for them to do for God, who kept nothing back they could give Him, and who gave what they gave in every way they could, according to their strength and their measure,—they who had more, gave more. How rich will he be who gave up all his riches for Christ! How honourable will he be who, for His sake, sought no honours whatever, but rather took pleasure in seeing himself abased ! How wise he will be who rejoiced when men accounted him as mad !—they did so of Wisdom Itself![3] How few there are of this kind now, because of our sins ! Now, indeed, they are all gone whom people regarded as mad,[4] because they saw them perform heroic acts, as true lovers of Christ.

[1] S. Luke xxiii. 28 : "Filiæ Jerusalem, nolite flere super Me, sed super vos ipsas flete."
[2] S. Matt. xxvii. 32 : "Hunc angariaverunt ut tolleret crucem Ejus."
[3] S. John x. 20 : "Dæmonium habet et insanit : quid Eum auditis ?"
[4] Sap. v. 4 : "Nos insensati vitam illorum æstimabamus insaniam."

16. O world, world! how thou art gaining credit because they are few who know thee! But do we suppose that God is better pleased when men account us wise and discreet persons? We think forthwith that there is but little edification given when people do not go about, every one in his degree, with great gravity, in a dignified way. Even in the friar, the ecclesiastic, and the nun, if they wear old and patched garments, we think it a novelty, and a scandal to the weak; and even if they are very recollected and given to prayer. Such is the state of the world, and so forgotten are matters of perfection, and those grand impetuosities of the Saints. More mischief, I think, is done in this way, than by any scandal that might arise if the religious showed in their actions, as they proclaim it in words, that the world is to be held in contempt. Out of scandals such as this, our Lord obtains great fruit. If some people take scandal, others are filled with remorse: anyhow, we should have before us some likeness of that which our Lord and His Apostles endured; for we have need of it now more than ever.

The Saint denounces pretences.

17. And what an excellent likeness in the person of that blessed friar, Peter of Alcantara, God has just taken from us![1] The world cannot bear such perfection now; it is said that men's health is grown feebler, and that we are not now in those former times. But this holy man lived in our day; he had a spirit strong as those of another age, and so he trampled on the world. If men do not go about barefooted, nor undergo sharp penances, as he did, there are many ways, as I have said before,[2] of trampling on the world; and our Lord teaches them when He finds the necessary courage. How great was the courage with which His Majesty filled the Saint I am speaking of! He did penance—oh, how sharp it was!—for seven-and-forty years, as all men know. I should like to speak of it, for I know it to be all true.

S. Peter of Alcantara.

18. He spoke of it to me and to another person, from whom he kept few or no secrets. As for me, it was the affection he bore me that led him to speak;

The penance of S. Peter of Alcantara,

---

[1] 18th Oct. 1562. As the Saint finished the first relation of her life in June 1562, this is one of the additions subsequently made.

[2] Ch. xiv. § 7.

for it was our Lord's will that he should undertake my defence, and encourage me, at a time when I was in great straits, as I said before, and shall speak of again.[1] He told me, I think, that for forty years he slept but an hour and a half out of the twenty-four, and that the most laborious penance he underwent, when he began, was this of overcoming sleep. For that purpose, he was always either kneeling or standing. When he slept, he sat down, his head resting against a piece of wood driven into the wall. Lie down he could not, if he wished it; for his cell, as every one knows, was only four feet and a half in length. In all these years, he never covered his head with his hood, even when the sun was hottest, or the rain heaviest. He never covered his feet: the only garment he wore was made of sackcloth, and that was as tight as it could be, with nothing between it and his flesh; over this, he wore a cloak of the same stuff. He told me that, in the severe cold, he used to take off his cloak, and open the door and the window of his cell, in order that when he put his cloak on again, after shutting the door and the window, he might give some satisfaction to his body in the pleasure it might have in the increased warmth. His ordinary practice was to eat but once in three days. He said to me, "Why are you astonished at it? it is very possible for any one who is used to it." One of his companions told me that he would be occasionally eight days without eating: that must have been when he was in prayer; for he was subject to trances, and to the impetuosities of the love of God, of which I was once a witness myself.

19. His poverty was extreme; and his mortification, from his youth, was such,—so he told me,—that he was three years in one of the houses of his Order without knowing how to distinguish one friar from another, otherwise than by the voice; for he never raised his eyes: and so, when he was obliged to go from one part of the house to the other, he never knew the way, unless he followed the friars. His journeys, also, were made in the same way. For many years, he never saw a woman's face. He told me that it was nothing to him then whether he saw it or not: but he was an

And his mortified life.

[1] Ch. xxvi. § 3, ch. xxxii. § 16.

aged man when I made his acquaintance; and his weakness was so great, that he seemed like nothing else but the roots of trees. With all his sanctity, he was very agreeable; though his words were few, unless when he was asked questions; he was very pleasant to speak to, for he had a most clear understanding.

Death of S. Peter of Alcantara. 20. Many other things I should like to say of him, if I were not afraid, my father, that you will say, Why does she meddle here? and it is in that fear I have written this. So I leave the subject, only saying that his last end was like his life—preaching to, and exhorting, his brethren. When he saw that the end was come, he repeated the Psalm,[1] "Lætatus sum in his quæ dicta sunt mihi;" and then, kneeling down, he died.

He appears to S. Teresa after his death. 21. Since then, it has pleased our Lord that I should find more help from him than during his life. He advises me in many matters. I have often seen him in great glory. The first time he appeared to me, he said: "O blessed penance, which has merited so great a reward!" with other things. A year before his death, he appeared to me, being then far away. I knew he was about to die, and so I sent him word to that effect, when he was some leagues from here. When he died, he appeared to me, and said that he was going to his rest. I did not believe it. I spoke of it to some persons, and within eight days came the news that he was dead—or, to speak more correctly, that he had begun to live for evermore.[2]

Power of S. Peter of Alcantara with God. 22. Behold here, then, how that life of sharp penance is perfected in such great glory: and now he is a greater comfort to me, I do believe, than he was on earth. Our Lord said to me on one occasion, that persons could not ask Him any thing in his name, and He not hear them. I have recommended many things to him that he was to ask of our Lord, and I have seen my petitions granted. God be blessed for ever! Amen.

[1] Ps. cxxi. The words in the MS. are: "Lætatun sun yn is que dita sun miqui" (*De la Fuente*).

[2] See ch. xxx. § 2.

23. But how I have been talking in order to stir you up never to esteem any thing in this life!—as if you did not know this, or as if you were not resolved to leave every thing, and had already done it! I see so much going wrong in the world, that though my speaking of it is of no other use than to weary me by writing of it, it is some relief to me that all I am saying makes against myself. Our Lord forgive me all that I do amiss herein; and you too, my father, for wearying you to no purpose. It seems as if I would make you do penance for my sins herein.

CHAPTER XXVIII.

VISIONS OF THE SACRED HUMANITY, AND OF THE GLORIFIED BODIES—IMAGINARY VISIONS—GREAT FRUITS THEREOF WHEN THEY COME FROM GOD.

1. I NOW resume our subject. I spent some days, not many, with that vision[1] continually before me. *Subject resumed.* It did me so much good, that I never ceased to pray. Even when I did cease, I contrived that it should be in such a way as that I should not displease Him whom I saw so clearly present, an eye-witness of my acts. And though I was occasionally afraid, because so much was said to me about delusions, that fear lasted not long, because our Lord reassured me.

2. It pleased our Lord, one day that I was in prayer, to show me His Hands, and His Hands only. *Our Lord shows the Saint His Hands.* The beauty of them was so great, that no language can describe it. This put me in great fear; for every thing that is strange, in the beginning of any new grace from God, makes me very much afraid. A few days later, I saw His divine Face, and I was utterly entranced. I could not understand why our Lord showed Himself in this way, seeing that, afterwards, He granted me the grace of seeing His whole Person. Later on, I understood that His Majesty was dealing with me according to the weakness of my nature. May He be

---

[1] Ch. xxvii. § 3.

blessed for ever! A glory so great was more than one so base and wicked could bear; and our merciful Lord, knowing this, ordered it in this way.

Beauty of glorified bodies. 3. You will think, my father, that it required no great courage to look upon Hands and Face so beautiful. But so beautiful are glorified bodies, that the glory which surrounds them renders those who see that which is so supernatural and beautiful beside themselves. It was so with me: I was in such great fear, trouble, and perplexity at the sight. Afterwards, there ensued a sense of safety and certainty, together with other results, so that all fear passed immediately away.[1]

The Saint beholds the Sacred Humanity. 4. On one of the feasts of S. Paul,[2] when I was at Mass, there stood before me the most Sacred Humanity,[3] as painters represent Him after the resurrection, in great beauty and majesty, as I particularly described it to you, my father, when you had insisted on it. It was painful enough to have to write about it, for I could not describe it without doing great violence to myself. But I described it as well as I could, and there is no reason why I should now recur to it. One thing, however, I have to say: if in heaven itself there were nothing else to delight our eyes but the great beauty of glorified bodies, that would be an excessive bliss, particularly the vision of the Humanity of Jesus

---

[1] Philipp. a SS. Trinitate, *Theolog. Mystic.* par. 2, tr. 3, art. 8: "Quamvis in principio visiones a dæmone fictæ aliquam habeant pacem ac dulcedinem, in fine tamen confusionem et amaritudinem in anima relinquunt; cujus contrarium est in divinis visionibus, quæ sæpe turbant in principio, sed semper in fine pacem animæ relinquunt." S. John of the Cross, *Spiritual Canticle*, st. 14, p. 84: "In the spiritual passage from the sleep of natural ignorance to the wakefulness of the supernatural understanding, which is the beginning of trance or ecstasy, the spiritual vision then revealed makes the soul fear and tremble."

[2] See ch. xxix. § 4.

[3] "The holy Mother, Teresa of Jesus, had these imaginary visions for many years, seeing our Lord continually present before her in great beauty, risen from the dead, with His wounds and the crown of thorns. She had a picture made of Him, which she gave to me, and which I gave to Don Fernando de Toledo, Duke of Alva" (Jerome Gratian, *Union del Alma*, cap. 5. Madrid, 1616).

Christ our Lord. If here below, where His Majesty shows Himself to us according to the measure which our wretchedness can bear, it is so great, what must it be there, where the fruition of it is complete!

5. This vision, though imaginary, I never saw with my bodily eyes, nor, indeed, any other, but only with the eyes of the soul. Those who understand these things better than I do, say that the intellectual vision is more perfect than this; and this, the imaginary vision, much more perfect than those visions which are seen by the bodily eyes. The latter kind of visions, they say, is the lowest; and it is by these that the devil can most delude us.[1] I did not know it then; for I wished, when this grace had been granted me, that it had been so in such a way that I could see it with my bodily eyes, in order that my confessor might not say to me that I indulged in fancies. *Intellectual and imaginary and bodily visions.*

6. After the vision was over, it happened that I too imagined—the thought came at once—I had fancied these things; so I was distressed, because I had spoken of them to my confessor, thinking that I might have been deceiving him.. There was another lamentation: I went to my confessor, and told him of my doubts. He would ask me whether I told him the truth so far as I knew it; or, if not, had I intended to deceive him? I would reply, that I told the truth; for, to the best of my belief, I did not lie, nor did I mean any thing of the kind; neither would I tell a lie for the whole world.[2] This he knew well enough; and, accordingly, he contrived to quiet me; and I felt so much the going to him with these doubts, that I cannot tell how Satan could have put it into my head that I invented those things for the purpose of tormenting myself. *Perplexities of the Saint.*

---

[1] Anton. a Sp. Sancto, *Direct. Mystic.* tr. iii. disp. 5, § 1, n. 315: "Visio corporea est infima, visio imaginaria est media, visio intellectualis est suprema." N. 322: "Apparitio visibilis, cum sit omnium infima, est magis exposita illusioni diaboli, nisi forte huic visioni corporali visio intellectualis adjungatur, ut in apparitione S. Gabrielis archangeli facta Beatæ Virgini."

[2] See ch. xxx. § 18.

7. But our Lord made such haste to bestow this grace upon me, and to declare the reality of it, that all doubts of the vision being a fancy on my part were quickly taken away, and ever since I see most clearly how silly I was. For if I were to spend many years in devising how to picture to myself any thing so beautiful, I should never be able, nor even know how, to do it; for it is beyond the reach of any possible imagination here below: the whiteness and brilliancy alone are inconceivable. It is not a brilliancy which dazzles, but a delicate whiteness and a brilliancy infused, furnishing the most excessive delight to the eyes, never wearied thereby, nor by the visible brightness which enables us to see a beauty so divine. It is a light so different from any light here below, that the very brightness of the sun we see, in comparison with the brightness and light before our eyes, seems to be something so obscure, that no one would ever wish to open his eyes again.

Doubts removed.

8. It is like most pellucid water running in a bed of crystal, reflecting the rays of the sun, compared with most muddy water on a cloudy day, flowing on the surface of the earth. Not that there is any thing like the sun present here, nor is the light like that of the sun: this light seems to be natural; and, in comparison with it, every other light is something artificial. It is a light which knows no night; but rather, as it is always light, nothing ever disturbs it. In short, it is such that no man, however gifted he may be, can ever, in the whole course of his life, arrive at any imagination of what it is. God puts it before us so instantaneously, that we could not open our eyes in time to see it, if it were necessary for us to open them at all. But whether our eyes be open or shut, it makes no difference whatever; for when our Lord wills, we must see it, whether we will or not. No distraction can shut it out, no power can resist it, nor can we attain to it by any diligence or efforts of our own. I know this by experience well, as I shall show you.

Another illustration of the divine light.

9. That which I wish now to speak of is the manner in which our Lord manifests Himself in these visions. I do not mean that I am going to explain how it is that a light so strong can enter the interior

The Saint never understood how these visions were wrought.

sense, or so distinct an image the understanding, so as to seem to be really there; for this must be work for learned men. Our Lord has not been pleased to let me understand how it is. I am so ignorant myself, and so dull of understanding, that, although people have very much wished to explain it to me, I have never been able to understand how it can be.

10. This is the truth : though you, my father, may think that I have a quick understanding, it is not so; for I have found out, in many ways, that my understanding can take in only, as they say, what is given to it to eat. Sometimes my confessor used to be amazed at my ignorance: and he never explained to me—nor, indeed, did I desire to understand—how God did this, nor how it could be. Nor did I ever ask; though, as I have said,[1] I had converse for many years with men of great learning. But I did ask them if this or that were a sin or not: as for every thing else, the thought that God did it all was enough for me. I saw there was no reason to be afraid, but great reason to praise Him. On the other hand, difficulties increase my devotion; and the greater the difficulty, the greater the increase. *Faith and reason.*

11. I will therefore relate what my experience has shown me; but how our Lord brought it about, you, my father, will explain better than I can, and make clear all that is obscure, and beyond my skill to explain. Now and then it seemed to me that what I saw was an image; but most frequently it was not so. I thought it was Christ Himself, judging by the brightness in which He was pleased to show Himself. Sometimes the vision was so indistinct, that I thought it was an image; but still not like a picture, however well painted—and I have seen many good pictures. It would be absurd to suppose that the one bears any resemblance whatever to the other, for they differ as a living person differs from his portrait, which, however well drawn, cannot be lifelike, for it is plain that it is a dead thing. But let this pass, though to the purpose, and literally true. *The Saint's explanation of visions.*

12. I do not say this by way of comparison, for comparisons are never exact, but because it is the *The Majesty of God in visions.*

[1] Ch. xxv. § 18.

truth itself, as there is the same difference here that there is between a living subject and the portrait thereof, neither more nor less: for if what I saw was an image, it was a living image,—not a dead man, but the living Christ: and He makes me see that He is God and man,—not as He was in the sepulchre, but as He was when He had gone forth from it, risen from the dead. He comes at times in majesty so great, that no one can have any doubt that it is our Lord Himself, especially after Communion: we know that He is then present, for faith says so. He shows Himself so clearly to be the Lord of that little dwelling-place, that the soul seems to be dissolved and lost in Christ. O my Jesus, who can describe the majesty wherein Thou showest Thyself! How utterly Thou art the Lord of the whole world, and of heaven, and of a thousand other and innumerable worlds and heavens, the creation of which is possible to Thee! The soul understands by that majesty wherein Thou showest Thyself that it is nothing for Thee to be Lord of all this.

Effects of the vision. 13. Here it is plain, O my Jesus, how slight is the power of all the devils in comparison with Thine, and how he who is pleasing unto Thee is able to tread all hell under his feet. Here we see why the devils trembled when Thou didst go down to Limbus, and why they might have longed for a thousand hells still lower, that they might escape from Thy terrible Majesty. I see that it is Thy will the soul should feel the greatness of Thy Majesty, and the power of Thy most Sacred Humanity, united with Thy Divinity. Here, too, we see what the day of judgment will be, when we shall behold the King in His majesty, and in the rigour of His justice against the wicked. Here we learn true humility, imprinted in the soul by the sight of its own wretchedness, of which now it cannot be ignorant. Here, also, is confusion of face, and true repentance for sins; for though the soul sees that our Lord shows how He loves it, yet it knows not where to go, and so is utterly dissolved.

Effects of the vision remain when the vision is forgotten. 14. My meaning is, that so exceedingly great is the power of this vision, when our Lord shows the soul much of His grandeur and majesty, that it is impossible, in my opinion, for any soul to endure it, if our Lord did not succour it in a most supernatural way, by throwing it into a trance or ecstasy, whereby the vision of the divine presence is lost in the fruition thereof. It is true that afterwards the vision is forgotten; but there remains so deep an impression of the majesty and beauty of God, that it is impossible to forget it, except when our Lord is pleased that the soul should suffer from aridity and desolation, of which I shall speak hereafter;[1] for then it seems to forget God Himself. The soul is itself no longer, it is always inebriated; it seems as if a living love of God, of the highest kind, made a new beginning within it; for though the former vision, which I said represented God without any likeness of Him,[2] is of a higher kind, yet because of our weakness, in order that the remembrance of the vision may last, and that our thoughts may be well occupied, it is a great matter that a presence so divine should remain and abide in our imagination. These two kinds of visions come almost always together, and they do so come; for we behold the excellency and beauty and glory of the most Holy Humanity with the eyes of the soul. And in the other way I have spoken of, — that of intellectual vision, — we learn how He is God, is mighty, can do all things, commands all things, governs all things, and fills all things with His love.

15. This vision is to be esteemed very highly; nor is there, in my opinion, any risk in it, because the fruits of it show that the devil has no power here. I think he tried three or four times to represent our Lord to me, in this way, by a false image of Him. He takes the appearance of flesh, but he cannot counterfeit the glory which it has when the vision is from God. Satan makes his representations in order to undo the true vision which the soul has had: but the soul resists instinctively, is troubled, disgusted, and restless; it loses that devotion and joy it previously had, and cannot pray at all. In the beginning, it so happened *The imaginary vision not dangerous.*

---

[1] Ch. xxx. §§ 9, 10. See S. John of the Cross, *Obscure Night*, bk. ii. ch. 7.

[2] Ch. xxvii. § 3.

to me three or four times. These satanic visions are very different things; and even he who shall have attained to the prayer of quiet only will, I believe, detect them by those results of them which I described when I was speaking of locutions.[1] They are most easily recognised; and if a soul consents not to its own delusion, I do not think that Satan will be able to deceive it, provided it walks in humility and singleness of heart. He who shall have had the true vision, coming from God, detects the false visions at once; for, though they begin with a certain sweetness and joy, the soul rejects them of itself; and the joy which Satan ministers must be, I think, very different—it shows no traces of pure and holy love: Satan very quickly betrays himself.

Tests of the reality of these visions. 16. Thus, then, as I believe, Satan can do no harm to any one who has had experience of these things; for it is the most impossible of all impossible things that all this may be the work of the imagination. There is no ground whatever for the supposition; for the very beauty and whiteness of one of our Lord's Hands[2] are beyond our imagination altogether. How is it that we see present before us, in a moment, what we do not remember, what we have never thought of, and, moreover, what, in a long space of time, the imagination could not compass, because, as I have just said,[3] it far transcends any thing we can comprehend in this life? This, then, is not possible. Whether we have any power in the matter or not will appear by what I am now going to say.

Fictitious visions unprofitable. 17. If the vision were the work of a man's own understanding,—setting aside that such a vision would not accomplish the great results of the true one, nor, indeed, any at all,—it would be as the act of one who tries to go to sleep, and yet continues awake, because sleep has not come. He longs for it, because of some necessity or weakness in his head: and so he lulls himself to sleep, and makes efforts to procure it, and now and then thinks he has succeeded; but, if the sleep be not real, it will not support him, nor supply strength to his head: on the contrary, his head will very often

---

[1] Ch. xxv. § 8.   [2] See § 2.   [3] § 7, *supra*.

be the worse for it. So will it be here, in a measure; the soul will be dissipated, neither sustained nor strengthened; on the contrary, it will be wearied and disgusted. But, in the true vision, the riches which abide in the soul cannot be described; even the body receives health and comfort.

18. I urged this argument, among others, when they told me that my visions came from the evil one, and that I imagined them myself,—and it was very often,—and made use of certain illustrations, as well as I could, and as our Lord suggested to me. But all was to little purpose; for as there were most holy persons in the place,—in comparison with whom I was a mass of perdition,—whom God did not lead by this way, they were at once filled with fear; they thought it all came through my sins. And so my state was talked about, and came to the knowledge of many; though I had spoken of it to no one, except my confessor, or to those to whom he commanded[1] me to speak of it. *The spirit of the Saint misunderstood.*

19. I said to them once, If they who thus speak of my state were to tell me that a person with whom I had just conversed, and whom I knew well, was not that person, but that I was deluding myself, and that they knew it, I should certainly trust them rather than my own eyes. But if that person left with me certain jewels, —and if, possessing none previously, I held the jewels in my hand as pledges of a great love,—and if I were now rich, instead of poor as before,—I should not be able to believe this that they said, though I might wish it. These jewels I could now show them, for all who knew me saw clearly that my soul was changed,—and so my confessor said; for the difference was very great in every way—not a pretence, but such as all might most clearly observe. As I was formerly so wicked, I said, I could not believe that Satan, if he wished to deceive me and take me down to hell, would have recourse to means so adverse to his purpose as this of rooting out my faults, implanting virtues and spiritual strength; for I saw clearly that I had become at once another person through the instrumentality of these visions. *The Saint's answer to those who tried her spirit.*

[1] See ch. xxiii. § 14.

20. My confessor, who was, as I said before,[1] one of the fathers of the Society of Jesus, and a really holy man, answered them in the same way,—so I learnt afterwards. He was a most discreet man, and of great humility; but this great humility of his brought me into serious trouble: for, though he was a man much given to prayer, and learned, he never trusted his own judgment, because our Lord was not leading him by this way. He had, therefore, much to suffer on my account, in many ways. I knew they used to say to him that he must be on his guard against me, lest Satan should delude him through a belief in any thing I might say to him. They gave instances of others who were deluded.[2] All this distressed me. I began to be afraid I should find no one to hear my confession,[3] and that all would avoid me. I did nothing but weep.

F. Baltasar Alvarez defends her.

21. It was a providence of God that he was willing to stand by me and hear my confession. But he was so great a servant of God, that he would have exposed himself to any thing for His sake. So he told me that if I did not offend God, nor swerve from the instructions he gave me, there was no fear I should be deserted by him. He encouraged me always, and quieted me. He bade me never to conceal any thing from him; and I never did.[4] He used to say that, so long as I did this, the devil, if it were the devil, could not hurt me; on the contrary, out of that evil which Satan wished to do me, our Lord would bring forth good. He laboured with all his might to make me perfect. As I was very much afraid myself, I obeyed him in every thing, though imperfectly. He had much to suffer on my account during three years of trouble and more, because he heard my confession all that time; for in the great persecutions that fell upon me, and the many harsh judgments of me which our Lord

And continues to direct her.

---

[1] Ch. xxiv. § 5.
[2] There were in Spain, and elsewhere, many women who were hypocrites, or deluded. Among others was the prioress of Lisbon, afterwards notorious, who deceived Luis of Granada (*De la Fuente*).
[3] *Inner Fortress*, vi. 1, § 4.
[4] Ch. xxvi. § 5; *Inner Fortress*, vi. 9, § 7.

permitted,—many of which I did not deserve,—every thing was carried to him, and he was found fault with because of me,—he being all the while utterly blameless.

22. If he had not been so holy a man, and if our Lord had not been with him, it would have been impossible for him to bear so much; for he had to answer those who regarded me as one going to destruction; and they would not believe what he said to them. On the other hand, he had to quiet me, and relieve me of my fears; when my fears increased, he had again to reassure me; for, after every vision which was strange to me, our Lord permitted me to remain in great fear. All this was the result of my being then, and of having been, a sinner. He used to console me out of his great compassion; and, if he had trusted to his own convictions, I should not have had so much to suffer; for God revealed the whole truth to him. I believe that he received this light from the Blessed Sacrament. *Sanctity of F. B. Alvarez.*

23. Those servants of God who were not satisfied had many conversations with me.[1] As I spoke to them carelessly, so they misunderstood my meaning in many things. I had a great regard for one of them; for my soul owed him more than I can tell. He was a most holy man, and I felt it most acutely when I saw that he did not understand me. He had a great desire for my improvement, and hoped our Lord would enlighten me. So, then, because I spoke, as I was saying, without careful consideration, they looked upon me as deficient in humility; and when they detected any of my faults—they might have detected many—they condemned me at once. They used to put certain questions to me, which I answered simply and carelessly. Then they concluded forthwith that I wished to teach them, and that I considered myself to be a learned woman. All this was carried to my confessor,—for certainly they desired my amendment,—and so he would reprimand me. This lasted some time, and I was distressed on many sides; but, with the graces which our Lord gave me, I bore it all. *The Saint misunderstood.*

[1] See ch. xxv. § 18.

230   THE LIFE OF S. TERESA.   [CH. XXIX

Want of intelligent direction painful.
24. I relate this in order that people may see what a great trial it is not to find any one who knows this way of the spirit by experience. If our Lord had not dealt so favourably with me, I know not what would have become of me. There were some things that were enough to take away my reason; and now and then I was reduced to such straits that I could do nothing but lift up my eyes to our Lord.[1] The contradiction of good people, which a wretched woman, weak, wicked, and timid as I am, must bear with, seems to be nothing when thus described; but I, who in the course of my life passed through very great trials, found this one of the heaviest.[2]

25. May our Lord grant that I may have pleased His Majesty a little herein; for I am sure that they pleased Him who condemned and rebuked me, and that it was all for my great good.

CHAPTER XXIX.

OF VISIONS—THE GRACES OUR LORD BESTOWED ON THE SAINT—THE ANSWERS OUR LORD GAVE HER FOR THOSE WHO TRIED HER.

Impotence of the imagination to form the imaginary visions.
1. I HAVE wandered far from the subject; for I undertook to give reasons why the vision was no work of the imagination. For how can we, by any efforts of ours, picture to ourselves the Humanity of Christ, and imagine His great beauty? No little time is necessary, if our conception is in any way to resemble it. Certainly, the imagination may be able to picture it, and a person may for a time contemplate that picture,—the form and the brightness of it,—and gradually make it more perfect, and so lay up that image in his memory. Who can hinder this, seeing that it could be fashioned by the understanding?

[1] 2 Paralip. xx. 12 : " Sed cum ignoremus quid agere debeamus, hoc solum habemus residui, ut oculos nostros dirigamus ad Te."
[2] See ch. xxx. § 6.

But as to the vision of which I am speaking, there are no means of bringing it about; only we must behold it when our Lord is pleased to present it before us, as He wills and what He wills; and there is no possibility of taking any thing away from it, or of adding any thing to it; nor is there any way of effecting it, whatever we may do, nor of seeing it when we like, nor of abstaining from seeing; if we try to gaze upon it—part of the vision in particular—the vision of Christ is lost at once.

2. For two years and a half God granted me this grace very frequently; but it is now more than three years since He has taken away from me its continual presence, through another of a higher nature, as I shall perhaps explain hereafter.[1] And though I saw Him speaking to me, and though I was contemplating His great beauty, and the sweetness with which those words of His came forth from His divine mouth,—they were sometimes uttered with severity, —and though I was extremely desirous to behold the colour of His eyes, or the form of them, so that I might be able to describe them, yet I never attained to the sight of them, and I could do nothing for that end; on the contrary, I lost the vision altogether. And though I see that He looks upon me at times with great tenderness, yet so strong is His gaze, that my soul cannot endure it; I fall into a trance so deep, that I lose the beautiful vision, in order to have a greater fruition of it all.

Cessation of the imaginary visions.

3. Accordingly, willing or not willing the vision has nothing to do with it. Our Lord clearly regards nothing but humility and confusion of face, the acceptance of what He wishes to give, and the praise of Himself, the Giver. This is true of all visions without exception: we can contribute nothing towards them—we cannot add to them, nor can we take from them; our own efforts can neither make nor unmake them. Our Lord would have us see most clearly that it is no work of ours, but of His Divine Majesty; we are therefore the less able to be proud of it: on the contrary, it makes us humble and afraid; for we see that, as our Lord can take from us the power of seeing what we

Visions wholly beyond our natural powers.

[1] Ch. xl.

would see, so also can He take from us these mercies and His grace, and we may be lost for ever. We must therefore walk in His fear while we are living in this our exile.

The different visions of our Lord which the Saint had.
4. Our Lord showed Himself to me almost always as He is after His resurrection. It was the same in the Host; only at those times when I was in trouble, and when it was His will to strengthen me, did He show His wounds. Sometimes I saw Him on the cross, in the Garden, crowned with thorns,—but that was rarely; sometimes also carrying His cross because of my necessities,—I may say so,—or those of others; but always in His glorified body. Many reproaches and many vexations have I borne while telling this—many suspicions and much persecution also. So certain were they to whom I spoke that I had an evil spirit, that some would have me exorcised. I did not care much for this; but I felt it bitterly when I saw that my confessors were afraid to hear me, or when I knew that they were told of any thing about me.

The Saint's confidence.
5. Notwithstanding all this, I never could be sorry that I had had these heavenly visions; nor would I exchange even one of them for all the wealth and all the pleasures of the world. I always regarded them as a great mercy from our Lord; and to me they were the very greatest treasure,—of this our Lord assured me often. I used to go to Him to complain of all these hardships; and I came away from prayer consoled, and with renewed strength. I did not dare to contradict those who were trying me; for I saw that it made matters worse, because they looked on my doing so as a failure in humility. I spoke of it to my confessor; he always consoled me greatly when he saw me in distress.

Indiscreet direction of one of the Saint's confessors.
6. As my visions grew in frequency, one of those who used to help me before—it was to him I confessed when the father-minister[1] could not hear me—began to say that I was certainly under the influence of Satan. He bade me, now that I had no power of resisting,

---
[1] Baltasar Alvarez was father-minister of the house of S. Giles, Avila, in whose absence she had recourse to another father of that house (*Ribera*, i. ch. 10).

always to make the sign of the cross when I had a vision, to point my finger at it by way of scorn,[1] and be firmly persuaded of its diabolic nature. If I did this, the vision would not recur. I was to be without fear on the point; God would watch over me, and take the vision away.[2] This was a great hardship for me; for, as I could not believe that the vision did not come from God, it was a fearful thing for me to do; and I could not wish, as I said before, that the visions should be withheld. However, I did at last as I was bidden. I prayed much to our Lord, that He would deliver me from delusions. I was always praying to that effect, and with many tears. I had recourse also to S. Peter and S. Paul; for our Lord had said to me— it was on their feast that He had appeared to me the first time[3]—that they would preserve me from delusion. I used to see them frequently most distinctly on my left hand; but that vision was not imaginary. These glorious Saints were my very good lords.

7. It was to me a most painful thing to make a show of contempt whenever I saw our Lord in a vision; for when I saw Him before me, if I were to be cut in pieces, I could not believe it was Satan. *The Saint's obedience on this point.* This was to me, therefore, a heavy kind of penance; and accordingly, that I might not be so continually crossing myself, I used to hold a crucifix in my hand. This I did almost always; but I did not always make signs of contempt, because I felt that too much. It reminded me of the insults which the Jews heaped upon Him; and so I prayed Him to forgive me, seeing that I did so in obedience to him who stood in His stead, and not to lay the blame on me, seeing that he was one of those whom He had placed as His ministers in His Church. He said to me, that I was not to distress myself—that I did well to obey; but He would make them see the truth of the matter. He seemed

[1] Y diese higas. "Higa es una manera de menosprecio que hacemos cerrando el puño, y mostrando el dedo pulgar por entre el dedo indice, y el medio" (*Cobarruvias, in voce*).

[2] See *Book of the Foundations*, ch. viii. § 3, where the Saint refers to this advice, and to the better advice given her later by F. Dominic Bañes, one of her confessors. See also *Inner Fortress*, vi. 9, § 7.

[3] See ch. xxvii. § 3, and ch. xxviii. § 4.

to me to be angry when they made me give up my prayer.[1] He told me to say to them that this was tyranny. He gave me reasons for believing that the vision was not satanic; some of them I mean to repeat by and by.

The cross of her rosary miraculously changed. 8. On one occasion, when I was holding in my hand the cross of my rosary, He took it from me into His own hand. He returned it; but it was then four large stones incomparably more precious than diamonds; for nothing can be compared with what is supernatural. Diamonds seem counterfeits and imperfect when compared with these precious stones. The five wounds were delineated on them with most admirable art. He said to me, that for the future that cross would appear so to me always; and so it did. I never saw the wood of which it was made, but only the precious stones. They were seen, however, by no one else,—only by myself.[2]

Our Lord consoles her. 9. When they had begun to insist on my putting my visions to a test like this, and resisting them, the graces I received were multiplied more and more. I tried to distract myself; I never ceased to be in prayer: even during sleep my prayer seemed to be continual; for now my love grew, I made piteous complaints to our Lord, and told Him I could not bear it. Neither was it in my power—though I desired, and, more than that, even strove—to give up thinking of Him. Nevertheless, I obeyed to the utmost of my power; but my power was little or nothing in the matter; and our Lord never released me from that obedience; but though He bade me obey my confessor, He reassured me in another way, and taught me what I was to say. He has continued to do so until now; and He gave me reasons so sufficient, that I felt myself perfectly safe.

The visions proved to be divine. 10. Not long afterwards, His Majesty began, according to His promise, to make it clear that it was He Himself who appeared, by the growth in me

.

[1] Ch. xxv. § 18.
[2] The cross was made of ebony (*Ribera*). It is not known where that cross is now. The Saint gave it to her sister, Doña Juana de Ahumada, who begged it of her. Some say that the Carmelites of Madrid possess it; and others, those of Valladolid (*De la Fuente*).

of the love of God so strong, that I knew not who could have infused it; for it was most supernatural, and I had not attained to it by any efforts of my own. I saw myself dying with a desire to see God, and I knew not how to seek that life otherwise than by dying. Certain great impetuosities[1] of love, though not so intolerable as those of which I have spoken before,[2] nor yet of so great worth, overwhelmed me. I knew not what to do; for nothing gave me pleasure, and I had no control over myself. It seemed as if my soul were really torn away from myself. Oh, supreme artifice of our Lord! how tenderly didst Thou deal with Thy miserable slave! Thou didst hide Thyself from me, and didst yet constrain me with Thy love, with a death so sweet, that my soul would never wish it over.

11. It is not possible for any one to understand these impetuosities if he has not experienced them himself. *A prayer which is not supernatural.* They are not an upheaving of the breast, nor those devotional sensations, not uncommon, which seem on the point of causing suffocation, and are beyond control. That prayer is of a much lower order; and those agitations should be avoided by gently endeavouring to be recollected; and the soul should be kept in quiet. This prayer is like the sobbing of little children, who seem on the point of choking, and whose disordered senses are soothed by giving them to drink. So here reason should draw in the reins, because nature itself may be contributing to it; and we should consider with fear that all this may not be perfect, and that much sensuality may be involved in it. The infant soul should be soothed by the caresses of love, which shall draw forth its love in a gentle way, and not, as they say, by force of blows. This love should be inwardly under control, and not as a caldron, fiercely boiling because too much fuel has been applied to it, and out of which every thing is lost. The source of the fire must be kept under control, and the flame must be quenched in sweet tears, and not with those painful tears which come out of these emotions, and which do so much harm.

12. In the beginning, I had tears of this kind. They left me with a disordered head and a wearied *Forced tears.*

[1] See *Relation*, i. § 3.   [2] Ch. xx. § 11.

spirit, and for a day or two afterwards unable to resume my prayer. Great discretion, therefore, is necessary at first, in order that every thing may proceed gently, and that the operations of the spirit may be within; all outward manifestations should be carefully avoided.

The impetuosities of supernatural love. 13. These other impetuosities are very different. It is not we who apply the fuel; the fire is already kindled, and we are thrown into it in a moment to be consumed. It is by no efforts of the soul that it sorrows over the wound which the absence of our Lord has inflicted on it; it is far otherwise; for an arrow is driven into the entrails to the very quick,[1] and into the heart at times, so that the soul knows not what is the matter with it, nor what it wishes for. It understands clearly enough that it wishes for God, and that the arrow seems tempered with some herb which makes the soul hate itself for the love of our Lord, and willingly lose its life for Him. It is impossible to describe or explain the way in which God wounds the soul, nor the very grievous pain inflicted, which deprives it of all self-consciousness; yet this pain is so sweet, that there is no joy in the world which gives greater delight. As I have just said,[2] the soul would wish to be always dying of this wound.

The soul wounded with love. 14. This pain and bliss together carried me out of myself, and I never could understand how it was. Oh, what a sight a wounded soul is!—a soul, I mean, so conscious of it, as to be able to say of itself that it is wounded for so good a cause; and seeing distinctly that it never did any thing whereby this love should come to it, and that it does come from that exceeding love which our Lord bears it. A spark seems to have fallen suddenly upon it, that has set it all on fire. Oh, how often do I remember, when in this state, those words of David: "Quemadmodum desiderat cervus ad fontes aquarum"![3] They seem to me to be literally true of myself.

---

[1] *Inner Fortress*, vi. 11, § 2; S. John of the Cross, *Spiritual Canticle*, st. 1, p. 22, Engl. trans.

[2] § 8.

[3] Ps. xli. 1: "As the longing of the hart for the fountains of waters, so is the longing of my soul for Thee, O my God."

15. When these impetuosities are not very violent, they seem to admit of a little mitigation—at least, the soul seeks some relief, because it knows not what to do—through certain penances; the painfulness of which, and even the shedding of its blood, are no more felt than if the body were dead. The soul seeks for ways and means to do something that may be felt, for the love of God; but the first pain is so great, that no bodily torture I know of can take it away. As relief is not to be had here, these medicines are too mean for so high a disease. Some slight mitigation may be had, and the pain may pass away a little, by praying God to relieve its sufferings: but the soul sees no relief except in death, by which it thinks to attain completely to the fruition of its good. At other times, these impetuosities are so violent, that the soul can do neither this nor any thing else; the whole body is contracted, and neither hand nor foot can be moved: if the body be upright at the time, it falls down, as a thing that has no control over itself. It cannot even breathe; all it does is to moan—not loudly, because it cannot: its moaning, however, comes from a keen sense of pain. *Effects of these impetuosities.*

16. Our Lord was pleased that I should have at times a vision of this kind: I saw an angel close by me, on my left side, in bodily form. This I am not accustomed to see, unless very rarely. Though I have visions of angels frequently, yet I see them only by an intellectual vision, such as I have spoken of before.[1] It was our Lord's will that in this vision I should see the angel in this wise. He was not large, but small of stature, and most beautiful—his face burning, as if he were one of the highest angels, who seem to be all of fire: they must be those whom we call cherubim.[2] Their names they never tell me; but I see very well that there is in heaven so great a difference between one angel and *Vision of an angel granted to the Saint.*

---

[1] Ch. xxvii. § 3.

[2] In the MS. of the Saint preserved in the Escurial, the word is "cherubines;" but all the editors before Don Vicente de la Fuente have adopted the suggestion, in the margin, of Bañes, who preferred "seraphim." F. Bouix, in his translation, corrected the mistake; but, with his usual modesty, did not call the reader's attention to it.

another, and between these and the others, that I cannot explain it.

The piercing of the heart of S. Teresa. 17. I saw in his hand a long spear of gold, and at the iron's point there seemed to be a little fire. He appeared to me to be thrusting it at times into my heart,[1] and to pierce my very entrails; when he drew it out, he seemed to draw them out also, and to leave me all on fire with a great love of God. The pain was so great, that it made me moan; and yet so surpassing was the sweetness of this excessive pain, that I could not wish to be rid of it. The soul is satisfied now with nothing less than God. The pain is not bodily, but spiritual; though the body has its share in it, even a large one. It is a caressing of love so sweet which now takes place between the soul and God, that I pray God of His goodness to make him experience it who may think that I am lying.[2]

18. During the days that this lasted, I went about as if beside myself. I wished to see, or speak with, no one, but only to cherish my pain, which was to me a greater bliss than all created things could give me.[3]

19. I was in this state from time to time, when-**Her continual ecstasies.** ever it was our Lord's pleasure to throw me into those deep trances, which I could not prevent even when I was in the company of others, and which, to my deep vexation, came to be publicly known. Since then, I do not feel that pain so much, but only that which I spoke of before, —I do not remember the chapter,[4]—which is in many ways

---

[1] See *Relation*, viii. § 16.

[2] "The most probable opinion is, that the piercing of the heart of the Saint took place in 1559. The hymn which she composed on that occasion was discovered in Seville in 1700 ("En las internas entrañas"). On the high altar of the Carmelite church in Alba de Tormes, the heart of the Saint thus pierced is to be seen; and I have seen it myself more than once" (*De la Fuente*).

[3] Brev. Rom. in fest. S. Teresiæ, Oct. 15, Lect. v.: "Tanto autem divini amoris incendio cor ejus conflagravit, ut merito viderit Angelum ignito jaculo sibi præcordia transverberantem." The Carmelites keep the feast of this piercing of the Saint's heart on the 27th of August.

[4] Ch. xx. § 11.

very different from it, and of greater worth. On the other hand, when this pain, of which I am now speaking, begins, our Lord seems to lay hold of the soul, and to throw it into a trance, so that there is no time for me to have any sense of pain or suffering, because fruition ensues at once. May He be blessed for ever, who hath bestowed such great graces on one who has responded so ill to blessings so great!

CHAPTER XXX.

S. PETER OF ALCANTARA COMFORTS THE SAINT—GREAT TEMPTATIONS AND INTERIOR TRIALS.

1. WHEN I saw that I was able to do little or nothing towards avoiding these great impetuosities, I began also to be afraid of them, because I could not understand how this pain and joy could subsist together. I knew it was possible enough for bodily pain and spiritual joy to dwell together; but the coexistence of a spiritual pain so excessive as this, and of joy so deep, troubled my understanding. Still, I tried to continue my resistance; but I was so little able, that I was now and then wearied. I used to take up the cross for protection, and try to defend myself against Him who, by the cross, is the Protector of us all. I saw that no one understood me. I saw it very clearly myself, but I did not dare to say so to any one except my confessor; for that would have been a real admission that I had no humility. *The Saint neither understood by others nor by herself.*

2. Our Lord was pleased to succour me in a great measure,—and, for the moment, altogether,—by bringing to the place where I was that blessed friar, Peter of Alcantara. Of him I spoke before, and said something of his penance.[1] Among other things, I have been assured that he wore continually, for twenty years, a girdle *S. Peter of Alcantara.*

[1] Ch. xxvii. §§ 17, 18, 19.

made of iron.[1] He is the author of certain little books, in Spanish, on prayer, which are now in common use; for, as he was much exercised therein, his writings are very profitable to those who are given to prayer. He kept the first rule of the blessed S. Francis in all its rigour, and did those things besides of which I spoke before.

3. When that widow, the servant of God and my friend, of whom I have already spoken,[2] knew that so great a man had come, she took her measures. *Doña Guiomar.* She knew the straits I was in, for she was an eye-witness of my afflictions, and was a great comfort to me. Her faith was so strong, that she could not help believing that what others said was the work of the devil was really the work of the Spirit of God; and as she is a person of great sense and great caution, and one to whom our Lord is very bountiful in prayer, it pleased His Majesty to let her see what learned men failed to discern. My confessors gave me leave to accept relief in some things from her, because in many ways she was able to afford it. Some of those graces which our Lord bestowed on me fell to her lot occasionally, together with instructions most profitable for her soul. So, then, when she knew that the blessed man was come, without saying a word to me, she obtained leave from the Provincial for me to stay eight days in her house, in order that I might the more easily confer with him. In that house, and in one church or another, I had many conversations with him the first time he came here; for, afterwards, I had many communications with him at diverse times.

4. I gave him an account, as briefly as I could, of my life, and of my way of prayer, with the utmost clearness in my power. *Conferences with S. Peter of Alcantara.* I have always held to this, to be perfectly frank and exact with those to whom I make known the state of my soul.[3] Even my first impulses I wish them to know; and as for doubtful and suspicious matters, I used to make the most of them by arguing against myself.

---

[1] Hoja de lata, "cierta hoja de hierro muy delgada" (Cobarruvias, *Tesoro, in voce*).
[2] Ch. xxiv. § 5. Doña Guiomar de Ulloa.
[3] Ch. xxvi. § 5.

Thus, then, without equivocation or concealment, I laid before him the state of my soul. I saw almost at once that he understood me, by reason of his own experience. That was all I required; for at that time I did not know myself as I do now, so as to give an account of my state. It was at a later time that God enabled me to understand myself, and describe the graces which His Majesty bestows upon me. It was necessary, then, that he who would clearly understand and explain my state should have had experience of it himself.

5. The light he threw on the matter was of the clearest; for as to these visions, at least, which were not imaginary, I could not understand how they could be. And it seemed that I could not understand, too, how those could be which I saw with the eyes of the soul; for, as I said before,[1] those visions only seemed to me to be of consequence which were seen with the bodily eyes: and of these I had none. The holy man enlightened me on the whole quession, explained it to me, and bade me not to be distressed, but to praise God, and to abide in the full conviction that this was the work of the Spirit of God; for, saving the faith, nothing could be more true, and there was nothing on which I could more firmly rely. He was greatly comforted in me, was most kind and serviceable, and ever afterwards took great care of me, and told me of his own affairs and labours; and when he saw that I had those very desires which in himself were fulfilled already,—for our Lord had given me very strong desires,—and also how great my resolution was, he delighted in conversing with me. *S. Peter of Alcantara instructs her.*

6. To a person whom our Lord has raised to this state, there is no pleasure or comfort equal to that of meeting with another whom our Lord has begun to raise in the same way. At that time, however, it must have been only a beginning with me, as I believe; and God grant I may not have gone back now. He was extremely sorry for me. He told me that one of the greatest trials in this world was that which I had borne,—namely, the contradiction of good people,[2]—and that more was in reserve for me: I had need, *Benefits of communication between spiritual persons.*

[1] Ch. vii. § 12.   [2] See ch. xxviii. § 24.

therefore, of some one—and there was no one in this city—who understood me; but he would speak to my confessor, and to that married nobleman, already spoken of,[1] who was one of those who tormented me most, and who, because of his great affection for me, was the cause of all these attacks. He was a holy but timid man, and could not feel safe about me, because he had seen how wicked I was, and that not long before. The holy man did so; he spoke to them both, explained the matter, and gave them reasons why they should reassure themselves, and disturb me no more. My confessor was easily satisfied,— not so the nobleman; for though they were not enough to keep him quiet, yet they kept him in some measure from frightening me so much as he used to do.

The advice of S. Peter of Alcantara. 7. We made an agreement that I should write to him and tell him how it fared with me, for the future, and that we should pray much for each other. Such was his humility, that he held to the prayers of a wretch like me. It made me very much ashamed of myself. He left me in the greatest consolation and joy, bidding me continue my prayer with confidence, and without any doubt that it was the work of God. If I should have any doubts, for my greater security, I was to make them known to my confessor, and, having done so, be in peace. Nevertheless, I was not able at all to feel that confidence, for our Lord was leading me by the way of fear; and so, when they told me that the devil had power over me, I believed them. Thus, then, not one of them was able to inspire me with confidence on the one hand, or fear on the other, in such a way as to make me believe either of them, otherwise than as our Lord allowed me. Accordingly, though the holy friar consoled and calmed me, I did not rely so much on him as to be altogether without fear, particularly when our Lord forsook me in the afflictions of my soul, of which I will now speak. Nevertheless, as I have said, I was very much consoled.

8. I could not give thanks enough to God, and to my glorious father S. Joseph, who seemed to me to have brought him here. He was the commissary-general of the

[1] Ch. xxiii. § 7.

custody[1] of S. Joseph, to whom, and to our Lady, I used to pray much.

9. I suffered at times—and even still, though not so often—the most grievous spiritual trials, together with bodily pains and afflictions arising from violent sicknesses; so much so, that I could scarcely control myself. At other times, my bodily sickness was more grievous; and, as I had no spiritual pain, I bore it with great joy: but, when both pains came upon me together, my distress was so heavy, that I was reduced to sore straits. *Spiritual and bodily pain.*

10. I forgot all the mercies our Lord had shown me, and remembered them only as a dream, to my great distress; for my understanding was so dull, that I had a thousand doubts and suspicions whether I had ever understood matters aright, thinking that perhaps all was fancy, and that it was enough for me to have deceived myself, without also deceiving good men. I looked upon myself as so wicked as to have been the cause, by my sins, of all the evils and all the heresies that had sprung up. This is but a false humility, and Satan invented it for the purpose of disquieting me, and trying whether he could thereby drive my soul to despair. I have now had so much experience, that I know this was his work; so he, seeing that I understand him, does not torment me in the same way as much as he used to do. That it is his work is clear from the restlessness and discomfort with which it begins, and the trouble it causes in the soul while it lasts; from the obscurity and distress, the aridity and indisposition for prayer and for every good work, which it produces. It seems to stifle the soul and trammel the body, so as to make them good for nothing. *Spiritual desolation.*

11. Now, though the soul acknowledges itself to be miserable, and though it is painful to us to see ourselves as we are, and though we have most deep convictions of our own wickedness,—deep as those spoken of just now,[2] and really felt,—yet true humility is not attended *True humility.*

---

[1] A "custody" is a division of the province, in the Order of S. Francis, comprising a certain number of convents.
[2] § 10.

with trouble; it does not disturb the soul; it causes neither obscurity nor aridity: on the contrary, it consoles. It is altogether different, bringing with it calm, sweetness, and light. It is no doubt painful; but, on the other hand, it is consoling, because we see how great is the mercy of our Lord in allowing the soul to have that pain, and how well the soul is occupied. On the one hand, the soul grieves over its offences against God; on the other, His compassion makes it glad. It has light, which makes it ashamed of itself; and it gives thanks to His Majesty, who has borne with it so long. That other humility, which is the work of Satan, furnishes no light for any good work; it pictures God as bringing upon every thing fire and sword; it dwells upon His justice; and the soul's faith in the mercy of God—for the power of the devil does not reach so far as to destroy faith—is of such a nature as to give me no consolation: on the contrary, the consideration of mercies so great helps to increase the pain, because I look upon myself as bound to render greater service.

False humility one of the most ingenious devices of Satan.
12. This invention of Satan is one of the most painful, subtle, and crafty that I have known him to possess; I should therefore like to warn you, my father, of it, in order that, if Satan should tempt you herein, you may have some light, and be aware of his devices, if your understanding should be left at liberty: because you must not suppose that learning and knowledge are of any use here; for though I have none of them myself, yet now that I have escaped out of his hands I see clearly that this is folly. What I understood by it is this: that it is our Lord's pleasure to give him leave and license, as He gave him of old to tempt Job;[1] though in my case, because of my wretchedness, the temptation is not so sharp.

Power of temptation.
13. It happened to me to be tempted once in this way; and I remember it was on the day before the vigil of Corpus Christi,—a feast to which I have great devotion, though not so great as I ought to have. The trial then lasted only till the day of the feast itself. But, on other occasions, it continued one, two, and even three weeks,

[1] Job i.

and—I know not—perhaps longer. But I was specially liable to it during the Holy Weeks, when it was my habit to make prayer my joy. Then the devil seizes on my understanding in a moment ; and occasionally, by means of things so trivial that I should laugh at them at any other time, he makes it stumble over any thing he likes. The soul, laid in-fetters, loses all control over itself, and all power of thinking of any thing but the absurdities he puts before it, which, being more or less unsubstantial, inconsistent, and disconnected, serve only to stifle the soul, so that it has no power over itself ; and accordingly—so it seems to me—the devils make a football of it, and the soul is unable to escape out of their hands. It is impossible to describe the sufferings of the soul in this state. It goes about in quest of relief, and God suffers it to find none. The light of reason, in the freedom of its will, remains, but it is not clear ; it seems to me as if its eyes were covered with a veil. As a person who, having travelled often by a particular road, knows, though it be night and dark, by his past experience of it, where he may stumble, and where he ought to be on his guard against that risk, because he has seen the place by day, so the soul avoids offending God: it seems to go on by habit—that is, if we put out of sight the fact that our Lord holds it by the hand, which is the true explanation of the matter.

14. Faith is then as dead, and asleep, like all the other virtues ; not lost, however,—for the soul truly believes all that the Church holds; but its profession *How temptation numbs the soul.* of the faith is hardly more than an outward profession of the mouth. And, on the other hand, temptations seem to press it down, and make it dull, so that its knowledge of God becomes to it as that of something which it hears of far away. So tepid is its love that, when it hears God spoken of, it listens and believes that He is what He is, because the Church so teaches ; but it recollects nothing of its own former experience. Vocal prayer or solitude is only a greater affliction, because the interior suffering—whence it comes, it knows not—is unendurable, and, as it seems to me, in some measure a counterpart of hell. So it is, as our Lord showed me in a vision ;[1] for the

[1] See ch. xxxii. § 1, &c.

soul itself is then burning in the fire, knowing not who has kindled it, nor whence it comes, nor how to escape it, nor how to put it out: if it seeks relief from the fire by spiritual reading, it cannot find any, just as if it could not read at all. On one occasion, it occurred to me to read a life of a Saint, that I might forget myself, and be refreshed with the recital of what he had suffered. Four or five times, I read as many lines; and, though they were written in Spanish, I understood them less at the end than I did when I began: so I gave it up. It so happened to me on more occasions than one, but I have a more distinct recollection of this.

Harshness of her confessors.
15. To converse with any one is worse, for the devil then sends so offensive a spirit of bad temper, that I think I could eat people up; nor can I help myself. I feel that I do something when I keep myself under control; or rather our Lord does so, when He holds back with His hand any one in this state from saying or doing something that may be hurtful to his neighbours and offensive to God. Then, as to going to our confessor, that is of no use; for the certain result is—and very often has it happened to me—what I shall now describe. Though my confessors, with whom I had to do then, and have to do still, are so holy, they spoke to me and reproved me with such harshness, that they were astonished at it afterwards when I told them of it. They said that they could not help themselves; for, though they had resolved not to use such language, and though they pitied me also very much,—yea, even had scruples on the subject, because of my grievous trials of soul and body,—and were, moreover, determined to console me, they could not refrain. They did not use unbecoming words—I mean, words offensive to God; yet their words were the most offensive that could be borne with in confession. They must have aimed at mortifying me. At other times, I used to delight in this, and was prepared to bear it; but it was then a torment altogether. I used to think, too, that I deceived them; so I went to them, and cautioned them very earnestly to be on their guard against me, for it might be that I deceived them. I saw well enough that I would not do so advisedly, nor tell them an

untruth;[1] but every thing made me afraid. One of them, on one occasion, when he had heard me speak of this temptation, told me not to distress myself; for, even if I wished to deceive him, he had sense enough not to be deceived. This gave me great comfort.

16. Sometimes, almost always,—at least, very frequently,—I used to find rest after Communion; now and then, even, as I drew near to the most Holy Sacrament, all at once my soul and body would be so well, that I was amazed.[2] It seemed to be nothing else but an instantaneous dispersion of the darkness that covered my soul: when the sun rose, I saw how silly I had been. *Effects of the Saint's Communions at this time.*

17. On other occasions, if our Lord spoke to me but one word, saying only, "Be not distressed, have no fear,"—as I said before,[3]—I was made whole at once; or, if I saw a vision, I was as if I had never been amiss. I rejoiced in God, and made my complaint to Him, because He permitted me to undergo such afflictions: yet the recompense was great; for almost always, afterwards, His mercies descended upon me in great abundance. The soul seemed to come forth as gold out of the crucible, more refined, and made glorious to behold, our Lord dwelling within it. These trials afterwards are light, though they once seemed to be unendurable; and the soul longs to undergo them again, if that be more pleasing to our Lord. And though trials and persecutions increase, yet, if we bear them without offending our Lord, rejoicing in suffering for His sake, it will be all the greater gain: I, however, do not bear them as they ought to be borne, but rather in a most imperfect way. At other times, my trials came upon me—they come still—in another form; and then it seems to me as if the very possibility of thinking a good thought, or desiring the accomplishment of it, were utterly taken from me: both soul and body are altogether useless and a heavy burden. However, when I am in this state, *Effects of the divine visitations.*

---

[1] See ch. xxviii. § 6.
[2] See *Way of Perfection*, ch. lxi. § 2; but ch. xxxiv. § 8 of the earlier editions.
[3] Ch. xx. § 23, ch. xxv. § 22, ch. xxvi. § 3.

I do not suffer from the other temptations and disquietudes, but only from a certain loathing of I know not what, and my soul finds pleasure in nothing.

The Saint tries the active life in vain. 18. I used to try exterior good works, in order to occupy myself partly by violence; and I know well how weak a soul is when grace is hiding itself. It did not distress me much, because the sight of my own meanness gave me some satisfaction. On other occasions, I find myself unable to pray or to fix my thoughts with any distinctness upon God, or any thing that is good, though I may be alone; but I have a sense that I know Him. It is the understanding and the imagination, I believe, which hurt me here; for it seems to me that I have a good will, disposed for all good; but the understanding is so lost, that it seems to be nothing else but a raving lunatic, which nobody can restrain, and of which I am not mistress enough to keep it quiet for a minute.[1]

Distractions. 19. Sometimes I laugh at myself, and recognise my wretchedness: I watch my understanding, and leave it alone to see what it will do. Glory be to God, for a wonder, it never runs on what is wrong, but only on indifferent things, considering what is going on here, or there, or elsewhere. I see then, more and more, the exceeding great mercy of our Lord to me, when He keeps this lunatic bound in the chains of perfect contemplation. I wonder what would happen if those people who think I am good knew of my extravagance. I am very sorry when I see my soul in such bad company; I long to see it delivered therefrom, and so I say to our Lord: When, O my God, shall I see my whole soul praising Thee, that it may have the fruition of Thee in all its faculties? Let me be no longer, O Lord, thus torn to pieces, and every one of them, as it were, running in a different direction. This has been often the case with me, but I think that my scanty bodily health was now and then enough to bring it about.

Scruples. 20. I dwell much on the harm which original sin has done us; that is, I believe, what has rendered us incapable of the fruition of so great a good. My sins, too, must be in fault; for, if I had not committed so many, I should

[1] "Un Credo."

have been more perfect in goodness. Another great affliction which I suffered was this: all the books which I read on the subject of prayer, I thought I understood thoroughly, and that I required them no longer, because our Lord had given me the gift of prayer. I therefore ceased to read those books, and applied myself to lives of Saints, thinking that this would improve me and give me courage; for I found myself very defective in every kind of service which the Saints rendered unto God. Then it struck me that I had very little humility, when I could think that I had attained to this degree of prayer; and so, when I could not come to any other conclusion, I was greatly distressed, until certain learned persons, and the blessed friar, Peter of Alcantara, told me not to trouble myself about the matter.

21. I see clearly enough that I have not yet begun to serve God, though He showers down upon me those very graces which He gives to many good people. I am a mass of imperfection, except in desire and in love; for herein I see well that our Lord has been gracious to me, in order that I may please Him in some measure. I really think that I love Him; but my conduct, and the many imperfections I discern in myself, make me sad. *The Saint's view of her own imperfections.*

22. My soul, also, is subject occasionally to a certain foolishness,—that is the right name to give it,—when I seem to be doing neither good nor evil, but following in the wake of others, as they say, without pain or pleasure, indifferent to life and death, pleasure and pain. I seem to have no feeling. The soul seems to me like a little ass, which feeds and thrives, because it accepts the food which is given it, and eats it without reflection. The soul in this state must be feeding on some great mercies of God, seeing that its miserable life is no burden to it, and that it bears it patiently; but it is conscious of no sensible movements or results, whereby it may ascertain the state it is in. *Spiritual food unconsciously supplied.*

23. It seems to me now like sailing with a very gentle wind, when one makes much way without knowing how; for in the other states, so great are the effects, that the soul sees almost at once an *Description of a soul filled with the love of God.*

improvement in itself, because the desires instantly are on fire, and the soul is never satisfied. This comes from those great impetuosities of love, spoken of before,[1] in those to whom God grants them. It is like those little wells I have seen flowing, wherein the upheaving of the sand never ceases. This illustration and comparison seem to me to be a true description of those souls who attain to this state; their love is ever active, thinking what it may do; it cannot contain itself, as the water remains not in the earth, but is continually welling upwards. So is the soul, in general; it is not at rest, nor can it contain itself, because of the love it has: it is so saturated therewith, that it would have others drink of it, because there is more than enough for itself, in order that they might help it to praise God.

24. I call to remembrance—oh, how often!— *The living water.* that living water of which our Lord spoke to the Samaritan woman. That Gospel[2] has a great attraction for me; and, indeed, so it had even when I was a little child, though I did not understand it then as I do now. I used to pray much to our Lord for that living water; and I had always a picture of it, representing our Lord at the well, with this inscription, "Domine, da mihi aquam."[3]

25. This love is also like a great fire, which re- *The anxieties of love.* quires fuel continually, in order that it may not burn out. So those souls I am speaking of, however much it may cost them, will always bring fuel, in order that the fire may not be quenched. As for me, I should be glad, considering what I am, if I had but straw even to throw upon it. And so it is with me occasionally—and, indeed, very often. At one time, I laugh at myself; and at another, I am very much distressed. The inward stirring of my love urges me to do something for the service of God; and I am not able to do more than adorn images with boughs and flowers, clean or

---

[1] Ch. xxix. § 11.

[2] S. John iv. 5-42 : the Gospel of Friday after the Third Sunday in Lent, where the words are, " hanc aquam."

[3] "Lord, give me this water" (S. John iv. 15). See ch. i. § 6 ; and *Way of Perfection*, ch. xxix. § 5: ch. xix. § 5 of the earlier editions.

arrange an oratory, or some such trifling acts, so that I am ashamed of myself. If I undertook any penitential practice, the whole was so slight, and was done in such a way, that if our Lord did not accept my good will, I saw it was all worthless, and so I laughed at myself. The failure of bodily strength, sufficient to do something for God, *Effects of weak health.* is no light affliction for those souls to whom He, in His goodness, has communicated this fire of His love in its fulness. It is a very great penance; for when souls are not strong enough to heap fuel on this fire, and die of fear that the fire may go out, it seems to me that they become fuel themselves, are reduced to ashes, or dissolved in tears, and burn away: and this is suffering enough, though it be sweet.

26. Let him, then, praise our Lord exceedingly, who has attained to this state; who has received the bodily strength requisite for penance; who has learning, ability, and power to preach, to hear confessions, and to draw souls unto God. Such a one neither knows nor comprehends the blessing he possesses, unless he knows by experience what it is to be powerless to serve God in any thing, and at the same time to be receiving much from Him. May He be blessed for ever, and may the angels glorify Him! Amen.

27. I know not if I do well to write so much in detail. But as you, my father, bade me again not to be troubled by the minuteness of my account, nor to omit any thing, I go on recounting clearly and truly all I can call to mind. But I must omit much; for if I did not, I should have to spend more time—and, as I said before,[1] I have so little to spend, and perhaps, after all, nothing will be gained.

[1] Ch. xiv. § 12.

CHAPTER XXXI.

OF CERTAIN OUTWARD TEMPTATIONS AND APPEARANCES OF SATAN—OF THE SUFFERINGS THEREBY OCCASIONED—COUNSELS FOR THOSE WHO GO ON UNTO PERFECTION.

1. Now that I have described certain temptations and troubles, interior and secret, of which Satan was the cause, I will speak of others which he wrought almost in public, and in which his presence could not be ignored.[1]

Satan appears to the Saint. 2. I was once in an oratory, when Satan, in an abominable shape, appeared on my left hand. I looked at his mouth in particular, because he spoke, and it was horrible. A huge flame seemed to issue out of his body, perfectly bright, without any shadow. He spoke in a fearful way, and said to me that, though I had escaped out of his hands, he would yet lay hold of me again. I was in great terror, made the sign of the cross as well as I could, and then the form vanished—but it reappeared instantly. This occurred twice. I did not know what to do; there was some holy water at hand; I took some, and threw it in the direction of the figure, and then Satan never returned.

The Saint buffeted by Satan. 3. On another occasion, I was tortured for five hours with such terrible pains, such inward and outward sufferings, that it seemed to me as if I could not bear them. Those who were with me were frightened; they knew not what to do, and I could not help myself. I am in the habit, when these pains and my bodily suffering are most unendurable, to make interior acts as well as I can, imploring our Lord, if it be His will, to give me patience, and then to let me suffer on, even to the end of the world. So, when I found myself suffering so cruelly, I relieved myself by making those acts and resolutions, in order that I might be able to endure the pain. It pleased our Lord to let me understand that it was the work of Satan; for I saw close beside me a most frightful little negro, gnashing his teeth in despair at

[1] 2 Cor. ii. 11: "Non enim ignoramus cogitationes ejus."

losing what he attempted to seize. When I saw him, I laughed, and had no fear; for there were some then present who were helpless, and knew of no means whereby so great a pain could be relieved. My body, head, and arms were violently shaken; I could not help myself: but the worst of all was the interior pain, for I could find no ease in any way. Nor did I dare to ask for holy water, lest they who were with me should be afraid, and find out what the matter really was.

4. I know by frequent experience that there is nothing which puts the devils to flight like holy water. They run away before the sign of the cross also, but they return immediately: great, then, must be the power of holy water. As for me, my soul is conscious of a special and most distinct consolation whenever I take it. Indeed, I feel almost always a certain refreshing, which I cannot describe, together with an inward joy, which comforts my whole soul. This is no fancy, nor a thing which has occurred once only; for it has happened very often, and I have watched it very carefully. I may compare what I feel with that which happens to a person in great heat, and very thirsty, drinking a cup of cold water—his whole being is refreshed. I consider that every thing ordained by the Church is very important; and I have a joy in reflecting that the words of the Church are so mighty, that they endow water with power, so that there shall be so great a difference between holy water and water that has never been blessed. Then, as my pains did not cease, I told them, if they would not laugh, I would ask for some holy water. They brought me some, and sprinkled me with it; but I was no better. I then threw some myself in the direction of the negro, when he fled in a moment. All my sufferings ceased, just as if some one had taken them from me with his hand; only I was wearied, as if I had been beaten with many blows. It was of great service to me to learn that if, by our Lord's permission, Satan can do so much evil to a soul and body not in his power, he can do much more when he has them in his possession. It gave me a renewed desire to be delivered from a fellowship so dangerous.

Virtue of the cross and of holy water.

5. Another time, and not long ago, the same thing happened to me, though it did not last so long, and I was alone at the moment. I asked for holy water; and they who came in after the devil had gone away,—they were two nuns, worthy of all credit, and who would not tell a lie for any thing,—perceived a most offensive smell, like that of brimstone. I smelt nothing myself; but the odour lasted long enough to become sensible to them.

Another buffeting of Satan.

6. On another occasion, I was in choir, when, in a moment, I became profoundly recollected. I went out, in order that the sisters might know nothing of it; yet those who were near heard the sound of heavy blows where I was, and I heard voices myself, as of persons in consultation, but I did not hear what they said: I was so absorbed in prayer, that I understood nothing, neither was I at all afraid. This took place almost always when our Lord was pleased that some soul or other, persuaded by me, advanced in the spiritual life. Certainly, what I am now about to describe happened to me once; there are witnesses to testify to it, particularly my present confessor, for he saw the account in a letter. I did not tell him from whom the letter came, but he knew perfectly who the person was.

In the choir.

7. There came to me a person who, for two years and a half, had been living in mortal sin of the most abominable nature I ever heard. During the whole of that time, he neither confessed it nor ceased from it; and yet he said Mass. He confessed his other sins; but of this one he used to say, How can I confess so foul a sin? He wished to give it up, but he could not prevail on himself to do so. I was very sorry for him, and it was a great grief to me to see God offended in such a way. I promised him that I would pray to God for his amendment, and get others who were better than I to do the same. I wrote to one person, and the priest undertook to get the letter delivered. It came to pass that he made a full confession at the first opportunity; for our Lord God was pleased, on account of the prayers of those most holy persons to whom I had recommended him, to have pity on this soul. I, too, wretched as I am, did all I could for the same end.

The Saint obtains the conversion of a great sinner.

8. He wrote to me, and said that he was so far improved, that he had not for some days repeated his sin; but he was so tormented by the temptation, that it seemed to him as if he were in hell already, so great were his sufferings. He asked me to pray to God for him. I recommended him to my sisters, through whose prayers I must have obtained this mercy from our Lord; for they took the matter greatly to heart; and he was a person whom no one could find out. I implored His Majesty to put an end to these torments and temptations, and to let the evil spirits torment me instead, provided I did not offend our Lord. Thus it was that for one month I was most grievously tormented; and then it was that those two assaults of Satan, of which I have just spoken, took place.

And suffers for it.

9 Our Lord was pleased to deliver him out of this temptation, so I was informed; for I told him what happened to myself that month. His soul gained strength, and he continued free; he could never give thanks enough to our Lord and to me, as if I had been of any service—unless it be that the belief he had that our Lord granted me such graces was of some advantage to him. He said that, when he saw himself in great straits, he would read my letters, and then the temptation left him. He was very much astonished at my sufferings, and at the manner of his own deliverance: even I myself am astonished, and I would suffer as much for many years for the deliverance of that soul. May our Lord be praised for ever! for the prayers of those who serve Him can do great things; and I believe the sisters of this house do serve Him. The devils must have been more angry with me only because I asked them to pray, and because our Lord permitted it on account of my sins. At that time, too, I thought the evil spirits would have suffocated me one night, and when the sisters threw much holy water about I saw a great troop of them rush away as if tumbling over a precipice. These cursed spirits have tormented me so often, and I am now so little afraid of them,—because I see they cannot stir without our Lord's permission,—that I should weary both you, my father, and myself, if I were to speak of these things in detail.

Effects of intercessory prayer.

10. May this I have written be of use to the true servant of God, who ought to despise these terrors, which Satan sends only to make him afraid! Let him understand that each time we despise those terrors, their force is lessened, and the soul gains power over them. There is always some great good obtained; but I will not speak of it, that I may not be too diffuse. I will speak, however, of what happened to me once on the night of All Souls. I was in an oratory, and, having said one Nocturn, was saying some very devotional prayers at the end of our Breviary, when Satan put himself on the book before me, to prevent my finishing my prayer. I made the sign of the cross, and he went away. I then returned to my prayer, and he, too, came back; he did so, I believe, three times, and I was not able to finish the prayer without throwing holy water at him. I saw certain souls at that moment come forth out of purgatory—they must have been near their deliverance, and I thought that Satan might in this way have been trying to hinder their release. It is very rarely that I saw Satan assume a bodily form; I know of his presence through the vision I have spoken of before,[1] the vision wherein no form is seen.

Satan afraid of contempt.

11. I wish also to relate what follows, for I was greatly alarmed at it: on Trinity Sunday, in the choir of a certain monastery, and in a trance, I saw a great fight between evil spirits and the angels. I could not make out what the vision meant. In less than a fortnight, it was explained clearly enough by the dispute that took place between persons given to prayer and many who were not, which did great harm to that house; for it was a dispute that lasted long, and caused much trouble. On another occasion, I saw a great multitude of evil spirits round about me, and, at the same time, a great light, in which I was enveloped, which kept them from coming near me. I understood it to mean that God was watching over me, that they might not approach me so as to make me offend Him. I knew the vision was real by what I saw occasionally in myself. The fact is, I know now how little power the evil spirits have,

The Saint sees devils fighting with angels.

[1] Ch. xxvii. § 4.

provided I am not out of the grace of God; I have scarcely any fear of them at all, for their strength is as nothing; if they do not find the souls they assail give up the contest, and become cowards, it is in this case that they show their power.

12. Now and then, during the temptations I am speaking of, it seemed to me as if all my vanity and weakness in times past had become alive again within me; so I had reason enough to commit myself into the hands of God. Then I was tormented by the thought that, as these things came back to my memory, I must be utterly in the power of Satan, until my confessor consoled me; for I imagined that even the first movement towards an evil thought ought not to have come near one who had received from our Lord such great graces as I had. *The Saint's distress at her temptations.*

13. At other times, I was much tormented—and even now I am tormented—when I saw people make much of me, particularly great people, and when they spake well of me. I have suffered, and still suffer, much in this way. I think at once of the life of Christ and of the Saints, and then my life seems the reverse of theirs, for they received nothing but contempt and ill-treatment. All this makes me afraid; I dare not lift up my head, and I wish nobody saw me at all. It is not thus with me when I am persecuted; then my soul is so conscious of strength, though the body suffers, and though I am in other ways afflicted, that I do not know how this can be; but so it is, —and my soul seems then to be a queen in its kingdom, having every thing under its feet. *The Saint's distress on account of the good opinion of others.*

14. I had such a thought now and then—and, indeed, for many days together. I regarded it as a sign of virtue and of humility; but I see clearly now that it was nothing else but a temptation. A Dominican friar, of great learning, showed it to me very plainly. When I considered that the graces which our Lord had bestowed upon me might come to the knowledge of the public, my sufferings became so excessive as greatly to disturb my soul. They went so far, that I made up my mind, while thinking of it, that I would rather be buried alive than *A Dominican father helps the Saint to unravel a temptation.*

s

have these things known. And so, when I began to be profoundly recollected, or to fall into a trance, which I could not resist even in public, I was so ashamed of myself, that I would not appear where people might see me.

Our Lord consoles the Saint. 15. Once, when I was much distressed at this, our Lord said to me, What was I afraid of? one of two things must happen—people would either speak ill of me, or give glory to Him. He made me understand by this, that those who believed in the truth of what was going on in me would glorify Him; and that those who did not would condemn me without cause: in both ways I should be the gainer, and I was therefore not to distress myself.[1] This made me quite calm, and it comforts me whenever I think of it.

The Saint tempted to leave the Convent of the Incarnation for another where she was not known. 16. This temptation became so excessive, that I wished to leave the house, and take my dower to another monastery, where enclosure was more strictly observed than in that wherein I was at this time. I had heard great things of that other house, which was of the same Order as mine; it was also at a great distance, and it would have been a great consolation to me to live where I was not known; but my confessor would never let me go. These fears deprived me in a great measure of all liberty of spirit; and I understood afterwards that this was not true humility, because it disturbed me so much. And our Lord taught me this truth: if I was convinced, and certainly persuaded, that all that was good in me came wholly and only from God, and if it did not distress me to hear the praises of others,—yea, rather, if I was pleased and comforted when I saw that God was working in them,—then neither should I be distressed if He showed forth His works in me.

The Saint wished her sins to be known to those who knew the graces God bestowed on her. 17. I fell, too, into another extreme. I begged of God, and made it a particular subject of prayer, that it might please His Majesty, whenever any one saw any good in me, that such a one might also become acquainted with my sins, in order that he might see that His graces were bestowed on me without any merit on my part: and I always greatly desire

[1] See *Inner Fortress*, vi. ch. iv. § 12.

this. My confessor told me not to do it. But almost to this day, if I saw that any one thought well of me, I used in a roundabout way, or anyhow, as I could, to contrive he should know of my sins:[1] that seemed to relieve me. But they have made me very scrupulous on this point. This, it appears to me, was not an effect of humility, but oftentimes the result of temptation. It seemed to me that I was deceiving every body —though, in truth, they deceived themselves, by thinking that there was any good in me.[2] I did not wish to deceive them, nor did I ever attempt it, only our Lord permitted it for some end; and so, even with my confessors, I never discussed any of these matters if I did not see the necessity of it, for that would have occasioned very considerable scruples.

18. All these little fears and distresses, and semblance of humility, I now see clearly were mere imperfections, and the result of my unmortified life; *(Trust in God the only remedy.)* for a soul left in the hands of God cares nothing about evil or good report, if it clearly comprehends, when our Lord is pleased to bestow upon it His grace, that it has nothing of its own. Let it trust the Giver; it will know hereafter why He reveals His gifts, and prepare itself for persecution, which in these times is sure to come, when it is our Lord's will it should be known of any one that He bestows upon him graces such as these; for a thousand eyes are watching that soul, while a thousand souls of another order are observed of none. In truth, there was no little ground for fear, and that fear should have been mine: I was therefore not humble, but a coward; for a soul which God permits to be thus seen of men may well prepare itself to be the world's martyr—because, if it will not die to the world voluntarily, that very world will kill it.

19. Certainly, I see nothing in the world that seems to me good except this, that it tolerates no faults in good people, and helps them to perfection by dint of complaints against them. I mean, that it *(Censoriousness and unreasonableness of the world.)* requires greater courage in one not yet perfect to walk in the

---

[1] *Way of Perfection*, ch. lxv. § 2; but ch. xxxvi. of the previous editions.

[2] See ch. x. § 10.

way of perfection than to undergo an instant martyrdom; for perfection is not attained to at once, unless our Lord grant that grace by a special privilege: yet the world, when it sees any one beginning to travel on that road, insists on his becoming perfect at once, and a thousand leagues off detects in him a fault, which after all may be a virtue. He who finds fault is doing the very same thing,—but, in his own case, viciously,—and he pronounces it to be so wrong in the other. He who aims at perfection, then, must neither eat nor sleep,— nor, as they say, even breathe; and the more men respect such a one, the more do they forget that he is still in the body; and, though they may consider him perfect, he is living on the earth, subject to its miseries, however much he may tread them under his feet. And so, as I have just said, great courage is necessary here; for, though the poor soul have not yet begun to walk, the world will have it fly; and, though its passions be not wholly overcome, men will have it that they must be under restraint, even upon trying occasions, as those of the Saints are, of whom they read, after they are confirmed in grace.

Why souls fail to advance. 20. All this is a reason for praising God, and also for great sorrow of heart, because very many go backwards who, poor souls, know not how to help themselves; and I too, I believe, would have gone back also, if our Lord had not so mercifully on His part done every thing for me. And until He, of His goodness, had done all, nothing was done by me, as you, my father, may have seen already, beyond falling and rising again. I wish I knew how to explain it, because many souls, I believe, delude themselves in this matter; they would fly before God gives them wings.

Causes of discouragement. 21. I believe I have made this comparison on another occasion,[1] but it is to the purpose here, for I see certain souls are very greatly afflicted on that ground. When these souls begin, with great fervour, courage, and desire, to advance in virtue,—some of them, at least outwardly, giving up all for God,—when they see in others, more advanced than themselves, greater fruits of virtue given them

[1] Ch. xiii. § 3.

by our Lord,—for we cannot acquire these of ourselves,—when they see in all the books written on prayer and on contemplation an account of what we have to do in order to attain thereto, but which they cannot accomplish themselves,—they lose heart. For instance, they read that we must not be troubled when men speak ill of us, that we are to be then more pleased than when they speak well of us; that we must despise our own good name, be detached from our kindred, avoid their company, which should be wearisome to us, unless they be given to prayer; with many other things of the same kind. The disposition to practise this must be, in my opinion, the gift of God; for it seems to me a supernatural good, contrary to our natural inclinations. Let them not distress themselves; let them trust in our Lord: what they now desire, His Majesty will enable them to attain to by prayer, and by doing what they can themselves; for it is very necessary for our weak nature that we should have great confidence, that we should not be faint-hearted, nor suppose that, if we do our best, we shall fail to obtain the victory at last. And as my experience here is large, I will say, by way of caution to you, my father, do not think—though it may seem so—that a virtue is acquired when we have not tested it by its opposing vice: we must always be suspicious of ourselves, and never negligent while we live; for much evil clings to us if, as I said before,[1] grace be not given to us fully to understand what every thing is: and in this life there is nothing without great risks.

22. I thought a few years ago, not only that I was detached from my kindred, but that they were a burden to me; and certainly it was so, for I could not endure their conversation. *The Saint's detachment from kindred.* An affair of some importance had to be settled, and I had to remain with a sister of mine, for whom I had always before had a great affection. The conversation we had together, though she is better than I am, did not please me; for it could not always be on subjects I preferred, owing to the difference of our conditions—she being married. I was therefore as much alone as I could; yet I felt that her troubles gave me more trouble than did those of my neighbours,

[1] Ch. xx. § 38.

and even some anxiety. In short, I found out that I was not so detached as I thought, and that it was necessary for me to flee from dangerous occasions, in order that the virtue which our Lord had begun to implant in me might grow; and so, by His help, I have striven to do from that time till now.

23. If our Lord bestows any virtue upon us, we must make much of it, and by no means run the risk of losing it; so it is in those things which concern our good name, and many other matters. You, my father, must believe that we are not all of us detached, though we think we are; it is necessary for us never to be careless on this point. If any one detects in himself any tenderness about his good name, and yet wishes to advance in the spiritual life, let him believe me and throw this embarrassment behind his back, for it is a chain which no file can sever; only the help of God, obtained by prayer and much striving on his part, can do it. It seems to me to be a hindrance on the road, and I am astonished at the harm it does. I see some persons so holy in their works, and they are so great as to fill people with wonder. O my God, why is their soul still on the earth? Why has it not arrived at the summit of perfection? What does it mean? What keeps him back who does so much for God? Oh, there it is!—self-respect; and the worst of it is, that these persons will not admit that they have it, merely because Satan now and then convinces them that they are under an obligation to observe it.

Self-respect.

24. Well, then, let them believe me : for the love of our Lord, let them give heed to the little ant, who speaks because it is His pleasure. If they take not this caterpillar away, though it does not hurt the whole tree, because some virtues remain, the worm will eat into every one of them. Not only is the tree not beautiful, but it also never thrives, neither does it suffer the others near it to thrive ; for the fruit of good example which it bears is not sound, and endures but a short time. I say it again and again, let our self-respect be ever so slight, it will have the same result as the missing of a note on the organ when it is played,—the whole music is out of tune. It is a thing which hurts the soul exceedingly in every way, but it is a pestilence in the way of prayer.

25. Are we striving after union with God ? and do we wish to follow the counsels of Christ,—who was loaded with reproaches and falsely accused,—and, at the same time, to keep our own reputation and credit untouched? We cannot succeed, for these things are inconsistent one with another. Our Lord comes to the soul when we do violence to ourselves, and strive to give up our rights in many things. Some will say, I have nothing that I can give up, nor have I any opportunity of doing so. I believe that our Lord will never suffer any one who has made so good a resolution as this to miss so great a blessing. His Majesty will make so many arrangements for him, whereby he may acquire this virtue,—more frequently, perhaps, than he will like. Let him put his hand to the work. I speak of the little nothings and trifles which I gave up when I began—or, at least, of some of them: the straws which I said[1] I threw into the fire ; for I am not able to do more. All this our Lord accepted : may He be blessed for evermore !

Necessity of denying self.

26. One of my faults was this : I had a very imperfect knowledge of my Breviary and of my duties in choir, simply because I was careless and given to vanities ; and I knew the other novices could have taught me. But I never asked them, that they might not know how little I knew. It suggested itself to me at once, that I ought to set a good example : this is very common. Now, however, that God has opened my eyes a little, even when I know a thing, but yet am very slightly in doubt about it, I ask the children. I have lost neither honour nor credit by it—on the contrary, I believe our Lord has been pleased to strengthen my memory. My singing of the Office was bad, and I felt it much if I had not learned the part intrusted to me,—not because I made mistakes before our Lord, which would have been a virtue, but because I made them before the many nuns who heard me. I was so full of my own reputation, that I was disturbed, and therefore did not sing what I had to sing even so well as I might have done. Afterwards, I ventured, when I did not know it very well, to say so. At first, I

The Saint conquers herself in the matter of self-respect.

[1] Ch. xxx. § 25.

felt it very much ; but afterwards I found pleasure in doing it. So, when I began to be indifferent about its being known that I could not sing well, it gave me no pain at all, and I sang much better. This miserable self-esteem took from me the power of doing that which I regarded as an honour, for every one regards as honourable that which he likes.

The great reward of slight services. 27. By trifles such as these, which are nothing,— and I am altogether nothing myself, seeing that this gave me pain,—by little and little, doing such actions, and by such slight performances,—they become of worth because done for God,—His Majesty helps us on towards greater things ; and so it happened to me in the matter of humility. When I saw that all the nuns except myself were making great progress, —I was always myself good for nothing,—I used to fold up their mantles when they left the choir. I looked on myself as doing service to angels who had been there praising God. I did so till they—I know not how—found it out ; and then I was not a little ashamed, because my virtue was not strong enough to bear that they should know of it. But the shame arose, not because I was humble, but because I was afraid they would laugh at me, the matter being so trifling.

28. O Lord, what a shame for me to lay bare so much wickedness, and to number these grains of sand, which yet I did not raise up from the ground in Thy service without mixing them with a thousand meannesses ! The waters of Thy grace were not as yet flowing beneath them, so as to make them ascend upwards. O my Creator, oh, that I had any thing worth recounting amid so many evil things, when I am recounting the great mercies I received at Thy hands ! So it is, O my Lord. I know not how my heart could have borne it, nor how any one who shall read this can help having me in abhorrence when he sees that mercies so great had been so ill-requited, and that I have not been ashamed to speak of these services. Ah ! they are only mine, O my Lord ; but I am ashamed I have nothing else to say of myself ; and that is it that makes me speak of these wretched beginnings, in order that he who has begun more nobly may have hope that our Lord, who has made much of mine, will make more of his. May it please His

Majesty to give me this grace, that I may not remain for ever at the beginning! Amen.[1]

CHAPTER XXXII.

OUR LORD SHOWS S. TERESA THE PLACE WHICH SHE HAD BY HER SINS DESERVED IN HELL—THE TORMENTS THERE—HOW THE MONASTERY OF S. JOSEPH WAS FOUNDED.

1. SOME considerable time after our Lord had bestowed upon me the graces I have been describing, and others also of a higher nature, I was one day in prayer, when I found myself in a moment, without knowing how, plunged apparently into hell. I understood that it was our Lord's will I should see the place which the devils kept in readiness for me, and which I had deserved by my sins. It was but a moment, but it seems to me impossible I should ever forget it even if I were to live many years. *[The Saint has a vision of hell.]*

2. The entrance seemed to be by a long and narrow pass, like a furnace, very low, dark, and close. The ground seemed to be saturated with water, mere mud, exceedingly foul, sending forth pestilential odours, and covered with loathsome vermin. At the end was a hollow place in the wall, like a closet, and in that I saw myself confined. All this was even pleasant to behold in comparison with what I felt there. There is no exaggeration in what I am saying. *[Description of the place prepared for herself.]*

3. But as to what I then felt, I do not know where to begin, if I were to describe it; it is utterly inexplicable. I felt a fire in my soul. I cannot see how it is possible to describe it. My bodily sufferings were unendurable. I have undergone most painful sufferings in this life, and, as the physicians say, the greatest that can be borne, *[The torments she endured.]*

[1] Don Vicente de la Fuente thinks the first "Life" ended here; that which follows was written under obedience to her confessor, F. Garcia of Toledo, and after the foundation of the monastery of S. Joseph, Avila.

such as the contraction of my sinews when I was paralysed,[1] without speaking of others of different kinds, yea, even those of which I have also spoken,[2] inflicted on me by Satan; yet all these were as nothing in comparison with what I felt then, especially when I saw that there would be no intermission, nor any end to them.

4. These sufferings were nothing in comparison with the anguish of my soul, a sense of oppression, of stifling, and of pain so keen, accompanied by so hopeless and cruel an infliction, that I know not how to speak of it. If I said that the soul is continually being torn from the body, it would be nothing, for that implies the destruction of life by the hands of another; but here it is the soul itself that is tearing itself in pieces. I cannot describe that inward fire or that despair, surpassing all torments and all pain. I did not see who it was that tormented me, but I felt myself on fire, and torn to pieces, as it seemed to me ; and, I repeat it, this inward fire and despair are the greatest torments of all.

Sense of despair.

5. Left in that pestilential place, and utterly without the power to hope for comfort, I could neither sit nor lie down ; there was no room. I was placed as it were in a hole in the wall ; and those walls, terrible to look on of themselves, hemmed me in on every side. I could not breathe. There was no light, but all was thick darkness. I do not understand how it is; though there was no light, yet every thing that can give pain by being seen was visible.

Description of hell.

6. Our Lord at that time would not let me see more of hell. Afterwards, I had another most fearful vision, in which I saw the punishment of certain sins. They were most horrible to look at; but, because I felt none of the pain, my terror was not so great. In the former vision, our Lord made me really feel those torments, and that anguish of spirit, just as if I had been suffering them in the body there. I know not how it was, but I understood distinctly that it was a great mercy that our Lord would have me see with mine own eyes the very place from which His compassion

Horrors of hell.

---

[1] See ch. v. § 14, ch. vi. § 1.   [2] Ch. xxxi. § 3.

saved me. I have listened to people speaking of these things, and I have at other times dwelt on the various torments of hell, though not often, because my soul made no progress by the way of fear; and I have read of the diverse tortures, and how the devils tear the flesh with red-hot pincers. But all is as nothing before this; it is a wholly different matter. In short, the one is a reality, the other a picture; and all burning here in this life is as nothing in comparison with the fire that is there.

7. I was so terrified by that vision,—and that terror is on me even now while I am writing,—that, though it took place nearly six years ago,[1] the natural warmth of my body is chilled by fear even now when I think of it. And so, amid all the pain and suffering which I may have had to bear, I remember no time in which I do not think that all we have to suffer in this world is as nothing. It seems to me that we complain without reason. I repeat it, this vision was one of the grandest mercies of our Lord. It has been to me of the greatest service, because it has destroyed my fear of trouble and of the contradiction of the world, and because it has made me strong enough to bear up against them, and to give thanks to our Lord, who has been my Deliverer, as it now seems to me, from such fearful and everlasting pains. *Effects of the vision on the Saint.*

8. Ever since that time, as I was saying, every thing seems endurable in comparison with one instant of sufferings such as those I had then to bear in hell. I am filled with fear when I see that, after frequently reading books which describe in some manner the pains of hell, I was not afraid of them, nor made any account of them. Where was I? How could I possibly take any pleasure in those things which led me directly to so dreadful a place? Blessed for ever be Thou, O my God! and, oh, how manifest is it that Thou didst love me much more than I did love Thee! How often, O Lord, didst Thou save me from that fearful prison! and how I used to get back to it contrary to Thy will! *No pains comparable to the pains of hell.*

[1] In 1558 (*De la Fuente*).

9. It was that vision that filled me with the very great distress which I feel at the sight of so many lost souls, especially of the Lutherans,—for they were once members of the Church by baptism,—and also gave me the most vehement desires for the salvation of souls; for certainly I believe that, to save even one from those overwhelming torments, I would most willingly endure many deaths. If here on earth we see one whom we specially love in great trouble or pain, our very nature seems to bid us compassionate him; and if those pains be great, we are troubled ourselves. What, then, must it be to see a soul in danger of pain, the most grievous of all pains, for ever? Who can endure it? It is a thought no heart can bear without great anguish. Here we know that pain ends with life at last, and that there are limits to it; yet the sight of it moves our compassion so greatly. That other pain has no ending; and I know not how we can be calm, when we see Satan carry so many souls daily away.

The contemplation of hell.

10. This also makes me wish that, in a matter which concerns us so much, we did not rest satisfied with doing less than we can do on our part,—that we left nothing undone. May our Lord vouchsafe to give us His grace for that end! When I consider that, notwithstanding my very great wickedness, I took some pains to please God, and abstained from certain things which I know the world makes light of,—that, in short, I suffered grievous infirmities, and with great patience, which our Lord gave me; that I was not inclined to murmur or to speak ill of any body; that I could not—I believe so—wish harm to any one; that I was not, to the best of my recollection, either avaricious or envious, so as to be grievously offensive in the sight of God; and that I was free from many other faults,—for, though so wicked, I had lived constantly in the fear of God,—I had to look at the very place which the devils kept ready for me. It is true that, considering my faults, I had deserved a still heavier chastisement; but for all that, I repeat it, the torment was fearful, and we run a great risk whenever we please ourselves. No soul should take either rest or pleasure that is liable to fall every moment into mortal sin. Let us, then, for the love of God, avoid all occasions

The Saint's humility.

of sin, and our Lord will help us, as He has helped me. May it please His Majesty never to let me out of His hands, lest I should turn back and fall, now that I have seen the place where I must dwell if I do. I entreat our Lord, for His Majesty's sake, never to permit it. Amen.

11. When I had seen this vision, and had learned other great and hidden things which our Lord, of His goodness, was pleased to show me,—namely, the joy of the blessed and the torment of the wicked,—I longed for the way and the means of doing penance for the great evil I had done, and of meriting in some degree, so that I might gain so great a good; and therefore I wished to avoid all society, and to withdraw myself utterly from the world. I was in spirit restless, yet my restlessness was not harassing, but rather pleasant. I saw clearly that it was the work of God, and that His Majesty had furnished my soul with fervour, so that I might be able to digest other and stronger food than I had been accustomed to eat. I tried to think what I could do for God, and thought that the first thing was to follow my vocation to a religious life, which His Majesty had given me, by keeping my rule in the greatest perfection possible. *Effects of these visions on the Saint.*

12. Though in that house in which I then lived there were many servants of God, and God was greatly served therein, yet, because it was very poor, the nuns left it very often and went to other places, where, however, we could serve God in all honour and observances of religion. The rule also was kept, not in its original exactness, but according to the custom of the whole Order, authorised by the Bull of Mitigation. There were other inconveniences also: we had too many comforts, as it seemed to me; for the house was large and pleasant. But this inconvenience of going out, though it was I that took most advantage of it, was a very grievous one for me; for many persons, to whom my superiors could not say no, were glad to have me with them. My superiors, thus importuned, commanded me to visit these persons; and thus it was so arranged that I could not be long together in the monastery. Satan, too, must have had a share *Relaxed rule of her convent.*

in this, in order that I might not be in the house, where I was of great service to those of my sisters to whom I continually communicated the instructions which I received from my confessors.

The beginning of the reform of the Carmelites.
13. It occurred once to a person with whom I was speaking to say to me and the others that it was possible to find means for the foundation of a monastery, if we were prepared to become nuns like those of the Barefooted Orders.[1] I, having this desire, began to discuss the matter with that widowed lady who was my companion,—I have spoken of her before,[2]—and she had the same wish that I had. She began to consider how to provide a revenue for the home. I see now that this was not the way,—only the wish we had to do so made us think it was; but I, on the other hand, seeing that I took the greatest delight in the house in which I was then living, because it was very pleasant to me, and, in my own cell, most convenient for my purpose, still held back. Nevertheless, we agreed to commit the matter with all earnestness to God.

S. Teresa is divinely encouraged.
14. One day, after Communion, our Lord commanded me to labour with all my might for this end. He made me great promises,—that the monastery would be certainly built; that He would take great delight therein; that it should be called S. Joseph's; that S. Joseph would keep guard at one door, and our Lady at the other; that Christ would be in the midst of us; that the monastery would be a star shining in great splendour; that, though the religious Orders were then relaxed, I was not to suppose that He was scantily served in them,—for what would become of the world, if there were no religious in it?—I was to tell my confessor what He commanded me, and that He asked him not to oppose nor thwart me in the matter.

Her hesitations.
15. So efficacious was the vision, and such was the nature of the words our Lord spoke to me, that I could not possibly doubt that they came from Him.

[1] This was said by Maria de Ocampo, niece of S. Teresa, then living in the monastery of the Incarnation, but not a religious ; afterwards Maria Bautista, Prioress of the Carmelites at Valladolid (*Ribera*, i. 13).

[2] Ch. xxiv. § 7. Doña Guiomar de Ulloa.

I suffered most keenly, because I saw in part the great anxieties and troubles that the work would cost me, and I was also very happy in the house I was in then; and though I used to speak of this matter in past times, yet it was not with resolution nor with any confidence that the thing could ever be done. I saw that I was now in a great strait; and when I saw that I was entering on a work of great anxiety, I hesitated; but our Lord spoke of it so often to me, and set before me so many reasons and motives, which I saw could not be gainsaid,—I saw, too, that such was His will; so I did not dare do otherwise than put the whole matter before my confessor, and give him an account in writing of all that took place.

16. My confessor did not venture definitely to bid me abandon my purpose; but he saw that naturally there was no way of carrying it out; because my friend, who was to do it, had very little or no means available for that end. He told me to lay the matter before my superior,[1] and do what he might bid me do. I never spoke of my visions to my superior, but that lady who desired to found the monastery communicated with him. The Provincial was very much pleased, for he loves the whole Order, gave her every help that was necessary, and promised to acknowledge the house. Then there was a discussion about the revenues of the monastery, and for many reasons we never would allow more than thirteen sisters together. Before we began our arrangements, we wrote to the holy friar, Peter of Alcantara, telling him all that was taking place; and he advised us not to abandon our work, and gave us his sanction on all points. *F. Baltasar Alvarez hesitates.*

17. As soon as the affair began to be known here, there fell upon us a violent persecution, which cannot be very easily described—sharp sayings and keen jests. People said it was folly in me, who was so well off in my monastery; as to my friend, the persecution was so continuous, that it wearied her. I did not know what to do, and I thought that people were partly in the right. When I was thus heavily afflicted, I commended myself to God, and His Majesty began to console *Persecution begins.*

[1] The Provincial of the Carmelites: Fr. Angel de Salasar (*De la Fuente*).

and encourage me. He told me that I could then see what the Saints had to go through who founded the religious Orders: that I had much heavier persecutions to endure than I could imagine, but I was not to mind them. He told me also what I was to say to my friend; and what surprised me most was, that we were consoled at once as to the past, and resolved to withstand everybody courageously. And so it came to pass; for among people of prayer, and indeed in the whole neighbourhood, there was hardly one who was not against us, and who did not think our work the greatest folly.

The Provincial opposes the Saint's work. 18. There was so much talking and confusion in the very monastery wherein I was, that the Provincial began to think it hard for him to set himself against every body; so he changed his mind, and would not acknowledge the new house. He said that the revenue was not certain, and too little, while the opposition was great. On the whole, it seemed that he was right; he gave it up at last, and would have nothing to do with it. It was a very great pain to us,—for we seemed now to have received the first blow, and i n particular to me, to find the Provincial against us; for when he approved of the plan, I considered myself blameless before all. They would not give absolution to my friend, if she did not abandon the project; for they said she was bound to remove the scandal.

Dona Guiomar consults F. Pedro Ibanez, Dominican. 19. She went to a very learned man, and a very great servant of God, of the Order of S. Dominic,[1] to whom she gave an account of all this matter. This was even before the Provincial had withdrawn his consent; for in this place we had no one who would give us advice; and so they said that it all proceeded solely from our obstinacy. That lady gave an account of every thing, and told the holy man how much she received from the property of her husband. Having a great desire that he would help us,—for he was the most learned man here, and there are few in his Order more learned than he,—I told him myself all we intended to do, and some of my motives. I never said a word of any revelation whatever, speaking only of the natural reasons which influenced

[1] F. Pedro Ibañez (*De la Fuente*).

me; for I would not have him give an opinion otherwise than on those grounds. He asked us to give him eight days before he answered, and also if we had made up our minds to abide by what he might say. I said we had; but though I said so, and though I thought so, I never lost a certain confidence that the monastery would be founded. My friend had more faith than I; nothing they could say could make her give it up. As for myself, though, as I said, it seemed to me impossible that the work should be finally abandoned, yet my belief in the truth of the revelation went no further than in so far as it was not against what is contained in the sacred writings, nor against the laws of the Church, which we are bound to keep. Though the revelation seemed to me to have come really from God, yet, if that learned man had told me that we could not go on without offending God and going against our conscience, I believe I should have given it up, and looked out for some other way; but our Lord showed me no other way than this.

20. The servant of God told me afterwards that he had made up his mind to insist on the abandonment of our project, for he had already heard the popular cry: moreover, he, as every body did, thought it folly; and a certain nobleman also, as soon as he knew that we had gone to him, had sent him word to consider well what he was doing, and to give us no help; that when he began to consider the answer he should make us, and to ponder on the matter, the object we had in view, our manner of life, and the Order, he became convinced that it was greatly for the service of God, and that we must not give it up. Accordingly, his answer was that we should make haste to settle the matter. He told us how and in what way it was to be done; and if our means were scanty, we must trust somewhat in God. If any one made any objections, they were to go to him—he would answer them; and in this way he always helped us, as I shall show by and by.[1]

The counsel of F. Pedro Ibanez.

21. This answer was a great comfort to us; so also was the conduct of certain holy persons who were usually against us: they were now pacified, and some of them even helped us. One of them was the saintly nobleman[2]

The opposition vanishes.

[1] Ch. xxxiii. § 8.   [2] Francis de Salcedo.

of whom I spoke before ;[1] he looked on it—so, indeed, it was—as a means of great perfection, because the whole foundation was laid in prayer. He saw also very many difficulties before us, and no way out of them,—yet he gave up his own opinion, and admitted that the work might be of God. Our Lord Himself must have touched his heart, as He also did that of the doctor, the priest and servant of God, to whom, as I said before,[2] I first spoke, who is an example to the whole city,—being one whom God maintains there for the relief and progress of many souls: he, too, came now to give us his assistance.

A house bought for a monastery. 22. When matters had come to this state, and always with the help of many prayers, we purchased a house in a convenient spot; and though it was small, I cared not at all for that, for our Lord had told me to go into it as well as I could,—that I should see afterwards what He would do; and how well I have seen it! I saw, too, how scanty were our means; and yet I believed our Lord would order these things by other ways, and be gracious unto us.

CHAPTER XXXIII.

THE FOUNDATION OF THE MONASTERY HINDERED—OUR LORD CONSOLES THE SAINT.

The Saint is required to abandon her work. 1. WHEN the matter was in this state—so near its conclusion, that on the very next day the papers were to be signed—then it was that the Father-Provincial changed his mind. I believe that the change was divinely ordered—so it appeared afterwards; for while so many prayers were made, our Lord was perfecting His work and arranging its execution in another way. When the Provincial refused us, my confessor bade me forthwith to think no more of it, notwithstanding the great trouble and distress which our Lord knows it cost me to bring it to this state. When the work was given

---

[1] Ch. xxiii. § 6. [2] Gaspar Daza. See ch. xxiii. § 6.

up and abandoned, people were the more convinced that it was altogether the foolishness of women; and the complaints against me were multiplied, although I had until then this commandment of my Provincial to justify me.

2. I was now very much disliked throughout the whole monastery, because I wished to found another with stricter enclosure. It was said I insulted my sisters; that I could serve God among them as well as elsewhere, for there were many among them much better than I; that I did not love the house, and that it would have been better if I had procured greater resources for it than for another. Some said I ought to be put in prison; others—but they were not many—defended me in some degree. I saw well enough that they were for the most part right, and now and then I made excuses for myself; though, as I could not tell them the chief reason, which was the commandment of our Lord, I knew not what to do, and so was silent. *The nuns of her own monastery are against her.*

3. In other respects God was most merciful unto me, for all this caused me no uneasiness; and I gave up our design with much readiness and joy, as if it cost me nothing. No one could believe it, not even those men of prayer with whom I conversed; for they thought I was exceedingly pained and sorry: even my confessor himself could hardly believe it. I had done, as it seemed to me, all that was in my power. I thought myself obliged to do no more than I had done to fulfil our Lord's commandment, and so I remained in the house where I was, exceedingly happy and joyful; though, at the same time, I was never able to give up my conviction that the work would be done. I had now no means of doing it, nor did I know how or when it would be done; but I firmly believed in its accomplishment. *The resignation of the Saint.*

4. I was much distressed at one time by a letter which my confessor wrote to me, as if I had done any thing in the matter contrary to his will. Our Lord also must have meant that suffering should not fail me there where I should feel it most; and so, amid the multitude of my persecutions, when, as it seemed to me, consolations should have come from my confessor, he told me that I ought to *Her confessor turns against her.*

recognise in the result that all was a dream; that I ought to lead a new life by ceasing to have any thing to do for the future with it, or even to speak of it any more, seeing the scandal it had occasioned. He made some further remarks, all of them very painful. This was a greater affliction to me than all the others together. I considered whether I had done any thing myself, and whether I was to blame for any thing that was an offence unto God; whether all my visions were illusions, all my prayers a delusion, and I, therefore, deeply deluded and lost. This pressed so heavily upon me, that I was altogether disturbed and most grievously distressed. But our Lord, who never failed me in all the trials I speak of, so frequently consoled and strengthened me, that I need not speak of it here. He told me then not to distress myself; that I had pleased God greatly, and had not sinned against Him throughout the whole affair; that I was to do what my confessors required of me, and be silent on the subject till the time came to resume it. I was so comforted and so happy, that the persecution which had befallen me seemed to be as nothing at all.

5. Our Lord now showed me what an exceedingly great blessing it is to be tried and persecuted for His sake; for the growth of the love of God in my soul, which I now discerned, as well as of many other virtues, was such as to fill me with wonder. It made me unable to abstain from desiring trials, and yet those about me thought I was exceedingly disheartened; and I must have been so, if our Lord in that extremity had not succoured me with His great compassion. Now was the beginning of those more violent impetuosities of the love of God of which I have spoken before,[1] as well as of those profounder trances. I kept silence, however, and never spoke of those graces to any one. The saintly Dominican[2] was as confident as I was that the work would be done; and as I would not speak of it, in order that nothing might take place contrary to the obedience I owed my confessor, he communicated with my companion, and they wrote letters to Rome and made their preparations.

Her consolations.

[1] Ch. xxi. § 8, ch. xxix. §§ 8, 9.
[2] Pedro Ibañez. See ch. xxxviii. § 15.

6. Satan also contrived now that persons should hear one from another that I had had a revelation in the matter; and people came to me in great terror, saying that the times were dangerous, that something might be laid to my charge, and that I might be taken before the Inquisitors. I heard this with pleasure, and it made me laugh, because I never was afraid of them; for I knew well enough that in matters of faith I would not break the least ceremony of the Church, that I would expose myself to die a thousand times rather than that any one should see me go against it or against any truth of Holy Writ. So I told them I was not afraid of that, for my soul must be in a very bad state if there was any thing the matter with it of such a nature as to make me fear the Inquisition; I would go myself and give myself up, if I thought there was any thing amiss; and if I should be denounced, our Lord would deliver me, and I should gain much. *[Timid people try to frighten the Saint.]*

7. I had recourse to my Dominican father; for I could rely upon him, because he was a learned man. I told him all about my visions, my way of prayer, the great graces our Lord had given me, as clearly as I could, and I begged him to consider the matter well, and tell me if there was any thing therein at variance with the Holy Writings, and give me his opinion on the whole matter. He reassured me much, and, I think, profited himself; for though he was exceedingly good, yet, from this time forth, he gave himself more and more to prayer, and retired to a monastery of his Order which was very lonely, that he might apply himself more effectually to prayer, where he remained more than two years. He was dragged out of his solitude by obedience, to his great sorrow: his superiors required his services; for he was a man of great abilities. I, too, on my part, felt his retirement very much, because it was a great loss to me, though I did not disturb him. But I knew it was a gain to him; for when I was so much distressed at his departure, our Lord bade me be comforted, not to take it to heart, for he was gone under good guidance. *[She consults F. Pedro Ibanez.]*

8. So, when he came back, his soul had made such great progress, and he was so advanced in the ways of the spirit, that he told me on his return he would *[The progress of F. Ibanez.]*

not have missed that journey for any thing in the world. And I, too, could say the same thing; for where he reassured and consoled me formerly by his mere learning, he did so now through that spiritual experience he had gained of supernatural things. And God, too, brought him here in time; for He saw that his help would be required in the foundation of the monastery which His Majesty willed should be laid.

9. I remained quiet after this for five or six months, neither thinking nor speaking of the matter; nor did our Lord once speak to me about it. I know not why, but I could never rid myself of the thought that the monastery would be founded. At the end of that time, the then Rector[1] of the Society of Jesus having gone away, His Majesty brought into his place another,[2] of great spirituality, high courage, strong understanding, and profound learning, at the very time when I was in great straits. As he who then heard my confession had a superior over him—the fathers of the Society are extremely strict about the virtue of obedience, and never stir but in conformity with the will of their superiors— so he would not dare, though he perfectly understood my spirit, and desired the accomplishment of my purpose, to come to any resolution; and he had many reasons to justify his conduct. I was at the same time subject to such great impetuosities of spirit, that I felt my chains extremely heavy; nevertheless, I never swerved from the commandment he gave me.

The Saint's patient silence.

10. One day, when in great distress, because I thought my confessor did not trust me, our Lord said to me, Be not troubled; this suffering will soon be over. I was very much delighted, thinking I should die shortly; and I was very happy whenever I recalled those words to remembrance. Afterwards I saw clearly that they referred to the coming of the rector of whom I am speaking, for never again had I any reason to be distressed. The rector that came

Our Lord consoles her.

[1] Dionisio Vasquez. Of him the Bollandists say that he was very austere and harsh to his subjects, notwithstanding his great learning : " homini egregie docto ac rebus gestis claro, sed in subditos, ut ex historia Societatis Jesu liquet, valde immiti" (§ 309).

[2] Gaspar de Salazar was made rector of the house in Avila in 1561, therein succeeding Vasquez (*Bollandists, ibid.*).

never interfered with the father-minister who was my confessor. On the contrary, he told him to console me,—that there was nothing to be afraid of,—and not to direct me along a road so narrow, but to leave the operations of the Spirit of God alone; for now and then it seemed as if these great impetuosities of the spirit took away the very breath of the soul.

11. The rector came to see me, and my confessor bade me speak to him in all freedom and openness. I used to feel the very greatest repugnance to speak of this matter; but so it was, when I went into the confessional, I felt in my soul something, I know not what. I do not remember to have felt so either before or after towards any one. I cannot tell what it was, nor do I know of any thing with which I could compare it. It was a spiritual joy, and a conviction in my soul that his soul must understand mine, that it was in unison with it, and yet, as I have said, I knew not how. If I had ever spoken to him, or had heard great things of him, it would have been nothing out of the way that I should rejoice in the conviction that he would understand me; but he had never spoken to me before, nor I to him, and, indeed, he was a person of whom I had no previous knowledge whatever. *She consults Father Gaspar de Salazar.*

12. Afterwards, I saw clearly that my spirit was not deceived; for my relations with him were in every way of the utmost service to me and my soul, because his method of direction is proper for those persons whom our Lord seems to have led far on the way, seeing that He makes them run, and not to crawl step by step. His plan is to render them thoroughly detached and mortified, and our Lord has endowed him with the highest gifts herein as well as in many other things beside. As soon as I began to have to do with him, I knew his method at once, and saw that he had a pure and holy soul, with a special grace of our Lord for the discernment of spirits. He gave me great consolation. Shortly after I had begun to speak to him, our Lord began to constrain me to return to the affair of the monastery, and to lay before my confessor and the father-rector many reasons and considerations why they should not stand in my way. Some of these reasons made them afraid, for the father-rector never *Father Salazar's method of direction.*

had a doubt of its being the work of the Spirit of God, because he regarded the fruits of it with great care and attention. At last, after much consideration, they did not dare to hinder me.[1]

Her confessor sanctions her plans.
13. My confessor gave me leave to prosecute the work with all my might. I saw well enough the trouble I exposed myself to, for I was utterly alone, and able to do so very little. We agreed that it should be carried on with the utmost secrecy; and so I contrived that one of my sisters,[2] who lived out of the town, should buy a house, and prepare it as if for herself, with money which our Lord gave us in a strange way for the purchase. It would take too much time to say how our Lord provided for us.[3] I made it a great point to do nothing against obedience; but I knew that if I spoke of it to my superiors all was lost, as on the former occasion, and worse even might happen. In holding the money, in finding the house, in treating for it, in putting it in order, I had so much to suffer; and, for the most part, I had to suffer alone, though my friend did what she could: she could do but little, and that was almost nothing. Beyond giving her name and her countenance, the whole of the trouble was mine; and that fell upon me in so many ways, that I am astonished now how I could have borne it.[4] Sometimes, in my

[1] S. Teresa was commanded by our Lord to ask F. Baltasar Alvarez to make a meditation on Ps. xci. 6: "Quam magnificata sunt opera Tua." The Saint obeyed, and the meditation was made. From that moment, as F. Alvarez afterwards told Father de Ribera (*Life of S. Teresa*, i. ch. xiv.), there was no further hesitation on the part of the Saint's confessor.

[2] Juana de Ahumada, wife of Juan de Ovalle.

[3] The money was a present from her brother, Don Lorenzo de Cepeda; and the Saint acknowledges the receipt of it, and confesses the use made of it, in a letter to her brother, written in Avila, Dec. 31, 1561 (*De la Fuente*).

[4] One day, she went with her sister—she was staying in her house—to hear a sermon in the church of S. Thomas. The zealous preacher denounced visions and revelations; and his observations were so much to the point, that there was no need of his saying that they were directed against S. Teresa, who was present. Her sister was greatly hurt, and persuaded the Saint to return to the monastery at once (*Reforma*, i. ch. xl. § 1).

affliction, I used to say: O my Lord, how is it that Thou commandest me to do that which seems impossible?—for, though I am a woman, yet, if I were free, it might be done; but when I am tied up in so many ways, without money, or the means of procuring it, either for the purpose of the Brief or for any other,—what, O Lord, can I do?

14. Once, when I was in one of my difficulties, not knowing what to do, unable to pay the workmen, S. Joseph, my true father and lord, appeared to me, and gave me to understand that money would not be wanting, and I must hire the workmen. So I did, though I was penniless; and our Lord, in a way that filled those who heard of it with wonder, provided for me. The house offered me was too small,—so much so, that it seemed as if it could never be made into a monastery,—and I wished to buy another, but had not the means, and there was neither way nor means to do so. I knew not what to do. There was another little house close to the one we had, which might have formed a small church. One day, after Communion, our Lord said to me, I have already bidden thee to go in anyhow. And then, as if exclaiming, said: Oh, covetousness of the human race, thinking that even the whole earth is too little for it! how often have I slept in the open air, because I had no place to shelter Me![1] I was alarmed, and saw that He had good reasons to complain. I went to the little house, arranged the divisions of it, and found that it would make a sufficient, though small, monastery. I did not care now to add to the site by purchase, and so I did nothing but contrive to have it prepared in such a way that it could be lived in. Every thing was coarse, and nothing more was done to it than to render it not hurtful to health—and that must be done every where.

The Saint takes possession of the new monastery.

15. As I was going to Communion on her feast, S. Clare appeared to me in great beauty, and bade me take courage, and go on with what I had begun; she would help me. I began to have a great devotion to S. Clare; and she has so truly kept her word, that a monastery of nuns of her Order in our neighbourhood helped us to live; and, what

S. Clare helps her.

[1] S. Luke ix. 58: "Filius autem hominis non habet ubi caput reclinet."

is of more importance, by little and little she so perfectly fulfilled my desire, that the poverty which the blessed Saint observes in her own house is observed in this, and we are living on alms. It cost me no small labour to have this matter settled by the plenary sanction and authority of the Holy Father,[1] so that it shall never be otherwise, and we possess no revenues. Our Lord is doing more for us—perhaps we owe it to the prayers of this blessed Saint; for, without our asking any body, His Majesty supplies most abundantly all our wants. May He be blessed for ever! Amen.

Her vision in the church of the Dominicans of Avila. Aug. 15, 1561. 16. On one of these days—it was the Feast of the Assumption of our Lady—I was in the church of the monastery of the Order of the glorious S. Dominic, thinking of the events of my wretched life, and of the many sins which in times past I had confessed in that house. I fell into so profound a trance, that I was as it were beside myself. I sat down, and it seemed as if I could neither see the Elevation nor hear Mass. This afterwards became a scruple to me. I thought then, when I was in that state, that I saw myself clothed with a garment of excessive whiteness and splendour. At first I did not see who was putting it on me. Afterwards I saw our Lady on my right hand, and my father S. Joseph on my left, clothing me with that garment. I was given to understand that I was then cleansed from my sins. When I had been thus clad—I was filled with the utmost delight and joy—our Lady seemed at once to take me by both hands. She said that I pleased her very much by being devout to the glorious S. Joseph; that I might rely on it my desires about the monastery were accomplished, and that our Lord and they too would be greatly honoured in it; that I was to be afraid of no failure whatever, though the obedience under which it would be placed might not be according to my mind, because they would watch over us, and because her Son had promised to be with us[2]—and, as a proof of this, she would give me that jewel. She then seemed to throw around my neck a most splendid necklace of gold, from

[1] Pius IV., on Dec. 5, 1562 (*Bouix*). See ch. xxxix. § 19.
[2] Ch. xxxii. § 14.

which hung a cross of great value. The stones and gold were so different from any in this world, that there is nothing wherewith to compare them. The beauty of them is such as can be conceived by no imagination,—and no understanding can find out the materials of the robe, nor picture to itself the splendours which our Lord revealed, in comparison with which all the splendours of earth, so to say, are a daubing of soot. This beauty, which I saw in our Lady, was exceedingly grand, though I did not trace it in any particular feature, but rather in the whole form of her face. She was clothed in white, and her garments shone with excessive lustre, which was not dazzling, but soft. I did not see S. Joseph so distinctly, though I saw clearly that he was there, as in the visions of which I spoke before,[1] in which nothing is seen. Our Lady seemed to be very young.

17. When they had been with me for a while,—I, too, in the greatest delight and joy, greater than I had ever had before, as I think, and with which I wished never to part,—I saw them, so it seemed, ascend up to heaven, attended by a great multitude of angels. I was left in great loneliness, though so comforted and raised up, so recollected in prayer and softened, that I was for some time unable to move or speak—being, as it were, beside myself. I was now possessed by a strong desire to be consumed for the love of God, and by other affections of the same kind. Every thing took place in such a way that I could never have a doubt— though I often tried—that the vision came from God.[2] It left me in the greatest consolation and peace. *Effects of the vision.*

18. As to that which the Queen of the Angels spoke about obedience, it is this : it was painful to me not to subject the monastery to the Order, and our Lord had told me that it was inexpedient to do so. He told me the reasons why it was in no wise convenient that I should do it, but I must send to Rome in a certain way, which He also explained ; He would

---

[1] See ch. xxvii.
[2] "Nuestro Señor," "our Lord," though inserted in the printed editions after the word "God," is not in the MS., according to Don V. de la Fuente.

take care that I found help there: and so I did. I sent to Rome, as our Lord directed me,—for we should never have succeeded otherwise,—and most favourable was the result.

The new monastery placed under the Bishop. 19. And as to subsequent events, it was very convenient to be under the Bishop,[1] but at that time I did not know him, nor did I know what kind of a superior he might be. It pleased our Lord that he should be as good and favourable to this house as it was necessary he should be on account of the great opposition it met with at the beginning, as I shall show hereafter,[2] and also for the sake of bringing it to the condition it is now in. Blessed be He who has done it all! Amen.

CHAPTER XXXIV.

THE SAINT LEAVES HER MONASTERY OF THE INCARNATION FOR A TIME, AT THE COMMAND OF HER SUPERIOR—CONSOLES AN AFFLICTED WIDOW.

Doña Luisa de la Cerda sends for the Saint to her house in Toledo. 1. Now, though I was very careful that no one should know what we were doing, all this work could not be carried on so secretly as not to come to the knowledge of divers persons; some believed in it, others did not. I was in great fear lest the Provincial should be spoken to about it when he came, and find himself compelled to order me to give it up; and if he did so, it would have been abandoned at once. Our Lord provided against it in this way. In a large city, more than twenty leagues distant, was a lady in great distress on account of her husband's death.[3] She was in such extreme affliction, that fears were entertained about her

[1] Don Alvaro de Mendoza, Bishop of Avila, afterwards of Palencia.

[2] See ch. xxxvi. § 19; *Way of Perfection,* ch. v. § 10; *Foundations,* ch. xxxi. § 1.

[3] Doña Luisa de la Cerda, sister of the Duke of Medina-Cœli, was now the widow of Arias Pardo, Marshal of Castille, Lord of Malagon and Paracuellos. Don Arias was nephew of Cardinal Tabera, Archbishop of Toledo (*De la Fuente*).

life. She had heard of me, a poor sinner,—for our Lord had provided that,—and men spoke well to her of me, for the sake of other good works which resulted from it. This lady knew the Provincial well; and as she was a person of some consideration, and knew that I lived in a monastery the nuns of which were permitted to go out, our Lord made her desire much to see me. She thought that my presence would be a consolation to her, and that she could not be comforted otherwise. She therefore strove by all the means in her power to get me into her house, sending messages to the Provincial, who was at a distance far away.

2. The Provincial sent me an order, charging me in virtue of my obedience to go immediately, with one companion. I knew of it on Christmas night. It caused me some trouble and much suffering to see that they sent for me because they thought there was some good in me; I, knowing myself to be so wicked, could not bear it. I commended myself earnestly to God, and during Matins, or the greater part of them, was lost in a profound trance. Our Lord told me I must go without fail, and give no heed to the opinions of people, for they were few who would not be rash in their counsel; and though I should have troubles, yet God would be served greatly: as to the monastery, it was expedient I should be absent till the Brief came, because Satan had contrived a great plot against the coming of the Provincial; that I was to have no fear,—He would help me. I repeated this to the rector, and he told me that I must go by all means, though others were saying I ought not to go, that it was a trick of Satan to bring some evil upon me there, and that I ought to send word to the Provincial. *The Saint ordered to go to Toledo.*

3. I obeyed the rector, and went without fear, because of what I had understood in prayer, though in the greatest confusion when I thought of the reasons why they sent for me, and how very much they were deceived. It made me more and more importunate with our Lord that He would not abandon me. It was a great comfort that there was a house of the Society of Jesus there whither I was going, and so I thought I should be in some degree safe under the direction of those fathers, as I had been here. *She goes to Toledo.*

4. It was the good pleasure of our Lord that the lady who sent for me should be so much consoled, that a visible improvement was the immediate result: she was comforted every day more and more. This was very remarkable, because, as I said before, her suffering had reduced her to great straits. Our Lord must have done this in answer to the many prayers which the good people of my acquaintance made for me, that I might prosper in my work. She had a profound fear of God, and was so good, that her great devotion supplied my deficiencies. She conceived a great affection for me—I, too, for her, because of her goodness; but all was as it were a cross for me; for the comforts of her house were a great torment, and her making so much of me made me afraid. I kept my soul continually recollected—I did not dare to be careless: nor was our Lord careless of me; for while I was there, He bestowed the greatest graces upon me, and those graces made me so free, and filled me with such contempt for all I saw,—and the more I saw, the greater my contempt,—that I never failed to treat those ladies, whom to serve would have been a great honour for me, with as much freedom as if I had been their equal.

The Saint's fears about worldly comforts.

5. I derived very great advantages from this, and I said so. I saw that she was a woman, and as much liable to passion and weakness as I was; that rank is of little worth, and the higher it is, the greater the anxiety and trouble it brings. People must be careful of the dignity of their state, which will not suffer them to live at ease; they must eat at fixed hours and by rule, for every thing must be according to their state, and not according to their constitutions; and they have frequently to take food fitted more for their state than for their liking.

Her contempt of the world.

6. So it was that I came to hate the very wish to be a great lady. God deliver me from this wicked, artificial life!—though I believe that this lady, notwithstanding that she was one of the chief personages of the realm, was a woman of great simplicity, and that few were more humble than she was. I was very sorry for her, for I saw how often she had to submit to much that was disagreeable to her, because

Great people slaves of their servants.

of the requirements of her rank. Then, as to servants, though this lady had very good servants, how slight is that little trust that may be put in them! One must not be conversed with more than another; otherwise, he who is so favoured is envied by the rest. This of itself is a slavery, and one of the lies of the world is that it calls such persons masters, who, in my eyes, are nothing else but slaves in a thousand ways.

7. It was our Lord's pleasure that the household of that lady improved in the service of His Majesty during my stay there, though I was not exempted from some trials and some jealousies on the part of some of its members, because of the great affection their mistress had for me. They perhaps must have thought I had some personal interest to serve. Our Lord must have permitted such matters, and others of the same kind, to give me trouble, in order that I might not be absorbed in the comforts which otherwise I had there; and He was pleased to deliver me out of it all with great profit to my soul. *Spiritual fruits of her stay at Toledo.*

8. When I was there, a religious person of great consideration, and with whom I had conversed occasionally some years ago,[1] happened to arrive. When I was at Mass, in a monastery of his Order, near the house in which I was staying, I felt a longing to know the state of his soul,—for I wished him to be a great servant of God,—and I rose up in order to go and speak to him. But as I was then recollected in prayer, it seemed to me a waste of time—for what had I to do in that matter?—and so I returned to my place. Three times, I think, I did this, and at last my good angel prevailed over the evil one, and I went and asked for him; and he came to speak to me in one of the confessionals. We began by asking one another of our past lives, for we had not seen one another for many years. I told him that my life had been one in which my soul had had many trials. He insisted much on my telling him what those trials were. I

[1] F. Vicente Barron, Dominican (see ch. v. § 8), according to F. Bouix, on the authority of Ribera and Yepez; but the Carmelite Father, Fr. Antonio of S. Joseph, in his note on the first Fragment (*Letters*, vol. iv. p. 408), says that it was Fr. Garcia of Toledo, brother of Don Fernando, Duke of Alva; and Don Vicente de la Fuente thinks the opinion of Fr. Antonio the more probable.

said that they were not to be told, and that I was not to tell them. He replied that the Dominican father,[1] of whom I have spoken, knew them, and that, as they were great friends, he could learn them from him, and so I had better tell them without hesitation.

The great gifts of F. V. Barron.
9. The fact is, that it was not in his power not to insist, nor in mine, I believe, to refuse to speak; for notwithstanding all the trouble and shame I used to feel formerly, I spoke of my state to him, and to the rector whom I have referred to before,[2] without any difficulty whatever; on the contrary, it was a great consolation to me; and so I told him all in confession. He seemed to me then more prudent than ever, though I had always looked upon him as a man of great understanding. I considered what high gifts and endowments for great services he had, if he gave himself wholly unto God. I had this feeling now for many years, so that I never saw any one who pleased me much without wishing at once he were given wholly unto God; and sometimes I feel this so keenly, that I can hardly contain myself. Though I long to see every body serve God, yet my desire about those who please me is very vehement, and so I importune our Lord on their behalf.

The Saint's prayers for F. V. Barron.
10. So it happened with respect to this religious. He asked me to pray much for him to God. There was no necessity for his doing so, because I could not do any thing else, and so I went back to my place where I was in the habit of praying alone, and began to pray to our Lord, being extremely recollected, in that my simple, silly way, when I speak without knowing very often what I am saying. It is love that speaks, and my soul is so beside itself, that I do not regard the distance between it and God. That love which I know His Majesty has for it makes it forget itself, and think itself to be one with Him; and so, as being one with Him, and not divided from Him, the soul speaks foolishly. When I had prayed with many tears that the soul of this religious might serve Him truly,—for, though I considered it good, it was not enough for me; I would have it much better,—I remember I said, "O Lord,

[1] Pedro Ibañez (*Bouix*).   [2] Ch. xxxiii. § 11.

Thou must not refuse me this grace; behold him,—he is a fit person to be our friend."

11. Oh, the great goodness and compassion of God! How He regards not the words, but the desire and the will with which they are spoken! How He suffered such a one as I am to speak so boldly before His Majesty! May He be blessed for evermore!

12. I remember that during those hours of prayer on that very night I was extremely distressed by the thought whether I was in the grace of God, and that I could never know whether I was so or not,—not that I wished to know it; I wished, however, to die, in order that I might not live a life in which I was not sure that I was not dead in sin, for there could be no death more dreadful for me than to think that I had sinned against God. I was in great straits at this thought. I implored Him not to suffer me to fall into sin, with great sweetness, dissolved in tears. Then I heard that I might console myself, and trust[1] that I was in a state of grace, because a love of God like mine, together with the graces and feelings with which His Majesty filled my soul, was of such a nature as to be inconsistent with a state of mortal sin. *The Saint's distress about her state.*

13. I was now confident that our Lord would grant my prayer as to that religious. He bade me repeat certain words to him. This I felt much, because I knew not how to speak to him; for this carrying messages to a third person, as I have said,[2] is what I have always felt the most, especially when I did not know how that person *Is made the instrument of the conversion of F. V. Barron.*

---

[1] Father Bouix says that here the word "confiar," "trust," in the printed text, has been substituted by some one for the words " estar cierta," " be certain," which he found in the MS. But Don Vicente de la Fuente retains the old reading " confiar," and makes no observation on the alleged discrepancy between the MS. and the printed text. The observation of F. Bouix, however, is more important, and deserves credit,—for Don Vicente may have failed, through mere inadvertence, to see what F. Bouix saw; and it is also to be remembered that Don Vicente does not say that the MS. on this point has been so closely inspected as to throw any doubt on the positive testimony of F. Bouix.

[2] Ch. xxxiii. § 12.

would take them, nor whether he would not laugh at me. This placed me in great difficulties, but at last I was so convinced I ought to do it, that I believe I made a promise to God I would not neglect that message; and because of the great shame I felt, I wrote it out, and gave it in that way. The result showed clearly enough that it was a message from God, for that religious resolved with great earnestness to give himself to prayer, though he did not do so at once. Our Lord would have him for Himself, so He sent me to tell him certain truths which, without my understanding them, were so much to the purpose that he was astonished. Our Lord must have prepared him to receive them as from His Majesty; and though I am but a miserable sinner myself, yet I made many supplications to our Lord to convert him thoroughly, and to make him hate the pleasures and the things of this life. And so he did—blessed be God!—for every time that he spoke to me I was in a manner beside myself; and if I had not seen it, I should never have believed that our Lord would have given him in so short a time graces so matured, and filled him so full of God, that he seemed to be alive to nothing on earth.

The gifts of God are given at His will.

14. May His Majesty hold him in His hand! If he will go on—and I trust in our Lord he will do so, now that he is so well grounded in the knowledge of himself—he will be one of the most distinguished servants of God, to the great profit of many souls, because he has in a short time had great experience in spiritual things: that is a gift of God, which He gives when He will and as He will, and it depends not on length of time nor extent of service. I do not mean that time and service are not great helps, but very often our Lord will not give to some in twenty years the grace of contemplation, while He gives it to others in one,—His Majesty knoweth why. We are under a delusion when we think that in the course of years we shall come to the knowledge of that which we can in no way attain to but by experience; and thus many are in error, as I have said[1] when they would understand spirituality without being spiritual themselves. I do not mean that a man who is not spiritual, if he is learned, may not direct

[1] Ch. xiv. § 10.

one that is spiritual; but it must be understood that in outward and inward things, in the order of nature, the direction must be an act of reason; and in supernatural things, according to the teaching of the sacred writings. In other matters, let him not distress himself, nor think that he can understand that which he understandeth not; neither let him quench the Spirit;[1] for now another Master, greater than he, is directing these souls, so that they are not left without authority over them.

15. He must not be astonished at this, nor think it impossible: all things are possible to our Lord;[2] he must strive rather to strengthen his faith, and humble himself, because in this matter our Lord imparts perhaps a deeper knowledge to some old woman than to him, though he may be a very learned man. Being thus humble, he will profit souls and himself more than if he affected to be a contemplative without being so; for, I repeat it, if he have no experience, if he have not a most profound humility, whereby he may see that he does not understand, and that the thing is not for that reason impossible, he will do himself but little good, and still less to his penitent. But if he is humble, let him have no fear that our Lord will allow either the one or the other to fall into delusion.

A director should be humble.

16. Now as to this father I am speaking of, as our Lord has given him light in many things, so has he laboured to find out by study that which in this matter can be by study ascertained; for he is a very learned man, and that of which he has no experience himself he seeks to find out from those who have it, and our Lord helps him by increasing his faith, and so he has greatly benefited himself and some other souls, of whom mine is one. As our Lord knew the trials I had to undergo, His Majesty seems to have provided that, when He took away unto Himself some of those who directed me, others might remain, who helped me in my great afflictions, and rendered me great services.

F. Garcia of Toledo.

17. Our Lord wrought a complete change in this father, so much so that he scarcely knew himself, so to speak. He has

---
[1] 1 Thess. v. 19: "Spiritum nolite extinguere."
[2] S. Matt. xix. 27: "Apud Deum autem omnia possibilia sunt."

given him bodily health, so that he may do penance, such as he never had before; for he was sickly. He has given him courage to undertake good works, with other gifts, so that he seems to have received a most special vocation from our Lord. May He be blessed for ever!

18. All these blessings, I believe, came to him through the graces our Lord bestowed upon him in prayer; for they are real. It has been our Lord's pleasure already to try him in certain difficulties, out of which he has come forth like one who knows the true worth of that merit which is gained by suffering persecutions. I trust in the munificence of our Lord that great good will, by his means, accrue to some of his Order and to the Order itself. This is beginning to be understood. I have had great visions on the subject, and our Lord has told me wonderful things of him and of the Rector of the Society of Jesus, whom I am speaking of,[1] and also of two other religious of the Order of S. Dominic, particularly of one who, to his own profit, has actually learned of our Lord certain things which I had formerly understood of him. But there were greater things made known of him to whom I am now referring: one of them I will now relate.

19. I was with him once in the parlour, when in my soul and spirit I felt what great love burned within him, and became as it were lost in ecstasy by considering the greatness of God, who had raised that soul in so short a time to a state so high. It made me ashamed of myself when I saw him listen with so much humility to what I was saying about certain matters of prayer, when I had so little myself that I could speak on the subject to one like him. Our Lord must have borne with me in this on account of the great desire I had to see that religious making great progress. My interview with him did me great good,—it seems as if it left a new fire in my soul, burning with desire to serve our Lord as in the beginning. O my Jesus! what is a soul on fire with Thy love! How we ought to prize it, and implore our Lord to let it live long upon earth! He who has this love should follow after such souls, if it be possible.

The fire of love.

[1] F. Gaspar de Salazar.

20. It is a great thing for a person ill of this disease to find another struck down by it,—it comforts him much to see that he is not alone ; they help one another greatly to suffer and to merit. They are strong with a double strength who are resolved to risk a thousand lives for God, and who long for an opportunity of losing them. They are like soldiers who, to acquire booty, and therewith enrich themselves, wish for war, knowing well that they cannot become rich without it. This is their work—to suffer. Oh, what a blessing it is when our Lord gives light to understand how great is the gain of suffering for Him ! This is never understood till we have left all things ; for if any body is attached to any one thing, that is a proof that he sets some value upon it ; and if he sets any value upon it, it is painful to be compelled to give it up. In that case, every thing is imperfect and lost. The saying is to the purpose here,—he who follows what is lost, is lost himself ; and what greater loss, what greater blindness, what greater calamity, can there be than making much of that which is nothing !

Blessings of detachment.

21. I now return to that which I had begun to speak of. I was in the greatest joy, beholding that soul. It seemed as if our Lord would have me see clearly the treasures He had laid up in it ; and so, when I considered the favour our Lord had shown me, in that I should be the means of so great a good, I recognised my own unworthiness for such an end. I thought much of the graces our Lord had given him, and held myself as indebted for them more than if they had been given to myself. So I gave thanks to our Lord, when I saw that His Majesty had fulfilled my desires and heard my petition that He would raise up persons like him. And now my soul, no longer able to bear the joy that filled it, went forth out of itself, losing itself that it might gain the more. It lost sight of the reflections it was making ; and the hearing of that divine language which the Holy Ghost seemed to speak threw me into a deep trance, which almost deprived me of all sense, though it did not last long. I saw Christ, in exceeding great majesty and glory, manifesting His joy at what was then passing. He told me as much, and it

Joy of the Saint at the graces bestowed on others.

was His pleasure that I should clearly see that He was always present at similar interviews, and how much He was pleased when people thus found their delight in speaking of Him.

Patience under false accusations. 22. On another occasion, when far away from this place, I saw him carried by angels in great glory. I understood by that vision that his soul was making great progress : so it was ; for an evil report was spread abroad against him by one to whom he had rendered a great service, and whose reputation and whose soul he had saved. He bore it with much joy. He did also other things greatly to the honour of God, and underwent more persecutions. I do not think it expedient now to speak further on this point; if, however, you, my father, who know all, should hereafter think otherwise, more might be said to the glory of our Lord.

The Saint's prophecies verified. 23. All the prophecies spoken of before,[1] relating to this house, as well as others, of which I shall speak hereafter, relating to it and to other matters, have been accomplished. Some of them our Lord revealed to me three years before they became known, others earlier, and others later. But I always made them known to my confessor, and to the widow my friend ; for I had leave to communicate with her, as I said before.[2] She, I know, repeated them to others, and these know that I lie not. May God never permit me, in any matter whatever,—much more in things of this importance,—to say any thing but the whole truth !

Sudden deaths of her sister and her brother-in-law. 24. One of my brothers-in-law[3] died suddenly; and as I was in great distress at this, because he had no opportunity of making his confession, our Lord said to me in prayer that my sister also was to die in the same way ; that I must go to her, and make her prepare herself for such an end. I told this to my confessor ; but as he would not let me go, I heard the same warning again ; and now, when he saw this, he told me I might go, and that I should lose nothing by going. My sister was living in the country ; and as I did

[1] Ch. xxvi. § 3.
[2] Ch. xxx. § 3. Doña Guiomar de Ulloa.
[3] Don Martin de Guzman y Barrientos, husband of Maria de Cepeda, the Saint's sister.

not tell her why I came, I gave her what light I could in all things. I made her go frequently to confession, and look to her soul in every thing. She was very good, and did as I asked her. Four or five years after she had begun this practice, and keeping a strict watch over her conscience, she died, with nobody near her, and without being able to go to confession. This was a blessing to her, for it was little more than a week since she had been to her accustomed confession. It was a great joy to me when I heard of her death. She was but a short time in purgatory.

25. I do not think it was quite eight days afterwards when, after Communion, our Lord appeared to me, and was pleased that I should see Him receive my sister into glory. During all those years, after our Lord had spoken to me, until her death, what I then learnt with respect to her was never forgotten either by myself or by my friend, who, when my sister was thus dead, came to me in great amazement at the fulfilment of the prophecy. God be praised for ever, who takes such care of souls that they may not be lost! *The Saint sees her sister received into glory.*

CHAPTER XXXV.

THE FOUNDATION OF THE HOUSE OF S. JOSEPH—THE OBSERVANCE OF HOLY POVERTY THEREIN—HOW THE SAINT LEFT TOLEDO.

1. WHEN I was staying with this lady,[1] already spoken of, in whose house I remained more than six months, our Lord ordained that a holy woman[2] of our *Mary of Jesus.*

[1] Doña Luisa de la Cerda.

[2] Maria of Jesus was the daughter of a Reporter of Causes in the Chancery of Granada; but his name and that of his wife are not known. Maria married, but became a widow soon afterwards. She then became a novice in the Carmelite monastery in Granada, and during her noviciate had revelations, like those of S. Teresa, about a reform of the Order. Her confessor made light of her revelations, and she then referred them to F. Gaspar de Salazar, a confessor of S. Teresa, who was then in Granada. He approved of them, and Maria left the noviciate and went to Rome with

Order should hear of me, who was more than seventy leagues away from the place. She happened to travel this way, and went some leagues out of her road that she might see me. Our Lord had moved her in the same year, and in the same month of the year, that He had moved me, to found another monastery of the Order; and as He had given her this desire, she sold all she possessed, and went to Rome to obtain the necessary faculties. She went on foot, and barefooted. She is a woman of great penance and prayer, and one to whom our Lord gave many graces; and our Lady appeared to her, and commanded her to undertake this work. Her progress in the service of our Lord was so much greater than mine, that I was ashamed to stand in her presence. She showed me Briefs she brought from Rome, and during the fortnight she remained with me we laid our plan for the founding of these monasteries.

Difficulties about the endowment of the monastery.
2. Until I spoke to her, I never knew that our rule, before it was mitigated, required of us that we should possess nothing;[1] nor was I going to found a monastery without revenue,[2] for my intention was that we should be without anxiety about all that was necessary for us, and I did not think of the many anxieties which the possession of property brings in its train. This holy woman, taught of our Lord, perfectly understood—though she could not read—what I was ignorant of, notwithstanding my having

---

two holy women of the Order of St. Francis. The three made the journey on foot, and, moreover, barefooted. Pope Pius IV. heard her prayer, and, looking at her torn and bleeding feet, said to her, "Woman of strong courage, let it be as thou wilt." She returned to Granada, but both the Carmelites and the city refused her permission to found her house there, and some went so far as to threaten to have her publicly whipped. Doña Leonor de Mascareñas gave her a house in Alcala de Henares, of which she took possession Sept. 11, 1562; but the house was formally constituted July 23, 1563, and subjected to the Bishop ten days after (*Reforma*, i. c. 56; and *Don Vicente*, vol. i. p. 255). The latter says that the Chronicler is in error when he asserts that this monastery of Maria of Jesus was endowed.

[1] The fourth chapter of the rule is: "Nullus fratrum dicat sibi aliquid esse proprium, sed sint vobis omnia communia."

[2] See ch. xxxii. § 16.

read the Constitutions[1] so often; and when she told me of it, I thought it right, though I feared they would never consent to this, but would tell me I was committing follies, and that I ought not to do any thing whereby I might bring suffering upon others. If this concerned only myself, nothing should have kept me back,—on the contrary, it would have been my great joy to think that I was observing the counsels of Christ our Lord; for His Majesty had already given me great longings for poverty.[2]

3. As for myself, I never doubted that this was the better part; for I had now for some time wished it were possible in my state to go about begging, for the love of God—to have no house of my own, nor any thing else. But I was afraid that others—if our Lord did not give them the same desire—might live in discontent. Moreover, I feared that it might be the cause of some distraction; for I knew some poor monasteries not very recollected, and I did not consider that their not being recollected was the cause of their poverty, and that their poverty was not the cause of their distraction: distraction never makes people richer, and God never fails those who serve Him. In short, I was weak in faith; but not so this servant of God. *The Saint's love of poverty.*

4. As I took the advice of many in every thing, I found scarcely any one of this opinion—neither my confessor, nor the learned men to whom I spoke of it. *The advice of others against her.* They gave me so many reasons the other way, that I did not know what to do. But when I saw what the rule required, and that poverty was the more perfect way, I could not persuade myself to allow an endowment. And though they did persuade me now and then that they were right, yet, when I returned to my prayer, and saw Christ on the cross, so poor and destitute, I could not bear to be rich, and I implored Him with tears so to order matters that I might be poor as He was.

---

[1] The Constitutions which the Saint read in the monastery of the Incarnation must have been the Constitutions grounded on the Mitigated Rule which was sanctioned by Eugenius IV. (*Romani Pontificis*, A.D. 1432).

[2] See *Relation*, i. § 10.

The Saint is dissuaded from her purpose.

5. I found that so many inconveniences resulted from an endowment, and saw that it was the cause of so much trouble, and even distraction, that I did nothing but dispute with the learned. I wrote to that Dominican friar[1] who was helping us, and he sent back two sheets by way of reply, full of objections and theology against my plan, telling me that he had thought much on the subject. I answered that, in order to escape from my vocation, the vow of poverty I had made, and the perfect observance of the counsels of Christ, I did not want any theology to help me, and in this case I should not thank him for his learning. If I found any one who would help me, it pleased me much. The lady in whose house I was staying was a great help to me in this matter. Some at first told me that they agreed with me; afterwards, when they had considered the matter longer, they found in it so many inconveniences, that they insisted on my giving it up. I told them that, though they changed their opinion so quickly, I would abide by the first.

S. Peter of Alcantara defends her.

6. At this time, because of my entreaties,—for the lady had never seen the holy friar, Peter of Alcantara,—it pleased our Lord to bring him to her house. As he was a great lover of poverty, and had lived in it for so many years, he knew well the treasures it contains, and so he was a great help to me; he charged me on no account whatever to give up my purpose. Now, having this opinion and sanction,—no one was better able to give it, because he knew what it was by long experience,—I made up my mind to seek no further advice.

And our Lord encourages her in a trance.

7. One day, when I was very earnestly commending the matter to God, our Lord told me that I must by no means give up my purpose of founding the monastery in poverty; it was His will, and the will of His Father: He would help me. I was in a trance; and the effects were such, that I could have no doubt it came from God. On another occasion, He said to me that endowments bred confusion, with other things in praise of poverty; and assured me that whosoever served Him would never be in

[1] F. Pedro Ibañez.

want of the necessary means of living: and this want, as I have said,[1] I never feared myself. Our Lord changed the dispositions also of the licentiate,—I am speaking of the Dominican friar,[2]—who, as I said, wrote to me that I should not found the monastery without an endowment. Now, I was in the greatest joy at hearing this; and having these opinions in my favour, it seemed to me nothing less than the possession of all the wealth of the world, when I had resolved to live in poverty for the love of God.

8. At this time, my Provincial withdrew the order and the obedience, in virtue of which I was staying in that house.[3] He left it to me to do as I liked: if I wished to return, I might do so; if I wished to remain, I might also do so for a certain time. But during that time the elections in my monastery[4] would take place, and I was told that many of the nuns wished to lay on me the burden of superiorship. The very thought of this alone was a great torment to me; for, though I was resolved to undergo readily any kind of martyrdom for God, I could not persuade myself at all to accept this; for, putting aside the great trouble it involved,—because the nuns were so many,—and other reasons, such as that I never wished for it, nor for any other office,—on the contrary, had always refused them,—it seemed to me that my conscience would be in great danger; and so I praised God that I was not then in my convent. I wrote to my friends, and asked them not to vote for me. *The Provincial permits her to leave Toledo.*

9. When I was rejoicing that I was not in that trouble, our Lord said to me that I was on no account to keep away; that as I longed for a cross, there was one ready for me, and that a heavy one: that I was not to throw it away, but go on with resolution; He would help me, and I must go at once. I was very much distressed, and did nothing but weep, because I thought that my cross was to be the office of prioress; and, as I have just said, I could not persuade myself that it would be at all good for my *Our Lord promises a cross to the Saint.*

---

[1] Ch. xi. § 2.   [2] F. Pedro Ibañez.
[3] The house of Doña Luisa, in Toledo.
[4] The monastery of the Incarnation, Avila.

soul—nor could I see any means by which it could be. I told my confessor of it, and he commanded me to return at once: that to do so was clearly the more perfect way; and that, because the heat was very great,—it would be enough if I arrived before the election,—I might wait a few days, in order that my journey might do me no harm.

<small>The Saint resolves to make the journey.</small> 10. But our Lord had ordered it otherwise. I had to go at once, because the uneasiness I felt was very great; and I was unable to pray, and thought I was failing in obedience to the commandments of our Lord, and that, as I was happy and contented where I was, I would not go to meet trouble. All my service of God there was lip-service: why did I, having the opportunity of living in greater perfection, neglect it? If I died on the road, let me die. Besides, my soul was in great straits, and our Lord had taken from me all sweetness in prayer. In short, I was in such a state of torment, that I begged the lady to let me go; for my confessor, when he saw the plight I was in, had already told me to go, God having moved him as He had moved me. The lady felt my departure very much, and that was another pain to bear; for it had cost her much trouble, and diverse importunities of the Provincial, to have me in her house.

<small>The Saint accepts the cross with joy.</small> 11. I considered it a very great thing for her to have given her consent, when she felt it so much; but, as she was a person who feared God exceedingly, —and as I told her, among many other reasons, that my going away tended greatly to His service, and held out the hope that I might possibly return,—she gave way, but with much sorrow. I was now not sorry myself at coming away, for I knew that it was an act of greater perfection, and for the service of God. So the pleasure I had in pleasing God took away the pain of quitting that lady,—whom I saw suffering so keenly,—and others to whom I owed much, particularly my confessor of the Society of Jesus, in whom I found all I needed. But the greater the consolations I lost for our Lord's sake, the greater was my joy in losing them. I could not understand it, for I had a clear consciousness of these two contrary feelings—pleasure, consolation, and joy in that which weighed down my

soul with sadness. I was joyful and tranquil, and had opportunities of spending many hours in prayer; and I saw that I was going to throw myself into a fire; for our Lord had already told me that I was going to carry a heavy cross,—though I never thought it would be so heavy as I afterwards found it to be,—and yet I went forth rejoicing. I was distressed because I had not already begun the fight, since it was our Lord's will that I should be in it. Thus His Majesty gave me strength, and established it in my weakness.[1]

12. As I have just said, I could not understand how this could be. I thought of this illustration: if I were possessed of a jewel, or any other thing which gave me great pleasure, and it came to my knowledge that a person whom I loved more than myself, and whose satisfaction I preferred to my own, wished to have it, it would give me great pleasure to deprive myself of it, because I would give all I possessed to please that person. Now, as the pleasure of giving pleasure to that person surpasses any pleasure I have in that jewel myself, I should not be distressed in giving away that or any thing else I loved, nor at the loss of that pleasure which the possession of it gave me. So now, though I wished to feel some distress when I saw that those whom I was leaving felt my going so much, yet, notwithstanding my naturally grateful disposition,—which, under other circumstances, would have been enough to cause me great pain,—at this time, though I wished to feel it, I could feel none. *The Saint analyses this state of mind.*

13. The delay of another day was so serious a matter in the affairs of this holy house, that I know not how they could have been settled if I had waited. Oh, God is great! I am often lost in wonder when I consider and see the special help which His Majesty gave me towards the establishment of this little cell of God,—for such I believe it to be,—the lodging wherein His Majesty delights; for once, when I was in prayer, He told me that this house was the paradise of His delight.[2] It seems, then, that His Majesty has chosen these whom he has drawn hither, among whom I am *The monastery of St. Joseph.*

[1] 2 Cor. xii. 9 : "Virtus in infirmitate perficitur."
[2] See *Way of Perfection*, ch. xxii.; but ch. xiii. ed. Doblado.

living very much ashamed of myself.[1] I could not have even wished for souls such as they are for the purpose of this house, where enclosure, poverty, and prayer are so strictly observed; they submit with so much joy and contentment, that every one of them thinks herself unworthy of the grace of being received into it,—some of them particularly; for our Lord has called them out of the vanity and dissipation of the world, in which, according to its laws, they might have lived contented. Our Lord has multiplied their joy, so that they see clearly how He has given them a hundredfold for the one thing they have left,[2] and for which they cannot thank His Majesty enough. Others He has advanced from well to better. To the young He gives courage and knowledge, so that they may desire nothing else, and also to understand that to live away from all things of this life is to live in greater peace even here below. To those who are no longer young, and whose health is weak, He gives — and has given—the strength to undergo the same austerities and penances with all the others.

<small>The love of God makes all things possible.</small> 14. O my Lord! how Thou dost show Thy power! There is no need to seek reasons for Thy will; for with Thee, against all natural reason, all things are possible: so that Thou teachest clearly there is no need of any thing but of loving Thee[3] in earnest, and really giving up every thing for Thee, in order that Thou, O my Lord, mightest make every thing easy. It is well said that

[1] See *Foundations*, ch. i. § 1.
[2] S. Matt. xix. 29 : "Et omnis qui reliquerit domum . . . . propter nomen Meum, centuplum accipiet, et vitam æternam possidebit."
[3] When the workmen were busy with the building, a nephew of the Saint, the child of her sister and Don Juan de Ovalle, was struck by some falling stones, and killed. The workmen took the child to his mother; and the Saint, then in the house of Doña Guiomar de Ulloa, was sent for. Doña Guiomar took the dead boy into her arms, gave him to the Saint, saying that it was a grievous blow to the father and mother, and that she must obtain his life from God. The Saint took the body, and, laying it in her lap, ordered those around her to cease their lamentations, of whom her sister was naturally the loudest, and be silent. Then, covering her face and her body with her veil, she prayed to God, and God gave the child his life again. The little boy soon after ran up to his aunt and thanked her for what she had done. In after years the child used to say to the

Thou feignest to make Thy law difficult:[1] I do not see it, nor do I feel that the way that leadeth unto Thee is narrow. I see it as a royal road, and not a pathway; a road upon which whosoever really enters, travels most securely. No mountain-passes and no cliffs are near it: these are the occasions of sin. I call that a pass,—a dangerous pass,—and a narrow road, which has on one side a deep hollow, into which one stumbles, and on the other a precipice, over which they who are careless fall, and are dashed to pieces. He who loves Thee, O my God, travels safely by the open and royal road, far away from the precipice: he has scarcely stumbled at all, when Thou stretchest forth Thy hand to save him. One fall—yea, many falls—if he does but love Thee, and not the things of the world, are not enough to make him perish; he travels in the valley of humility. I cannot understand what it is that makes men afraid of the way of perfection.

15. May our Lord of His mercy make us see what a poor security we have in the midst of dangers so manifest, when we live like the rest of the world; and that true security consists in striving to advance in the way of God! Let us fix our eyes upon Him, and have no fear that the Sun of Justice will ever set, or suffer us to travel to our ruin by night, unless we first look away from Him. People are not afraid of living in the midst of lions, every one of whom seems eager to tear them: I am speaking of honours, pleasures, and the like joys, as the world calls them: and herein the devil seems to make us afraid of ghosts. I am astonished a thousand times, and ten thousand times would I relieve myself by weeping, and proclaim aloud my own great blindness and wickedness, if, perchance, it might help in some measure to open their eyes. May He, who is almighty, of His goodness open their eyes, and never suffer mine to be blind again!

Our true safety lies in perfection.

Saint that, as she had deprived him of the bliss of heaven by bringing him back to life, she was bound to see that he did not suffer loss. Don Gonzalo died three years after S. Teresa, when he was twenty-eight years of age (*Reforma*, i. c. 40, § 2).

[1] Ps. xciii. 20: "Qui fingis laborem in præcepto."

CHAPTER XXXVI.

THE FOUNDATION OF THE MONASTERY OF S. JOSEPH—PERSECUTION AND TEMPTATIONS—GREAT INTERIOR TRIAL OF THE SAINT, AND HER DELIVERANCE.

The Saint leaves Toledo.
1. HAVING now left that city,[1] I travelled in great joy, resolved to suffer most willingly whatever our Lord might be pleased to lay upon me. On the night of my arrival here,[2] came also from Rome the commission and the Brief for the erection of the monastery.[3] I was astonished myself, and so were those who knew how our Lord had hastened my coming, when they saw how necessary it was, and in what a moment our Lord had brought me back.[4] I found here the Bishop[5] and the holy friar, Peter of Alcantara, and that nobleman,[6] the great servant of God, in whose house the holy man was staying; for he was a man who was in the habit of receiving the servants of God in his house. These two prevailed on the Bishop to accept the monastery, which was no small thing, because it was founded in poverty; but he was so great a lover of those whom he saw determined to serve our Lord, that he was immediately drawn to give them His protection. It was the approbation of the holy old man,[7] and the great trouble he took to make now this one, now that one, help us, that did the whole work. If I had not come at the moment, as I have just said, I do not see how it could have been done; for the holy man was here but a short time,—I think not quite eight days,—during which he was also ill; and

[1] Toledo.   [2] Avila. In the beginning of June 1562.
[3] See ch. xxxiv. § 2. The Brief was dated Feb. 7, 1562, the third year of Pius IV. (*De la Fuente*).
[4] The Brief was addressed to Doña Aldonza de Guzman, and to Doña Guiomar de Ulloa, her daughter.
[5] Don Alvaro de Mendoza (*De la Fuente*).
[6] Don Francisco de Salcedo.
[7] S. Peter of Alcantara. "Truly this is the house of S. Joseph," were the Saint's words when he saw the rising monastery; "for I see it is the little hospice of Bethlehem" (*De la Fuente*).

almost immediately afterwards our Lord took him to Himself.[1] It seems as if His Majesty reserved him till this affair was ended, because now for some time—I think for more than two years—he had been very ill.

2. Every thing was done in the utmost secrecy; and if it had not been so, I do not see how any thing could have been done at all; for the people of the city were against us, as it appeared afterwards. Our Lord ordained that one of my brothers-in-law[2] should be ill, and his wife away, and himself in such straits that my superiors gave me leave to remain with him. Nothing, therefore, was found out, though some persons had their suspicions; still, they did not believe. It was very wonderful, for his illness lasted only no longer than was necessary for our affair; and when it was necessary he should recover his health, that I might be disengaged, and he leave the house empty, our Lord restored him; and he was astonished at it himself.[3]

The providential illness of the Saint's brother-in-law.

3. I had much trouble in persuading this person and that to allow the foundation; I had to nurse the sick man, and obtain from the workmen the hasty preparation of the house, so that it might have the form of a monastery: but much remained still to be done. My friend was not here,[4] for we thought it best she should be away, in order the better to hide our purpose. I saw that every thing depended on haste, for many reasons, one of which was that I was afraid I might be ordered back to my monastery at any moment. I was troubled by so many things, that I suspected my cross had been sent me, though it seemed but a light one in comparison with that which I understood our Lord meant me to carry.

Her troubles and anxieties about the new foundation.

[1] In less than three months, perhaps; for S. Peter died in the sixty-third year of his age, Oct. 18, 1562, and in less than eight weeks after the foundation of the monastery of S. Joseph.

[2] Señor Juan de Ovalle.

[3] When he saw that the Saint had made all her arrangements, he knew the meaning of his illness, and said to her, "It is not necessary I should be ill any longer" (*Ribera*, i. c. 17).

[4] Doña Guiomar de Ulloa was now in her native place, Ciudad Toro.

4. When every thing was settled, our Lord was pleased that some of us should take the habit on S. Bartholomew's Day. The most Holy Sacrament began to dwell in the house at the same time.[1] With full sanction and authority, then, our monastery of our most glorious father S. Joseph was founded in the year 1562.[2] I was there myself to give the habit, with two nuns[3] of the house to which we belonged, who happened then to be absent from it. As the house which thus became a monastery was that of my brother-in-law—I said before[4] that he had bought it, for the purpose of concealing our plan—I was there myself with the permission of my 'superiors; and I did nothing without the advice of learned men, in order that I might not break, in a single point, my vow of obedience. As these persons considered what I was doing to be most advantageous for the whole Order, on many accounts, they told me—though I was acting secretly, and taking care my superiors should know nothing—that I might go on. If they had told me that there was the slightest imperfection in the whole matter, I would have given up the founding of a thousand monasteries,—how much more, then, this one! I am certain of this; for though I longed to withdraw from every thing more and more, and to follow my rule and vocation in the greatest perfection and seclusion, yet I wished to do so only conditionally; for if I should have learnt that it would be for the greater honour of our Lord to abandon it,

The monastery of S. Joseph founded August 24, 1562.

[1] The Mass was said by Gaspar Daza. See *infra*, § 18; *Reforma*, i. c. xliv. § 3.

[2] The bell which the Saint had provided for the convent weighed less than three pounds, and remained in the monastery for a hundred years, till it was sent, by order of the General, to the monastery of Pastrana, where the general chapters were held. There the friars assembled at the sound of the bell, which rang for the first Mass of the Carmelite Reform (*Reforma*, i. c. xliv. § 1).

[3] They were Doña Ines and Doña Ana de Tapia, cousins of the Saint. There were present also Don Gonzalo de Aranda, Don Francisco Salcedo, Julian of Avila, priest; Doña Juana de Ahumada, the Saint's sister; with her husband, Juan de Ovalle. The Saint herself retained her own habit, making no change, because she had not the permission of her superiors (*Reforma*, i. c. xliv. § 3).

[4] Ch. xxxiii. § 14.

I would have done so, as I did before on one occasion,[1] in all peace and contentment.

5. I felt as if I were in bliss, when I saw the most Holy Sacrament reserved, with four poor orphans,[2]— for they were received without a dowry,—and great servants of God, established in the house. It was our aim from the beginning to receive only those who, by their example, might be the foundation on which we could build up what we had in view—great perfection and prayer—and effect a work which I believed to be for the service of our Lord, and to the honour of the habit of His glorious Mother. This was my anxiety. It was also a great consolation to me that I had done that which our Lord had so often commanded me to do, and that there was one church more in this city dedicated to my glorious father S. Joseph. Not that I thought I had done any thing myself, for I have never thought so, and do not think so even now; I always looked upon it as the work of our Lord. My part in it was so full of imperfections, that I look upon myself rather as a person in fault than as one to whom any thanks are due. But it was a great joy to me when I saw His Majesty make use of me, who am so worthless, as His instrument in so grand a work. I was therefore in great joy,—so much so, that I was, as it were, beside myself, lost in prayer.

And in perfect poverty.

6. When all was done—it might have been about three or four hours afterwards—Satan returned to the spiritual fight against me, as I shall now relate. He suggested to me that perhaps I had been wrong in what I had

The Saint tempted by Satan.

---

[1] Ch. xxxiii. § 3.
[2] The first of these was Antonia de Henao, a penitent of S. Peter of Alcantara, and who wished to enter a religious house far away from Avila, her home. S. Peter kept her for S. Teresa. She was called from this day forth Antonia of the Holy Ghost. The second was Maria de la Paz, brought up by Doña Guiomar de Ulloa. Her name was Maria of the Cross. The third was Ursola de los Santos. She retained her family name as Ursola of the Saints. It was Gaspar Daza who brought her to the Saint. The fourth was Maria de Avila, sister of Julian the priest, and she was called Mary of S. Joseph. It was at this house, too, that the Saint herself exchanged her ordinary designation of Doña Teresa de Ahumada for Teresa of Jesus (*Reforma*, i. c. xliv. § 2).

done; perhaps I had failed in my obedience, in having brought it about without the commandment of the Provincial. I did certainly think that the Provincial would be displeased because I had placed the monastery under the jurisdiction of the Bishop[1] without telling him of it beforehand; though, as he would not acknowledge the monastery himself, and as I had not changed mine, it seemed to me that perhaps he would not care much about the matter. Satan also suggested whether the nuns would be contented to live in so strict a house, whether they could always find food, whether I had not done a silly thing, and what had I to do with it, when I was already in a monastery? All our Lord had said to me, all the opinions I had heard, and all the prayers which had been almost uninterrupted for more than two years, were completely blotted out of my memory, just as if they had never been. The only thing I remembered was my own opinion; and every virtue, with faith itself, was then suspended within me, so that I was without strength to practise any one of them, or to defend myself against so many blows.

7. The devil also would have me ask myself how *Her extreme distress.* I could think of shutting myself up in so strict a house, when I was subject to so many infirmities; how could I bear so penitential a life, and leave a house large and pleasant, where I had been always so happy, and where I had so many friends?—perhaps I might not like those of the new monastery; I had taken on myself a heavy obligation, and might possibly end in despair. He also suggested that perhaps it was he himself who had contrived it, in order to rob me of my peace and rest, so that, being unable to pray, I might be disquieted, and so lose my soul. Thoughts of this kind he put before me; and they were so many, that I could think of nothing else; and with them came such distress, obscurity, and darkness of soul as I can never describe. When I found myself in this state, I went and placed myself before the most Holy Sacrament, though I could not pray to Him; so great was my anguish, that I was like one in the agony of death. I could not make the matter known to any one, because no confessor had as yet been appointed.

[1] See *Foundations*, ch. ii. § 1, and ch. xxxi. § 1.

8. O my God, how wretched is this life! No joy is lasting; every thing is liable to change. Only a moment ago, I do not think I would have exchanged my joy with any man upon earth; and the very grounds of that joy so tormented me now, that I knew not what to do with myself. Oh, if we did but consider carefully the events of our life, every one of us would learn from experience how little we ought to make either of its pleasures or of its pains! Certainly this was, I believe, one of the most distressing moments I ever passed in all my life; my spirit seemed to forecast the great sufferings in store for me, though they never were so heavy as this was, if it had continued. But our Lord would not let His poor servant suffer, for in all my troubles He never failed to succour me; so it was now. He gave me a little light, so that I might see it was the work of the devil, and might understand the truth, namely, that it was nothing else but an attempt on his part to frighten me with his lies. So I began to call to mind my great resolutions to serve our Lord, and my desire to suffer for His sake; and I thought that if I carried them out, I must not seek to be at rest; that if I had my trials, they would be meritorious; and that if I had troubles, and endured them in order to please God, it would serve me for purgatory. What was I, then, afraid of? If I longed for tribulations, I had them now; and my gain lay in the greatest opposition. Why, then, did I fail in courage to serve One to whom I owed so much? *Unimportance of events in this life.*

9. After making these and other reflections, and doing great violence to myself, I promised before the most Holy Sacrament to do all in my power to obtain permission to enter this house, and, if I could do it with a good conscience, to make a vow of enclosure. When I had done this, the devil fled in a moment, and left me calm and peaceful, and I have continued so ever since; and the enclosure, penances, and other rules of this house are to me, in their observance, so singularly sweet and light, the joy I have is so exceedingly great, that I am now and then thinking what on earth I could have chosen which should be more delightful. I know not whether this may not be the cause of my being in better health than I *How she overcomes Satan.*

was ever before, or whether it be that our Lord, because it is needful and reasonable that I should do as all the others do, gives me this comfort of keeping the whole rule, though with some difficulty. However, all who know my infirmities are astonished at my strength. Blessed be He who giveth it all, and in whose strength I am strong !

<small>Why the temptation was permitted.</small> 10. Such a contest left me greatly fatigued, and laughing at Satan; for I saw clearly it was he. As I have never known what it is to be discontented because I am a nun—no, not for an instant—during more than twenty-eight years of religion, I believe that our Lord suffered me to be thus tempted, that I might understand how great a mercy He had shown me herein, and from what torment He had delivered me, and that if I saw any one in like trouble I might not be alarmed at it, but have pity on her, and be able to console her.

<small>Excitement of the nuns of the monastery of the Incarnation.</small> 11. Then, when this was over, I wished to rest myself a little after our dinner; for during the whole of that night I had scarcely rested at all, and for some nights previously I had had much trouble and anxiety, while every day was full of toil; for the news of what we had done had reached my monastery, and was spread through the city. There arose a great outcry, for the reasons I mentioned before,[1] and there was some apparent ground for it. The prioress[2] sent for me to come to her immediately. When I received the order, I went at once, leaving the nuns in great distress. I saw clearly enough that there were troubles before me; but as the work was really done, I did not care much for that. I prayed and implored our Lord to help me, and my father S. Joseph to bring me back to his house. I offered up to him all I was to suffer, rejoicing greatly that I had the opportunity of suffering for his honour and of doing him service. I went persuaded that I should be put in prison at once; but this would have been a great comfort, because I should have nobody to speak to, and might have some rest and solitude, of which I was in great need; for so much intercourse with people had worn me out.

[1] Ch. xxxiii. §§ 1, 2.   [2] Of the Incarnation.

12. When I came and told the prioress what I had done, she was softened a little. They all sent for the Provincial, and the matter was reserved for him. When he came, I was summoned to judgment, rejoicing greatly at seeing that I had something to suffer for our Lord. I did not think I had offended against his Majesty, or against my Order, in any thing I had done; on the contrary, I was striving with all my might to exalt my Order, for which I would willingly have died,—for my whole desire was that its rule might be observed in all perfection. I thought of Christ receiving sentence, and I saw how this of mine would be less than nothing. I confessed my fault, as if I had been very much to blame; and so I seemed to every one who did not know all the reasons. After the Provincial had rebuked me sharply—though not with the severity which my fault deserved, nor according to the representations made to him—I would not defend myself, for I was determined to bear it all; on the contrary, I prayed him to forgive and punish, and be no longer angry with me. *The Saint is reprimanded by the Provincial.*

13. I saw well enough that they condemned me on some charges of which I was innocent, for they said I had founded the monastery that I might be thought much of, and to make myself a name, and for other reasons of that kind. But on other points I understood clearly that they were speaking the truth, as when they said that I was more wicked than the other nuns. They asked, how could I, who had not kept the rule in that house, think of keeping it in another of stricter observance? They said I was giving scandal in the city, and setting up novelties. All this neither troubled nor distressed me in the least, though I did seem to feel it, lest I should appear to make light of what they were saying. *The Saint submits to the censure of the Provincial,*

14. At last the Provincial commanded me to explain my conduct before the nuns, and I had to do it. As I was perfectly calm, and our Lord helped me, I explained every thing in such a way that neither the Provincial nor those who were present found any reason to condemn me. Afterwards I spoke more plainly to the Provincial alone; *Who orders her to give her explanation.*

he was very much satisfied, and promised, if the new monastery prospered, and the city became quiet, to give me leave to live in it. Now the outcry in the city was very great, as I am going to tell. Two or three days after this, the governor, certain members of the council of the city and of the Chapter, came together, and resolved that the new monastery should not be allowed to exist, that it was a visible wrong to the state, that the most Holy Sacrament should be removed, and that they would not suffer us in any way to go on with our work.

Serious danger of the monastery.   15. They assembled all the Orders—that is, two learned men from each—to give their opinion. Some were silent, others condemned; in the end, they resolved that the monastery should be broken up. Only one[1] —he was of the Order of S. Dominic, and objected, not to the monastery itself, but to the foundation of it in poverty— said that there was no reason why it should be thus dissolved, that the matter ought to be well considered, that there was time enough, that it was the affair of the bishop, with other things of that kind. This was of great service to us, for they were angry enough to proceed to its destruction at once, and it was fortunate they did not. In short, the monastery must exist; our Lord was pleased to have it, and all of them could do nothing against His will. They gave their reasons, and showed their zeal for good, and thus, without offending God, made me suffer together with all those who were in favour of the monastery; there were not many, but they suffered much persecution. The inhabitants were so excited, that they talked of

[1] F. Domingo Bañes, the great commentator on S. Thomas. On the margin of the MS., Bañes has with his own hand written : "This was at the end of August 1562. I was present, and gave this opinion. I am writing this in May" (the day of the month is not legible) " 1575, and the mother has now founded nine monasteries *en gran religion*" (*De la Fuente*). At this time Bañes did not know, and had never seen, the Saint ; he undertook her defence simply because he saw that her intentions were good, and the means she made use of for founding the monastery lawful, seeing that she had received the commandment to do so from the Pope. Bañes testifies thus in the depositions made in Salamanca in 1591, in the Saint's process. See vol. ii. p 376 of Don Vicente's edition.

nothing else; every one condemned me, and hurried to the Provincial and to my monastery.

16. I was no more distressed by what they said of me than if they had said nothing; but I was afraid the monastery would be destroyed: that was painful; so also was it to see those persons who helped me lose their credit and suffer so much annoyance. But as to what was said of myself I was rather glad, and if I had had any faith I should not have been troubled at all; but a slight failing in one virtue is enough to put all the others to sleep. I was therefore extremely distressed during the two days on which those assemblies of which I have spoken were held. In the extremity of my trouble, our Lord said to me: "Knowest thou not that I am the Almighty? what art thou afraid of?" He made me feel assured that the monastery would not be broken up, and I was exceedingly comforted. The informations taken were sent up to the king's council, and an order came back for a report on the whole matter. *The Saint's patience and confidence.*

17. Here was the beginning of a grand lawsuit: the city sent delegates to the court, and some must be sent also to defend the monastery: but I had no money, nor did I know what to do. Our Lord provided for us; for the Father-Provincial never ordered me not to meddle in the matter. He is so great a lover of all that is good, that, though he did not help us, he would not be against our work. Neither did he authorise me to enter the house till he saw how it would end. Those servants of God who were in it were left alone, and did more by their prayers than I did with all my negotiations, though the affair needed the utmost attention. Now and then every thing seemed to fail; particularly one day, before the Provincial came, when the prioress ordered me to meddle no more with it, and to give it up altogether. I betook myself to God, and said, "O Lord, this house is not mine; it was founded for Thee; and now that there is no one to take up the cause, do Thou protect it." I now felt myself in peace, and as free from anxiety as if the whole world were on my side in the matter; and at once I looked upon it as safe.[1] *The Saint has to defend the monastery.*

[1] See ch. xxxix. § 24.

The Saint's friends suffer for her. 18. A very great servant of God, and a lover of all perfection, a priest[1] who had helped me always, went to the court on this business, and took great pains. That holy nobleman[2] of whom I have often spoken laboured much on our behalf, and helped us in every way. He had much trouble and persecution to endure, and I always found a father in him, and do so still. All those who helped us, our Lord filled with such fervour as made them consider our affair as their own, as if their own life and reputation were at stake; and yet it was nothing to them, except in so far as it regarded the service of our Lord. His Majesty visibly helped the priest I have spoken of before,[3] who was also one of those who gave us great help when the Bishop sent him as his representative to one of the great meetings. There he stood alone against all; at last he pacified them by means of certain propositions, which obtained us a little respite. But that was not enough; for they were ready to spend their lives, if they could but destroy the monastery. This servant of God was he who gave the habit and reserved the most Holy Sacrament, and he was the object of much persecution. This attack lasted about six months: to relate in detail the heavy trials we passed through would be too tedious.

An endowment proposed for the monastery. 19. I wondered at what Satan did against a few poor women, and also how all people thought that merely twelve women, with a prioress, could be so hurtful to the city,—for they were not to be more,—I say this to those who opposed us,—and living such austere lives; for if any harm or error came of it, it would all fall upon them. Harm to the city there could not be in any way; and yet the people thought there was so much in it, that they opposed us with a good conscience. At last they resolved they would tolerate us if we were endowed, and in consideration of that would suffer us to remain. I was so distressed at the trouble of all those who were on our side—more than at my own— that I thought it would not be amiss, till the people were

---

[1] Gonzalo de Aranda (*De la Fuente*).
[2] Don Francisco de Salcedo (*ibid.*).
[3] Ch. xxiii. § 6; Gaspar Daza (*ibid.*).

pacified, to accept an endowment, but afterwards to resign it. At other times, too, wicked and imperfect as I am, I thought that perhaps our Lord wished it to be so, seeing that, without accepting it, we could not succeed; and so I consented to the compromise.

20. The night before the settlement was to be made, I was in prayer,—the discussion of the terms of it had already begun,—when our Lord said to me that I must do nothing of the kind; for if we began with an endowment, they would never allow us to resign it. He said some other things also. The same night, the holy friar, Peter of Alcantara, appeared to me. He was then dead.[1] But he had written to me before his death—for he knew the great opposition and persecution we had to bear—that he was glad the foundation was so much spoken against; it was a sign that our Lord would be exceedingly honoured in the monastery, seeing that Satan was so earnest against it; and that I was by no means to consent to an endowment. He urged this upon me twice or thrice in that letter, and said that if I persisted in this every thing would succeed according to my wish. *The Saint is warned by our Lord not to accept an endowment.*

21. At this time I had already seen him twice since his death, and the great glory he was in, and so I was not afraid,—on the contrary, I was very glad; for he always appeared as a glorified body in great happiness, and the vision made me very happy too. I remember that he told me, the first time I saw him, among other things, when speaking of the greatness of his joy, that the penance he had done was a blessed thing for him, in that it had obtained so great a reward. But, as I think I have spoken of this before,[2] I will now say no more than that he showed himself severe on this occasion: he merely said that I was on no account to accept an endowment, and asked why it was I did not take his advice. He then disappeared. I remained in astonishment, and the next day told the nobleman—for I went to him in all my trouble, as to one who did more than others for us in the matter—what had taken place, and charged him not to consent to the endowment, but to let the lawsuit go on. He was more *S. Peter of Alcantara appears to the Saint.*

[1] He died Oct. 18, 1562.   [2] Ch. xxvii. § 18.

firm on this point than I was, and was therefore greatly pleased; he told me afterwards how much he disliked the compromise.

The Saint is troubled by the advice of a prudent person.

22. After this, another personage—a great servant of God, and with good intentions—came forward, who, now that the matter was in good train, advised us to put it in the hands of learned men. This brought on trouble enough; for some of those who helped me agreed to do so; and this plot of Satan was one of the most difficult of all to unravel. Our Lord was my helper throughout. Writing thus briefly, it is impossible for me to explain what took place during the two years that passed between the beginning and the completion of the monastery: the last six months and the first six months were the most painful.

Father Pedro Ibanez helps her.

23. When at last the city was somewhat calm, the licentiate father, the Dominican friar[1] who helped us, exerted himself most skilfully on our behalf. Though not here at the time, our Lord brought him here at a most convenient moment for our service, and it seems that His Majesty brought him for that purpose only. He told me afterwards that he had no reasons for coming, and that he heard of our affair as if by chance. He remained here as long as we wanted him: and on going away he prevailed, by some means, on the Father-Provincial to permit me to enter this house, and to take with me some of the nuns[2]—such a permission seemed impossible in so short a time—for the performance of the Divine Office, and the training of those who were in this house: the day of our coming was a most joyful day for me.[3]

[1] "El Padre Presentado, Dominico. Presentado en algunas Religiones es cierto titulo de grado que es respeto del Maestro Como Licenciado'' (*Covarruvias, in voce* Presente). The father was Fra Pedro Ibañez. See ch. xxxviii. § 15.

[2] From the monastery of the Incarnation. These were Ana of S. John, Ana of All the Angels, Maria Isabel, and Isabel of S. Paul. S. Teresa was a simple nun, living under obedience to the prioress of S. Joseph, Ana of S. John, and intended so to remain. But the nuns applied to the Bishop of Avila and to the Provincial of the Order, who, listening to the complaints of the sisters, compelled the Saint to be their prioress. See *Reforma*, i. c. xlvii. § 4.

[3] Mid-Lent of 1563.

24. While praying in the church, before I went into the house, and being as it were in a trance, I saw Christ; who, as it seemed to me, received me with great affection, placed a crown on my head, and thanked me for what I had done for His Mother. On another occasion, when all of us remained in the choir in prayer after Compline, I saw our Lady in exceeding glory, in a white mantle, with which she seemed to cover us all. I understood by that the high degree of glory to which our Lord would raise the religious of this house. *Takes possession of the monastery of S. Joseph.*

25. When we had begun to sing the Office, the people began to have a great devotion to the monastery: more nuns were received, and our Lord began to stir up those who had been our greatest persecutors to become great benefactors, and give alms to us. *The people flock to the monastery with their alms.* In this way they came to approve of what they had condemned; and so, by degrees, they withdrew from the lawsuit, and would say that they now felt it to be a work of God, since His Majesty had been pleased to carry it on in the face of so much opposition. And now there is not one who thinks that it would have been right not to have founded the monastery: so they make a point of furnishing us with alms; for without any asking on our part, without begging of any one, our Lord moves them to succour us; and so we always have what is necessary for us, and I trust in our Lord it will always be so.[1] As the sisters are few in number, if they do their duty as our Lord at present by His grace enables them to do, I am confident that they will always have it, and that they need not be a burden nor troublesome to any body; for our Lord will care for them, as He has hitherto done.

26. It is the greatest consolation to me to find myself among those who are so detached. Their occupation is to learn how they may advance in the service of God. Solitude is their delight; and the thought of being visited by any one, even of their nearest kindred, is a trial, unless it helps them to kindle more and more their love of the Bridegroom. Accordingly, none come to this house who *The nuns of S. Joseph.*

---

[1] See *Way of Perfection*, ch. ii.

do not aim at this; otherwise they neither give nor receive any pleasure from their visits. Their conversation is of God only; and so he whose conversation is different does not understand them, and they do not understand him.

<small>The rule of our Lady of Mount Carmel.</small> 27. We keep the rule of our Lady of Carmel, not the rule of the Mitigation, but as it was settled by Fr. Hugo, Cardinal of Santa Sabina, and given in the year 1248, in the fifth year of the pontificate of Innocent IV., Pope. All the trouble we had to go through, as it seems to me, will have been endured to good purpose.

<small>But the sisters have added to it.</small> 28. And now, though the rule be somewhat severe,—for we never eat flesh except in cases of necessity, fast eight months in the year, and practise some other austerities besides, according to the primitive rule,[1]—yet the sisters think it light on many points, and so they have other observances, which we have thought necessary for the more perfect keeping of it. And I trust in our Lord that what we have begun will prosper more and more, to the promise which His Majesty gave me.

<small>Another house founded at Alcala.</small> 29. The other house, which the holy woman of whom I spoke before[2] laboured to establish, has been also blessed of our Lord, and is founded in Alcala: it did not escape serious opposition, nor fail to endure many trials. I know that all duties of religion are observed in it, according to our primitive rule. Our Lord grant that

---

[1] *Brockie*, iii. 20: " Jejunium singulis diebus, exceptis Dominicis, observetis a Festo Exaltationis Sanctæ Crucis usque ad diem Dominicæ Resurrectionis, nisi infirmitas seu debilitas corporis, aut alia justa causa, jejunium solvi suadeat; quia necessitas non habet legem. Ab esu carnium semper abstineatis, nisi pro infirmitatis aut nimiæ debilitatis remedio sint sumendæ." That is the seventh section of the rule.

[2] See ch. xxxv. § 1. Maria of Jesus had founded her house in Alcala de Henares; but the austerities practised in it, and the absence of the religious mitigations which long experience had introduced, were too much for the fervent nuns there assembled. Maria of Jesus begged Doña Leonor de Mascareñas to persuade S. Teresa to come to Alcala. The Saint went to the monastery, and was received there with joy, and even entreated to take the house under her own government (*Reforma*, ii. c. x. §§ 3, 4).

all may be to the praise and glory of Himself and of the glorious Virgin Mary, whose habit we wear. Amen.

30. I think you must be wearied, my father, by the tedious history of this monastery; and yet it is most concise, if you compare it with our labours, and the wonders which our Lord has wrought here. There are many who can bear witness to this on oath. I therefore beg of your reverence, for the love of God, should you think fit to destroy the rest of this my writing, to preserve that part of it which relates to this monastery, and give it, when I am dead, to the sisters who may then be living in it. It will encourage them greatly, who shall come here both to serve God and to labour, that what has been thus begun may not fall to decay, but ever grow and thrive, when they see how much our Lord has done through one so mean and vile as I. As our Lord has been so particularly gracious to us in the foundation of this house, it seems to me that she will do very wrong, and that she will be heavily chastised of God, who shall be the first to relax the perfect observance of the rule, which our Lord has here begun and countenanced, so that it may be kept with so much sweetness: it is most evident that the observance of it is easy, and that it can be kept with ease, by the arrangement made for those who long to be alone with their Bridegroom Christ, in order to live for ever in Him. <small>Observance of the rule.</small>

31. This is to be the perpetual aim of those who are here, to be alone with Him alone. They are not to be more in number than thirteen: I know this number to be the best, for I have had many opinions about it; and I have seen in my own experience, that to preserve our spirit, living on alms, without asking of any one, a larger number would be inexpedient. May they always believe one who with much labour, and by the prayers of many people, accomplished that which must be for the best! That this is most expedient for us will be seen from the joy and cheerfulness, and the few troubles, we have all had in the years we have lived in this house, as well as from the better health than usual of us all. If any one thinks the rule hard, let her lay the fault on her want of the true spirit, and not on the rule of the <small>End of the foundation.</small>

house, seeing that delicate persons, and those not saints,—because they have the true spirit,—can bear it all with so much sweetness. Let others go to another monastery, where they may save their souls in the way of their own spirit.

CHAPTER XXXVII.

THE EFFECTS OF THE DIVINE GRACES IN THE SOUL—THE INESTIMABLE GREATNESS OF ONE DEGREE OF GLORY.

The Saint resumes the account of her interior life.

1. IT is painful to me to recount more of the graces which our Lord gave me than these already spoken of; and they are so many, that nobody can believe they were ever given to one so wicked: but in obedience to our Lord, who has commanded me to do it,[1] and you, my fathers, I will speak of some of them to His glory. May it please His Majesty it may be to the profit of some soul! For if our Lord has been thus gracious to so miserable a thing as myself, what will He be to those who shall serve Him truly? Let all people resolve to please His Majesty, seeing that He gives such pledges as these even in this life.[2]

Degrees of glory.

2. In the first place, it must be understood that, in those graces which God bestows on the soul, there are diverse degrees of joy: for in some visions the joy and sweetness and comfort of them so far exceed those of others, that I am amazed at the different degrees of fruition even in this life; for it happens that the joy and consolation which God gives in a vision or a trance are so different, that it seems impossible for the soul to be able to desire any thing more in this world: and so, in fact, the soul does not desire, nor would it ask for, a greater joy. Still, since our Lord has

---

[1] The Saint, having interrupted her account of her interior life in order to give the history of the foundation of the monastery of S. Joseph, Avila,—the first house of the Reformed Carmelites,—here resumes that account, broken off at the end of § 10 of ch. xxxii.

[2] Ephes. i. 14 : "Pignus hæreditatis nostræ."

made me understand how great a difference there is in heaven itself between the fruition of one and that of another, I see clearly enough that here also, when our Lord wills, He gives not by measure;[1] and so I wish that I myself observed no measure in serving His Majesty, and in using my whole life and strength and health therein; and I would not have any fault of mine rob me of the slightest degree of fruition.

3. And so I say that if I were asked which I preferred, to endure all the trials of the world until the end of it, and then receive one slight degree of glory additional, or without any suffering of any kind to enter into glory of a slightly lower degree, I would accept—oh, how willingly!—all those trials for one slight degree of fruition in the contemplation of the greatness of God; for I know that he who understands Him best, loves Him and praises Him best. I do not mean that I should not be satisfied, and consider myself most blessed, to be in heaven, even if I should be in the lowest place; for as I am one who had that place in hell, it would be a great mercy of our Lord to admit me at all; and may it please His Majesty to bring me thither, and take away His eyes from beholding my grievous sins. What I mean is this,—if it were in my power, even if it cost me every thing, and our Lord gave me the grace to endure much affliction, I would not through any fault of mine lose one degree of glory. Ah, wretched that I am, who by so many faults had forfeited all!

For one degree of glory the Saint would endure all sufferings.

4. It is also to be observed that, in every vision or revelation which our Lord in His mercy sent me, a great gain accrued to my soul, and that in some of the visions this gain was very great. The vision of Christ left behind an impression of His exceeding beauty, and it remains with me to this day. One vision alone of Him is enough to effect this; what, then, must all those visions have done, which our Lord in His mercy sent me? One exceedingly great blessing has resulted therefrom, and it is this,— I had one very grievous fault, which was the source of much

Effects of the visions.

[1] S. John iii. 34: "Non enim ad mensuram dat Deus spiritum."

evil; namely, whenever I found any body well disposed towards myself, and I liked him, I used to have such an affection for him as compelled me always to remember and think of him, though I had no intention of offending God: however, I was pleased to see him, to think of him and of his good qualities. All this was so hurtful, that it brought my soul to the very verge of destruction.

<small>The vision of our Lord's beauty.</small> 5. But ever since I saw the great beauty[1] of our Lord, I never saw any one who in comparison with Him seemed even endurable, or that could occupy my thoughts. For if I but turn mine eyes inwardly for a moment to the contemplation of the image which I have within me, I find myself so free, that from that instant every thing I see is loathsome in comparison with the excellences and graces of which I had a vision in our Lord. Neither is there any sweetness, nor any kind of pleasure, which I can make any account of, compared with that which comes from hearing but one word from His divine mouth. What, then, must it be when I hear so many? I look upon it as impossible—unless our Lord, for my sins, should permit the loss of this remembrance—that I should have the power to occupy myself with any thing in such a way as that I should not instantly recover my liberty by thinking of our Lord.

<small>The Saint's freedom of spirit, and detachment from creatures.</small> 6. This has happened to me with some of my confessors, for I always have a great affection for those who have the direction of my soul. As I really saw in them only the representatives of God, I thought my will was always there where it is most occupied; and as I felt very safe in the matter, I always showed myself glad to see them.[2] They, on the other hand, servants of God, and fearing Him, were afraid that I was attaching and binding myself too much to them, though in a holy way, and treated me with rudeness. This took place after I had become so ready to obey them; for before that time I had no affection whatever for them. I used to laugh to myself, when I saw

[1] Ch. xxviii. §§ 1-5.
[2] See ch. xl. § 25; *Way of Perfection*, ch. vii. § 1; but ch. iv. of the previous editions.

how much they were deceived. Though I was not always putting before them how little I was attached to any body, as clearly as I was convinced of it myself, yet I did assure them of it; and they, in their further relations with me, acknowledged how much I owed to our Lord in the matter. These suspicions of me always arose in the beginning.

7. My love of, and trust in, our Lord, after I had seen Him in a vision, began to grow, for my converse with Him was so continual. I saw that, though He was God, He was man also; that He is not surprised at the frailties of men; that He understands our miserable nature, liable to fall continually, because of the first sin, for the reparation of which He had come. I could speak to Him as to a friend, though He is my Lord, because I do not consider Him as one of our earthly lords, who affect a power they do not possess, who give audience at fixed hours, and to whom only certain persons may speak. If a poor man have any business with these, it will cost him many goings and comings, and currying favour with others, together with much pain and labour before he can speak to them. Ah, if such a one has business with a king! Poor people, not of gentle blood, cannot approach him, for they must apply to those who are his friends; and certainly these are not persons who tread the world under their feet; for they who do this speak the truth, fear nothing, and ought to fear nothing; they are not courtiers, because it is not the custom of a court, where they must be silent about those things they dislike, must not even dare to think about them, lest they should fall into disgrace. *Our Lord easy of access.*

8. O King of glory, and Lord of all kings! oh, how Thy kingly dignity is not hedged about by trifles of this kind! Thy kingdom is for ever. We do not require chamberlains to introduce us into Thy presence. The very vision of Thy person shows us at once that Thou alone art to be called Lord. Thy Majesty is so manifest, that there is no need of a retinue or guard to make us confess that Thou art King. An earthly king without attendants would be hardly acknowledged; and though he might wish ever so much to be recognised, people will not own *Contrast between the heavenly and an earthly king.*

him when he appears as others; it is necessary that his dignity should be visible, if people are to believe in it. This is reason enough why kings should affect so much state; for if they had none, no one would respect them; this their semblance of power is not in themselves, and their authority must come to them from others.

The majesty and humility of God.
9. O my Lord! O my King! who can describe Thy Majesty? It is impossible not to see that Thou art Thyself the great Ruler of all, that the beholding of Thy Majesty fills men with awe. But I am filled with greater awe, O my Lord, when I consider Thy humility, and the love Thou hast for such as I am. We can converse and speak with Thee about every thing whenever we will; and when we lose our first fear and awe at the vision of Thy Majesty, we have a greater dread of offending Thee,—not arising out of the fear of punishment, O my Lord, for that is as nothing in comparison with the loss of Thee!

The divine visions are known by their fruits.
10. Thus far of the blessings of this vision, without speaking of others, which abide in the soul when it is past. If it be from God, the fruits thereof show it, when the soul receives light; for, as I have often said,[1] the will of our Lord is that the soul should be in darkness, and not see this light. It is, therefore, nothing to be wondered at that I, knowing myself to be so wicked as I am, should be afraid.

God leaves the soul in darkness.
11. It is only just now it happened to me to be for eight days in a state wherein it seemed that I did not, and could not, confess my obligations to God, or remember His mercies; but my soul was so stupefied and occupied with I know not what nor how: not that I had any bad thoughts; only I was so incapable of good thoughts, that I was laughing at myself, and even rejoicing to see how mean a soul can be if God is not always working in it.[2] The soul sees clearly that God is not away from it in this state, and that it is not in those great tribulations which I have spoken of as being occasionally mine. Though it heaps up fuel, and does the little it can do of itself, it cannot make the fire of the love of

[1] See ch. xx. § 14.   [2] See ch. xxx. § 19.

God burn: it is a great mercy that even the smoke is visible, showing that it is not altogether quenched. Our Lord will return and kindle it; and until then the soul —though it may lose its breath in blowing and arranging the fuel—seems to be doing nothing but putting it out more and more.

12. I believe that now the best course is to be absolutely resigned, confessing that we can do nothing, and so apply ourselves—as I said before[1]—to something else which is meritorious. Our Lord, it may be, takes away from the soul the power of praying, that it may betake itself to something else, and learn by experience how little it can do in its own strength. What the soul should do when it cannot pray.

13. It is true I have this day been rejoicing in our Lord, and have dared to complain of His Majesty. I said unto Him: How is it, O my God, that it is not enough for Thee to detain me in this wretched life, and that I should have to bear with it for the love of Thee, and be willing to live where every thing hinders the fruition of Thee; where, besides, I must eat and sleep, transact business, and converse with every one, and all for Thy love? how is it, then,—for Thou well knowest, O my Lord, all this to be the greatest torment unto me,—that, in the rare moments when I am with Thee, Thou hidest Thyself from me? How is this consistent with Thy compassion? How can that love Thou hast for me endure this? I believe, O Lord, if it were possible for me to hide myself from Thee, as Thou hidest Thyself from me—I think and believe so—such is Thy love, that Thou wouldest not endure it at my hands. But Thou art with me, and seest me always. O my Lord, I beseech Thee look to this; it must not be; a wrong is done to one who loves Thee so much. The Saint's loving complaint.

14. I happened to utter these words, and others of the same kind, when I should have been thinking rather how my place in hell was pleasant in comparison with the place I deserved. But now and then my love makes me foolish, so that I lose my senses; only it is with all Excesses of love.

[1] See ch. xxx. §§ 18, 25.

the sense I have that I make these complaints, and our Lord bears it all. Blessed be so good a King!

Exigencies of the world's laws. 15. Can we be thus bold with the kings of this world? And yet I am not surprised that we dare not thus speak to a king, for it is only reasonable that men should be afraid of him, or even to the great lords who are his representatives. The world is now come to such a state, that men's lives ought to be longer than they are, if we are to learn all the new customs and ceremonies of good breeding, and yet spend any time in the service of God. I bless myself at the sight of what is going on. The fact is, I did not know how I was to live when I came into this house. Any negligence in being much more ceremonious with people than they deserve is not taken as a jest; on the contrary, they look upon it as an insult deliberately offered; so that it becomes necessary for you to satisfy them of your good intentions, if there happens, as I have said, to have been any negligence; and even then, God grant they may believe you.

Weariness of worldly observances. 16. I repeat it,—I certainly did not know how to live; for my poor soul was worn out. It is told to employ all its thoughts always on God, and that it is necessary to do so if it would avoid many dangers. On the other hand, it finds it will not do to fail in any one point of the world's law, under the penalty of affronting those who look upon these things as touching their honour. I was worn out in unceasingly giving satisfaction to people; for, though I tried my utmost, I could not help failing in many ways in matters which, as I have said, are not slightly thought of in the world.

The Saint insists on simplicity, and laughs at the world's rites. 17. Is it true that in religious houses no explanations are necessary, for it is only reasonable we should be excused these observances? Well, that is not so; for there are people who say that monasteries ought to be courts in politeness and instruction. I certainly cannot understand it. I thought that perhaps some saint may have said that they ought to be courts to teach those who wish to be the courtiers of heaven, and that these people misunderstood their meaning; for if a man be careful to please God continually, and to hate the world, as he ought to do, I do not see how he can be equally careful to please those who live in the world in these matters which are continually changing. If they could be learnt once for all, it might be borne with: but as to the way of addressing letters, there ought to be a professor's chair founded, from which lectures should be given, so to speak, teaching us how to do it; for the paper should on one occasion be left blank in one corner, and on another in another corner; and a man must be addressed as the illustrious who was not hitherto addressed as the magnificent.

18. I know not where this will stop: I am not yet fifty, and yet I have seen so many changes during my life, that I do not know how to live. What will they do who are only just born, and who may live many years? Certainly I am sorry for those spiritual people who, for certain holy purposes, are obliged to live in the world; the cross they have to carry is a dreadful one. If they could all agree together, and make themselves ignorant, and be willing to be considered so in these sciences, they would set themselves free from much trouble. But what folly am I about! from speaking of the greatness of God I am come to speak of the meanness of the world! Since our Lord has given me the grace to quit it, I wish to leave it altogether. Let them settle these matters who maintain these follies with so much labour. God grant that in the next life, where there is no changing, we may not have to pay for them! Amen.

The burden of the world's laws.

CHAPTER XXXVIII.

CERTAIN HEAVENLY SECRETS, VISIONS, AND REVELATIONS—
THE EFFECTS OF THEM IN HER SOUL.

1. ONE night I was so unwell that I thought I might be excused making my prayer; so I took my rosary, that I might employ myself in vocal prayer, trying not to be recollected in my understanding, though out-

The Saint has a vision of heaven.

wardly I was recollected, being in my oratory. These little precautions are of no use when our Lord will have it otherwise. I remained there but a few moments thus, when I was rapt in spirit with such violence that I could make no resistance whatever. It seemed to me that I was taken up to heaven; and the first persons I saw there were my father and my mother. I saw other things also; but the time was no longer than that in which the *Ave Maria* might be said, and I was amazed at it, looking on it all as too great a grace for me. But as to the shortness of the time, it might have been longer, only it was all done in a very short space.

<small>The Saint tells her confessor of the vision.</small> 2. I was afraid it might be an illusion; but as I did not think so, I knew not what to do, because I was very much ashamed to go to my confessor about it. It was not, as it seemed to me, because I was humble, but because I thought he would laugh at me, and say: Oh, what a S. Paul!—she sees the things of heaven; or a S. Jerome. And because these glorious Saints had had such visions, I was so much the more afraid, and did nothing but cry; for I did not think it possible for me to see what they saw. At last, though I felt it exceedingly, I went to my confessor; for I never dared to keep secret any thing of this kind, however much it distressed me to speak of them, owing to the great fear I had of being deceived. When my confessor saw how much I was suffering, he consoled me greatly, and gave me plenty of good reasons why I should have no fear.

<small>Joyous effects of the vision.</small> 3. It happened, also, as time went on, and it happens now from time to time, that our Lord showed me still greater secrets. The soul, even if it would, has neither the means nor the power to see more than what He shows it; and so, each time, I saw nothing more than what our Lord was pleased to let me see. But such was the vision, that the least part of it was enough to make my soul amazed, and to raise it so high that it esteems and counts as nothing all the things of this life. I wish I could describe, in some measure, the smallest portion of what I saw; but when I think of doing it, I find it impossible; for the mere difference alone between the light we have here below, and that which is seen

in a vision,—both being light,—is so great, that there is no comparison between them; the brightness of the sun itself seems to be something exceedingly loathsome. In a word, the imagination, however strong it may be, can neither conceive nor picture to itself this light, nor any one of the things which our Lord showed me in a joy so supreme that it cannot be described; for then all the senses exult so deeply and so sweetly, that no description is possible; and so it is better to say nothing more.

4. I was in this state once for more than an hour, our Lord showing me wonderful things. He seemed as if He would not leave me. He said to me: "See, My daughter, what they lose who are against Me; do not fail to tell them of it." Ah, my Lord, how little good my words will do them, who are made blind by their own conduct, if Thy Majesty will not give them light! Some, to whom Thou hast given it, there are, who have profited by the knowledge of Thy greatness; but as they see it revealed to one so wicked and base as I am, I look upon it as a great thing if there should be any found to believe me. Blessed be Thy name, and blessed be Thy compassion; for I can trace, at least in my own soul, a visible improvement. Afterwards I wished I had continued in that trance for ever, and that I had not returned to consciousness, because of an abiding sense of contempt for every thing here below; all seemed to be filth; and I see how meanly we employ ourselves who are detained on earth. *Excellence of the vision.*

5. When I was staying with that lady of whom I have been speaking,[1] it happened to me once when I was suffering from my heart,—for, as I have said,[2] I suffered greatly at one time, though not so much now,—that she, being a person of great charity, brought out her jewels set in gold, and precious stones of great price, and particularly a diamond, which she valued very much. She thought this might amuse me; but I laughed to myself, and was very sorry to see what men made much of; for I thought of what our Lord had laid up for us, and considered how impossible it was for me, *The Saint's contempt of earthly goods.*

[1] Ch. xxxiv. Doña Luisa de la Cerda, at Toledo.   [2] Ch. iv. § 6.

even if I made the effort, to have any appreciation whatever of such things, provided our Lord did not permit me to forget what He was keeping for us.

Detachment a grace of God. 6. A soul in this state attains to a certain freedom, which is so complete that none can understand it who does not possess it. It is a real and true detachment, independent of our efforts; God effects it all Himself; for His Majesty reveals the truth in such a way, that it remains so deeply impressed on our souls as to make it clear that we of ourselves could not thus acquire it in so short a time.

Detachment takes away the fear of death. 7. The fear of death, also, was now very slight in me, who had always been in great dread of it; now it seems to me that death is a very light thing for one who serves God, because the soul is in a moment delivered thereby out of its prison, and at rest. This elevation of the spirit, and the vision of things so high, in these trances seem to me to have a great likeness to the flight of the soul from the body, in that it finds itself in a moment in the possession of these good things. We put aside the agonies of its dissolution, of which no great account is to be made; for they who love God in truth, and are utterly detached from the things of this life, must die with the greater sweetness.

Visions made the Saint long for heaven. 8. It seems to me, also, that the rapture was a great help to recognise our true home, and to see that we are pilgrims here;[1] it is a great thing to see what is going on there, and to know where we have to live; for if a person has to go and settle in another country, it is a great help to him, in undergoing the fatigues of his journey, that he has discovered it to be a country where he may live in the most perfect peace. Moreover, it makes it easy for us to think of the things of heaven, and to have our conversation there.[2] It is a great gain, because the mere looking up to heaven makes the soul recollected; for as our Lord has been pleased to reveal heaven in some degree, my soul dwells upon it in thought; and it happens occasionally that they who are about me, and with whom I find consolation, are those

---

[1] 1 S. Pet. ii. 11 : "Advenas et peregrinos."
[2] Philipp. iii. 20 : "Nostra autem conversatio in cœlis est."

whom I know to be living in heaven, and that I look upon them only as really alive; while those who are on earth are so dead, that the whole world seems unable to furnish me with companions, particularly when these impetuosities of love are upon me. Every thing seems a dream, and what I see with the bodily eyes an illusion. What I have seen with the eyes of the soul is that which my soul desires; and as it finds itself far away from those things, that is death.

9. In a word, it is a very great mercy which our Lord gives to that soul to which He grants the like visions, for they help it in much, and also in carrying *The great blessing of these visions.* a heavy cross, since nothing satisfies it, and every thing is against it; and if our Lord did not now and then suffer these visions to be forgotten, though they recur again and again to the memory, I know not how life could be borne. May He be blessed and praised for ever and ever! I implore His Majesty by that Blood which His Son shed for me, now that, of His good pleasure, I know something of these great blessings, and begin to have the fruition of them, that it may not be with me as it was with Lucifer, who by his own fault forfeited it all. I beseech Thee, for Thine own sake, not to suffer this; for I am at times in great fear, though at others, and most frequently, the mercy of God reassures me, for He who has delivered me from so many sins will not withdraw His hand from under me, and let me be lost. I pray you, my father, to beg this grace for me always.

10. The mercies, then, hitherto described, are not, in my opinion, so great as those which I am now going to speak of, on many accounts, because of the great blessings they have brought with them, and because of the great fortitude which my soul derived from them; and yet every one separately considered is so great, that there is nothing to be compared with them.

11. One day—it was the eve of Pentecost—I went after Mass to a very lonely spot, where I used to pray very often, and began to read about the feast *The Saint discerns her own progress.* in the book of a Carthusian;[1] and reading of the marks by

[1] The *Life of Christ*, by Ludolf of Saxony.

which beginners, proficients, and the perfect may know that they have the Holy Ghost, it seemed to me, when I had read of these three states, that by the goodness of God, so far as I could understand, the Holy Ghost was with me. I praised God for it; and calling to mind how on another occasion, when I read this, I was very deficient,—for I saw most distinctly at that time how deficient I was then from what I saw I was now,—I recognised herein the great mercy of our Lord to me, and so began to consider the place which my sins had earned for me in hell, and praised God exceedingly, because it seemed as if I did not know my own soul again, so great a change had come over it.

The Saint falls into a trance,

12. While thinking of these things, my soul was carried away with extreme violence, and I knew not why. It seemed as if it would have gone forth out of the body, for it could not contain itself, nor was it able to hope for so great a good. The impetuosity was so excessive that I had no power left, and, as I think, different from what I had been used to. I knew not what ailed my soul, nor what it desired, for it was so changed. I leaned for support, for I could not sit, because my natural strength had utterly failed.

And sees a dove hovering over herself,

13. Then I saw over my head a dove, very different from those we usually see, for it had not the same plumage, but wings formed of small shells shining brightly. It was larger than an ordinary dove; I thought I heard the rustling of its wings. It hovered above me during the space of an *Ave Maria*. But such was the state of my soul, that in losing itself it lost also the sight of the dove. My spirit grew calm with such a guest; and yet, as I think, a grace so wonderful might have disturbed and frightened it; and as it began to rejoice in the vision, it was delivered from all fear, and with the joy came peace, my soul continuing entranced. The joy of this rapture was exceedingly great; and for the rest of that festal time I was so amazed and bewildered that I did not know what I was doing, nor how I could have received so great a grace. I neither heard nor saw any thing, so to speak, because of my great inward joy. From that day forth I perceived in myself a very great progress

in the highest love of God, together with a great increase in the strength of my virtues. May He be blessed and praised for ever! Amen.

14. On another occasion I saw that very dove above the head of one of the Dominican fathers; but it seemed to me that the rays and brightness of the wings were far greater. I understood by this that he was to draw souls unto God. *And over a Dominican friar.*

15. At another time I saw our Lady putting a cope of exceeding whiteness on that Licentiate of the same Order, of whom I have made mention more than once.[1] She told me that she gave him that cope in consideration of the service he had rendered her by helping to found this house,[2] that it was a sign that she would preserve his soul pure for the future, and that he should not fall into mortal sin. I hold it for certain that so it came to pass, for he died within a few years; his death and the rest of his life were so penitential, his whole life and death so holy, that, so far as any thing can be known, there cannot be a doubt on the subject. One of the friars present at his death told me that, before he breathed his last, he said to him that S. Thomas was with him.[3] He died in great joy, longing to depart out of this land of exile. *Sanctity of F. Pedro Ibanez.*

16. Since then he has appeared to me more than once in exceedingly great glory, and told me certain things. He was so given to prayer, that when he was dying, and would have interrupted it if he could because of his great weakness, he was not able to do so; for he was often in a trance. He wrote to me not long before he died, and asked me what he was to do; for as soon as he had said Mass he fell into a trance, which lasted a long time, and which he could not hinder. At last God gave him the reward of the many services of his whole life. *The Saint saw him in her visions.*

---

[1] F. Pedro Ibañez. See ch. xxxiii. § 5, ch. xxxvi. § 23. "This father died Prior of Trianos," is written on the margin of the MS. by F. Bañes (*De la Fuente*).

[2] S. Joseph, Avila, where S. Teresa was living at this time.

[3] See below, § 41.

17. I had certain visions, too, of the great graces which our Lord bestowed upon that rector of the Society of Jesus, of whom I have spoken already more than once;[1] but I will not say any thing of them now, lest I should be too tedious. It was his lot once to be in great trouble, to suffer great persecution and distress. One day, when I was hearing Mass, I saw Christ on the cross at the elevation of the Host. He spoke certain words to me, which I was to repeat to that father for his comfort, together with others, which were to warn him beforehand of what was coming, and to remind him of what He had suffered on his behalf, and that he must prepare for suffering. This gave him great consolation and courage; and every thing came to pass afterwards as our Lord had told me.

The Saint's great veneration for the Jesuits.   18. I have seen great things of members of the Order to which this father belongs, which is the Society of Jesus, and of the whole Order itself; I have occasionally seen them in heaven with white banners in their hands, and I have had other most wonderful visions, as I am saying, about them, and therefore have a great veneration for this Order; for I have had a great deal to do with those who are of it, and I see that their lives are conformed to that which our Lord gave me to understand about them.

Our Lord makes the Saint consider her former life.   19. One night, when I was in prayer, our Lord spoke to me certain words, whereby He made me remember the great wickedness of my past life. They filled me with shame and distress; for though they were not spoken with severity, they caused a feeling and a painfulness which were too much for me: and we feel that we make greater progress in the knowledge of ourselves when we hear one of these words, than we can make by a meditation of many days on our own misery, because these words impress the truth upon us at the same time in such a way that we cannot

---

[1] F. Gaspar de Salasar: see ch. xxxiii. § 10, ch. xxxiv. § 14. It appears from the 179th letter of the Saint (lett. 20, vol. i. of the Doblado edition), that F. Salasar was reported to his Provincial, F. Juan Suarez, as having a desire to quit the Society for the Carmelite Order.

resist it. He set before me the former inclinations of my will to vanities, and told me to make much of the desire I now had that my will, which had been so ill employed, should be fixed on Him, and that He would accept it.

20. On other occasions He told me to remember how I used to think it an honourable thing to go against His honour; and, again, to remember my debt to Him, for when I was most rebellious He was bestowing His graces upon me. If I am doing any thing wrong—and my wrong-doings are many—His Majesty makes me see it in such a way that I am utterly confounded; and as I do so often, that happens often also. I have been found fault with by my confessors occasionally; and on betaking myself to prayer for consolation, have received a real reprimand. *And her resistance to His will.*

21. To return to what I was speaking of. When our Lord made me remember my wicked life, I wept; for as I considered that I had then never done any good, I thought He might be about to bestow upon me some special grace; because most frequently, when I receive any particular mercy from our Lord, it is when I have been previously greatly humiliated, in order that I may the more clearly see how far I am from deserving it. I think our Lord must do it for that end. *Great graces follow after humiliations.*

22. Almost immediately after this I was so raised up in spirit that I thought myself to be, as it were, out of the body; at least, I did not know that I was living in it.[1] I had a vision of the most Sacred Humanity in exceeding glory, greater than I had ever seen It in before. I beheld It in a wonderful and clear way in the bosom of the Father. I cannot tell how it was, for I saw myself, without seeing, as it seemed to me, in the presence of God. My amazement was such that I remained, as I believe, some days before I could recover myself. I had continually before me, as present, the Majesty of the Son of God, though not so distinctly as in the vision. I understood this well enough; but the vision remained so impressed on my *A vision of the Sacred Humanity in the bosom of the Father.*

[1] 2 Cor. xii. 2: "Sive in corpore nescio, sive extra corpus nescio."

imagination, that I could not get rid of it for some time, though it had lasted but a moment; it is a great comfort to me, and also a great blessing.

Fruits of the vision. 23. I have had this vision on three other occasions, and it is, I think, the highest vision of all the visions which our Lord in His mercy showed me. The fruits of it are the very greatest, for it seems to purify the soul in a wonderful way, and destroy, as it were utterly, altogether the strength of our sensual nature. It is a grand flame of fire, which seems to burn up and annihilate all the desires of this life. For though now—glory be to God!—I had no desire after vanities, I saw clearly in the vision how all things are vanity, and how hollow are all the dignities of earth; it was a great lesson, teaching me to raise up my desires to the Truth alone. It impresses on the soul a sense of the presence of God such as I cannot in any way describe, only it is very different from that which it is in our own power to acquire on earth. It fills the soul with profound astonishment at its own daring, and at any one else being able to dare to offend His most awful Majesty.

The Saint filled with awe at Communion. 24. I must have spoken now and then of the effects of visions,[1] and of other matters of the same kind, and I have already said that the blessings they bring with them are of various degrees; but those of this vision are the highest of all. When I went to Communion once I called to mind the exceeding great majesty of Him I had seen, and considered that it was He who is present in the most Holy Sacrament, and very often our Lord was pleased to show Himself to me in the Host; the very hairs on my head stood,[2] and I thought I should come to nothing.

God's greatness and man's vileness. 25. O my Lord! ah, if Thou didst not throw a veil over Thy greatness, who would dare, being so foul and miserable, to come in contact with Thy great Majesty? Blessed be Thou, O Lord; may the angels and all creation praise Thee, who orderest all things according to the measure of our weakness, so that, when we have the fruition of Thy sovereign mercies, Thy great power may not

---

[1] See ch. xxviii. [2] Job iv. 15: "Inhorruerunt pili carnis meæ."

terrify us, so that we dare not, being a frail and miserable race, persevere in that fruition!

26. It might happen to us as it did to the labourer—I know it to be a certain fact—who found a treasure beyond his expectations, which were mean. *An illustration.* When he saw himself in possession of it, he was seized with melancholy, which by degrees brought him to his grave through simple distress and anxiety of mind, because he did not know what to do with his treasure. If he had not found it all at once, and if others had given him portions of it by degrees, maintaining him thereby, he might have been more happy than he had been in his poverty, nor would it have cost him his life.

27. O Thou Treasure of the poor! how marvellously Thou sustainest souls, showing to them, not all at once, but by little and little, the abundance of Thy riches! *God hiding Himself in the Host.* When I behold Thy great Majesty hidden beneath that which is so slight as the Host is, I am filled with wonder, ever since that vision, at Thy great wisdom; and I know not how it is that our Lord gives me the strength and courage necessary to draw near to Him, were it not that He who has had such compassion on me, and still has, gives me strength, nor would it be possible for me to be silent, or refrain from making known marvels so great.

28. What must be the thoughts of a wretched person such as I am, full of abominations, and who has spent her life with so little fear of God, when she draws near to our Lord's great Majesty, at the moment He is pleased to show Himself to my soul? *The Saint's confession of her unworthiness.* How can I open my mouth, that has uttered so many words against Him, to receive that most glorious Body, purity and compassion itself? The love that is visible in His most beautiful Face, sweet and tender, pains and distresses the soul, because it has not served Him, more than all the terrors of His Majesty. What should have been my thoughts, then, on those two occasions when I saw what I have described? Truly, O my Lord and my joy, I am going to say that in some way, in these great afflictions of my soul, I have done something in Thy service. Ah! I

know not what I am saying, for I am writing this as if the words were not mine,[1] because I am troubled, and in some measure beside myself, when I call these things to remembrance. If these thoughts were really mine, I might well say that I had done something for Thee, O my Lord; but as I can have no good thought if Thou givest it not, no thanks are due to me; I am the debtor, O Lord, and it is Thou who art the offended One.

29. Once, when I was going to Communion, I saw with the eyes of the soul, more distinctly than with those of the body, two devils of most hideous shape; their horns seemed to encompass the throat of the poor priest; and I beheld my Lord, in that great majesty of which I have spoken,[2] held in the hands of that priest, in the Host he was about to give me. It was plain that those hands were those of a sinner, and I felt that the soul of that priest was in mortal sin. What must it be, O my Lord, to look upon Thy beauty amid shapes so hideous! The two devils were so frightened and cowed in Thy presence, that they seemed as if they would have willingly run away, hadst Thou but given them leave. So troubled was I by the vision, that I knew not how I could go to Communion. I was also in great fear, for I thought, if the vision was from God, that His Majesty would not have allowed me to see the evil state of that soul.[3]

A horrible vision.

30. Our Lord Himself told me to pray for that priest; that He had allowed this in order that I might understand the power of the words of consecration, and how God failed not to be present, however wicked the priest might be who uttered them; and that I might see His great goodness in that He left Himself in the very hands of His enemy, for my good and for the good of all. I understood clearly how the priests are under greater obligations to be holy

The words of consecration in the Mass.

---

[1] The biographers of the Saint say that she often found, on returning from an ecstasy, certain passages written, but not by herself: this seems to be alluded to here (*De la Fuente*).

[2] § 22.

[3] S. John of the Cross, *Ascent of Mount Carmel*, bk. ii. ch. xxvi. vol. i. p. 183.

than other persons; and what a horrible thing it is to receive this most Holy Sacrament unworthily, and how great is the devil's dominion over a soul in mortal sin. It did me a great service, and made me fully understand what I owe to God. May He be blessed for evermore!

31. At another time I had a vision of a different kind, which frightened me very much. I was in a place where a certain person died, who, as I understood, had led a very bad life, and that for many years. But he had been ill for two years, and in some respects seemed to have reformed. He died without confession; nevertheless, I did not think he would be damned. When the body had been wrapped in the winding-sheet, I saw it laid hold of by a multitude of devils, who seemed to toss it to and fro, and also to treat it with great cruelty. I was terrified at the sight, for they dragged it about with great hooks. But when I saw it carried to the grave with all the respect and ceremoniousness common to all, I began to think of the goodness of God, who would not allow that person to be dishonoured, but would have the fact of his being His enemy concealed. *A vision of a lost soul.*

32. I was almost out of my senses at the sight. During the whole of the funeral service, I did not see one of the evil spirits. Afterwards, when the body was about to be laid in the grave, so great a multitude of them was therein waiting to receive it, that I was beside myself at the sight, and it required no slight courage on my part not to betray my distress. I thought of the treatment which that soul would receive, when the devils had such power over the wretched body. Would to God that all who live in mortal sin might see what I then saw,—it was a fearful sight; it would go, I believe, a great way towards making them lead better lives. *The Office of the Dead.*

33. All this made me know more of what I owe to God, and of the evil from which He has delivered me. I was in great terror. I spoke of it to my confessor, and I thought it might be an illusion of Satan, in order to take away my good opinion of that person, who yet was not accounted a very good Christian. The truth is, that, whether *Effect of this vision on the Saint.*

it was an illusion or not, it makes me afraid whenever I think of it.

The Saint learns that the Provincial was dead, 34. Now that I have begun to speak of the visions I had concerning the dead, I will mention some matters which our Lord was pleased to reveal to me in relation to certain souls. I will confine myself to a few for the sake of brevity, and because they are not necessary; I mean that they are not for our profit. They told me that one who had been our Provincial—he was then of another province—was dead. He was a man of great virtue, with whom I had had a good deal to do, and to whom I was under many obligations for certain kindnesses shown me. When I heard that he was dead, I was exceedingly troubled, because I trembled for his salvation, seeing that he had been superior for twenty years. That is what I dread very much; for the cure of souls seems to me to be full of danger. I went to an oratory in great distress, and gave up to him all the good I had ever done in my whole life,—it was little enough,—and prayed our Lord that His merits might fill up what was wanting, in order that this soul might be delivered from purgatory.

And sees him ascend to heaven. 35. While I was thus praying to our Lord as well as I could, he seemed to me to rise up from the depths of the earth on my right hand, and I saw him ascend to heaven in exceeding great joy. He was a very old man then, but I saw him as if he were only thirty years old, and I thought even younger, and there was a brightness in his face. This vision passed away very quickly; but I was so exceedingly comforted by it, that I could never again mourn his death, although many persons were distressed at it, for he was very much beloved. So greatly comforted was my soul, that nothing disturbed it, neither could I doubt the truth of the vision; I mean that it was no illusion.

Nevertheless, she begs people to pray for him. 36. I had this vision about a fortnight after he was dead; nevertheless, I did not omit to obtain prayers for him, and I prayed myself, only I could not pray with the same earnestness that I should have done if I had not seen that vision. For when our Lord showed him thus to me, it seemed to me afterwards, when I prayed for him to His Majesty,—and I could not help it,—that I was like one who gave alms to a rich man. Later on I heard an account of the death he died in our Lord—he was far away from here; it was one of such great edification, that he left all wondering to see how recollected, how penitent, and how humble he was when he died.

37. A nun, who was a great servant of God, died in this house. On the next day one of the sisters was reciting the lesson in the Office of the Dead, which was said in choir for that nun's soul, and I was standing myself to assist her in singing the versicle, when, in the middle of the lesson, I saw the departed nun, as I believe, in a vision; her soul seemed to rise on my right hand like the soul of the Provincial, and ascend to heaven. This vision was not imaginary, like the preceding, but like those others of which I have spoken before;[1] it is not less certain, however, than the other visions I had. *A vision of a nun.*

38. Another nun died in this same house of mine: she was about eighteen or twenty years of age, and had always been sickly. She was a great servant of God, attentive in choir, and a person of great virtue. I certainly thought that she would not go to purgatory, on account of her exceeding merits, because the infirmities under which she had laboured were many. While I was saying the Office, before she was buried,—she had been dead about four hours,—I saw her rise in the same place and ascend to heaven. *Another.*

39. I was once in one of the colleges of the Society of Jesus, and in one of those great sufferings which, as I have said,[2] I occasionally had, and still have, both in soul and body, and then so grievously that I was not able, as it seemed to me, to have even one good thought. The night before, one of the brothers of that house had died in it; and I, as well as I could, was commending his soul to God, and hearing the Mass which another father of that Society was saying for him, when I became recollected at once, and saw him go up to heaven in great glory, and our Lord with *Of a Jesuit.*

[1] See ch. xxvii. [2] Ch. xxx. § 9.

him. I understood that His Majesty went with him by way of special grace.

40. Another brother of our Order, a good friar, *Of a Carmelite friar.* was very ill; and when I was at Mass, I became recollected, and saw him dead, entering into heaven without going through purgatory. He died, as I afterwards learned, at the very time of my vision. I was amazed that he had not gone to purgatory. I understood that, having become a friar and carefully kept the rule, the Bulls of the Order had been of use to him, so that he did not pass into purgatory. I do not know why I came to have this revealed to me; I think it must be because I was to learn that it is not enough for a man to be a friar in his habit—I mean, to wear the habit—to attain to that state of high perfection which that of a friar is.

41. I will speak no more of these things, because, as I have just said,[1] there is no necessity for it, though our Lord has been so gracious to me as to show me much. But in all the visions I had, I saw no souls escape purgatory except this Carmelite father, the holy friar Peter of Alcantara, and that Dominican father of whom I spoke before.[2] It pleased our Lord to let me see the degree of glory to which some souls have been raised, showing them to me in the places they occupy. There is a great difference between one place and another.

CHAPTER XXXIX.

OTHER GRACES BESTOWED ON THE SAINT—THE PROMISES OF OUR LORD TO HER—DIVINE LOCUTIONS AND VISIONS.

1. I WAS once importuning our Lord exceed-*The Saint obtains the restoration of a person's sight.* ingly to restore the sight of a person who had claims upon me, and who was almost wholly blind. I was very sorry for him, and afraid our Lord would not hear me because of my sins. He appeared to me as at other times, and began to show the wound in His left hand; with the

---

[1] § 34.   [2] § 15. Fr. Pedro Ibañez.

other He drew out the great nail that was in it, and it seemed to me that, in drawing the nail, He tore the flesh. The greatness of the pain was manifest, and I was very much distressed thereat. He said to me, that He who had borne that for my sake would still more readily grant what I asked Him, and that I was not to have any doubts about it. He promised me there was nothing I should ask that He would not grant; that He knew I should ask nothing that was not for His glory, and that He would grant me what I was now praying for. Even during the time when I did not serve Him, I should find, if I considered it, I had asked nothing that He had not granted in an ampler manner than I had known how to ask; how much more amply still would He grant what I asked for, now that He knew I loved Him! I was not to doubt. I do not think that eight days passed before our Lord restored that person to sight. My confessor knew it forthwith. It might be that it was not owing to my prayer; but, as I had had the vision, I have a certain conviction that it was a grace accorded to me. I gave thanks to His Majesty.

2. Again, a person was exceedingly ill of a most painful disease; but, as I do not know what it was, I do not describe it by its name here. What he had gone through for two months was beyond all endurance; and his pain was so great that he tore his own flesh. My confessor, the rector of whom I have spoken,[1] went to see him; he was very sorry for him, and told me that I must anyhow go myself and visit him; he was one whom I might visit, for he was my kinsman. I went, and was moved to such a tender compassion for him that I began, with the utmost importunity, to ask our Lord to restore him to health. Herein I saw clearly how gracious our Lord was to me, so far as I could judge; for immediately, the next day, he was completely rid of that pain. *The Saint heals one of her kindred.*

3. I was once in the deepest distress, because I knew that a person to whom I was under great obligations was about to commit an act highly offensive to God and dishonourable to himself. He was determined upon it. I was so much harassed by this that I did not know *The Saint's distress at the sins of others.*

[1] Ch. xxxiii. § 10. F. Gaspar de Salazar.

what to do in order to change his purpose; and it seemed to me as if nothing could be done. I implored God, from the bottom of my heart, to find a way to hinder it; but till I found it I could find no relief for the pain I felt. In my distress, I went to a very lonely hermitage,—one of those belonging to this monastery,—in which there is a picture of Christ bound to the pillar; and there, as I was imploring our Lord to grant me this grace, I heard a voice of exceeding gentleness, speaking, as it were, in a whisper.[1] My whole body trembled, for it made me afraid. I wished to understand what was said, but I could not, for it all passed away in a moment.

The Saint believes that her prayer was heard. 4. When my fears had subsided, and that was immediately, I became conscious of an inward calmness, a joy and delight, which made me marvel how the mere hearing a voice,—I heard it with my bodily ears,—without understanding a word, could have such an effect on the soul. I saw by this that my prayer was granted, and so it was; and I was freed from my anxieties about a matter not yet accomplished, as it afterwards was, as completely as if I saw it done. I told my confessors of it, for I had two at this time, both of them learned men, and great servants of God.

The Saint obtains the conversion of a person in peril of sin. 5. I knew of a person who had resolved to serve God in all earnestness, and had for some days given himself to prayer, in which he had received many graces from our Lord, but who had abandoned his good resolutions because of certain occasions of sin in which he was involved, and which he would not avoid; they were extremely perilous. This caused me the utmost distress, because the person was one for whom I had a great affection, and one to whom I owed much. For more than a month I believe I did nothing else but pray to God for his conversion. One day, when I was in prayer, I saw a devil close by in a great rage, tearing to pieces some paper which he had in his hands. That sight consoled me greatly, because it seemed that my prayer had been heard. So it was, as I learnt afterwards; for that person had made his confession with great contrition, and returned to God so sincerely, that I trust in

[1] 3 Kings xix. 12 : " Sibilus auræ tenuis."

His Majesty he will always advance further and further. May He be blessed for ever! Amen.

6. In answer to my prayers, our Lord has very often rescued souls from mortal sins, and led others on to greater perfection. But as to the delivering of souls out of purgatory, and other remarkable acts, so many are the mercies of our Lord herein, that were I to speak of them I should only weary myself and my reader. But He has done more by me for the salvation of souls than for the health of the body. This is very well known, and there are many to bear witness to it. *The intercession of the Saint.*

7. At first it made me scrupulous, because I could not help thinking that our Lord did these things in answer to my prayer; I say nothing of the chief reason of all—His pure compassion. But now these graces are so many, and so well known to others, that it gives me no pain to think so. I bless His Majesty, and abase myself, because I am still more deeply in His debt; and I believe that He makes my desire to serve Him grow, and my love revive. *The Saint tempted to be scrupulous.*

8. But what amazes me most is this: however much I may wish to pray for those graces which our Lord sees not to be expedient, I cannot do it; and if I try, I do so with little earnestness, force, and spirit: it is impossible to do more, even if I would. But it is not so as to those which His Majesty intends to grant. These I can pray for constantly, and with great importunity; though I do not carry them in my memory, they seem to present themselves to me at once.[1] *Two ways of praying.*

9. There is a great difference between these two ways of praying, and I know not how to explain it. As to the first, when I pray for those graces which our Lord does not mean to grant,—even though they concern me very nearly,—I am like one whose tongue is tied; who, though he would speak, yet cannot; or, if he speaks, sees that people do not listen to him. And yet I do not fail to force myself to pray, though not conscious of that fervour which I have when praying for those graces which our Lord intends to *The Saint explains the two ways.*

[1] See S. John of the Cross, *Ascent of Mount Carmel*, bk. iii. ch. i.

give. In the second case, I am like one who speaks clearly and intelligibly to another, whom he sees to be a willing listener.

<small>Vocal prayer and contemplation.</small> 10. The prayer that is not to be heard is, so to speak, like vocal prayer; the other is a prayer of contemplation so high that our Lord shows Himself in such a way as to make us feel He hears us, and that He delights in our prayer, and that He is about to grant our petition. Blessed be He for ever who gives me so much, and to whom I give so little! For what is he worth, O my Lord, who does not utterly abase himself to nothing for Thee? How much, how much, how much,—I might say so a thousand times,—I fall short of this! It is on this account that I do not wish to live,—though there be other reasons also,—because I do not live according to the obligations which bind me to Thee. What imperfections I trace in myself! what remissness in Thy service! Certainly, I could wish occasionally I had no sense, that I might be unconscious of the great evil that is in me. May He who can do all things help me!

<small>The Saint in the house of Doña Luisa.</small> 11. When I was staying in the house of that lady of whom I have spoken before,[1] it was necessary for me to be very watchful over myself, and keep continually in mind the intrinsic vanity of all the things of this life, because of the great esteem I was held in, and of the praises bestowed on me. There was much there to which I might have become attached, if I had looked only to myself; but I looked to Him who sees things as they really are, not to let me go out of His hand. Now that I speak of seeing things as they really are, I remember how great a trial it is for those to whom God has granted a true insight into the things of earth to have to discuss them with others. They wear so many disguises, as our Lord once told me,—and much of what I am saying of them is not from myself, but rather what my heavenly Master has taught me; and therefore, in speaking of them, when I say distinctly I understood this, or our Lord told me this, I am very scrupulous neither to add nor to take away one single syllable; so, when I do not clearly

[1] Ch. xxxiv. § 1.

remember every thing exactly, that must be taken as coming from myself, and some things, perhaps, are so altogether. I do not call mine that which is good, for I know there is no other good in me but only that which our Lord gave me when I was so far from deserving it: I call that mine which I speak without having had it made known to me by revelation.

12. But, O my God, how is it that we too often judge even spiritual things, as we do those of the world, by our own understanding, wresting them grievously from their true meaning? We think we may measure our progress by the years which we have given to the exercise of prayer; we even think we can prescribe limits to Him who bestows His gifts not by measure[1] when He wills, and who in six months can give to one more than to another in many years. This is a fact which I have so frequently observed in many persons, that I am surprised how any of us can deny it. *God gives to whom He will.*

13. I am certainly convinced that he will not remain under this delusion who possesses the gift of discerning spirits, and to whom our Lord has given real humility; for such a one will judge of them by the fruits, by the good resolutions and love,—and our Lord gives him light to understand the matter; and herein He regards the progress and advancement of souls, not the years they may have spent in prayer; for one person may make greater progress in six months than another in twenty years, because, as I said before, our Lord gives to whom He will, particularly to him who is best disposed. *The progress of the soul not to be measured by time.*

14. I see this in certain persons of tender years who have come to this monastery,—God touches their hearts, and gives them a little light and love. I speak of that brief interval in which He gives them sweetness in prayer, and then they wait for nothing further, and make light of every difficulty, forgetting the necessity even of food; for they shut themselves up for ever in a house that is unendowed, as persons who make no account of their life, for His sake, who, they know, loves them. They give up every thing, *The nuns of S. Joseph.*

---

[1] S. John iii. 34 : "Non enim ad mensuram dat Deus spiritum."

even their own will; and it never enters into their mind that they might be discontented in so small a house, and where enclosure is so strictly observed. They offer themselves wholly in sacrifice to God.

The Saint thinks herself inferior to her novices at S. Joseph.

15. Oh, how willingly do I admit that they are better than I am! and how I ought to be ashamed of myself before God! What His Majesty has not been able to accomplish in me in so many years,—it is long ago since I began to pray, and He to bestow His graces upon me,—He accomplished in them in three months, and in some of them even in three days, though He gives them much fewer graces than He gave to me: and yet His Majesty rewards them well; most assuredly they are not sorry for what they have done for Him.

All souls are not to be directed in the same way.

16. I wish, therefore, we reminded ourselves of those long years which have gone by since we made our religious profession. I say this to those persons, also, who have given themselves long ago to prayer, but not for the purpose of distressing those who in a short time have made greater progress than we have made, by making them retrace their steps, so that they may proceed only as we do ourselves. We must not desire those who, because of the graces God has given them, are flying like eagles, to become like chickens whose feet are tied. Let us rather look to His Majesty, and give these souls the reins, if we see that they are humble; for our Lord, who has had such compassion upon them, will not let them fall into the abyss.

We must not judge other souls by our own.

17. These souls trust themselves in the hands of God, for the truth, which they learn by faith, helps them to do it; and shall not we also trust them to Him, without seeking to measure them by our measure, which is that of our meanness of spirit? We must not do it; for if we cannot ascend to the heights of their great love and courage,—without experience none can comprehend them,—let us humble ourselves, and not condemn them; for, by this seeming regard to their progress, we hinder our own, and miss the opportunity our Lord gives us to humble ourselves, to ascertain our own shortcomings, and learn how

much more detached and more near to God these souls must be than we are, seeing that His Majesty draws so near to them Himself.

18. I have no other intention here, and I wish to have no other, than to express my preference for the prayer that in a short time results in these great effects, which show themselves at once; for it is impossible they should enable us to leave all things only to please God, if they were not accompanied with a vehement love. I would rather have that prayer than that which lasted many years, but which at the end of the time, as well as at the beginning, never issued in a resolution to do any thing for God, with the exception of some trifling services, like a grain of salt, without weight or bulk, and which a bird might carry away in its mouth. Is it not a serious and mortifying thought that we are making much of certain services which we render our Lord, but which are too pitiable to be considered, even if they were many in number? This is my case, and I am forgetting every moment the mercies of our Lord. I do not mean that His Majesty will not make much of them Himself, for He is good; but I wish I made no account of them myself, or even perceived that I did them, for they are nothing worth. *The Saint prefers the prayer which most quickly does its work.*

19. But, O my Lord, do Thou forgive me, and blame me not, if I try to console myself a little with the little I do, seeing that I do not serve Thee at all; for if I rendered Thee any great services, I should not think of these trifles. Blessed are they who serve Thee in great deeds; if envying these, and desiring to do what they do, were of any help to me, I should not be so far behind them as I am in pleasing Thee; but I am nothing worth, O my Lord; do Thou make me of some worth, Thou who lovest me so much. *The Saint regards herself as the unprofitable servant.*

20. During one of those days, when this monastery, which seems to have cost me some labour, was fully founded by the arrival of the Brief from Rome, which empowered us to live without an endowment;[1] and I was comforting myself at seeing the whole affair concluded, *The Saint is astonished at her own imperfections.*

[1] See ch. xxxiii. § 14.

and thinking of all the trouble I had had, and giving thanks to our Lord for having been pleased to make some use of me, —it happened that I began to consider all that we had gone through. Well, so it was; in every one of my actions, which I thought were of some service, I traced so many faults and imperfections, now and then but little courage, very frequently a want of faith; for until this moment, when I see every thing accomplished, I never absolutely believed; neither, however, on the other hand, could I doubt what our Lord said to me about the foundation of this house. I cannot tell how it was; very often the matter seemed to me, on the one hand, impossible; and, on the other hand, I could not be in doubt: I mean, I could not believe that it would not be accomplished. In short, I find that our Lord Himself, on His part, did all the good that was done, while I did all the evil. I therefore ceased to think of the matter, and wished never to be reminded of it again, lest I should do myself some harm by dwelling on my many faults. Blessed be He who, when He pleases, draws good out of all my failings! Amen.

Length of time given to prayer not necessarily meritorious.

21. I say, then, there is danger in counting the years we have given to prayer; for, granting that there is nothing in it against humility, it seems to me to imply something like an appearance of thinking that we have merited, in some degree, by the service rendered. I do not mean that there is no merit in it at all, nor that it will not be well rewarded; yet if any spiritual person thinks, because he has given himself to prayer for many years, that he deserves any spiritual consolations, I am sure he will never attain to spiritual perfection. Is it not enough that a man has merited the protection of God, which keeps him from committing those sins into which he fell before he began to pray, but he must also, as they say, sue God for His own money?

There is no humility in asking spiritual consolation,

22. This does not seem to me to be deep humility, and yet it may be that it is; however, I look on it as great boldness, for I, who have very little humility, have never ventured upon it. It may be that I never asked for it, because I had never served Him; perhaps,

if I had served Him, I should have been more importunate than all others with our Lord for my reward.

23. I do not mean that the soul makes no progress in time, or that God will not reward it, if its prayer has been humble; but I do mean that we should forget the number of years we have been praying, because all that we can do is utterly worthless in comparison with one drop of blood out of those which our Lord shed for us. And if the more we serve Him, the more we become His debtors, what is it, then, we are asking for? for, if we pay one farthing of the debt, He gives us back a thousand ducats. For the love of God, let us leave these questions alone, for they belong to Him. Comparisons are always bad, even in earthly things; what, then, must they be in that, the knowledge of which God has reserved to Himself? His Majesty showed this clearly enough, when those who came late and those who came early to His vineyard received the same wages.[1] *Because we can never pay what we owe to God.*

24. I have sat down so often to write, and have been so many days writing these three leaves,—for, as I have said,[2] I had, and have still, but few opportunities,—that I forgot what I had begun with, namely, the following vision.[3] *The Saint interrupted while writing her Life.*

25. I was in prayer, and saw myself on a wide plain all alone. Round about me stood a great multitude of all kinds of people, who hemmed me in on every side; all of them seemed to have weapons of war in their hands, to hurt me: some had spears, others swords; some had daggers, and others very long rapiers. In short, I could not move away in any direction without exposing myself to the hazard of death, and I was alone, without any one to take my part. In this distress of mind, not knowing what to do, I lifted up my eyes to heaven, and saw Christ, not in heaven, but high above me in the air, holding out His hand to me, and there protecting me in such a way that I was no longer afraid of all that *A vision.*

---

[1] S. Matt. xx. 9-14: "Volo autem et huic novissimo dare sicut et tibi."

[2] Ch. x. § 13.

[3] The Saint had this vision when she was in the house of Doña Luisa de la Cerda in Toledo, and it was fulfilled in the opposition she met with in the foundation of S. Joseph of Avila. See ch. xxxvi. § 18.

multitude, neither could they, though they wished it, do me any harm.

26. At first the vision seemed to have no results; *Merits of the vision.* but it has been of the greatest help to me, since I understood what it meant. Not long afterwards, I saw myself, as it were, exposed to the like assault, and I saw that the vision represented the world, because every thing in it takes up arms against the poor soul. We need not speak of those who are not great servants of our Lord, nor of honours, possessions, and pleasures, with other things of the same nature; for it is clear that the soul, if it be not watchful, will find itself caught in a net,—at least, all these things labour to ensnare it; more than this, so also do friends and relatives, and—what frightens me most—even good people. I found myself afterwards so beset on all sides, good people thinking they were doing good, and I knowing not how to defend myself, nor what to do.

27. O my God, if I were to say in what way, *The great trials of the Saint.* and in how many ways, I was tried at that time, even after that trial of which I have just spoken, what a warning I should be giving to men to hate the whole world utterly! It was the greatest of all the persecutions I had to undergo. I saw myself occasionally so hemmed in on every side, that I could do nothing else but lift up my eyes to heaven, and cry unto God.[1] I recollected well what I had seen in the vision, and it helped me greatly not to trust much in any one, for there is no one that can be relied on except God. In all my great trials, our Lord—He showed it to me—sent always some one on His part to hold out his hand to help me, as it was shown to me in the vision, so that I might attach myself to nothing, but only please our Lord; and this has been enough to sustain the little virtue I have in desiring to serve Thee: be Thou blessed for evermore!

28. On one occasion I was exceedingly dis- *Our Lord consoles her* quieted and troubled, unable to recollect myself, fighting and struggling with my thoughts, running

[1] 2 Paralip. xx. 12: "Hoc solum habemus residui, ut oculos nostros dirigamus ad Te."

upon matters which did not relate to perfection; and, moreover, I did not think I was so detached from all things as I used to be. When I found myself in this wretched state, I was afraid that the graces I had received from our Lord were illusions, and the end was that a great darkness covered my soul. In this my distress our Lord began to speak to me: He bade me not to harass myself, but learn, from the consideration of my misery, what it would be if He withdrew Himself from me, and that we were never safe while living in the flesh. It was given me to understand how this fighting and struggling are profitable to us, because of the reward, and it seemed to me as if our Lord were sorry for us who live in the world. Moreover, He bade me not to suppose that He had forgotten me; He would never abandon me, but it was necessary I should do all that I could myself.

29. Our Lord said all this with great tenderness and sweetness; He also spoke other most gracious words, which I need not repeat. His Majesty, further showing His great love for me, said to me very often: "Thou art Mine, and I am thine." I am in the habit of saying myself, and I believe in all sincerity: "What do I care for myself?—I care only for Thee, O my Lord." *With many words.*

30. These words of our Lord, and the consolations He gives me, fill me with the utmost shame, when I remember what I am. I have said it before, I think,[1] and I still say now and then to my confessor, that it requires greater courage to receive these graces than to endure the heaviest trials. When they come, I forget, as it were, all I have done, and there is nothing before me but a picture of my wretchedness, and my understanding can make no reflections; this, also, seems to me at times to be supernatural. *Effects of the divine locutions.*

31. Sometimes I have such a vehement longing for Communion; I do not think it can be expressed. One morning it happened to rain so much as to make it seem impossible to leave the house. When I had gone out, I was so beside myself with that longing, that if spears had been pointed at my heart, I should have rushed upon *The Saint's longing for Communion.*

[1] Ch. xx. § 4.

them; the rain was nothing. When I entered the church, I fell into a deep trance, and saw heaven open—not a door only, as I used to see at other times. I beheld the throne which, as I have told you, my father, I saw at other times, with another throne above it, whereon, though I saw not, I understood by a certain inexplicable knowledge that the Godhead dwelt.

The trance lasted two hours. 32. The throne seemed to me to be supported by certain animals; I believe I saw the form of them: I thought they might be the Evangelists. But now the throne was arrayed, and Him who sat on it I did not see, but only an exceedingly great multitude of angels, who seemed to me more beautiful, beyond all comparison, than those I had seen in heaven. I thought they were, perhaps, the seraphim or cherubim, for they were very different in their glory, and seemingly all on fire. The difference is great, as I said before;[1] and the joy I then felt cannot be described, either in writing or by word of mouth; it is inconceivable to any one who has not had experience of it. I felt that every thing man can desire was all there together, and I saw nothing; they told me, but I know not who, that all I could do there was to understand that I could understand nothing, and see how every thing was nothing in comparison with that. So it was; my soul afterwards was vexed to see that it could rest on any created thing: how much more, then, if it had any affection thereto; for every thing seemed to me but an ant-hill. I communicated, and remained during Mass. I know not how it was: I thought I had been but a few minutes, and was amazed when the clock struck; I had been two hours in that trance and joy.

The fire of divine love. 33. I was afterwards amazed at this fire, which seems to spring forth out of the true love of God; for though I might long for it, labour for it, and annihilate myself in the effort to obtain it, I can do nothing towards procuring a single spark of it myself, because it all comes of the good pleasure of His Majesty, as I said on another occasion.[2] It seems to burn up the old man, with his faults, his lukewarmness, and misery; so that it is like the phœnix, of

[1] Ch. xxix. § 16.   [2] Ch. xxix. § 11.

which I have read that it comes forth, after being burnt, out of its own ashes into a new life. Thus it is with the soul: it is changed into another, whose desires are different, and whose strength is great. It seems to be no longer what it was before, and begins to walk renewed in purity in the ways of our Lord. When I was praying to Him that thus it might be with me, and that I might begin His service anew, He said to me: "The comparison thou hast made is good; take care never to forget it, that thou mayest always labour to advance."

34. Once, when I was doubting, as I said just now,[1] whether these visions came from God or not, our Lord appeared, and, with some severity, said to me: "O children of men, how long will you remain hard of heart!" I was to examine myself carefully on one subject, —whether I had given myself up wholly to Him, or not. If I had,—and it was so,—I was to believe that He would not suffer me to perish. I was very much afflicted when He spoke thus, but He turned to me with great tenderness and sweetness, and bade me not to distress myself, for He knew already that, so far as it lay in my power, I would not fail in any thing that was for His service; that He himself would do what I wished,— and so He did grant what I was then praying for; that I was to consider my love for Him, which was daily growing in me, for I should see by this that these visions did not come from Satan; that I must not imagine that God would ever allow the devil to have so much power over the souls of His servants as to give them such clearness of understanding and such peace as I had. *Our Lord removes the Saint's doubts.*

35. He gave me also to understand that, when such and so many persons had told me the visions were from God, I should do wrong if I did not believe them.[2] *Directors to be trusted.*

36. Once, when I was reciting the psalm *Quicunque vult*,[3] I was given to understand the mystery of One God and Three Persons with so much clearness, that I was greatly astonished and consoled at the same *The mystery of the Trinity revealed to the Saint.*

---

[1] § 28.   [2] See ch. xxviii. §§ 19, 20.
[3] Commonly called the Creed of S. Athanasius.

time. This was of the greatest help to me, for it enabled me to know more of the greatness and marvels of God; and when I think of the most Holy Trinity, or hear It spoken of, I seem to understand the mystery, and a great joy it is.

The Saint sees the Assumption in a vision. 37. One day—it was the Feast of the Assumption of the Queen of the Angels, and our Lady—our Lord was pleased to grant me this grace. In a trance He made me behold her going up to heaven, the joy and solemnity of her reception there, as well as the place where she now is. To describe it is more than I can do; the joy that filled my soul at the sight of such great glory was excessive. The effects of the vision were great; it made me long to endure still greater trials: and I had a vehement desire to serve our Lady, because of her great merits.

A vision in a Jesuit house. 38. Once, in one of the colleges of the Society of Jesus, when the brothers of the house were communicating, I saw an exceedingly rich canopy above their heads. I saw this twice; but I never saw it when others were receiving Communion.

CHAPTER XL.

VISIONS, REVELATIONS, AND LOCUTIONS.

The Saint in a trance. 1. ONE day, in prayer, the sweetness of which was so great that, knowing how unworthy I was of so great a blessing, I began to think how much I had deserved to be in that place which I had seen prepared for me in hell,—for, as I said before,[1] I never forget the way I saw myself there,—as I was thinking of this, my soul began to be more and more on fire, and I was carried away in spirit in a way I cannot describe. It seemed to me as if I had been absorbed in, and filled with, that grandeur of God which, on another occasion, I had felt.[2] In that majesty it was given me to understand one truth, which is the fulness of all truth, but I cannot tell how, for I saw nothing. It was said to me,

[1] Ch. xxxii. § 1.   [2] Ch. xxviii. § 14.

I saw not by whom, but I knew well enough it was the Truth Itself: "This I am doing to thee is not a slight matter; it is one of those things for which thou owest Me much; for all the evil in the world comes from ignorance of the truths of the holy writings in their clear simplicity, of which not one iota shall pass away."[1] I thought that I had always believed this, and that all the faithful also believed it. Then He said: "Ah, My daughter, they are few who love Me in truth; for if men loved Me, I should not hide My secrets from them. Knowest thou what it is to love Me in truth? It is to admit every thing to be a lie which is not pleasing unto Me. Now thou dost not understand it, but thou shalt understand it clearly hereafter, in the profit it will be to thy soul."

2. Our Lord be praised, so I found it; for after this vision I look upon every thing which does not tend to the service of God as vanity and lies. I cannot tell how much I am convinced of this, nor how sorry I am for those whom I see living in darkness, not knowing the truth. I derived other great blessings also from this, some of which I will here speak of, others I cannot describe. *Blessing of believing every word of God.*

3. Our Lord at the same time uttered a special word of most exceeding graciousness. I know not how it was done, for I saw nothing; but I was filled, in a way which also I cannot describe, with exceeding strength and earnestness of purpose to observe with all my might every thing contained in the divine writings. I thought that I could rise above every possible hindrance put in my way. *The Saint hears ineffable words.*

4. Of this divine truth, which was put before me I know not how, there remains imprinted within me a truth—I cannot give it a name—which fills me with a new reverence for God; it gives me a notion of His majesty and power in a way which I cannot explain. I can understand that it is something very high. I had a very great desire never to speak of any thing but of those deep truths which far surpass all that is spoken of here in the world, —and so the living in it began to be painful to me. *Effects of them.*

---

[1] S. Matt. v. 18: "Iota unum aut unus apex non præteribit a lege."

5. The vision left me in great tenderness, joy, and humility. It seemed to me, though I knew not how, that our Lord now gave me great things; and I had no suspicion whatever of any illusion. I saw nothing; but I understood how great a blessing it is to make no account of any thing which does not lead us nearer unto God. I also understood what it is for a soul to be walking in the truth, in the presence of the Truth itself. What I understood is this: that our Lord gave me to understand that He is Himself the very Truth.

Effects of the vision.

6. All this I am speaking of I learnt at times by means of words uttered; at other times I learnt some things without the help of words, and that more clearly than those other things which were told me in words. I understood exceedingly deep truths concerning the Truth, more than I could have done through the teaching of many learned men. It seems to me that learned men never could have thus impressed upon me, nor so clearly explained to me, the vanity of this world.

Difference between natural and supernatural teaching.

7. The Truth of which I am speaking, and which I was given to see, is Truth Itself, in Itself. It has neither beginning nor end. All other truths depend on this Truth, as all other loves depend on this love, and all other grandeurs on this grandeur. I understood it all, notwithstanding that my words are obscure in comparison with that distinctness with which it pleased our Lord to show it to me. What think you must be the power of His Majesty, seeing that in so short a time it leaves so great a blessing and such an impression on the soul? O Grandeur! Majesty of mine! what is it Thou art doing, O my Lord Almighty! Consider who it is to whom Thou givest blessings so great! Dost Thou not remember that this my soul has been an abyss of lies and a sea of vanities, and all my fault? Though Thou hadst given me a natural hatred of lying, yet I did involve myself in many lying ways. How is this, O my God? how can it be that mercies and graces so great should fall to the lot of one who has so ill deserved them at Thy hands?

The Truth.

8. Once, when I was with the whole community reciting the Office, my soul became suddenly recollected, and seemed to me all bright as a mirror, clear behind, sideways, upwards, and downwards; and in the centre of it I saw Christ our Lord, as I usually see Him. It seemed to me that I saw Him distinctly in every part of my soul, as in a mirror, and at the same time the mirror was all sculptured—I cannot explain it—in our Lord Himself by a most loving communication which I can never describe. I know that this vision was a great blessing to me, and is still whenever I remember it, particularly after Communion. *The Saint has a vision of her own soul.*

9. I understood by it, that, when a soul is in mortal sin, this mirror becomes clouded with a thick vapour, and utterly obscured, so that our Lord is neither visible nor present, though He is always present in the conservation of its being. In heretics, the mirror is, as it were, broken in pieces, and that is worse than being dimmed. There is a very great difference between seeing this and describing it, for it can hardly be explained. But it has done me great good; it has also made me very sorry on account of those times when I dimmed the lustre of my soul by my sins, so that I could not see our Lord. *Meaning of the vision.*

10. This vision seems to me very profitable to recollected persons, to teach them to look upon our Lord as being in the innermost part of their soul. It is a method of looking upon Him which penetrates us more thoroughly, and is much more fruitful, than that of looking upon Him as external to us, as I have said elsewhere,[1] and as it is laid down in books on prayer, where they speak of where we are to seek God. The glorious S. Augustin,[2] in particular, says so, when he says that neither in the streets of the city, nor in pleasures, nor in any place whatever where he sought Him, did he find Him as he found Him within himself. *God to be sought within ourselves.*

[1] Ch. iv. § 10.
[2] "Ecce quantum spatiatus sum in memoria mea quærens Te, Domine; et non Te inveni extra eam.... Ex quo didici Te, manes in memoria mea, et illic Te invenio cum reminiscor Tui et delector in Te" (*Confess.* x. 24). See *Way of Perfection*, ch. xiv. § 1; but ch. xxviii. of previous editions.

This is clearly the best way; we need not go up to heaven, nor any further than our own selves, for that would only distress the spirit and distract the soul, and bring but little fruit.

Outward effects of a trance. 11. I should like to point out one result of a deep trance; it may be that some are aware of it. When the time is over during which the soul was in union, wherein all its powers were wholly absorbed,—it lasts, as I have said,[1] but a moment,—the soul continues still to be recollected, unable to recover itself even in outward things; for the two powers—the memory and the understanding—are, as it were, in a frenzy, extremely disordered. This, I say, happens occasionally, particularly in the beginnings. I am thinking whether it does not result from this: that our natural weakness cannot endure the vehemence of the spirit, which is so great, and that the imagination is enfeebled. I know it to be so with some. I think it best for these to force themselves to give up prayer at that time, and resume it afterwards, when they may recover what they have lost, and not do every thing at once, for in that case much harm might come of it. I know this by experience, as well as the necessity of considering what our health can bear.

12. Experience is necessary throughout, so also *Necessity of a director.* is a spiritual director; for when the soul has reached this point, there are many matters which must be referred to the director. If, after seeking such a one, the soul cannot find him, our Lord will not fail that soul, seeing that He has not failed me, who am what I am. They are not many, I believe, who know by experience so many things, and without experience it is useless to treat a soul at all, for nothing will come of it, save only trouble and distress. But our Lord will take this also into account, and for that reason it is always best to refer the matter to the director. I have already more than once said this,[2] and even all I am saying now, only I do not distinctly remember it; but I do see that it is of great importance, particularly to women, that they should

---

[1] Ch. xx. § 26.
[2] Ch. xxv. § 18, ch. xxvi. § 6. See S. John of the Cross, *Mount Carmel*, bk. ii. ch. xxii.

go to their confessor, and that he should be a man of experience herein. There are many more women than men to whom our Lord gives these graces; I have heard the holy friar Peter of Alcantara say so, and, indeed, I know it myself. He used to say that women made greater progress in this way than men did; and he gave excellent reasons for his opinion, all in favour of women; but there is no necessity for repeating them here.

13. Once, when in prayer, I had a vision, for a moment,—I saw nothing distinctly, but the vision was most clear,—how all things are seen in God, and how all things are comprehended in Him. *All things are, and are seen, in God.* I cannot in any way explain it, but the vision remains most deeply impressed on my soul, and is one of those grand graces which our Lord wrought in me, and one of those which put me to the greatest shame and confusion whenever I call my sins to remembrance. I believe, if it had pleased our Lord that I had seen this at an earlier time, or if they saw it who sin against Him, we should have neither the heart nor the daring to do so. I had the vision, I repeat it, but I cannot say that I saw any thing; however, I must have seen something, seeing that I explain it by an illustration, only it must have been in a way so subtile and delicate that the understanding is unable to reach it, or I am so ignorant in all that relates to these visions, which seem to be not imaginary. In some of these visions there must be something imaginary, only, as the powers of the soul are then in a trance, they are not able afterwards to retain the forms, as our Lord showed them to it then, and as He would have it rejoice in them.

14. Let us suppose the Godhead to be a most brilliant diamond, much larger than the whole world, *The illustration.* or a mirror like that to which I compared the soul in a former vision,[1] only in a way so high that I cannot possibly describe it; and that all our actions are seen in that diamond, which is of such dimensions as to include every thing, because nothing can be beyond it. It was a fearful thing for me to see, in so short a time, so many things together in that brilliant

[1] § 9.

diamond, and a most piteous thing too, whenever I think of it, to see such foul things as my sins present in the pure brilliancy of that light.

Horrible nature of sin. 15. So it is, whenever I remember it, I do not know how to bear it, and I was then so ashamed of myself that I knew not where to hide myself. Oh, that some one could make this plain to those who commit most foul and filthy sins, that they may remember their sins are not secret, and that God most justly resents them, seeing that they are wrought in the very presence of His Majesty, and that we are demeaning ourselves so irreverently before Him! I saw, too, how completely hell is deserved for only one mortal sin, and how impossible it is to understand the exceeding great wickedness of committing it in the sight of majesty so great, and how abhorrent to His nature such actions are. In this we see more and more of His mercifulness, who, though we all know His hatred of sin, yet suffers us to live.

The day of judgment. 16. The vision made me also reflect, that if one such vision as this fills the soul with such awe, what will it be in the day of judgment, when His Majesty will appear distinctly, and when we too shall look on the sins we have committed! O my God, I have been, oh, how blind! I have often been amazed at what I have written; and you, my father, be you not amazed at any thing, but that I am still living,—I, who see such things, and know myself to be what I am. Blessed for ever be He who has borne with me so long!

The Saint sees herself close unto God. 17. Once, in prayer, with much recollection, sweetness, and repose, I saw myself, as it seemed to me, surrounded by angels, and was close unto God. I began to intercede with His Majesty on behalf of the Church. I was given to understand the great services which a particular Order would render in the latter days, and the courage with which its members would maintain the faith.

Prophecy concerning an Order not then in a high estate. 18. I was praying before the most Holy Sacrament one day; I had a vision of a Saint, whose Order was in some degree fallen. In his hands he held a large book, which he opened, and then told me to read certain words, written in large and very legible letters; they were to this effect: "In times to come this Order will flourish; it will have many martyrs."[1]

19. On another occasion, when I was at Matins in choir, six or seven persons, who seemed to me to be of this Order, appeared and stood before me with swords in their hands. The meaning of that, as I think, is that they are to be defenders of the faith; for at another time, when I was in prayer, I fell into a trance, and stood in spirit on a wide plain, where many persons were fighting; and the members of this Order were fighting with great zeal. Their faces were beautiful, and as it were on fire. Many they laid low on the ground defeated, others they killed. It seemed to me to be a battle with heretics. *A vision relating to the same Order.*

20. I have seen this glorious Saint occasionally, and he has told me certain things, and thanked me for praying for his Order, and he has promised to pray for me to our Lord. I do not say which Orders these are,—our Lord, if it so pleased Him, could make them known, —lest the others should be aggrieved. Let every Order, or every member of them by himself, labour, that by his means our Lord would so bless his own Order that it may serve Him in the present grave necessities of His Church. Blessed are they whose lives are so spent. *And to the Saint referred to before.*

[1] Yepez says that the Order here spoken of is the Carmelite, and Ribera understands the Saint to refer to that of S. Dominic. The Bollandists, n. 1638-1646, on the whole, prefer the authority of Ribera to that of Yepez, and give good reasons for their preference, setting aside as insufficient the testimony of Fray Luis of the Assumption, who says he heard himself from the Venerable Anne of S. Bartholomew that the Order in question is the Order of our Lady of Mount Carmel. Don Vicente, the Spanish editor, rejects the opinion of Ribera, on the ground that it could not have been truly said of the Dominicans in the sixteenth century that the Order was in "some degree fallen," for it was in a most flourishing state. He therefore was inclined to believe that the Saint referred to the Augustinians or to the Franciscans. But, after he had printed this part of his book, he discovered among the MSS. in the public library of Madrid a letter of Anne of S. Bartholomew, addressed to Fray Luis of the Assumption, in which the saintly companion of S. Teresa says that the "Order was ours." Don Vicente has published the letter in the Appendix, p. 566.

21. I was once asked by a person to pray God to let him know whether his acceptance of a bishopric would be for the service of God. After Communion our Lord said to me: "When he shall have clearly and really understood that true dominion consists in possessing nothing, he may then accept it." I understood by this that he who is to be in dignity must be very far from wishing or desiring it, or at least he must not seek it.

The Saint consulted by one to whom a bishopric was offered.

22. These and many other graces our Lord has given, and is giving continually, to me a sinner. I do not think it is necessary to speak of them, because the state of my soul can be ascertained from what I have written; so also can the spirit which our Lord has given me. May He be blessed for ever, who has been so mindful of me!

23. Our Lord said to me once, consoling me, that I was not to distress myself,—this He said most lovingly,—because in this life we could not continue in the same state.[1] At one time I should be fervent, at another not; now disquieted, and again at peace, and tempted; but I must hope in Him, and fear not.

Changes in the spiritual life.

24. I was one day thinking whether it was a want of detachment in me to take pleasure in the company of those who had the care of my soul, and to have an affection for them, and to comfort myself with those whom I see to be very great servants of God.[2] Our Lord said to me : " It is not a virtue in a sick man to abstain from thanking and loving the physician who seems to restore him to health when he is in danger of death. What should I have done without these persons? The conversation of good people was never hurtful; my words should always be weighed, and holy; and I was not to cease my relations with them, for they would do me good rather than harm."

Our Lord bids the Saint continue her relations with good people.

25. This was a great comfort to me, because, now and then, I wished to abstain from converse with all people; for it seemed to me that I was

She is greatly consoled.

---

[1] Job xiv. 2: "Nunquam in eodem statu permanet."
[2] See ch. xxxvii. §§ 4, 6.

attached to them. Always, in all things, did our Lord console me, even to the showing me how I was to treat those who were weak, and some other people also. Never did He cease to take care of me. I am sometimes distressed to see how little I do in His service, and how I am forced to spend time in taking care of a body so weak and worthless as mine is, more than I wish.

26. I was in prayer one night, when it was time to go to sleep. I was in very great pain, and my usual sickness was coming on.[1] I saw myself so great a slave to myself, and, on the other hand, the spirit asked for time for itself. I was so much distressed that I began to weep exceedingly, and to be very sorry. This has happened to me not once only, but, as I am saying, very often; and it seems to make me weary of myself, so that at the time I hold myself literally in abhorrence. Habitually, however, I know that I do not hate myself, and I never fail to take that which I see to be necessary for me. May our Lord grant that I do not take more than is necessary!—I am afraid I do. *The Saint's distress because she had to take care of her health.*

27. When I was thus distressed, our Lord appeared unto me. He comforted me greatly, and told me I must do this for His love, and bear it; my life was necessary now. And so, I believe, I have never known real pain since I resolved to serve my Lord and my Consoler with all my strength; for though He would leave me to suffer a little, yet He would console me in such a way that I am doing nothing when I long for troubles. And it seems to me there is nothing worth living for but this, and suffering is what I most heartily pray to God for. I say to Him sometimes, with my whole heart: "O Lord, either to die or to suffer! I ask of Thee nothing else for myself." It is a comfort to me to hear the clock strike, because I seem to have come a little nearer to the vision of God, in that another hour of my life has passed away. *The Saint's longing for suffering.*

28. At other times I am in such a state that I do not feel that I am living, nor yet do I desire to die; but I am lukewarm, and darkness surrounds me on every side, as I said before;[2] for I am very often *The Saint's vision became known against her will.*

[1] See ch. vii. § 19. [2] Ch. xxx. § 11.

in great trouble. It pleased our Lord that the graces He wrought in me should be published abroad,[1] as He told me some years ago they should be. It was a great pain to me, and I have borne much on that account even to this day, as you, my father, know, because every man explains them in his own sense. But my comfort herein is that it is not my fault that they are become known, for I was extremely cautious never to speak of them but to my confessors, or to persons who I knew had heard of them from them. I was silent, however, not out of humility, but because, as I said before,[2] it gave me great pain to speak of them even to my confessors.

The Saint's contentment. 29. Now, however,—to God be the glory!—though many speak against me, but out of a zeal for goodness, and though some are afraid to speak to me, and even to hear my confession, and though others have much to say about me, because I see that our Lord willed by this means to provide help for many souls,—and also because I see clearly and keep in mind how much He would suffer, if only for the gaining of one,—I do not care about it at all.

The Saint's indifference to the opinions of men. 30. I know not why it is so, but perhaps the reason may in some measure be that His Majesty has placed me in this corner out of the way, where the enclosure is so strict, and where I am as one that is dead. I thought that no one would remember me, but I am not so much forgotten as I wish I was, for I am forced to speak to some people. But as I am in a house where none may see me, it seems as if our Lord had been pleased to bring me to a haven, which I trust in His Majesty will be secure. Now that I am out of the world, with companions holy and few in number, I look down on the world as from a great height, and care very little what people say or know about me. I think much more of one soul's advancement, even if it were but slight, than of all that people may say of me; and since I am settled here it has pleased our Lord that all my desires tend to this.

[1] Ch. xxxi. §§ 16, 17.   [2] Ch. xxviii. § 6.

31. He has made my life to me now a kind of sleep; for almost always what I see seems to me to be seen as in a dream, nor have I any great sense either of pleasure or of pain. If matters occur which may occasion either, the sense of it passes away so quickly that it astonishes me, and leaves an impression as if I had been dreaming,—and this is the simple truth; for if I wished afterwards to delight in that pleasure, or be sorry over that pain, it is not in my power to do so: just as a sensible person feels neither pain nor pleasure in the memory of a dream that is past; for now our Lord has roused my soul out of that state, which, because I was not mortified nor dead to the things of this world, made me feel as I did, and His Majesty does not wish me to become blind again. *The Saint's life.*

32. This is the way I live now, my lord and father; do you, my father, pray to God that He would take me to Himself, or enable me to serve Him. May it please His Majesty that what I have written may be of some use to you, my father! I have so little time,[1] and therefore my trouble has been great in writing; but it will be a blessed trouble if I have succeeded in saying any thing that will cause one single act of praise to our Lord. If that were the case, I should look upon myself as sufficiently rewarded, even if you, my father, burnt at once what I have written. I would rather it were not burnt before those three saw it, whom you, my father, know of, because they are, and have been, my confessors; for if it be bad, it is right they should lose the good opinion they have of me; and if it be good, they are good and learned men, and I know they will recognise its source, and give praise to Him who hath spoken through me.

33. May His Majesty ever be your protector, and make you so great a saint that your spirit and light may show the way to me a miserable creature, so wanting in humility and so bold as to have ventured to write on subjects so high! May our Lord grant I have not fallen into any errors in the matter, for I had the intention and the desire to be accurate and obedient, and also that through me He might, in some mea-

[1] See ch. xiv. § 12.

sure, have glory,—because that is what I have been praying for these many years; and as my good works are inefficient for that end, I have ventured to put in order this my disordered life. Still, I have not wasted more time, nor given it more attention, than was necessary for writing it; yet I have put down all that has happened to me with all the simplicity and sincerity possible.

34. May our Lord, who is all-powerful, grant—and He can if He will—that I may attain to the doing of His will in all things! May He never suffer this soul to be lost, which He so often, in so many ways, and by so many means, has rescued from hell and drawn unto Himself! Amen.

IHS.

The Holy Spirit be ever with you, my father.[1] Amen. It would not be any thing improper if I were to magnify my labour in writing this, to oblige you to be very careful to recommend me to our Lord; for indeed I may well do so, considering what I have gone through in giving this account of myself, and in retracing my manifold wretchedness. But, still, I can say with truth that I felt it more difficult to speak of the graces which I have received from our Lord than to speak of my offences against His Majesty. You, my father, commanded me to write at length; that is what I have done, on condition that you will do what you promised, namely, destroy every thing in it that has the appearance of being wrong. I had not yet read it through after I had written it, when your reverence sent for it. Some things in it may not be very clearly explained, and there may be some repetitions; for the time I could give to it was so short, that I could not stop to see what I was writing. I entreat your reverence to correct it and have it copied, if it is to be sent on to the Father-Master, Avila,[2] for perhaps some one may recog-

[1] This letter, which seems to have accompanied the "Life," is printed among the other letters of the Saint, and is addressed to her confessor, the Dominican friar, Pedro Ibañez. It is the fifteenth letter in the first volume of the edition of Madrid; but it is not dated there.

[2] Juan de Avila, commonly called the Apostle of Andalusia.

nise the handwriting. I wish very much you would order it so that he might see it, for I began to write it with a view to that. I shall be greatly comforted if he shall think that I am on a safe road, now that, so far as it concerns me, there is nothing more to be done.

Your reverence will do in all things that which to you shall seem good, and you will look upon yourself as under an obligation to take care of one who trusts her soul to your keeping. I will pray for the soul of your reverence to our Lord, so long as I live. You will, therefore, be diligent in His service, in order that you may be able to help me; for your reverence will see by what I have written how profitable it is to give oneself, as your reverence has begun to do, wholly unto Him who gives Himself to us so utterly without measure.

Blessed be His Majesty for ever! I hope of His mercy we shall see one another one day, when we, your reverence and myself, shall see more clearly the great mercies He has shown us, and when we shall praise Him for ever and ever. Amen.

This book was finished in June 1562.

"This date refers to the first account which the holy Mother Teresa of Jesus wrote of her life; it was not then divided into chapters. Afterwards she made this copy, and inserted in it many things which had taken place subsequent to this date, such as the foundation of the monastery of S. Joseph of Avila, as in p. 169.[1]—FRAY D⁰. BAÑES."

[1] *i.e.* of the MS. See p. 271 of this translation.

THE RELATIONS OR MANIFESTATIONS

OF HER

SPIRITUAL STATE

WHICH

S. TERESA SUBMITTED TO HER CONFESSORS.

THE RELATIONS.

RELATION I.

SENT TO S. PETER OF ALCANTARA IN 1560 FROM THE MONASTERY OF THE INCARNATION, AVILA.[1]

1. THE method of prayer I observe at present is this : when I am in prayer, it is very rarely that I can use the understanding, because the soul becomes at once recollected, remains in repose, or falls into a trance, so that I cannot in any way

[1] Fra Anton. de San Joseph, in his notes on this Relation, usually published among the letters of the Saint, ed. Doblado, vol. ii. letter 11, says it was written for S. Peter of Alcantara when he came to Avila in 1560, at the time when the Saint was so severely tried by her confessors and the others who examined her spirit, and were convinced that her prayer was a delusion of Satan : see the *Life*, ch. xxv. § 18. The following notes were discovered among the papers of the Saint in the monastery of the Incarnation, and are supposed to refer to this Relation. The Chronicler of the Order, Fra Francis de Santa Maria, is inclined to the belief that they were written by S. Peter of Alcantara, to whom the Relation is addressed, and the more so because Ribera does not claim them for any member of the Society, notwithstanding the reference to them in §§ 22, 28.

" 1. The end God has in view is the drawing a soul to Himself; that of the devil is the withdrawing it from God. Our Lord never does any thing whereby any one may be separated from Him, and the devil does nothing whereby any one may be made to draw near unto God. All the visions and the other operations in the soul of this person draw her nearer unto God, and make her more humble and obedient.

" 2. It is the teaching of S. Thomas that an angel of light may be recognised by the peace and quietness he leaves in the soul. She is

have the use of the faculties and the senses,—so much so, that the hearing alone is left; but then it does not help me to understand any thing.

never visited in this way, but she afterwards abides in peace and joy; so much so, that all the pleasures of earth together are not comparable to one of these visitations.

" 3. She never commits a fault, nor falls into an imperfection, without being instantly rebuked by Him who speaks interiorly to her.

" 4. She has never prayed for nor wished for them; all she wishes for is to do the will of God our Lord in all things.

" 5. Every thing herein is consistent with the Scriptures and the teaching of the Church, and most true, according to the most rigorous principles of scholastic theology.

" 6. This soul is most pure and sincere, with the most fervent desires of being pleasing unto God, and of trampling on every earthly thing.

" 7. She has been told that whatever she shall ask of God, being good, she shall have. She has asked much, and things not convenient to put on paper lest it should be wearisome; all of which our Lord has granted.

" 8. When these operations are from God, they are always directed to the good of the recipient, to that of the community, or of some other. That she has profited by them she knows by experience, and she knows it, too, of other persons also.

" 9. No one converses with her, if he be not in evil dispositions, who is not moved thereby to devotion, even though she says nothing about it.

" 10. She is growing daily in the perfection of virtues, and learns by these things the way of a higher perfection. And thus, during the whole time in which she had visions, she was making progress, according to the doctrine of S. Thomas.

" 11. The spirit that speaks to her soul never tells her any thing in the way of news, or what is unbecoming, but only that which tends to edification.

" 12. She has been told of some persons that they were full of devils; but this was for the purpose of enabling her to understand the state of a soul which has sinned mortally against our Lord.

" 13. The devil's method is, when he attempts to deceive a soul, to advise that soul never to speak of what he says to it; but the spirit that speaks to this soul warns her to be open with learned men, servants of our Lord, and that the devil may deceive her if she should conceal any thing through shame.

" 14. So great is the progress of her soul in this way, and the edification she ministers in the good example given, that more than forty nuns in her monastery practise great recollection.

2. It often happens, when I am not even thinking of the things of God, but engaged in other matters, and when prayer seems to be beyond my power, whatever efforts I might make, because of the great aridity I am in, bodily pains contributing thereto, that this recollection

Effects of raptures.

"15. These supernatural things occur after long praying, when she is absorbed in God, on fire with His love, or at Communion.

"16. They kindle in her a most earnest desire to be on the right road, and to escape the delusions of Satan.

"17. They are in her the cause of the deepest humility; she understands that what she receives comes to her from the hand of our Lord, and how little worth she is herself.

"18. When they are withheld, any thing that occurs is wont to pain and distress her; but when she is in this state, she remembers nothing; all she is conscious of is a great longing for suffering, and so great is it that she is amazed at it.

"19. They are to her sources of joy and consolation in her troubles, when people speak ill of her, and in her infirmities,—and she has fearful pains about the heart, sicknesses, and many other afflictions, all of which leave her when she has these visions.

"20. With all this, she undergoes great penances, fasting, the discipline, and mortifications.

"21. All that on earth may give her any pleasure, and her trials, which are many, she bears with equal tranquillity of mind, without losing the peace and quiet of her soul.

"22. Her resolution never to offend our Lord is so earnest that she has made a vow never to leave undone what she knows herself, or is told by those who understand the matter better, to be the more perfect. And though she holds the members of the Society to be saints, and believes that our Lord made use of them to bestow on her graces so great, she told me that, if she knew it would be more perfect to have nothing more to do with them, she would never speak to them again, nor see them, notwithstanding the fact that it was through them that her mind had been quieted and directed in these things.

"23. The sweetnesses she commonly receives, her sense of God, her languishing with love, are certainly marvellous, and through these she is wont to be enraptured the whole day long.

"24. She frequently falls into a trance when she hears God spoken of with devotion and earnestness, and cannot resist the rapture, do what she can; and in that state her appearance is such that she excites very great devotion.

"25. She cannot bear to be directed by any one who will not tell her of her faults, and rebuke her; all that she accepts with great humility.

"26. Moreover, she cannot endure people who are in a state of per-

or elevation of spirit comes upon me so suddenly that I cannot withstand it, and the fruits and blessings it brings with it are in a moment mine: and this, without my having had a vision, or heard any thing, or knowing where I am, except that when the soul seems to be lost I see it make great progress, which I could not have made if I had laboured for a whole year, so great is my gain.

3. At other times certain excessive impetuosities
Impetuosities. occur, accompanied with a certain fainting away of the soul for God, so that I have no control over myself;[1] my life seems to have come to an end, and so it makes me cry out and call upon God; and this comes upon me with great vehemence. Sometimes I cannot remain sitting, so

fection, if they do not labour to become perfect, according to the spirit of their rule.

" 27. She is most detached from her kindred, has no desire to converse with people, and loves solitude. She has a great devotion to the saints, and on their feasts, and on the days on which the Church celebrates the mysteries of the faith, is filled with most fervent affections for our Lord.

" 28. If all the members of the Society, and all the servants of God upon earth, tell her that her state is an effect of the operations of Satan, or were to say so, she is in fear and trembling before the visions occur; but as soon as she is in prayer, and recollected, she cannot be persuaded, were they to tear her into a thousand pieces, that it is any other than God who is working in her and speaking to her.

" 29. God has given her a most wonderfully strong and valiant spirit: she was once timid; now she tramples on all the evil spirits. She has put far away from herself all the littleness and silliness of women ; she is singularly free from scruples, and most sincere.

" 30. Besides, our Lord has given her the gift of most sweet tears, great compassion for her neighbours, the knowledge of her own faults, a great reverence for good people, and self-abasement ; and I am certain that she has done good to many, of whom I am one.

" 31. She is continually reminding herself of God, and has a sense of His presence. All the locutions have been verified, and every one of them accomplished ; and this is a very great test.

" 32. Her visions are a source of great clearness in her understanding, and an admirable illumination in the things of God.

" 33. It was said to her that she should lead those who were trying her spirit to look into the Scriptures, and that they would not find that any soul desirous of pleasing God had been so long deceived."

[1] See *Life*, ch. xxix. §§ 9-13.

great is the oppression of the heart; and this pain comes on without my doing any thing to cause it, and the nature of it is such that my soul would be glad never to be without it while I live. And the longings I have are longings not to live; and they come on because it seems as if I must live on without being able to find any relief, for relief comes from the vision of God, which comes by death, and death is what I cannot take; and with all this my soul thinks that all except itself are filled with consolations, and that all find help in their troubles, but not itself. The distress thus occasioned is so intense that, if our Lord did not relieve it by throwing it into a trance, whereby all is made calm, and the soul rests in great quiet and is satisfied, now by seeing something of that which it desires, now by hearing other things, it would seem to be impossible for it to be delivered from this pain.

4. At other times there come upon me certain desires to serve God, with a vehemence so great *Desires.* that I cannot describe it, and accompanied with a certain pain at seeing how unprofitable I am. It seems to me then that there is nothing in the world, neither death nor martyrdom, that I could not easily endure. This conviction, too, is not the result of any reflection, but comes in a moment. I am wholly changed, and I know not whence cometh such great courage. I think I should like to raise my voice, and publish to all the world how important it is for men not to be satisfied with the common way, and how great the good is that God will give us if we prepare ourselves to receive it. I say it again, these desires are such that I am melted away in myself, for I seem to desire what I cannot have. The body seems to me to hold me in prison, through its inability to serve God and my state[1] in any thing; for if it were not for the body, I might do very great things, so far as my strength would allow; and thus, because I see myself without any power whatever to serve God, I feel this pain in a way wholly indescribable; the issue is delight, recollection, and the consolation of God.

[1] De la Fuente thinks she means the religious state.

Penance. 5. Again, it has happened, when these longings to serve Him come upon me, that I wish to do penance, but I am not able. It would be a great relief to me, and it does relieve and cheer me, though what I do is almost nothing, because of my bodily weakness; and yet, if I were to give way to these my longings, I believe I should observe no moderation.

Solitude. 6. Sometimes, if I have to speak to any one, I am greatly distressed, and I suffer so much that it makes me weep abundantly; for my whole desire is to be alone, and solitude comforts me, though at times I neither pray nor read, and conversation—particularly of kindred and connections—seems oppressive, and myself to be as a slave, except when I speak to those whose conversation is of prayer and matters of the soul,—in these I find comfort and joy;[1] yet these occasionally are too much for me, and I would rather not see them, but go where I might be alone: though this is not often the case, for those especially who direct my conscience always console me.

Food. 7. At other times it gives me much pain that I must eat and sleep, and that I see I cannot forego these things, being less able to do so than any one. I submit that I may serve God, and thus I offer up those actions to Him. Time seems to me too short, and that I have not enough for my prayer, for I should never be tired of being alone. I am always wishing I had time for reading, for I have been always fond of reading. I read very little, for when I take up a book I become recollected through the pleasure it gives me, and thus my reading is turned into prayer: and it is but rarely, for I have many occupations; and though they are good, they do not give me the pleasure which reading would give. And thus I am always wishing for more time, and every thing becomes disagreeable, so I believe, because I see I cannot do what I wish and desire.

Raptures. 8. All these desires, with an increase in virtue, have been given me by our Lord since He raised me to this prayer of quiet, and sent these raptures. I find

[1] See *Life*, ch. xxiv. § 8, and ch. xxxi. § 22.

myself so improved that I look on myself as being a mass of perdition before this. These raptures and visions leave me in possession of the blessings I shall now speak of; and I maintain that, if there be any good in me, they are the occasions of it.

9. I have made a very strong resolution never to offend God, not even venially. I would rather die a thousand deaths than do any thing of the kind knowingly. I am resolved never to leave undone any thing I may consider to be the more perfect, or more for the honour of our Lord, if he who has the care of my soul and directs me tells me I may do it. Cost me what pain it might, I would not leave such an act undone for all the treasure of the world. If I were to do so, I do not think I could have the face to ask any thing of God our Lord, or to make my prayer; and yet, for all this, I have many faults and imperfections. I am obedient to my confessor,[1] though imperfectly; but if I know that he wishes or commands any thing, I would not leave that undone, so far as I understand it; if I did so, I should think myself under a grievous delusion. *Obedience, and the vow of greater perfection.*

10. I have a longing for poverty, though not free from imperfection; however, I believe, if I had wealth, I would not reserve any revenue, nor hoard money for myself, nor do I care for it; I wish to have only what is necessary. Nevertheless, I feel that I am very defective in this virtue; for, though I desire nothing for myself, I should like to have something to give away: still, I desire no revenue, nor any thing for myself.[2] *Poverty.*

11. In almost all the visions I have had, I have found good, if it be not a delusion of Satan; herein I submit myself to the judgment of my confessors. *Visions.*

12. As to fine and beautiful things, such as water, fields, perfume, music, &c., I think I would rather not have them, so great is the difference between them and what I am in the habit of seeing, and so all pleasure in them is gone from me.[3] Hence it is that I care *Pleasurable sights.*

---

[1] See *Life*, ch. xxiii. § 19.   [2] See *Life*, ch. xxxv. § 2.
[3] See *Life*, ch. ix. § 6, and ch. xiv. § 7.

not for them, unless it be at the first sight: they never make any further impression; to me they seem but dirt.

13. If I speak or converse with people in the world—for I cannot help it—even about prayer, and if the conversation be long, though to pass away the time, I am under great constraint if it be not necessary, for it gives me much pain.

Conversation with others.

14. Amusements, of which I used to be fond, and worldly things, are all disagreeable to me now, and I cannot look at them.

Pastimes.

15. The longings, which I said I have,[1] of loving and serving and seeing God, are not helped by any reflections, as formerly, when I thought I was very devout, and shed many tears; but they flow out of a certain fire and heat so excessive that, I repeat it, if God did not relieve them by throwing me into a trance, wherein the soul seems to find itself satisfied, I believe my life would come to an end at once.

Effects of rapture.

16. When I see persons making great progress, and thus resolved, detached, and courageous, I love them much; and I should like to have my conversation with such persons, and I think they help me on. People who are afraid, and seemingly cautious in those things, the doing of which is perfectly reasonable here, seem to vex me, and drive me to pray to God and the saints to make them undertake such things as these which now frighten us. Not that I am good for any thing myself, but because I believe that God helps those who, for His sake, apply themselves to great things, and that He never abandons any one who puts his trust in Him only. And I should like to find any one who would help me to believe so, and to be without thought about food and raiment, but leave it all in the hands of God.[2]

Good people.

17. This leaving in the hands of God the supply of all I need is not to be understood as excluding all labour on my part, but merely solicitude—I mean, the solicitude

Resignation.

---

[1] See § 3, above.
[2] S. Matt. vi. 31: "Nolite ergo solliciti esse, dicentes: Quid manducabimus, ... aut quo operiemur?"

of care. And since I have attained to this liberty, it goes well with me, and I labour to forget myself as much as I can. I do not think it is a year ago since our Lord gave me this liberty.

18. Vain-glory[1]—glory be to God!—so far as I know, there is no reason why I should have any; for I see plainly that in these things which God sends me I have no part myself: on the contrary, God makes me conscious of my own wretchedness; for whatever reflections I might be able to make, I could never come to the knowledge of such deep truths as I attain to in a single rapture. *Vain-glory.*

19. When I speak of these things a few days after, they seem to me as if they had happened to another person. Previously, I thought it a wrong to me that they should be known to others; but I see now that I am not therefore any the better, but rather worse, seeing that I make so little progress after receiving mercies so great. And certainly, in every way, it seems to me that there was not in the world any body worse than myself; and so the virtues of others seem to me much more meritorious than mine, and that I do nothing myself but receive graces, and that God must give to others at once all that He is now giving unto me; and I pray Him not to reward me in this life; and so I believe that God has led me along this way because I am weak and wicked. *Humility.*

20. When I am in prayer, and even almost always when I am able to reflect at all, I cannot, even if I tried, pray to God for rest, or desire it; for I see that His life was one of suffering, and that I ask Him to send me, giving me first the grace to bear it. *Resignation to the will of God.*

21. Every thing of this kind, and of the highest perfection, seems to make so deep an impression on me in prayer, that I am amazed at the sight of truths so great and so clear that the things of the world seem to be folly; and so it is necessary for me to take pains to reflect on the way I demeaned myself formerly in the things of the world, for it seems to me folly to feel for deaths and the troubles of the world,—at least, that sorrow for, or love of, *Vanity of the world.*

---

[1] See *Life*, ch. vii. § 2.

kindred and friends should last long. I say I have to take pains when I am considering what I was, and what I used to feel.

Rash judgments.
22. If I see people do any thing which clearly seems to be sin, I cannot make up my mind that they have offended God; and if I dwell upon this at all,—which happens rarely or never,—I never can make up my mind, though I see it plainly enough. It seems to me that every body is as anxious to serve God as I am. And herein God has been very gracious unto me, for I never dwell on an evil deed, to remember it afterwards; and if I do remember it, I see some virtue or other in that person. In this way these things never weary me, except generally: but heresies do; they distress me very often, and almost always when I think of them they seem to me to be the only trouble which should be felt. And also I feel, when I see people who used to give themselves to prayer fall away; this gives me pain, but not much, because I strive not to dwell upon it.

Excessive neatness.
23. I find, also, that I am improved in the matter of that excessive neatness which I was wont to observe,[1] though not wholly delivered from it. I do not discern that I am always mortified in this; sometimes, however, I do.

Recollectedness.
24. All this I have described, together with a very constant dwelling in thought on God, is the ordinary state of my soul, so far as I can understand it. And if I must be busy about something else, without my seeking it, as I said before,[2] I know not who makes me awake,—and this not always, only when I am busy with things of importance; and such—glory be to God!—only at intervals demand my attention, and do not occupy me at all times.

Submission to the will of God.
25. For some days—they are not many, however— for three, or four, or five, all my good and fervent thoughts, and my visions, seem to be withdrawn, yea, even forgotten, so that, if I were to seek for it, I know of no good that can ever have been in me. It seems to have been all a dream, or, at least, I can call nothing to mind.

---

[1] See *Life*, ch. ii. § 2.   [2] § 2, above.

Bodily pains at the same time distress me. My understanding is troubled, so that I cannot think at all about God, neither do I know under what law I live. If I read any thing, I do not understand it; I seem to be full of faults, and without any resolution whatever to practise virtue; and the great resolution I used to have is come to this, that I seem to be unable to resist the least temptation or slander of the world. It suggests itself to me then that I am good for nothing, if any one would have me undertake more than the common duties. I give way to sadness, thinking I have deceived all those who trusted me at all. I should like to hide myself where nobody could see me; but my desire for solitude arises from want of courage, not from love of virtue. It seems to me that I should like to dispute with all who contradict me; I am under the influence of these impressions, only God has been so gracious unto me, that I do not offend more frequently than I was wont to do, nor do I ask Him to deliver me from them, but only, if it be His will I should always suffer thus, to keep me from offending Him; and I submit myself to His will with my whole heart, and I see that it is a very great grace bestowed upon me that He does not keep me constantly in this state.

26. One thing astonishes me; it is that, while I am in this state, through a single word of those I am in the habit of hearing, or a single vision, or a little self-recollection, lasting but an *Ave Maria*, or through my drawing near to communicate, I find my soul and body so calm, so sound, the understanding so clear, and myself possessing all the strength and all the good desires I usually have. And this I have had experience of very often—at least, when I go to Communion; it is more than six months ago that I felt a clear improvement in my bodily health,[1] and that occasionally brought about through raptures, and I find it last sometimes more than three hours, at other times I am much stronger for a whole day; and I do not think it is fancy, for I have considered the matter, and reflected on it. Accordingly, when I am thus recollected, I fear no illness. The truth is, that when I pray, as I was accustomed to do before, I feel no improvement.

Effects of her prayer.

[1] See *Life*, ch. xx. § 29.

27. All these things of which I am speaking make me believe that it comes from God; for when I see what I once was, that I was in the way of being lost, and that soon, my soul certainly is astonished at these things, without knowing whence these virtues came to me; I did not know myself, and saw that all was a gift, and not the fruit of my labours. I understand in all truthfulness and sincerity, and see that I am not deluded, that it has been not only the means of drawing me to God in His service, but of saving me also from hell. This my confessors know, who have heard my general confession.

Work of God.

28. Also, when I see any one who knows anything about me, I wish to let him know my whole life,[1] because my honour seems to me to consist in the honour of our Lord, and I care for nothing else. This He knows well, or I am very blind; for neither honour, nor life, nor praise, nor good either of body or of soul, can interest me, nor do I seek or desire any advantage, only His glory. I cannot believe that Satan has sought so many means of making my soul advance, in order to lose it after all. I do not hold him to be so foolish. Nor can I believe it of God, though I have deserved to fall into delusions because of my sins, that He has left unheeded so many prayers of so many good people for two years, and I do nothing else but ask every body to pray to our Lord that He would show me if this be for His glory, or lead me by another way.[2] I do not believe that these things would have been permitted by His Majesty to be always going on if they were not His work. These considerations, and the reasons of so many saintly men, give me courage when I am under the pressure of fear that they are not from God, I being so wicked myself. But when I am in prayer, and during those days when I am in repose, and my thoughts fixed on God, if all the learned and holy men in the world came together and put me to all conceivable tortures, and I, too, desirous of agreeing with them, they could not make me believe that this is the work of Satan, for I cannot. And when they would have had me believe it, I was afraid,

Her sincerity.

[1] See *Life*, ch. xxxi. § 17.   [2] See *Life*, ch. xxv. § 20.

seeing who it was that said so; and I thought that they must be saying what was true, and that I, being what I was, must have been deluded. But all they had said to me was destroyed by the first word, or recollection, or vision that came, and I was able to resist no longer, and believed it was from God.[1]

29. However, I can think that Satan now and then may intermeddle here, and so it is, as I have seen and said; but he produces different results, nor can he, as it seems to me, deceive any one possessed of any experience. Nevertheless, I say that, though I do certainly believe this to be from God, I would never do any thing, for any consideration whatever, that is not judged by him who has the charge of my soul to be for the better service of our Lord, and I never had any intention but to obey without concealing any thing, for that is my duty. I am very often rebuked for my faults, and that in such a way as to pierce me to the very quick; and I am warned when there is, or when there may be, any danger in what I am doing. These rebukes and warnings have done me much good, in often reminding me of my former sins, which make me exceedingly sorry. *Wiles of Satan.*

30. I have been very long, but this is the truth, —that, when I rise from my prayer, I see that I have received blessings which seem too briefly described. Afterwards I fall into many imperfections, and am unprofitable and very wicked. And perhaps I have no perception of what is good, but am deluded; still, the difference in my life is notorious, and compels me to think over all I have said—I mean, that which I verily believe I have felt. These are the perfections which I feel our Lord has wrought in me, who am so wicked and so imperfect. I refer it all to your judgment, my father, for you know the whole state of my soul. *Effects of her prayer.*

[1] See *Life*, ch. xxv. § 18.

RELATION II.

TO ONE OF HER CONFESSORS, FROM THE HOUSE OF DOÑA LUISA DE LA CERDA, IN 1562.[1]

JESUS.

I THINK it is more than a year since this was written; God has all this time protected me with His hand, so that I have not become worse; on the contrary, I see a great change for the better in all I have to say: may He be praised for it all!

Raptures. 1. The visions and revelations have not ceased, but they are of a much higher kind. Our Lord has taught me a way of prayer, wherein I find myself far more advanced, more detached from the things of this life, more courageous, and more free.[2] I fall into a trance more frequently, for these ecstasies at times come upon me with great violence, and in such a way as to be outwardly visible, I having no power to resist them; and even when I am with others—for they come in such a way as admits of no disguising them, unless it be by letting people suppose that, as I am subject to disease of the heart, they are fainting-fits; I take great pains, however, to resist them when they are coming on—sometimes I cannot do it.

Poverty. 2 As to poverty, God seems to have wrought great things in me; for I would willingly be without even what is necessary, unless given me as an alms; and therefore my longing is extreme that I may be in such a state as to depend on alms alone for my food. It seems to me that to live, when I am certain of food and raiment without fail, is not so complete an observance of my vow or of the counsel of Christ as it would be to live where no revenue is possessed, and I should be in want at times; and as to the blessings that come with true poverty, they seem to me to be great, and I would not miss them. Many times do I find myself with such

---

[1] Addressed, it is believed, to her confessor, F. Pedro Ibañez. This Relation corresponds with ch. xxxiv. of the *Life* (*De la Fuente*).

[2] See *Life*, ch. xxvii.

great faith, that I do not think God will ever fail those who serve Him, and without any doubt whatever that there is, or can be, any time in which His words are not fulfilled: I cannot persuade myself to the contrary, nor can I have any fear; and so, when they advise me to accept an endowment, I feel it keenly, and betake myself unto God.

3. I think I am much more compassionate towards the poor than I used to be, having a great pity for them and a desire to help them; for if I regarded only my good will, I should give them even the habit I wear. I am not fastidious with respect to them, even if I had to do with them or touched them with my hands,—and this I now see is a gift of God; for though I used to give alms for His love, I had no natural compassion. I am conscious of a distinct improvement herein. *Compassion.*

4. As to the evil speaking directed against me, —which is considerable, and highly injurious to me, and done by many,—I find myself herein also very much the better. I think that what they say makes scarcely any more impression upon me than it would upon an idiot. I think at times, and nearly always, that it is just. I feel it so little, that I see nothing in it that I might offer to God, as I learn by experience that my soul gains greatly thereby; on the contrary, the evil speaking seems to be a favour. And thus, the first time I go to prayer, I have no ill-feeling against them; the first time I hear it, it creates in me a little resistance, but it neither disturbs nor moves me; on the contrary, when I see others occasionally disturbed, I am sorry for them. So it is, I put myself out of the question; for all the wrongs of this life seem to me so light, that it is not possible to feel them, because I imagine myself to be dreaming, and see that all this will be nothing when I am awake. *Insensibility to detraction.*

5. God is giving me more earnest desires, a greater love of solitude, a much greater detachment, as I said, with the visions; by these He has made me know what all that is, even if I gave up all the friends I have, both men and women and kindred. This is the least part of it: my kindred are rather a very great weariness to me; I leave them *Kindred.*

in all freedom and joy, provided it be to render the least service unto God; and thus on every side I find peace.

Prophecies. 6. Certain things, about which I have been warned in prayer, have been perfectly verified. Thus, considering the graces received from God, I find myself very much better; but, considering my service to Him in return, I am exceedingly worthless, for I have received greater consolation than I have given, though sometimes that gives me grievous pain. My penance is very scanty, the respect shown me great, much against my will very often.[1] However, in a word, I see that I live an easy, not a penitential, life; God help me, as He can!

The world not trusted. 7. It is now nine months, more or less, since I wrote this with mine own hand; since then I have not turned my back on the graces which God has given me; I think I have received, so far as I can see, a much greater liberty of late. Hitherto I thought I had need of others, and I had more reliance on worldly helps. Now I clearly understand that all men are bunches of dried rosemary, and that there is no safety in leaning on them, for if they are pressed by contradictions or evil speaking they break down. And so I know by experience that the only way not to fall is to cling to the cross, and put our trust in Him who was nailed thereto. I find Him a real Friend, and with Him I find myself endowed with such might that, God never failing me, I think I should be able to withstand the whole world if it were against me.

Love of others. 8. Having a clear knowledge of this truth, I used to be very fond of being loved by others; now I do not care for that, yea, rather, their love seems to weary me in some measure, excepting theirs who take care of my soul, or theirs to whom I think I do good. Of the former I wish to be loved, in order that they may bear with me; and of the latter, that they may be more inclined to believe me when I tell them that all is vanity.

9. In the very grievous trials, persecutions, and contradic-

---

[1] See *Life*, ch. xxxi. § 15.

tions of these months,[1] God gave me great courage; and the more grievous they were, the greater the courage, without weariness in suffering. Not only had I no ill-feeling against those who spoke evil of me, but I had, I believe, conceived a deeper affection for them. I know not how it was; certainly it was a gift from the hand of our Lord.

10. When I desire any thing, I am accustomed naturally to desire it with some vehemence; now my desires are so calm, that I do not even feel that I am pleased when I see them fulfilled. Sorrow and joy, excepting in that which relates to prayer, are so moderated, that I seem to be without sense, and in that state I remain for some days. *Desires.*

11. The vehement longings to do penance which come, and have come, upon me are great; and if I do any penance, I feel it to be so slight in comparison with that longing, that I regard it sometimes, and almost always, as a special consolation; however, I do but little, because of my great weakness. *Penance.*

12. It is a very great pain to me very often, and at this moment most grievous, that I must take food, particularly if I am in prayer. It must be very great, for it makes me weep much, and speak the language of affliction, almost without being aware of it, and that is what I am not in the habit of doing, for I do not remember that I ever did so in the very heaviest trials of my life: I am not a woman in these things, for I have a hard heart. *Food.*

13. I feel in myself a very earnest desire, more so than usual, that God may find those who will serve Him, particularly learned men, in all detachment, and who will not cleave to any thing of this world, for I see it is all a mockery; for when I see the great needs of the Church, I look upon it as a mockery to be distressed about aught else. I do nothing but pray to God for such men, because I see that one person, who is wholly perfect in the true fervour of the love of God, will do more good than many who are lukewarm. *Needs of the Church.*

[1] The Saint is supposed to refer to the troubles she endured during the foundation of the monastery of S. Joseph.

Faith. 14. In matters concerning the faith, my courage seems to me much greater. I think I could go forth alone by myself against all the Lutherans, and convince them of their errors. I feel very keenly the loss of so many souls. I see many persons making great progress; I see clearly it was the pleasure of God that such progress should have been helped by me; and I perceive that my soul, of His goodness, grows daily more and more in His love.

Vain-glory. 15. I think I could not be led away by vain-glory, even if I seriously tried, and I do not see how I could imagine any one of my virtues to be mine, for it is not long since I was for many years without any at all; and now, so far as I am concerned, I do nothing but receive graces, without rendering any service in return, being the most worthless creature in the world. And so it is that I consider at times how all, except myself, make progress; I am good for nothing in myself. This is not humility only, but the simple truth; and the knowledge of my being so worthless makes me sometimes think with fear that I must be under some delusion. Thus I see clearly that all my gain has come through the revelations and the raptures, in which I am nothing myself, and do no more to effect them than the canvas does for the picture painted on it. This makes me feel secure and be at rest; and I place myself in the hands of God, and trust my desires; for I know for certain that my desires are to die for Him, and to lose all ease, and that whatever may happen.

Life in God. 16. There are days wherein I remember times without number the words of S. Paul,[1]—though certainly they are not true of me,—that I have neither life, nor speech, nor will of my own, but that there is One in me by whom I am directed and made strong; and I am, as it were, beside myself, and thus life is a very grievous burden to me. And the greatest oblation I make to God, as the highest service on my part, is that I, when I feel it so painfully to be absent from Him, am willing to live on for the love of Him. I would have my life also full of great tribulations and persecutions;

---

[1] Gal. ii. 20: "Vivo autem, jam non ego: vivit vero in me Christus."

now that I am unprofitable, I should like to suffer; and I would endure all the tribulations in the world to gain ever so little more merit—I mean, by a more perfect doing of His will.

17. Every thing that I have learnt in prayer, though it may be two years previously, I have seen fulfilled. What I see and understand of the grandeurs of God, and of the way He has shown them, is so high, that I scarcely ever begin to think of them but my understanding fails me,—for I am as one that sees things far higher than I can understand, —and I become recollected. *Prophecies.*

18. God so keeps me from offending Him, that I am verily amazed at times. I think I discern the great care He takes of me, without my taking scarcely any care at all, being, as I was, before these things happened to me, a sea of wickedness and sins, and without a thought that I was mistress enough of myself to leave them undone. And the reason why I would have this known is that the great power of God might be made manifest. Unto Him be praise for ever and ever! Amen.

JESUS.

This Relation here set forth, not in my handwriting, is one that I gave to my confessor, and which he with his own hand copied, without adding or diminishing a word. He was a most spiritual man and a theologian: I discussed the state of my soul with him, and he with other learned men, among whom was Father Mancio.[1] They found nothing in it that is not in perfect agreement with the holy writings. This makes me calm now, though, while God is leading me by this way, I feel that it is necessary for me to put no trust whatever in myself. And so I have always done, though it is painful enough. You, my father, will be careful that all this goes under the seal of confession, according to my request.

[1] A celebrated Dominican, professor of theology in Salamanca (*Bouix*).

RELATION III.

OF VARIOUS GRACES GRANTED TO THE SAINT FROM THE YEAR 1568 TO 1571 INCLUSIVE.

1. WHEN I was in the monastery of Toledo, and some people were advising me not to allow any but noble persons to be buried there,[1] our Lord said to me: "Thou wilt be very inconsistent, My daughter, if thou regardest the laws of the world. Look at Me, poor and despised of men: are the great people of the world likely to be great in My eyes? or is it descent or virtue that is to make you esteemed?"

True greatness.

2. After Communion, the second day of Lent, in S. Joseph of Malagon, our Lord Jesus Christ appeared to me in an imaginary vision, as He is wont to do; and when I was looking upon Him I saw that He had on His head, instead of the crown of thorns, a crown of great splendour, over the part where the wounds of that crown must have been. And as I have a great devotion to the crowning with thorns, I was exceedingly consoled, and began to think how great the pain must have been because of the many wounds, and to be sorrowful. Our Lord told me not to be sad because of those wounds, but for the many wounds which men inflict upon Him now. I asked Him what I could do by way of reparation; for I was resolved to do any thing. He replied: "This is not the time for rest;" that I must hasten on the foundations, for He would take His rest with the souls which entered the monasteries; that I must admit all who offered themselves, because there were many souls that did not serve Him because they had no place wherein to do it; that those monasteries which were to be founded in small towns should be like this; that the merit of those in them would be as great, if they only desired to do that which was done in the other houses; that I

A vision of our Lord.

[1] Alonzo Ramirez wished to have the right of burial in the new monastery, but the nobles of Toledo looked on his request as unreasonable. See *Foundations*, chs. xiv. and xv.

must contrive to put them all under the jurisdiction of one superior,[1] and take care that anxieties about means of bodily maintenance did not destroy interior peace, for He would help us, so that we should never be in want of food. Especial care was to be had of the sick sisters; the prioress who did not provide for and comfort the sick was like the friends of Job: He sent them sickness for the good of their souls, and careless superiors risked the patience of their nuns. I was to write the history of the foundation of the monasteries. I was thinking how there was nothing to write about in reference to the foundation of Medina, when He asked me, what more did I want to see than that the foundation there was miraculous? By this He meant to say that He alone had done it, when it seemed impossible.[2] I resolved to execute His commands.

3. Our Lord told me something I was to tell another, and as I was considering how I did not understand it at all,— though I prayed to Him, and was thinking it might be from Satan,—He said to me that it was not, and that He Himself would warn me when the time came.

4. Once, when I was thinking how much more purely they live who withdraw themselves from all business, and how ill it goes with me, and how many faults I must be guilty of, when I have business to transact, I heard this: "It cannot be otherwise, My daughter; but strive thou always after a good intention in all things, and detachment; lift up thine eyes to Me, and see that all thine actions may resemble Mine." *Detachment.*

5. Thinking how it was that I scarcely ever fell into a trance of late in public, I heard this: "It is not necessary now; thou art sufficiently esteemed for My purpose; we are considering the weakness of the wicked." *Why the Saint's trances were no longer public.*

6. One Tuesday after the Ascension,[3] having prayed for a while after Communion in great distress, because I was so distracted that I could fix my *A vision of the most Holy Trinity.*

[1] See *Way of Perfection*, ch. viii.; but ch. v. of the previous editions
[2] See *Book of the Foundations*, ch. iii.
[3] In the copy kept in Toledo, the day is Tuesday after the Assumption (*De la Fuente*).

mind on nothing, I complained of our poor nature to our Lord. The fire began to kindle in my soul, and I saw, as it seemed to me, the most Holy Trinity[1] distinctly present in an intellectual vision, whereby my soul understood through a certain representation, as a figure of the truth, so far as my dullness could understand, how God is Three and One; and thus it seemed to me that all the Three Persons spoke to me, that They were distinctly present in my soul, saying unto me, "that from that day forth I should see that my soul had grown better in three ways, and that each one of the Three Persons had bestowed on me a distinct grace,—in charity, in suffering joyfully, in a sense of that charity in my soul, accompanied with fervour." I learnt the meaning of those words of our Lord, that the Three Divine Persons will dwell in the soul that is in a state of grace.[2] Afterwards giving thanks to our Lord for so great a mercy, and finding myself utterly unworthy of it, I asked His Majesty with great earnestness how it was that He, after showing such mercies to me, let me go out of His hand, and allowed me to become so wicked; for on the previous day I had been in great distress on account of my sins, which I had set before me. I saw clearly then how much our Lord on His part had done, ever since my infancy, to draw me to Himself by means most effectual, and yet that all had failed. Then I had a clear perception of the surpassing love of God for us, in that He forgives us all this when we turn to Him, and for me more than for any other, for many reasons. The vision of the Three Divine Persons—one God—made so profound an impression on my soul, that if it had continued it would have been impossible for me not to be recollected in so divine a company. What I saw and heard besides is beyond my power to describe.

7. Once, when I was about to communicate,—it was shortly before I had this vision,—the Host being still in the ciborium, for it had not yet been given me, I saw something like a dove, which moved its wings with a sound. It disturbed me so much, and

---

[1] Ch. xxvii. § 10.
[2] S. John xiv. 23: "Ad eum veniemus, et mansionem apud eum faciemus."

so carried me away out of myself, that it was with the utmost difficulty I received the Host. All this took place in S. Joseph of Avila. It was Father Francis Salcedo who was giving me the most Holy Sacrament. Hearing Mass another day, I saw our Lord glorious in the Host; He said to me that his sacrifice was acceptable unto Him.

8. I heard this once: "The time will come when many miracles will be wrought in this church; it will be called the holy church." It was in S. Joseph of Avila, in the year 1571.

9. I retain to this day, which is the commemoration of S. Paul, the presence of the Three Persons of which I spoke in the beginning;[1] They are present almost continually in my soul. I, being accustomed to the presence of Jesus Christ only, always thought that the vision of the Three Persons was in some degree a hindrance, though I know the Three Persons are but One God. To-day, while thinking of this, our Lord said to me "that I was wrong in imagining that those things which are peculiar to the soul can be represented by those of the body; I was to understand that they were very different, and that the soul had a capacity for great fruition." It seemed to me as if this were shown to me thus: as water penetrates and is drunk in by the sponge, so, it seemed to me, did the Divinity fill my soul, which in a certain sense had the fruition and possession of the Three Persons. And I heard Him say also: "Labour thou not to hold Me within thyself enclosed, but enclose thou thyself within Me." It seemed to me that I saw the Three Persons within my soul, and communicating Themselves to all creatures abundantly without ceasing to be with me.

10. A few days after this, thinking whether they were right who disapproved of my going out to make new foundations, and whether it would not be better for me if I occupied myself always with prayer, I heard this: "During this life, the true gain consists not in striving after greater joy in Me, but in doing My will." It seemed to me, considering what S. Paul says about women, how they should stay at home,[2]

Obedience.

[1] See § 6.
[2] Tit. ii. 5: "Sobrias, domus curam habentes."

—people reminded me lately of this, and, indeed, I had heard it before,—it might be the will of God I should do so too. He said to me: "Tell them they are not to follow one part of Scripture by itself, without looking to the other parts also; perhaps, if they could, they would like to tie My hands."

The monastery of the Incarnation. 11. One day after the Octave of the Visitation, in one of the hermitages of Mount Carmel, praying to God for one of my brothers, I said to our Lord,— I do not know whether it was only in thought or not, for my brother was in a place where his salvation was in peril,—" If I saw one of Thy brethren, O Lord, in this danger, what would I not do to help him!" It seemed to me there was nothing that I could do which I would not have done. Our Lord said to me: "O daughter, daughter! the nuns of the Incarnation are thy sisters, and thou holdest back. Take courage, then. Behold, this is what I would have thee do: it is not so difficult as it seems; and though it seems to thee that by going thither thy foundations will be ruined, yet it is by thy going that both these and the monastery of the Incarnation will gain; resist not, for My power is great."[1]

Doña Catalina de Cardona. 12. Once, when thinking of the great penance practised by Doña Catalina de Cardona,[2] and how I might have done more, considering the desires which our Lord had given me at times, if it had not been for my obedience to my confessors, I asked myself whether it would not be as well if I disobeyed them for the future in this matter. Our Lord said to me: "No, My daughter; thou art on the sound and safe road. Seest thou all her penance? I think more of thy obedience."

Vision of a soul in grace. 13. Once, when I was in prayer, He showed me by a certain kind of intellectual vision the condition of a soul in a state of grace; in its company I saw by intellectual vision the most Holy Trinity, from whose companionship the soul derived a power which was a dominion

[1] This took place in 1571, when the Saint had been appointed prioress of the monastery of the Incarnation at Avila; the very house she had left in order to found that of S. Joseph, to keep the rule in its integrity.
[2] See *Book of the Foundations*, ch. xxviii.

over the whole earth. I understood the meaning of those words in the Canticle: "Let my Beloved come into His garden and eat."[1] He showed me also the condition of a soul in sin, utterly powerless, like a person tied and bound and blindfold, who, though anxious to see, yet cannot, being unable to walk or to hear, and in grievous obscurity. I was so exceedingly sorry for such souls, that, to deliver only one, any trouble seemed to me light. I thought it impossible for any one who saw this as I saw it,—and I can hardly explain it,—willingly to forfeit so great a good or continue in so evil a state.

14. One day, in very great distress about the state of the Order, and casting about for means to succour it, our Lord said to me: "Do thou what is in thy power, and leave Me to Myself, and be not disquieted by any thing; rejoice in the blessing thou hast received, for it is a very great one. My Father is pleased with thee, and the Holy Ghost loves thee."

15. "Thou art ever desiring trials, and, on the other hand, declining them. I order things according to what I know thy will is, and not according to thy sensuality and weakness. Be strong, for thou seest how I help thee; I have wished thee to gain this crown. Thou shalt see the Order of the Virgin greatly advanced in thy days." I heard this from our Lord about the middle of February 1571. *Order of Carmel.*

16. On the eve of S. Sebastian, the first year of my being in the monastery of the Incarnation[2] as prioress there, at the beginning of the *Salve*, I saw the Mother of God descend with a multitude of angels to the stall of the prioress, where the image of our Lady is, and sit there herself. I think I did not see the image then, but only our Lady. She seemed to be like that picture of her which the Countess[3] gave me; but I had no time to ascertain this, because I fell at once into a trance. Multitudes of angels seemed to me to be above the canopies of the stalls, and on the desks in front of them; but I saw no bodily forms, for the vision was *A vision of our Lady.*

[1] Cant. v. 1 : "Veniat dilectus meus in hortum suum, et comedat."
[2] A.D. 1572.
[3] Maria de Velasco and Aragon, Countess of Osorno (*Ribera*, lib. iii. c. 1).

intellectual. She remained there during the *Salve*, and said to me: " Thou hast done well to place me here ; I will be present when the sisters sing the praises of my Son, and will offer them to Him." After this I remained in that prayer which I still practise, and which is that of keeping my soul in the company of the most Holy Trinity ; and it seemed to me that the Person of the Father drew me to Himself, and spoke to me most comfortable words. Among them were these, while showing how He loved me: " I give thee My Son, and the Holy Ghost, and the Virgin : what canst thou give Me ?"[1]

17. On the Octave of the Holy Ghost, our Lord was gracious unto me, and gave me hopes of this house,[2] that it would go on improving—I mean the souls that are in it.

18. On the Feast of the Magdalene, our Lord again confirmed a grace I had received in Toledo, electing me, in the absence of a certain person, in her place.

<small>S. John of the Cross mortifies the Saint at her Communion.</small> 19. In the monastery of the Incarnation, and in the second year of my being prioress there, on the Octave of S. Martin, when I was going to Communion, the Father Fr. John of the Cross,[3]—it was he who was giving me the most Holy Sacrament,—divided the Host between me and another sister. I thought it was done, not because there was any want of Hosts, but that he wished to mortify me because I had told him how much I delighted in Hosts of a large size. Yet I was not ignorant that the size of the Host is of no moment ; for I knew that our Lord is whole and entire in the smallest particle. His Majesty said to me: " Have no fear, My daughter ; for no one will be able to separate thee from Me,"—giving me to understand that the size of the Host mattered not.

<small>Spiritual betrothal.</small> 20. Then appearing to me, as on other occasions, in an imaginary vision, most interiorly, He held out His right hand and said : " Behold this nail ! it is

[1] See *Relation* iv. § 2.
[2] The monastery of the Incarnation, Avila (*De la Fuente*).
[3] S. John of the Cross, at the instance of the Saint, was sent to Avila, with another father of the reformed Carmelites, to be confessor of the nuns of the Incarnation, who then disliked the observance of the primitive rule.

the pledge of thy being My bride from this day forth. Until now thou hadst not merited it; from henceforth thou shalt regard my honour, not only as of one who is Thy Creator, King, and God, but as thine, My veritable bride; My honour is thine, and thine is Mine." This grace had such an effect on me, that I could not contain myself: I became as one that is foolish, and said to our Lord: " Either ennoble my vileness or cease to bestow such mercies on me, for certainly I do not think that nature can bear them." I remained thus the whole day, as one utterly beside herself. Afterwards I became conscious of great progress, and greater shame and distress to see that I did nothing in return for graces so great.

21. Our Lord said this to me one day : " Thinkest thou, My daughter, that meriting lies in fruition? *Merit.* No ; merit lies only in doing, in suffering, and in loving. You never heard that S. Paul had the fruition of heavenly joys more than once ; while he was often in sufferings.[1] Thou seest how My whole life was full of dolors, and only on Mount Tabor hast thou heard of Me in glory.[2] Do not suppose, when thou seest My Mother hold Me in her arms, that she had that joy unmixed with heavy sorrows. From the time that Simeon spoke to her, My Father made her see in clear light all I had to suffer. The grand Saints of the desert, as they were led by God, so also did they undergo heavy penances; besides, they waged serious war with the devil and with themselves, and much of their time passed away without any spiritual consolation whatever. Believe me, My daughter, his trials are the heaviest whom My Father loves most; trials are the measure of His love. How can I show My love for thee better than by desiring for thee what I desired for Myself? Consider My wounds ; thy pains will never reach to them. This is the way of truth; thus shalt thou help Me to weep over the ruin of those who are in the world, for thou knowest how all their desires, anxieties, and thoughts tend the other way." When I began my prayer that day, my headache was so violent that I thought

[1] 2 Cor. xi. 27: " In labore et ærumna, in vigiliis multis."
[2] S. Matt. xvii. 2: " Et transfiguratus est ante eos."

I could not possibly go on. Our Lord said to me: "Behold, now, the reward of suffering. As thou, on account of thy health, wert unable to speak to Me, I spoke to thee and comforted thee." Certainly, so it was; for the time of my recollection lasted about an hour and a half, more or less. It was then that He spoke to me the words I have just related, together with all the others. I was not able to distract myself, neither knew I where I was; my joy was so great as to be indescribable; my headache was gone, and I was amazed, and I had a longing for suffering. He also told me to keep in mind the words He said to His Apostles: "The servant is not greater than his lord."[1]

RELATION IV.

OF THE GRACES THE SAINT RECEIVED IN SALAMANCA AT THE END OF LENT 1571.

Raptures.

1. I FOUND myself the whole of yesterday in great desolation, and, except at Communion, did not feel that it was the day of the Resurrection. Last night, being with the community, I heard one[2] of them singing how hard it is to be living away from God. As I was then suffering, the effect of that singing on me was such that a numbness began in my hands, and no efforts of mine could hinder it; but as I go out of myself in raptures of joy, so then my soul was thrown into a trance through the excessive pain, and remained entranced; and until this day I had not felt this. A few days previously I thought that the vehement impulses were not so great as they used to be, and now it seems to me that the reason is what I have described; I know not if it is so. Hitherto the pain had not gone so far as to make me beside myself; and as it is so unendurable, and as I retained the

[1] S. John xiii. 16: "Non est servus major domino suo."
[2] Isabel of Jesus, born in Segovia, and whose family name was Jimenas, told Ribera (*vide* lib. iv. c. x.) that she was the singer, being then a novice in Salamanca.

control of my senses, it made me utter loud cries beyond my power to restrain. Now that it has grown, it has reached this point of piercing me; and I understand more of that piercing which our Lady suffered; for until to-day, as I have just said, I never knew what that piercing was. My body was so bruised, that I suffer even now when I am writing this; for my hands are as if the joints were loosed, and in pain.[1] You, my father, will tell me when you see me whether this trance be the effect of suffering, or whether I felt it, or whether I am deceived.

2. I was in this great pain till this morning; and, being in prayer, I fell into a profound trance; and it seemed to me that our Lord had taken me up in spirit to His Father, and said to Him: "Whom Thou hast given to Me, I give to Thee;"[2] and He seemed to draw me near to Himself. This is not an imaginary vision, but one most certain, and so spiritually subtile that it cannot be explained. He spoke certain words to me which I do not remember. Some of them referred to His grace, which He bestows on me. He kept me by Him for some time.

3. As you, my father, went away yesterday so soon, and I consider the many affairs which detain you, so that it is impossible for me to have recourse to you for comfort even when necessary,—for I see that your occupations are most urgent,—I was for some time in pain and sadness. As I was then in desolation,—as I said before,—that helped me; and as nothing on earth, I thought, had any attractions for me, I had a scruple, and feared I was beginning to lose that liberty. This took place last night; and to-day our Lord answered my doubt, and said to me "that I was not to be surprised; for as men seek for companions with whom they may speak of their sensual satisfactions, so the soul—when there is any one who understands it—seeks those to whom it may communicate its pleasures and its pains, and is sad and mourns when it can find none." He said to me: "Thou art prosperous now, and thy works please Me." As He remained with me for some time, I remembered that I had told you, my father, that these

Detachment.

[1] See *Fortress of the Soul*, vi. ch. xi.
[2] See *Relation* iii. § 16.

visions pass quickly away; He said to me "that there was a difference between these and the imaginary visions, and that there could not be an invariable law concerning the graces He bestowed on us; for it was expedient to give them now in one way, now in another."

4. After Communion, I saw our Lord most distinctly close beside me; and He began to comfort me with great sweetness, and said to me, among other things: "Thou beholdest Me present, my daughter,—it is I. Show Me thy hands." And to me He seemed to take them and to put them to His side, and said: "Behold My wounds; thou art not without Me. Finish the short course of thy life." By some things He said to me, I understood that, after His Ascension, He never came down to the earth except in the most Holy Sacrament to communicate Himself to any one. He said to me, that when He rose again He showed Himself to our Lady, because she was in great trouble; for sorrow had so pierced her soul that she did not even recover herself at once in order to have the fruition of that joy. By this I saw how different was my piercing.[1] But what must that of the Virgin have been? He remained long with her then because it was necessary to console her.

The Resurrection.

5. On Palm Sunday, at Communion, I was in a deep trance,—so much so, that I was not able even to swallow the Host; and, still having It in my mouth, when I had come a little to myself, I verily believed that my mouth was all filled with Blood; and my face and my whole body seemed to be covered with It, as if our Lord had been shedding It at that moment. I thought It was warm, and the sweetness I then felt was exceedingly great; and our Lord said to me: "Daughter, My will is that My Blood should profit thee; and be not thou afraid that My compassion will fail thee. I shed It in much suffering, and, as thou seest, thou hast the fruition of It in great joy. I reward thee well for the pleasure thou gavest Me to-day." He said this because I have been in the habit of going to Communion, if possible, on this day for more than thirty years, and of

Effects of Communion.

[1] See above, § 1.

labouring to prepare my soul to be the host of our Lord; for I considered the cruelty of the Jews to be very great, after giving Him so grand a reception, in letting Him go so far for supper; and I used to picture Him as remaining with me, and truly in a poor lodging, as I see now. And thus I used to have such foolish thoughts—they must have been acceptable to our Lord, for this was one of the visions which I regard as most certain; and, accordingly, it has been a great blessing to me in the matter of Communion.

6. Previous to this, I had been, I believe, for three days in that great pain, which I feel sometimes more than at others, because I am away from God; and during those days it had been very great, and seemingly more than I could bear. Being thus exceedingly wearied by it, I saw it was late to take my collation, nor could I do so,—for if I do not take it a little earlier, it occasions great weakness because of my sickness; and then, doing violence to myself, I took up some bread to prepare for collation, and on the instant Christ appeared, and seemed to be breaking the bread and putting it into my mouth. He said to me: "Eat, My daughter, and bear it as well as thou canst. I condole with thee in thy suffering; but it is good for thee now." My pain was gone, and I was comforted; for He seemed to be really with me then, and the whole of the next day; and with this my desires were then satisfied. The word "condole" made me strong; for now I do not think I am suffering at all.

[Sidenote: Pain of the absence from God.]

RELATION V.

OBSERVATIONS ON CERTAIN POINTS OF SPIRITUALITY.

1. "What is it that distresses thee, little sinner? Am I not thy God? Dost thou not see how ill I am treated here? If thou lovest Me, why art thou not sorry for Me? Daughter, light is very different from darkness. I am faithful; no one will be lost without knowing it. He must

[Sidenote: Light.]

be deceiving himself who relies on spiritual sweetnesses; the true safety lies in the witness of a good conscience.[1] But let no one think that of himself he can abide in the light, any more than he can hinder the natural night from coming on; for that depends on My grace. The best means he can have for retaining the light is the conviction in his soul that he can do nothing of himself, and that it comes from Me; for, even if he were in the light, the instant I withdraw, night will come. True humility is this: the soul's knowing what itself can do, and what I can do. Do not neglect to write down the counsels I give thee, that thou mayest not forget them. Thou seekest to have the counsels of men in writing; why, then, thinkest thou that thou art wasting time in writing down those I give thee? The time will come when thou shalt require them all."

On Union.

2. "Do not suppose, My daughter, that to be near to Me is union; for they who sin against Me are near Me, though they do not wish it. Nor is union the joys and comforts of union,[2] though they be of the very highest kind, and though they come from Me. These very often are means of winning souls, even if they are not in a state of grace." When I heard this, I was in a high degree lifted up in spirit. Our Lord showed me what the spirit was, and what the state of the soul was then, and the meaning of those words of the *Magnificat*, "Exultavit spiritus meus." He showed me that the spirit was the higher part of the will.

Union. 3. To return to union; I understood it to be a spirit, pure, and raised up above all the things of earth, with nothing remaining in it that would swerve from the will of God, being a spirit and a will resigned to His will, and in detachment from all things, occupied in God in such a way as to leave no trace of any love of self, or of any created thing whatever.[3] Thereupon, I considered

[1] 2 Cor. i. 12: "Gloria nostra hæc est, testimonium conscientiæ nostræ."
[2] See S. John of the Cross, *Mount Carmel*, bk. ii. ch. v.
[3] See *Foundations*, ch. v. § 2.

that, if this be union, it comes to this, that, as my soul is always abiding in this resolution, we can say of it that it is always in this prayer of union; and yet it is true that the union lasts but a very short time. It was suggested to me that, as to living in justice, meriting and making progress, it will be so; but it cannot be said that the soul is in union, as it is when in contemplation; and I thought I understood, yet not by words heard, that the dust of our wretchedness, faults, and imperfections, wherein we bury ourselves, is so great, that it is not possible to live in such pureness as the spirit is in when in union with God, raised up and out of our wretched misery. And I think, if it be union to have our will and spirit in union with the will and Spirit of God, that it is not possible for any one not in a state of grace to attain thereto; and I have been told so. Accordingly, I believe it is very difficult to know when the soul is in union; to have that knowledge is a special grace of God, because nobody can tell whether he is in a state of grace or not.[1]

4. You will show me in writing, my father, what you think of this, and how I am in the wrong, and send me this paper back.

5. I had read in a book that it was an imperfection to possess pictures well painted,—and I would *Poverty.* not, therefore, retain in my cell one that I had; and also, before I had read this, I thought that it was poverty to possess none, except those made of paper,—and, as I read this afterwards, I would not have any of any other material. I learnt from our Lord, when I was not thinking at all about this, what I am going to say: "that this mortification was not right. Which is better, poverty or charity? But as love was the better, whatever kindled love in me, that I must not give up, nor take away from my nuns; for the book spoke of much adorning and curious devices—not of pictures.[2] What Satan was doing among the Lutherans was the taking away from them all those means by which their love might be the more quickened; and thus they were going to perdition. Those who are loyal to

[1] Eccl. ix. 1: "Nescit homo utrum amore an odio dignus sit."
[2] See S. John of the Cross, *Mount Carmel*, bk. iii. ch. xxxiv.

Me, My daughter, must now, more than ever, do the very reverse of what they do." I understood that I was under great obligations to serve our Lady and S. Joseph, because, when I was utterly lost, God, through their prayers, came and saved me.

Visions. 6. One day, after the Feast of S. Matthew,[1] I was as is usual with me, after seeing in a vision the most Holy Trinity, and how It is present in a soul in a state of grace.[2] I understood the mystery most clearly, in such a way that, after a certain fashion and comparisons, I saw It in an imaginary vision. And though at other times I have seen the most Holy Trinity in an intellectual vision, for some days after the truth of it did not rest with me,—as it does now, I mean,—so that I could dwell upon it. I see now that it is just as learned men told me; and I did not understand it as I do now, though I believed them without the least hesitation; for I never had any temptations against the faith.

7. It seems to us ignorant women that the Persons *Pictures of the Trinity.* of the most Holy Trinity are all Three, as we see Them painted, in one Person, after the manner of those pictures which represent a body with three faces; and thus it causes such astonishment in us that we look on it as impossible, and so there is nobody who dares to think of it; for the understanding is perplexed, is afraid it may come to doubt the truth, and that robs us of a great blessing.

8. What I have seen is this: Three distinct Persons, *Vision of the Trinity.* each one by Himself visible, and by Himself speaking.[3] And afterwards I have been thinking that the Son alone took human flesh, whereby this truth is known. The Persons love, communicate, and know Themselves. Then, if each one is by Himself, how can we say that the Three are one Essence, and so believe? That is a most deep truth,

---

[1] The §§ 6, 7, and 8 are the thirteenth letter of the second volume, ed. Doblado.

[2] See *Relation* iii. § 13.

[3] Antonio de San Joseph, in his notes on this passage, is anxious to save the Thomist doctrine that one of the Divine Persons cannot be seen without the other, and so he says that the Saint speaks of the Three Persons as she saw Them—not as They are in Themselves.

and I would die for it a thousand times. In the Three Persons there is but one will and one power and one might; neither can One be without Another : so that of all created things there is but one sole Creator. Could the Son create an ant without the Father ? No ; because the power is all one. The same is to be said of the Holy Ghost. Thus, there is one God Almighty, and the Three Persons are one Majesty. Is it possible to love the Father without loving the Son and the Holy Ghost ? No ; for he who shall please One of the Three pleases the Three Persons ; and he who shall offend One offends All. Can the Father be without the Son and without the Holy Ghost ? No ; for They are one substance, and where One is there are the Three ; for They cannot be divided. How, then, is it that we see the Three Persons distinct ? and how is it that the Son, not the Father, nor the Holy Ghost, took human flesh ? This is what I have never understood ; theologians know it. I know well that the Three were there when that marvellous work was done, and I do not busy myself with much thinking thereon. All my thinking thereon comes at once to this : that I see God is almighty, that He has done what He would, and so can do what He will. The less I understand it, the more I believe it, and the greater the devotion it excites in me. May He be blessed for ever ! Amen.

9. If our Lord had not been so gracious with me as He has been, I do not think I should have had the courage to do what has been done, nor strength to undergo the labours endured, with the contradictions and the opinions of men. And accordingly, since the beginning of the foundations, I have lost the fears I formerly had, thinking that I was under delusions,—and I had a conviction that it was the work of God : having this, I ventured upon difficult things, though always with advice and under obedience. I see in this that when our Lord willed to make a beginning of the Order, and of His mercy made use of me, His Majesty had to supply all that I was deficient in, which was every thing, in order that the work might be effected, and that His greatness might be the more clearly revealed in one so wicked.

Courage.

10. Antiochus was unendurable to himself, and to those

who were about him, because of the stench of his many sins.[1]

11. Confession is for faults and sins, and not for virtues, nor for any thing of the kind relating to prayer. These things are to be treated of out of confession with one who understands the matter,—and let the prioress see to this; and the nun must explain the straits she is in, in order that the proper helps may be found for her; for Cassian says that he who does not know the fact, as well as he who has never seen or learnt, that men can swim, will think, when he sees people throw themselves into the river, that they will all be drowned.[2]

Matter of Confession.

12. Our Lord would have Joseph tell the vision to his brethren, and have it known, though it was to cost Joseph so much.

13. How the soul has a sense of fear when God is about to bestow any great grace upon it; that sense is the worship of the spirit, as that of the four[3] elders spoken of in Scripture.

14. How, when the faculties are suspended, it is to be understood that certain matters are suggested to the soul, to be by it recommended to God; that an angel suggests them, of whom it is said in the Scriptures that he was burning incense and offering up the prayers of the saints.[4]

15. How there are no sins where there is no knowledge; and thus our Lord did not permit the king to sin with the wife of Abraham, for he thought that she was his sister, not his wife.

---

[1] 2 Maccab. ix. 10, 12: "Eum nemo poterat propter intolerantiam fœtoris portare, ... nec ipse jam fœtorem suum ferre posset."

[2] Cassian. *Collat.* vii. cap. iv. p. 311: "Nec enim si quis ignarus natandi, sciens pondus corporis sui ferre aquarum liquorem non posse, experimento suæ voluerit imperitiæ definire, neminem penitus posse liquidis elementis solida carne circumdatum sustineri."

[3] Antonio de San Joseph says that the Saint meant to write four-and-twenty, in allusion to Apoc. iv.

[4] Apoc. viii. 4.

RELATION VI.

THE VOW OF OBEDIENCE TO FATHER GRATIAN WHICH THE SAINT MADE IN 1575.

1. IN the year 1575, in the month of April, when I was founding the monastery of Veas, Fra Jerome of the Mother of God Gratian happened to come thither.[1] I began to go to confession to him from time to time, though not looking upon him as filling the place of the other confessors I had, so as to be wholly directed by him. One day, when I was taking food, but without any interior recollection whatever, my soul began to be recollected in such a way that I thought I must fall into a trance; and I had a vision, that passed away with the usual swiftness, like a meteor. I seemed to see close beside me Jesus Christ our Lord, in the form wherein His Majesty is wont to reveal Himself, with F. Gratian on His right. Our Lord took his right hand and mine, and, joining them together, said to me that He would have me accept him in His place for my whole life, and that we were both to have one mind in all things, for so it was fitting. I was profoundly convinced that this was the work of God, though I remembered with regret two of my confessors whom I frequented in turn for a long time, and to whom I owed much; that one for whom I have a great affection especially caused a terrible resistance. Nevertheless, not being able to persuade myself that the vision was a delusion, because it had a great power and influence over me, and also because it was said to me on two other occasions that I was not to be afraid, that He wished this,—the words were different,—I made up my mind at last to act upon them, understanding it to be our Lord's will, and to follow that counsel so long as I should live. I had never before so acted with any one, though I had consulted many persons of great learning and holiness, and who watched over my soul with great care,—but neither had I received any

(marginal note: Fra Jerome Gratian.)

---
[1] See *Foundations*, ch. xxii.

such direction as that I should make no change; for as to my confessors, of some I understood that they would be profitable to me, and so also of these.

Peace.

2. When I had resolved on this, I found myself in peace and comfort so great that I was amazed, and assured of our Lord's will; for I do not think that Satan could fill the soul with peace and comfort such as this : and so, whenever I think of it, I praise our Lord, and remember the words, " posuit fines tuos pacem,"[1] and I wish I could wear myself out in the praises of God.

The vow.

3. It must have been about a month after this my resolve was made, on the second day after Pentecost, when I was going to found the monastery in Seville, that we heard Mass in a hermitage in Ecija, and rested there during the hottest part of the day. Those who were with me remained in the hermitage while I was by myself in the sacristy belonging to it. I began to think of one great grace which I received of the Holy Ghost, on one of the vigils of His feast,[2] and a great desire arose within me of doing Him some most special service, and I found nothing that was not already done,—at least, resolved upon,—for all I do must be faulty; and I remembered that, though I had already made a vow of obedience, it might be made in greater perfection, and I had an impression it would be pleasing unto Him if I promised that which I was already resolved upon, to live under obedience to the Father-Master Fr. Jerome. On the one hand, I seemed to be doing nothing, because I was already bent on doing it; on the other hand, it would be a very serious thing, considering that our interior state is not made known to the superiors who receive our vows, and that they change, and that, if one is not doing his work well, another comes in his place; and I believed I should have none of my liberty all my life long, either outwardly or inwardly, and this constrained me greatly to abstain from making the vow. This repugnance of the will made me ashamed, and I saw that, now I had something I could do for God, I was not doing

[1] Ps. cxlvii. 3 : " He hath made thy borders peace."
[2] Perhaps the Saint refers to what she has written in her *Life*, ch. xxxviii. §§ 11, 12.

it; it was a sad thing for my resolution to serve Him. The fact is, that the objection so pressed me, that I do not think I ever did any thing in my life that was so hard—not even my profession—unless it be that of my leaving my father's house to become a nun.[1] The reason of this was that I had forgotten my affection for him, and his gifts for directing me; yea, rather, I was looking on it then as a strange thing, which has surprised me; feeling nothing but a great fear whether the vow would be for the service of God or not: and my natural self—which is fond of liberty—must have been doing its work, though for years now I have no pleasure in it. But it seemed to me a far other matter to give up that liberty by a vow, as in truth it is. After a protracted struggle, our Lord gave me great confidence; and I saw it was the better course, the more I felt about it: if I made this promise in honour of the Holy Ghost, He would be bound to give him light for the direction of my soul; and I remembered at the same time that our Lord had given him to me as my guide. Thereupon I fell upon my knees, and, to render this tribute of service to the Holy Ghost, made a promise to do whatever he should bid me do while I lived, provided nothing were required of me contrary to the law of God and the commands of superiors whom I am more bound to obey. I adverted to this, that the obligation did not extend to things of little importance,—as if I were to be importunate with him about any thing, and he bade me cease, and I neglected his advice and repeated my request,—nor to things relating to my convenience. In a word, his commands were not to be about trifles, done without reflection; and I was not knowingly to conceal from him my faults and sins, or my interior state; and this, too, is more than we allow to superiors. In a word, I promised to regard him as in the place of God, outwardly and inwardly. I know not if it be so, but I seemed to have done a great thing in honour of the Holy Ghost—at least, it was all I could do, and very little it was in comparison with what I owe Him.

4. I give God thanks, who has created one capable of this work: I have the greatest confidence that His Majesty will

[1] *Life*, ch. iv. § 1.

bestow on him great graces; and I myself am so happy and joyous, that I seem to be in every way free from myself; and though I thought that my obedience would be a burden, I have attained to the greatest freedom. May our Lord be praised for ever!

RELATION VII.

MADE FOR RODRIGO ALVAREZ, S.J., IN THE YEAR 1575, ACCORDING TO DON VICENTE DE LA FUENTE; BUT IN 1576, ACCORDING TO THE BOLLANDISTS AND F. BOUIX.

1. THIS nun took the habit forty years ago, and from the first began to reflect on the mysteries of the Passion of Christ our Lord, and on her own sins, for some time every day, without thinking at all of any thing supernatural, but only of created things, or of such subjects as suggested to her how soon the end of all things must come, discerning in creatures the greatness of God and His love for us.

2. This made her much more willing to serve Him: she was never under the influence of fear, and made no account of it, but had always a great desire to see God honoured and His glory increased. To that end were all her prayers directed, without making any for herself; for she thought that it mattered little if she had to suffer in purgatory in exchange for the increase of His glory even in the slightest degree.

3. In this she spent about two-and-twenty years in great aridities, and never did it enter into her thoughts to desire any thing else; for she regarded herself as one who, she thought, did not deserve even to think about God, except that His Majesty was very merciful to her in allowing her to remain in His presence, saying her prayers, reading also in good books.

Visions. 4. It must be about eighteen years since she began to arrange about the first monastery of Barefooted Carmelites which she founded. It was in Avila, three or two years before,—I believe it is three,—she began to think that she occasionally heard interior locutions, and had visions and revelations interiorly. She saw with the eyes of the soul, for she never saw any thing with her bodily eyes, nor heard any thing with her bodily ears: twice, she thinks, she heard a voice, but she understood not what was said. It was a sort of making things present when she saw these things interiorly; they passed away like a meteor most frequently. The vision, however, remained so impressed on her mind, and produced such effects, that it was as if she saw those things with her bodily eyes, and more.

5. She was then by nature so very timid, that she would not dare to be alone even by day, at times. *Confessors of the Saint.* And as she could not escape from these visitations, though she tried with all her might, she went about in very great distress, afraid that it was a delusion of Satan, and began to consult spiritual men of the Society of Jesus about it, among whom were Father Araoz, who was Commissary of the Society, and who happened to go to that place, and Father Francis, who was Duke of Gandia,—him she consulted twice;[1] also a Provincial, now in Rome, called Gil Gonzalez, and him also who is now Provincial of Castille,—this latter, however, not so often,—Father Baltasar Alvarez, who is now Rector in Salamanca; and he heard her confession for six years at this time; also the present Rector of Cuenca, Salazar by name; the Rector of Segovia, called Santander; the Rector of Burgos, whose name is Ripalda,—and he thought very ill of her when he heard of these things, till after he had conversed with her; the Doctor Paul Hernandez in Toledo, who was a Consultor of the Inquisition, him who was Rector in Salamanca when she talked to him; the Doctor Gutierrez, and other fathers, some of the Society, whom she knew to be spiritual men, these she sought out, if any were in those places where she went to found monasteries.

6. With the Father Fra Peter of Alcantara, who was a holy man of the Barefooted Friars of S. Francis, *S. Peter of Alcantara.* she had many communications, and he it was who insisted so much upon it that her spirit should be regarded as good. They were more than six years trying her spirit minutely, as it is already described at very great length,[2] as

[1] See *Life*, ch. xxiv. § 4.   [2] See *Life*, ch. xxv. § 18.

will be shown hereafter: and she herself in tears and deep affliction; for the more they tried her, the more she fell into raptures, and into trances very often,—not, however, deprived of her senses.

7. Many prayers were made, and many Masses were said, that our Lord would lead her by another way,[1] for her fear was very great when she was not in prayer; though in every thing relating to the state of her soul she was very much better, and a great difference was visible, there was no vain-glory, nor had she any temptation thereto, nor to pride; on the contrary, she was very much ashamed and confounded when she saw that people knew of her state, and except with her confessors, or any one who would give her light, she never spoke of these things, and it was more painful to speak of them than if they had been grave sins; for it seemed to her that people must laugh at her,[2] and that these things were womanish imaginations, which she had always heard of with disgust.

Soto.

8. About thirteen years ago, more or less, after the house of S. Joseph was founded, into which she had gone from the other monastery, came the present Bishop of Salamanca, Inquisitor, I think, of Toledo, previously of Seville, Soto by name.[3] She contrived to have a conference with him for her greater security, and told him every thing. He replied, that there was nothing in all this that concerned his office, because every thing that she saw and heard confirmed her the more in the Catholic faith, in which she always was, and is, firm, with

[1] See *Life*, ch. xxv. § 20, and ch. xxvii. § 1.
[2] See *Life*, ch. xxvi. § 5.
[3] Don Francisco de Soto y Salazar was a native of Bonilla de la Sierra, and Vicar-General of the Bishops of Astorga and Avila, and Canon of Avila; Inquisitor of Cordova, Seville, and Toledo; Bishop, successively, of Albarracin, Segorve, and Salamanca. He died at Merida in 1576, poisoned, it was suspected, by the sect of the Illuminati, who were alarmed at his faithful zeal and holy life (*Palafox*, note to letter 19, vol i. ed. Doblado). "She went to the Inquisitor Don Francisco Soto de Salazar—he was afterwards Bishop of Salamanca—and said to him: 'My lord, I am subject to certain extraordinary processes in prayer, such as ecstasies, raptures, and revelations, and do not wish to be deluded or deceived by Satan, or to do any thing that is not absolutely safe. I give

most earnest desires for the honour of God and the good of souls, willing to suffer death many times for one of them.

9. He told her, when he saw how distressed she was, to give an account of it all, and of her whole life, without omitting any thing, to the Master Avila, who was a man of great learning in the way of prayer, and to rest content with the answer he should give. She did so, and described her sins and her life. He wrote to her and comforted her, giving her great security. The account I gave was such that all those learned men who saw it—they were my confessors—said that it was very profitable for instruction in spiritual things; and they commanded her to make copies of it, and write another little book[1] for her daughters,—she was prioress,—wherein she might give them some instructions. *Advises her to write.*

10. Notwithstanding all this, she was not without fears at times, for she thought that spiritual men also might be deceived like herself. She told her confessor that he might discuss these things with certain learned men, though they were not much given to prayer, for she had no other desire but that of knowing whether what she experienced was in conformity with the sacred writings or not. Now and then she took comfort in thinking that—though she herself, because of her sins, deserved to fall into delusions—our Lord would not suffer so many good men, anxious to give her light, to be led into error. *Her fear of delusions.*

11. Having this in view, she began to communicate with fathers of the Order of the glorious S. Dominic, to which, before these things took place, she had been *Dominicans.*

---

myself up to the Inquisition to try me, and examine my ways of going on, submitting myself to its orders.' The Inquisitor replied: 'Señora, the business of the Inquisition is not to try the spirits, nor to examine ways of prayer, but to correct heretics. Do you, then, commit your experience to writing, in all simplicity and truth, and send it to the Father-Master Avila, who is a man of great spirituality and learning, and extremely conversant with matters of prayer; and when you shall have his answer, you may be sure there is nothing to be afraid of'" (Jerome Gratian, *Lucidario*, cap. iii.).

[1] This book is the *Way of Perfection*, written by direction of F. Bañes.

to confession,—she does not say to them, but to the Order.[1] These are they with whom she afterwards had relations. The Father Fra Vicente Barron, at that time Consultor of the Holy Office, heard her confessions for eighteen months in Toledo, and he had done so very many years before these things began. He was a very learned man. He reassured her greatly, as did also the fathers of the Society spoken of before. All used to say, If she does not sin against God, and acknowledges her own misery, what has she to be afraid of? She confessed to the Father Fra Pedro Ibañez, who was reader in Avila; to the Father-Master Fra Dominic Bañes, who is now in Valladolid as rector of the college of S. Gregory, I confessed for six years, and whenever I had occasion to do so communicated with him by letter; also to the Master Chaves; to the Father-Master Fra Bartholomew of Medina, professor in Salamanca, of whom she knew that he thought ill of her; for she, having heard this, thought that he, better than any other, could tell her if she was deceived, because he had so little confidence in her. This was more than two years ago. She contrived to go to confession to him, and gave him a full account of every thing while she remained there; and he saw what she had written,[2] for the purpose of attaining to a better understanding of the matter. He reassured her so much, and more than all the rest, and remained her very good friend.

Meneses.

12. She went to confession also to Fra Philip de Meneses, when she founded the monastery of Valladolid, for he was rector of the college of S. Gregory. He, having before that heard of her state, had gone to Avila, that he might speak to her,—it was an act of great charity,—being desirous of ascertaining whether she was deluded, so that he might enlighten her, and, if she was not, defend her when he heard her spoken against; and he was much satisfied.

[1] The Saint had such great affection for the Order of S. Dominic, that she used to say of herself, "Yo soy la Dominica in passione," meaning thereby that she was in her heart a Dominicaness, and a child of the Order (*Palafox*, note to letter 16, vol. i. ed. Doblado).

[2] When this father had read the *Life*, he had it copied, with the assent of F. Gratian, and gave the copy thus made to the Duchess of Alba (*De la Fuente*).

13. She also conferred particularly with Salinas, Dominican Provincial, a man of great spirituality; with another licentiate named Lunar, who was prior of S. Thomas of Avila; and, in Segovia, with a Reader, Fra Diego de Yangües.

14. Of these Dominicans some never failed to give themselves greatly to prayer, and perhaps all did. Some others also she consulted; for in so many years, and because of the fear she was in, she had opportunities of doing so, especially as she went about founding monasteries in so many places. Her spirit was tried enough, for every body wished to be able to enlighten her, and thereby reassured her and themselves. She always, at all times, wished to submit herself to whatever they enjoined her, and she was therefore distressed when, as to these spiritual things, she could not obey them. Both her own prayer, and that of the nuns she has established, are always carefully directed towards the propagation of the faith; and it was for that purpose, and for the good of her Order, that she began her first monastery.

15. She used to say that, if any of these things tended to lead her against the Catholic faith and the law of God, she would not need to seek for learned men nor tests, because she would see at once that they came from Satan. She never undertook any thing merely because it came to her in prayer; on the contrary, when her confessors bade her do the reverse, she did so without being in the least troubled thereat, and she always told them every thing. For all that they told her that these things came from God, she never so thoroughly believed them that she could swear to it herself, though it did seem to her that they were spiritually safe, because of the effects thereof, and of the great graces which she at times received; but she always desired virtues more than any thing else; and this it is that she has charged her nuns to desire, saying to them that the most humble and mortified will be the most spiritual.

Banes.

16. All that is told and written she communicated to the Father-Master Fra Dominic Bañes, who is now in Valladolid, and who is the person with whom she has had, and has still, the most frequent communications. He sent her writings to the Holy Office in Madrid, so it is said. In all

this she submits herself to the Catholic faith and the Roman Church. Nobody has found fault with them, because these things are not in the power of any man, and our Lord does not require what is impossible.

17. The reason why so much is known about her is that, as she was in fear about herself, and described her state to so many, these talked to one another on the subject, and also the accident that happened to what she had written.[1] This has been to her a very grievous torment and cross, and has cost her many tears. She says that this distress is not the effect of humility, but of the causes already mentioned. Our Lord seems to have given permission[2] for this torture; for if one spoke more harshly of her than others, by little and little he spoke more kindly of her.

18. She took the greatest pains not to submit the state of her soul to any one who she thought would believe that these things came from God, for she was instantly afraid that the devil would deceive them both. If she saw any one timid about these things, to him she laid bare her secrets with the greater joy; though also it gave her pain when, for the purpose of trying her, these things were treated with contempt, for she thought some were really from God, and she would not have people, even if they had good cause, condemn them so absolutely; neither would she have them believe that all were from God; and because she knew perfectly well that delusion was possible, therefore it was that she never thought herself altogether safe in a matter wherein there might be danger.

19. She used to strive with all her might never in any way to offend God, and was always obedient; and by these means she thought she might obtain her deliverance, by the help of God, even if Satan were the cause.

20. Ever since she became subject to these supernatural visitations, her spirit is always inclined to seek after that which is most perfect, and she had almost always a great desire to suffer; and in the persecutions she underwent, and they were many, she was comforted, and had a particular affection for her persecutors. She had a great desire to be poor and lonely, and

[1] See *Foundations*, ch. xvii. § 12, note.   [2] *Life*, ch. xxiii. § 15.

to depart out of this land of exile in order to see God. Through these effects, and others like them, she began to find peace, thinking that a spirit which could leave her with these virtues could not be an evil one, and they who had the charge of her soul said so; but it was a peace that came from diminished weariness, not from the cessation of fear.

21. The spirit she is of never urged her to make any of these things known, but to be always obedient.[1] As it has been said already,[2] she never saw any thing with her bodily eyes, but in a way so subtile and so intellectual that at first she sometimes thought that all was the effect of imagination; at other times she could not think so. These things were not continual, but occurred for the most part when she was in some trouble: as on one occasion, when for some days she had to bear unendurable interior pains, and a restlessness of soul arising out of the fear that she was deluded by Satan, as it is described at length in the account she has given of it,[3] and where her sins, for they have been so public, are mentioned with the rest; for the fear she was in made her forget her own good name.

22. Being thus in distress such as cannot be described, at the mere hearing interiorly these words,[4] "It is I, be not afraid," her soul became so calm, courageous, and confident, that she could not understand whence so great a blessing had come; for her confessor had not been able—and many learned men, with many words, had not been able—to give her that peace and rest which this one word had given her. And thus, at other times, some vision gave her strength, for without that she could not have borne such great trials and contradictions, together with infirmities without number, and which she still has to bear, though they are not so many,—for she is never free from some suffering or other, more or less intense. Her ordinary state is constant pain, with many other infirmities, though since she became a nun they are more troublesome, if she is doing any thing in the service of our Lord. And the mercies He shows her pass quickly out of memory, though she often

[1] *Life*, ch. xxvi. § 6.
[2] § 4.
[3] *Life*, ch. xxv. § 19.
[4] *Life*, ch. xxv. § 22.

dwells on those mercies,—but she is not able to dwell so long upon these as upon her sins; these are always a torment to her, most commonly as filth smelling foully.

23. That her sins are so many, and her service of God so scanty, must be the reason why she is not tempted to vainglory. There never was any thing in any of these spiritual visitations that was not wholly pure and clean, nor does she think it can be otherwise if the spirit be good and the visions supernatural, for she utterly neglects the body and never thinks of it, being wholly intent upon God.

24. She is also living in great fear about sinning against God, and doing His will in all things; this is her continual prayer. And she is, she thinks, so determined never to swerve from this, that there is nothing her confessors might enjoin her, which she considers to be for the greater honour of our Lord, that she would not undertake and perform, by the help of our Lord. And confident that His Majesty helps those who have resolved to advance His service and glory, she thinks no more of herself and of her own progress, in comparison with that, than if she did not exist, so far as she knows herself, and her confessors think so too.

25. All that is written in this paper is the simple truth, and they, and all others who have had any thing to do with her for these twenty years, can justify it. Most frequently her spirit urged her to praise God, and she wished that all the world gave itself up to that, even though it should cost her exceedingly. Hence the desire she has for the good of souls; and from considering how vile are the things of this world, and how precious are interior things, with which nothing can be compared, she has attained to a contempt of the world.

26. As for the vision about which you, my father, wish to know something, it is of this kind: she sees nothing either outwardly or inwardly, for the vision is not imaginary; but, without seeing any thing, she understands what it is, and where it is, more clearly than if she saw it, only nothing in particular presents itself to her. She is like a person who feels that another is close beside her; but because she is in the dark she sees him not, yet is certain that he is there present. Still, this comparison is

not exact; for he who is in the dark, in some way or other, through hearing a noise or having seen that person before, knows he is there, or knew it before; but here there is nothing of the kind, for without a word, inward or outward, the soul clearly perceives who it is, where he is, and occasionally what he means.[1] Why, or how, she perceives it, she knoweth not; but so it is; and while it lasts, she cannot help being aware of it. And when it is over,—though she may wish ever so much to retain the image thereof,—she cannot do it, for it is then clear to her that it would be, in that case, an act of the imagination, not the vision itself,—that is not in her power; and so it is with the supernatural things. And it is from this it comes to pass that he in whom God works these graces despises himself, and becomes more humble than he was ever before, for he sees that this is a gift of God, and that he can neither add to it nor take from it. The love and the desire become greater of serving our Lord, who is so mighty that He can do that which is more than our imagination can conceive here, as there are things which men, however learned they may be, can never know. Blessed for ever and ever be He who bestows this! Amen.

RELATION VIII.

ADDRESSED TO F. RODRIGO ALVAREZ.

1. THESE interior things of the spirit are so difficult to describe, and, still more, in such a way as to be understood,—the more so as they pass quickly away,—that, if obedience did not help me, it would be a chance if I succeeded, especially in such difficult things. I implore you, my father, to take for granted that it is not in my mind to think this to be correct, for it may well be that I do not understand the matter; but what I can assure you of is this, that I will speak of nothing I have not had experience of at times, and, indeed, often.

2. I think it will please you, my father, if I begin by

[1] See *Life*, ch. xxvii. § 5.

discussing that which is at the root of supernatural things; for that which relates to devotion, tenderness, tears, and meditations, which is in our power here to acquire by the help of our Lord, is understood.

3. The first prayer of which I was conscious,—in *Supernatural prayer.* my opinion, supernatural,—so I call that which no skill or effort of ours, however much we labour, can attain to, though we should prepare ourselves for it, and that preparation must be of great service,—is a certain interior recollection[1] of which the soul is sensible; the soul seems to have other senses within itself then, which bear some likeness to the exterior senses it possesses; and thus the soul, withdrawing into itself, seeks to go away from the tumult of its outward senses, and accordingly it drags them away with itself; for it closes the eyes on purpose that it may neither see, nor hear, nor understand any thing but that whereon the soul is then intent, which is to be able to converse with God alone. In this prayer there is no suspension of the faculties and powers of the soul; it retains the full use of them; but the use of them is retained that they may be occupied with God. This will be easily understood by him whom our Lord shall have raised to this state; but by him whom He has not, not; at least, such a one will have need of many words and illustrations.

4. Out of this recollection grow a certain quietude *Prayer of quiet.* and inward peace most full of comfort; for the soul is in such a state that it does not seem to it that it wants any thing; for even speaking wearies it,—I mean by this, vocal prayer and meditation; it would do nothing but love. This lasts some time, and even a long time.

5. Out of this prayer comes usually what is called *Sleep of the faculties.* a sleep of the faculties; but they are not so absorbed nor so suspended as that it can be called a trance; nor is it altogether union.

6. Sometimes, and even often, the soul is aware *Union of the will only.* that the will alone is in union; and this it sees very clearly,—that is, it seems so to it. The will is

[1] *Inner Fortress*, iv. ch. iii.

wholly intent upon God, and the soul sees that it has no power to rest on, or do, any thing else; and at the same time the two other faculties are at liberty to attend to other matters of the service of God,—in a word, Martha and Mary are together.[1] I asked Father Francis[2] if this was a delusion, for it made me stupid; and his reply was, that it often happened.

7. When all the faculties of the soul are in union, it is a very different state of things; for they can then do nothing whatever, because the understanding is as it were surprised. The will loves more than the understanding knows; but the understanding does not know that the will loves, nor what it is doing, so as to be able in any way to speak of it. As to the memory, the soul, I think, has none then, nor any power of thinking, nor are the senses awake, but rather as lost, so that the soul may be the more occupied with the object of its fruition: so it seems to me. They are lost but for a brief interval; it passes quickly away. By the wealth of humility, and other virtues and desires, left in the soul after this may be learnt how great the blessing is that flows from this grace, but it cannot be told what it is; for, though the soul applies itself to the understanding of it, it can neither understand nor explain it. This, if it be real, is, in my opinion, the greatest grace wrought by our Lord on this spiritual road,—at least, it is one of the greatest.

Union of all the faculties.

8. Raptures and trance, in my opinion, are all one, only I am in the habit of using the word trance instead of rapture because the latter word frightens people; and, indeed, the union of which I am speaking may also be called a trance. The difference between union and trance is this, that the latter lasts longer and is more visible outwardly, because the breathing gradually diminishes, so that it becomes impossible to speak or to open the eyes; and though this very thing occurs when the soul is in union, there is more violence in a trance, for the natural warmth vanishes, I know not how, when the rapture is deep; and in all these kinds of prayer there is more or less of this. When it is deep, as I was saying, the hands become cold, and

Rapture and union.

---

[1] See *Life*, ch. xvii. § 5.   [2] Compare *Life*, ch. xxiv. § 4.

sometimes stiff and straight as pieces of wood; as to the body, if the rapture comes on when it is standing or kneeling, it remains so;[1] and the soul is so full of the joy of that which our Lord is setting before it, that it seems to forget to animate the body, and abandons it. If the rapture lasts, the nerves are made to feel it.

9. It seems to me that our Lord will have the soul *Effects of rapture.* know more of that, the fruition of which it has, in a trance than in union, and accordingly in a rapture the soul receives most commonly certain revelations of His Majesty, and the effects thereof on the soul are great,—a forgetfulness of self, through the longing it has that God our Lord, who is so high, may be known and praised. In my opinion, if the rapture be from God, the soul cannot fail to obtain a deep conviction of its own helplessness, and of its wretchedness and ingratitude, in that it has not served Him who, of His own goodness only, bestows upon it graces so great; for the feeling and the sweetness are so high above all things that may be compared therewith that, if the recollection of them did not pass away, all the satisfactions of earth would be always loathsome to it; and hence comes the contempt for all the things of the world.

10. The difference between trance and transport[2] *Trance and transport.* is this,—in a trance the soul gradually dies to outward things, losing the senses and living unto God. A transport comes on by one sole act of His Majesty, wrought in the innermost part of the soul with such swiftness that it is as if the higher part thereof were carried away, and the soul leaving the body. Accordingly it requires courage at first to throw itself into the arms of our Lord, that He may take it whithersoever He will; for, until His Majesty establishes it in peace there whither He is pleased to take it—by take it I mean the admitting of it to the knowledge of deep things—it certainly requires in the beginning to be firmly resolved to die for Him, because the poor soul does not know what this means—that is, at first. The virtues, as it seems to me, remain stronger after this, for there is a growth in detachment, and the power of

[1] See *Life*, ch. xx. § 23.
[2] "Arrobamiento y arrebatamiento."

God, who is so mighty, is the more known, so that the soul loves and fears Him. For so it is, He carries away the soul, no longer in our power, as the true Lord thereof, which is filled with a deep sorrow for having offended Him, and astonishment that it ever dared to offend a Majesty so great, with an exceedingly earnest desire that none may henceforth offend Him, and that all may praise Him. This, I think, must be the source of those very fervent desires for the salvation of souls, and for some share therein, and for the due praising of God.

11. The flight of the spirit—I know not how to call it—is a rising upwards from the very depths of the soul. I remember only this comparison, and I made use of it before, as you know, my father, in that writing where these and other ways of prayer are explained at length,[1] and such is my memory that I forget things at once. It seems to me that soul and spirit are one and the same thing; but only as a fire, if it is great and ready for burning; so, like fire burning rapidly, the soul, in that preparation of itself which is the work of God, sends up a flame,—the flame ascends on high, but the fire thereof is the same as that below, nor does the flame cease to be fire because it ascends: so here, in the soul, something so subtile and so swift seems to issue from it, that ascends to the higher part, and goes thither whither our Lord wills. I cannot go further with the explanation; it seems a flight, and I know of nothing else wherewith to compare it: I know that it cannot be mistaken, for it is most evident when it occurs, and that it cannot be hindered.

Flight of the spirit.

12. This little bird of the spirit seems to have escaped out of this wretchedness of the flesh, out of the prison of this body, and now, disentangled therefrom, is able to be the more intent on that which our Lord is giving it. The flight of the spirit is something so fine, of such inestimable worth, as the soul perceives it, that all delusion therein seems impossible, or any thing of the kind, when it occurs. It was afterwards that fear arose, because she who received this grace was so wicked; for she saw what good reasons she had to be

Fruits of it.

[1] See *Life*, chs. xx. and xxi.

afraid of every thing, though in her innermost soul there remained an assurance and a confidence wherein she was able to live, but not enough to make her cease from the anxiety she was in not to be deceived.

Impetus. 13. By impetus I mean that desire which at times rushes into the soul, without being preceded by prayer, and that is most frequently the case; it is a sudden remembering that the soul is away from God, or of a word it has heard to that effect. This remembering is occasionally so strong and vehement that the soul in a moment becomes as if the reason were gone, just like a person who suddenly hears most painful tidings of which he knew not before, or is surprised; such a one seems deprived of the power of collecting his thoughts for his own comfort, and is as one lost. So is it in this state, except that the suffering arises from this, that there abides in the soul a conviction that it would be well worth dying in it. It seems that whatever the soul then perceives does but increase its suffering, and that our Lord will have its whole being find no comfort in any thing, nor remember that it is His will that it should live: the soul seems to itself to be in great and indescribable loneliness, and abandoned of all, because the world, and all that is in it, gives it pain; and because it finds no companionship in any created thing, the soul seeks its Creator alone, and this it sees to be impossible unless it dies; and as it must not kill itself, it is dying to die, and there is really a risk of death, and it sees itself hanging between heaven and earth, not knowing what to do with itself. And from time to time God gives it a certain knowledge of Himself, that it may see what it loses, in a way so strange that no explanation of it is possible; and there is no pain in the world—at least, I have felt none—that is equal or like unto this, for if it lasts but half an hour the whole body is out of joint, and the bones so racked, that I am not able to write with my hands: the pains I endure are most grievous.[1]

Effects thereof. 14. But nothing of all this is felt till the impetus shall have passed away. He to whom it comes has enough to do in enduring that which is going on

[1] *Life*, ch. xx. § 16; *Inner Fortress*, vi. c. xi.

within him, nor do I believe that he would feel if he were grievously tortured: he is in possession of all his senses, can speak, and even observe; walk about he cannot,—the great blow of that love throws him down to the ground. If we were to die to have this, it would be of no use, for it cannot be except when God sends it. It leaves great effects and blessings in the soul. Some learned men say that it is this, others that it is that, but no one condemns it. The Master-Father d'Avila wrote to me and said it was good, and so say all. The soul clearly understands that it is a great grace from our Lord; were it to occur more frequently, life would not last long.

15. The ordinary impetus is, that this desire of serving God comes on with a certain tenderness, accompanied with tears, out of a longing to depart from this land of exile; but as the soul retains its freedom, wherein it reflects that its living on is according to our Lord's will, it takes comfort in that thought, and offers its life to Him, beseeching Him that it may last only for His glory. This done, it bears all. *The ordinary impetus.*

16. Another prayer very common is a certain kind of wounding;[1] for it really seems to the soul as if an arrow were thrust through the heart, or through itself. Thus it causes great suffering, which makes the soul complain; but the suffering is so sweet, that it wishes it never would end. The suffering is not one of sense, neither is the wound physical; it is in the interior of the soul, without any appearance of bodily pain; but as I cannot explain it except by comparing it with other pains, I make use of these clumsy expressions,—for such they are when applied to this suffering. I cannot, however, explain it in any other way. It is, therefore, neither to be written of nor spoken of, because it is impossible for any one to understand it who has not had experience of it,—I mean, how far the pain can go; for the pains of the spirit are very different from those of earth. I gather, therefore, from this, that the souls in hell and purgatory suffer more than we can imagine, by considering these pains of the body. *Wound of the soul.*

[1] See *Life*, ch. xxix. § 16.

17. At other times, this wound of love seems to issue from the inmost depth of the soul; great are the effects of it; and when our Lord does not inflict it, there is no help for it, whatever we may do to obtain it; nor can it be avoided when it is His pleasure to inflict it. The effects of it are those longings after God, so quick and so fine that they cannot be described; and when the soul sees itself hindered and kept back from entering, as it desires, on the fruition of God, it conceives a great loathing for the body, on which it looks as a thick wall which hinders it from that fruition which it then seems to have entered upon within itself, and unhindered by the body. It then comprehends the great evil that has befallen us through the sin of Adam in robbing us of this liberty.[1]

Wound of love.

18. This prayer I had before the raptures and the great impetuosities I have been speaking of. I forgot to say that these great impetuosities scarcely ever leave me, except through a trance or great sweetness in our Lord, whereby He comforts the soul, and gives it courage to live on for His sake.

19. All this that I speak of cannot be the effect of the imagination; and I have some reasons for saying this, but it would be wearisome to enter on them: whether it be good or not is known to our Lord. The effects thereof, and how it profits the soul, pass all comprehension, as it seems to me.

20. I see clearly that the Persons are distinct, as I saw it yesterday when you, my father, were talking to the Father-Provincial; only I saw nothing, and heard nothing, as, my father, I have already told you. But there is a strange certainty about it, though the eyes of the soul see nothing; and when the Presence is withdrawn, that withdrawal is felt. How it is, I know not; but I do know very well that it is not an imagination, because I cannot reproduce the vision when it is over, even if I were to perish in the effort; but I have tried to do so. So is it with all that I have spoken of here, so far as I can see; for, as I have been in this state for so many years, I have been able to observe, so that I can say so with this confidence. The truth is,—and you, my father,

Visions of the most Holy Trinity.

[1] *Life*, ch. xvii. § 9.

should attend to this,—that, as to the Person who always speaks, I can certainly say which of Them He seems to me to be; of the others I cannot say so much. One of Them I know well has never spoken. I never knew why, nor do I busy myself in asking more of God than He is pleased to give, because in that case, I believe, I should be deluded by Satan at once; nor will I ask now, because of the fear I am in.

21. I think the First spoke to me at times; but, as I do not remember that very well now, nor what it was that He spoke, I will not venture to say so. It is all written,—you, my father, know where,—and more at large than it is here; I know not whether in the same words or not.[1] Though the Persons are distinct in a strange way, the soul knows One only God. I do not remember that our Lord ever seemed to speak to me but in His Human Nature; and—I say it again—I can assure you that this is no imagination.

22. What, my father, you say about the water, I know not; nor have I heard where the earthly paradise is. I have already said that I cannot but listen to what our Lord tells me; I hear it because I cannot help myself; but, as for asking His Majesty to reveal any thing to me, that is what I have never done. In that case, I should immediately think I was imagining things, and that I must be in a delusion of Satan. God be praised, I have never been curious about things, and I do not care to know more than I do.[2] What I have learnt, without seeking to learn, as I have just said, has been a great trouble to me, though it has been the means, I believe, which our Lord made use of to save me, seeing that I was so wicked; good people do not need so much to make them serve His Majesty.

23. I remember another way of prayer which I had before the one I mentioned first,—namely, a presence of God, which is not a vision at all. It seems that any one, if he recommends himself to His Majesty, even if he only prays vocally, finds Him; every one, at all times, can do this, if we except seasons of aridity. May He grant I may not by my own fault lose mercies so great, and may He have compassion on me!

[1] See *Relation* iii. § 6.
[2] See S. John of the Cross, *Ascent of Mount Carmel*, bk. ii. ch. xxii.

RELATION IX.

OF CERTAIN SPIRITUAL GRACES SHE RECEIVED IN TOLEDO AND AVILA IN THE YEARS 1576 AND 1577.

Father Yepes.
1. I HAD begun to go to confession to a certain person[1] in the city wherein I am at present staying, when he, though he had much good will towards me, and always has had since he took upon himself the charge of my soul, ceased to come here; and one night, when I was in prayer, and thinking how he failed me, I understood that God kept him from coming because it was expedient for me to treat of the affairs of my soul with a certain person on the spot.[2] I was distressed because I had to form new relations—it might be he would not understand me, and would disturb me—and because I had a great affection for him who did me this charity, though I was always spiritually content when I saw or heard the latter preach; also, I thought it would not do because of his many occupations. Our Lord said to me: "I will cause him to hear and understand thee. Make thyself known unto him; it will be some relief to thee in thy troubles." The latter part was addressed to me, I think, because I was then so worn out by the absence of God. His Majesty also said that He saw very well the trouble I was in; but it could not be otherwise while I lived in this land of exile: all was for my good; and he comforted me greatly. So it has been: he comforts me, and seeks opportunities to do so; he has understood me, and given me great relief; he is a most learned and holy man.

Detachment.
2. One day,—it was the Feast of the Presentation,—I was praying earnestly to God for a certain person, and thinking that after all the possession of property

[1] F. Yepes, then prior of S. Jerome's, Toledo (*De la Fuente*).
[2] Don Alonzo Velasquez, canon of Toledo, to whom Relation xi. is addressed. The Saint speaks of this in a letter to Fra Gratian in 1576. The letter is numbered 82 in the edition of Don Vicente, and 23 in the fourth volume of the edition of Doblado.

and of freedom was unfitting for that high sanctity which
I wished him to attain to; I reflected on his weak health, and
on the spiritual health which he communicated to souls; and I
heard these words: "He serves Me greatly; but the great
thing is to follow Me stripped of every thing, as I was on
the cross. Tell him to trust in Me." These last words were
said because I thought he could not, with his weak health, attain
to such perfection.

3. Once, when I was thinking of the pain it was
to me to take my food and do no penance, I under- Self-delusion.
stood that there was at times more of self-love in that
feeling than of a desire for penance.

4. Once, when I was in great distress because of my
offences against God, He said to me: "All thy sins in My
sight are as if they were not. For the future, be strong; for thy
troubles are not over."

5. One day, in prayer, I felt my soul in God in such a way
that it seemed to me as if the world did not exist, I was so
absorbed in Him. He made me then understand that verse
of the *Magnificat*, "Et exultavit spiritus meus," so that I
can never forget it.

6. Once, when I was thinking how people sought to destroy
this monastery of the Barefooted Carmelites, and that they
purposed, perhaps, to bring about the destruction of them all
by degrees, I heard: "They do purpose it; nevertheless, they
will never see it done, but very much the reverse."

7. Once, in deep recollection, I was praying to God for
Eliseus;[1] I heard this: "He is My true son; I will never fail
him," or to that effect; but I am not sure of the latter words.

8. Having one day conversed with a person who
had given up much for God, and calling to mind The Saint's betrothal.
that I had given up nothing for Him, and had never
served Him in any thing, as I was bound to do, and then considering the many graces He had wrought in my soul, I began
to be exceedingly weary; and our Lord said to me: "Thou
knowest of the betrothal between thee and Myself, and therefore all I have is thine; and so I give thee all the labours and

[1] Fra Jerome Gratian (*De la Fuente*).

sorrows I endured, and thou canst therefore ask of My Father as if they were thine." Though I have heard that we are partakers therein,[1] now it was in a way so different that it seemed as if I had become possessed of a great principality; for the affection with which He wrought this grace cannot be described. The Father seemed to ratify the gift; and from that time forth I look at our Lord's Passion in a very different light, as on something that belongs to me; and that gives me great comfort.[2]

9. On the Feast of the Magdalene, when thinking of the great love I am bound to have for our Lord, according to the words He spoke to me in reference to this Saint, and having great desires to imitate her, our Lord was very gracious unto me, and said, I was to be henceforward strong; for I had to serve Him more than I had hitherto done.[3] He filled me with a desire not to die so soon, that I might have the time to occupy myself therein; and I remained with a great resolution to suffer.

10. On one occasion, I understood how our Lord was in all things, and how He was in the soul; and the illustration of a sponge filled with water was suggested to me.

Kindred. 11. When my brothers came,—and I owe so much to one of them,[4]—I remained in conversation with him concerning his soul and his affairs, which wearied and distressed me; and as I was offering this up to our Lord, and thinking that I did it all because I was under obligations to him, I remembered that by our Constitutions[5] we are commanded to separate ourselves from our kindred, and I was set thinking whether I was under any obligation, our Lord said to me: "No, My daughter; the regulations of the Order must be

[1] 1 S. Pet. iv. 13: "Communicantes Christi passionibus, gaudete."
[2] This took place in 1575, when she was going to found her monastery in Seville (*Ribera*, iv. 10).
[3] See § 3, above.
[4] This was in 1575, when the Saint was founding the monastery of Seville; and the brother was Don Lorenzo, returned from the Indies, and who now placed himself under the direction of his sister (*De la Fuente*).
[5] In the chapter "De la Clausura," § 3: "De tratar con deudos se desvien lo mas que pudieren."

only in conformity with My law." The truth is, that the end of the Constitutions is, that we are not to be attached to our kindred ; and to converse with them, as it seems to me, is rather wearisome, and it is painful to have any thing to do with them.

12. After Communion, on S. Augustin's Day, I understood, and, as it were, saw,—I cannot tell how, *Vision of the Trinity.* unless it was by an intellectual vision which passed rapidly away,—how the Three Persons of the most Holy Trinity, whom I have always imprinted in my soul, are One. This was revealed in a representation so strange, and in a light so clear, that the impression made upon me was very different from that which I have by faith. From that time forth I have never been able to think of One of the Three Divine Persons without thinking of the Three ; so that to-day, when I was considering how, the Three being One, the Son alone took our flesh upon Him, our Lord showed me how, though They are One, They are also distinct. These are marvels which make the soul desire anew to be rid of the hindrance which the body interposes between it and the fruition of them. Though this passes away in a moment, there remains a gain to the soul incomparably greater than any it might have made by meditation during many years ; and all without knowing how it happens.

13. I have a special joy on the Feast of our Lady's Nativity. When this day was come, I thought it would be well to renew our vows ; and thereupon I saw our Lady, by an illuminative vision ; and it seemed as if we made them before her, and that they were pleasing unto her. I had this vision constantly for some days, and our Lady was by me on my left hand. One day, after Communion, it seemed to me that my soul was really one with the most Holy Body of our Lord, then present before me ; and that wrought a great work and blessing in me.

14. I was once thinking whether I was to be sent to reform a certain monastery ;[1] and, distressed at it, I heard : "What art

[1] The monastery of Paterna, of the unreformed Carmelites. This was in 1576 (*De la Fuente*).

thou afraid of? What canst thou lose?—only thy life, which thou hast so often offered to Me. I will help thee." This was in prayer, which was of such a nature as to ease my soul exceedingly.

15. Once, having a desire to render some service to our Lord, I considered that I could serve Him but poorly, and said to myself: "Why, O Lord, dost Thou desire my works?" And He answered: "To see thy good will, My child."

16. Once our Lord gave me light in a matter that I was very glad to understand, and I immediately forgot it, so that I was never able to call it again to mind; and so, when I was trying to remember it, I heard: "Thou knowest now that I speak to thee from time to time. Do not omit to write down what I say; for, though it may not profit thee, it may be that it will profit others." As I was thinking whether I, for my sins, had to be of use to others, and be lost myself, He said to me: "Have no fear."

17. I was once recollected in that companionship which I ever have in my soul, and it seemed to me that God was present therein in such a way that I remembered how S. Peter said: "Thou art Christ, the Son of the living God;"[1] for the living God was in my soul. This is not like other visions, for it overpowers faith; so that it is impossible to doubt of the indwelling of the Trinity in our souls by presence, power, and essence. To know this truth is of the very highest gain; and as I stood amazed to see His Majesty in a thing so vile as my soul, I heard: "It is not vile, My child, for it is made in My image."[2] I also learnt something of the reason why God delights in souls more than in any other creatures: it is so subtile that, though the understanding quickly comprehended it, I cannot tell it.

18. When I was in such distress, because of the troubles of our father,[3] that I had no rest, and after Communion one

---

[1] S. Matt. xvi. 16: "Tu es Christus, Filius Dei vivi."
[2] Gen. i. 26: "Ad imaginem et similitudinem Nostram."
[3] Fra Jerome Gratian. This took place during the persecution that fell on the reformed Carmelites at the end of the year 1575, and during the following year. See the last paragraph of this Relation (*De la Fuente;* see, also, Relation vi. § 1).

day was making most earnestly my petition to our Lord that, as He had given him to me, I might not lose him, He said to me: "Have no fear."

19. Once, with that presence of the Three Persons which I have in my soul, I was in light so clear that no doubt of the presence of the true and living God was possible; and I then came to the knowledge of things which afterwards I could not speak of. One of these things was, how the person of the Son only took human flesh. I cannot, as I have just said, explain it at all; for some of these things were wrought in the secret recesses of the soul, and the understanding seems to grasp them only as one who in his sleep, or half awake, thinks he comprehends what is told him. I was thinking how hard it was to remain alive, seeing that it was living on that robbed us of that marvellous companionship; and so I said to myself: "O Lord, show me some way whereby I may bear this life!" He said unto me: "Think, My child, when life is over, thou canst not serve Me as thou art serving Me now, and eat for Me, and sleep for Me. Whatsoever thou doest, let it be done for Me as if thou wert no longer living, but I; for that is what S. Paul said."[1]

20. Once, after Communion, I saw how His Father within our soul accepts the most Holy Body of Christ. I have understood and seen how the Divine Persons are there, and how pleasing is this offering of His Son, because He has His joy and delight in Him, so to speak, here on earth; for it is not the Humanity only that is with us in our souls, but the Divinity as well, and thus is it so pleasing and acceptable unto Him, and gives us graces so great. I understood also that He accepts the sacrifice, though the priest be in sin; but then the grace of it is not communicated to his soul as it is to their souls who are in a state of grace: not that the inflowings of grace, which proceed from this Communion wherein the Father accepts the sacrifice, cease to flow in their strength, but because of his fault who has to receive them; as it is not the fault of the sun that it does not illumine a lump of pitch, when its rays strike it, as it illumines a globe of crystal. If I could now

[1] Galat. ii. 20: "Vivo autem, jam non ego; vivit vero in me Christus."

describe it, I should be better understood; it is a great matter to know this, because there are grand secrets within us when we are at Communion. It is sad that these bodies of ours do not allow us to have the fruition thereof.

21. During the Octave of All Saints,[1] I had two or three days of exceeding anguish, the result of my remembrance of my great sins, and I was also in great dread of persecutions, which had no foundation except that great accusations were brought against me, and all my resolutions to suffer any thing for God failed me: though I sought to encourage myself, and made corresponding acts, and saw that all would be a great gain for me, it was to little purpose, for the fear never left me. It was a sharp warfare. I came across a letter, in which my good father[2] had written that S. Paul said that God does not suffer us to be tempted beyond our power to bear.[3] This was a very great relief to me, but was not enough; yea, rather, on the next day I was in great distress at his absence, for I had no one to go to in this trouble, for I seemed to be living in great loneliness. And it added to my grief to see that I now find no one but he who can comfort me, and he must be more than ever away, which is a very sore trouble.

22. The next night after this, reading in a book, I found another saying of S. Paul, with which I began to be comforted; and being slightly recollected, I remained thinking how I had our Lord before present within me, so that I truly saw Him to be the living God. While thinking on this He spoke to me, and I saw Him in my inmost being, as it were beside my heart, in an intellectual vision; His words were: "I am here, only I will have thee see how little thou canst do without Me." I was on the instant reassured, and all my fears left me; and while at Matins that very night our Lord Himself, in an intellectual vision so clear as to seem almost imaginary, laid Himself in my arms, as He is painted in the pictures of our Lady of

[1] A.D. 1577 (*De la Fuente*).
[2] Jerome Gratian (*id.*).
[3] 1 Cor. x. 13 : "Fidelis autem Deus est, qui non patietur vos tentari supra id quod potestis."

Anguish.[1] The vision made me very much afraid, for it was so clear, and so close to me, that it made me think whether it was an illusion or not. He said to me, "Be not afraid of it, for the union of My Father with thy soul is incomparably closer than this." The vision has remained with me till now. What I have said of our Lord continued more than a month: now it has left me.

23. I was one night in great distress, because it was then a long time since I had heard any thing of my father;[2] and, moreover, he was not well the last time he wrote to me. However, my distress was not so great as that I felt before, for I had hopes, and distress like that I never was in since; but still my anxiety hindered my prayer. He appeared to me on the instant; it could not have been the effect of imagination, for I saw a light within me, and himself coming by the way joyous, with a face all fair. It must have been the light I saw that made his face fair, for all the saints in heaven seem so; and I considered whether it be the light and splendour proceeding from our Lord that renders them thus fair. I heard this: "Tell him to begin at once without fear, for the victory is his."

24. One day, after he came, when I was at night giving thanks to our Lord for the many mercies He had given unto me, He said to me: "O my child, what canst thou ask that I have not done?"

25. Our Lord said to me one day, in the monastery of Veas, that I was to present my petition to Him, for I was His bride. He promised to grant whatever I might ask of Him, and, as a pledge, gave me a very beautiful ring, with a stone set in it like an amethyst, but of a brilliancy very unlike, which He put on my finger. I write this to my own confusion, considering the goodness of God, and my wretched life; for I have

---

[1] Don Vicente says, that here is a proof—if any were wanting—that the Saint wrote this after her sojourn in Seville; because in Avila and in Castile and Aragon the expression is, "our Lady of Dolors;" while in Andalucia it is our Lady of Anguish—"Nuestra Señora de las Angustias."

[2] Fra Jerome Gratian.

deserved hell. Ah, my daughters, pray to God for me, and be devout to S. Joseph, who can do much. This folly I write .... folly I write. .....

26. On the eve of S. Laurence, at Communion, I was so distracted and dissipated in mind, that I had no power over it, and began to envy those who dwell in desert places; thinking that, as they see and hear nothing, they are exempt from distractions. I heard this: "Thou art greatly deceived, My daughter; on the contrary, the temptations of Satan are more violent there. Have patience; while life lasts, it cannot be helped." While dwelling on this, I became suddenly recollected, and I saw a great light within me, so that I thought I was in another world, and my spirit found itself interiorly in a forest and in a garden of delights, which made me remember those words of the Canticle:[1] "Veniat dilectus meus in hortum suum." I saw my Eliseus[2] there, not at all swarthy, but in strange beauty: around his head was a garland of precious stones; a multitude of damsels went before him with palms in their hands, all singing hymns of praise unto God. I did nothing but open my eyes, to see whether I could not distract myself from the vision, but that failed to divert my attention; and I thought there was music also,—the singing of birds and of angels,—which filled my soul with joy, though I did not hear any. My soul was in joy, and did not consider that there was nobody else there. I heard these words: "He has merited to be among you, and all this rejoicing which thou beholdest will take place on the day he shall set aside for the honour of My Mother;[3] and do thou make haste, if thou wouldst reach the place where he is." This vision lasted more than an hour and a half. In this respect—differently from my other visions—I could not turn away from it, and it filled me with delight. The effect of the vision was a great affection for Eliseus, and a

[1] Cant. v. 1.
[2] This was the name given to Fra Jerome Gratian, when the Saint was driven, by the persecution raised against her, to distinguish her friends by other designations than those by which they were usually known: this fragment cannot have been written before the year 1578 (*De la Fuente*).
[3] See the last section.

more frequent thinking of him in that beauty. I have had a fear of its being a temptation, for work of the imagination it could not possibly be.¹

27. The day after the presentation of the Brief,² as I was in the most eager expectation, which utterly disturbed me, so that I could not even pray,—for I had been told that our father was in great straits because they would not let him come away, and that there was a great tumult,—I heard these words: "O woman of little faith, be quiet; every thing is going on perfectly well." It was the Feast of the Presentation of our Lady, in the year 1575. I resolved within myself, if our Lady obtained from her Son that we might see ourselves and our father free of these friars, to ask him to order the solemn celebration of that feast every year in our monasteries of the Barefooted Carmelites. When I made this resolution, I did not remember what I had heard in a former vision, that he would establish this solemnity. Now, in reading again this little paper, I think this must be the feast referred to.³

RELATION X.

OF A REVELATION TO THE SAINT AT AVILA, 1579, AND OF CERTAIN DIRECTIONS CONCERNING THE GOVERNMENT OF THE ORDER.

IN S. Joseph of Avila, on Pentecost eve, in the hermitage of Nazareth, thinking of one of the greatest graces our Lord had given me on that day some twenty years before,⁴ more or

---

¹ Don Vicente published §§ 25 and 26 as fragments separately (vol. i. pp.524-526); but, as they seem to form a part of the series of events spoken of in this Relation, they have been placed here.

² Fra Jerome Gratian exhibited the Brief which made him Visitor-Apostolic to the unreformed Carmelites, who were very angry thereat, and rude in their vexation.

³ See § 26.

⁴ See *Life*, ch. xxxviii. § 11.

less, my spirit was vehemently stirred and grew hot within me,[1] and I fell into a trance. In that profound recollection I heard our Lord say what I am now going to tell: I was to say to the Barefooted Fathers, as from Him, that they must strive to observe four things; and that so long as they observed them, the Order would increase more and more; and if they neglected them, they should know that they were falling away from their first estate.

The first is, the superiors of the monasteries are to be of one mind.

The second, even if they have many monasteries, to have but few friars in each.

The third, to converse little with people in the world, and that only for the good of their souls.

The fourth, to teach more by works than by words.

This happened in the year 1579; and because it is a great truth, I have put my name to it.

TERESA DE JESUS.

RELATION XI.

WRITTEN FROM PALENCIA IN MAY 1581, AND ADDRESSED TO DON ALONZO VELASQUEZ, BISHOP OF OSMA, WHO HAD BEEN, WHEN CANON OF TOLEDO, ONE OF THE SAINT'S CONFESSORS.[2]

JESUS.

1. OH, that I could clearly explain to your Lordship the peace and quiet my soul has found! for it has so great a certainty of the fruition of God, that it seems to be as if already in posses-

---

[1] Ps. xxxix. 3 : "Concaluit cor meum intra me."
[2] This Relation is usually printed among the letters of the Saint, and Don Vicente did not change the practice, assigning as his reason the Saint's reference in § 4 to certain transactions in which she was engaged. The letter is the 333d, and the 4th of vol. ii., ed Doblado, and is probably the latest account of the state of her soul, for she died on October 4 in the following year.

sion,[1] though the joy is withheld. I am as one to whom another has granted by deed a large revenue, into the enjoyment and use of which he is to come at a certain time, but until then has nothing but the right already given him to the revenue. In gratitude for this, my soul would abstain from the joy of it, because it has not deserved it; it wishes only to serve Him, even if in great suffering, and at times it thinks it would be very little if, till the end of the world, it had to serve Him who has given it this right; for, in truth, it is in some measure no longer subject, as before, to the miseries of this world; though it suffers more, it seems as if only the habit were struck, for my soul is, as it were, in a fortress with authority, and accordingly does not lose its peace. Still, this confidence does not remove from it its great fear of offending God, nor make it less careful to put away every hindrance to His service, yea, rather, it is more careful than before. But it is so forgetful of its own interests as to seem, in some measure, to have lost itself, so forgetful of self is it in this. Every thing is directed to the honour of God, to the doing of His will more and more, and the advancement of His glory.

2. Though this be so, yet, in all that relates to health and the care of the body, it seems to me that I am more careful than I was, that I mortify myself less in my food, and do fewer penances: it is not so with the desires I had; they seem to be greater. All this is done that I may be the better able to serve God in other things, for I offer to Him very often, as a great sacrifice, the care I take of my body, and that wearies me much, and I try it sometimes in acts of mortification; but, after all, this cannot be done without losing health, and I must not neglect what my superiors command. Herein, and in the wish for health, much self-love also must insinuate itself; but, as it seems to me, I feel that it would give me more pleasure, and it gave me more pleasure when I was strong, to do penance, for, at least, I seemed to be doing something, and was giving a good example, and I was free from the vexation which arises out of the fact that I am not serving God at all.

[1] See *Inner Fortress*, vii. ch. ii.

Your Lordship will see what it will be best to do in the matter.

3. The imaginary visions have ceased, but the intellectual vision of the Three Persons and of the Sacred Humanity seems ever present, and that, I believe, is a vision of a much higher kind; and I understand now, so I think, that the visions I had came from God, because they prepared my soul for its present state; they were given only because I was so wretched and so weak: God led me by the way which He saw was necessary; but they are, in my opinion, of great worth when they come from God.

4. The interior locutions have not left me, for, whenever it is necessary, our Lord gives me certain directions; and now, in Palencia, were it not for these, there would have been committed a great blunder, though not a sin.[1]

5. The acts and desires do not seem to be so vigorous as they used to be, for, though they are great, I have one much greater to see the will of God accomplished and His glory increased; for as the soul is well aware that His Majesty knoweth what is expedient herein, and is so far removed from all self-seeking, these acts and desires quickly end, and, as it seems to me, have no strength. Hence the fear I have at times, though without disquietude and pain as formerly, that my soul is dulled, and that I am doing nothing, because I can do no penance; acts of desire for suffering, for martyrdom, and of the vision of God, have no strength in them, and, most frequently, I cannot make them. I seem to live only for eating and drinking, and avoiding pain in every thing; and yet this gives me none, except that sometimes, as I said before, I am afraid that this is a delusion; but I cannot believe it, because, so far as I can see, I am not under the sway of any strong attachment to any created thing, not even to all the bliss of heaven, but only to the love of God; and this does not grow less,—on the contrary, I believe it is growing, together with the longing that all men may serve Him.

6. But, for all this, one thing amazes me: I have not the feelings I had formerly, so strong and so interior, which tor-

[1] This relates to the taking of the hermitage of our Lady de la Calle, in Palencia (*De la Fuente*). See *Foundations*, ch. xxix.

mented me when I saw souls go to their ruin, and when I used to think I had offended God. I cannot have these feelings now, though I believe my desire that God be not sinned against is not less than it was.

7. Your Lordship must consider that in all this, in my present as well as in my previous state, I can do no more, and that it is not in my power to serve Him better: I might do so, if I were not so wicked. I may say, also, that if I were now to make great efforts to wish to die, I could not, nor can I make the acts I used to make, nor feel the pains I felt for having offended God, nor the great fears I had for so many years when I thought I was under a delusion: and accordingly I have no need of learned men, or of speaking to any body at all, only to satisfy myself that I am going the right road now, and whether I can do any thing. I have consulted certain persons on this point, with whom I had taken counsel on the others, with Fra Dominic, the Master Medina, and certain members of the Society. I will be satisfied with the answer which you, my Lord, may give me, because of the great trust I have in your Lordship. Consider it carefully, for the love of God! Neither do I cease to learn that certain souls of people connected with me when they died are in heaven: of others I learn nothing. La soledad que me hace pensar no se puede dar aquel sentido á el que mama los pechos de mi madre, la ida de Egito![1]

8. I am at peace within; and my likings and dislikings have so little power to take from me the Presence of the Three Persons, of which, while it continues, it is so impossible to doubt, that I seem clearly to know by experience what is recorded by S. John, that God will make His dwelling in the soul:[2] and not only by grace, but because He will have the soul feel that presence, and it brings with it so many blessings, particularly this, that there is no need to run after reflections to learn that God is there. This is almost always the state I am in, except when my great infirmities oppress me. Some-

[1] This passage, Don Vicente observes, was omitted in all editions prior to his: he does not know what it means; and the translator can give no corresponding English words.
[2] S. John xiv. 23: "Mansionem apud eum faciemus."

times God will have me suffer without any inward comfort; but my will never swerves—not even in its first movements—from the will of God. This resignation to His will is so efficacious, that I desire neither life nor death, except for some moments, when I long to see God; and then the Presence of the Three Persons becomes so distinct as to relieve the pain of the absence, and I wish to live—if such be His good pleasure—to serve Him still longer. And if I might help, by my prayers, to make but one soul love Him more, and praise Him, and that only for a short time, I think that of more importance than to dwell in glory.

The unworthy servant and daughter
of your Lordship,

TERESA DE JESUS.

INDEX.

ABECEDARIO, Tercer, iv. 8.
Agony in raptures, xx. 15.
Ahumada, de, Antonio, iv. 1.
Ahumada, de, Doña Beatriz, mother of S. Teresa, death of, i. 7 ; seen in heaven by the Saint, xxxviii. 1.
Ahumada, de, Juana, sister of the Saint, xxxiii. 13.
Alcala, monastery founded in, xxxvi. 29, note.
Alcantara. See S. Peter of Alcantara.
Almsgiving of the Saint, i. 6, Rel. ii. 3.
Alvarez, F. Baltasar, xxiv. 6, xxxv. 10 ; mortifies the Saint, xxvi. 4 ; humility of, xxviii. 20 ; promise of, to protect the Saint, xxviii. 21 ; always consoled the Saint, xxix. 5 ; hesitates about the new foundation, xxxii. 16 ; commands the Saint to abandon it, xxxiii. 4 ; orders her to proceed, xxxiii. 13.
Alvarez, F. Rodrigo, Rel. viii.
Amendment of life, the work of prayer, viii. 6-11.
Amusements, vii. 1, Rel. i. 14.
Angels and evil spirits, vision of, xxxi. 11.
Angel, the Saint's vision of the, xxix. 16.
Answers to the Saint's prayers, xxxix. 1-7.
Antony, S., of Padua, xxii. 10.
Aranda, de, Don Gonzalo, xxxvi. 18.
Aridity, how it comes on in the second state of prayer, xv. 15.
Art, the, of serving God, xii. 2.
Ascent of the Mount, xxiii. 13.
Assumption, the, vision of, xxxix. 37.

Attachments, evil effects of worldly, xi. 5, xxiii. 5.
Augustin, S., Confessions of, ix. 8 ; effect of reading them on the Saint, ix. 9 ; saying of, xiii. 4.
Avila, birthplace of S. Teresa, troubled by the new foundation, xxxvi. 14.
Avila, Juan of, Rel. vii. 9.

BAÑES, Fr. Dom., xxxvi. 15; transmits the Saint's writings to the Inquisition, Rel. vii. 16.
Barrientos. See Martin.
Barron, Fra Vicente, confessor of the Saint's father, vii. 26 ; hears the confession of the Saint, vii. 27, xix. 19.
Beauty of our Lord, xxviii. 2, xxix. 2, xxxvii. 5 ; unimaginable, xxviii. 7.
Beginners, must toil, xi. 13 ; and persevere, xi. 16 ; not to be afraid of the cross, xi. 25 ; must be content, xii. 2 ; certain temptations of, vii. 16, xiii. 9 ; must begin humbly, xv. 19.
Bernard, S., xxii. 10.
Betrothal, spiritual, of the Saint, Rel. ix. 8, 25.
Bird, the soul likened to a, xviii. 13, xix. 22.
Bishopric, a, the Saint consulted about the acceptance of, xi. 21.
Blessed, the, joys of, x. 3.
Blindness healed through the prayer of the Saint, xxxix. 1.
Body, the, shares the joy of the soul in certain states of prayer, xvii. 14, xviii. 15 ; state of, in raptures, xx. 2, 4, 23 ; our Lord seen by the Saint always in His glorified, xxix. 4.

Book, a living, xxvi. 6.
Books insufficient without a director, xxii. 3.
Borja, de, S. Francis. See Francis.
Brief, the, sanctioning the observances of S. Joseph's, xxxiv. 2, xxxvi. 1, xxxix. 20.
Brizeño, Doña Maria, ii. 12; influences the Saint, iii. 1.
Bulls, the Sabbatine, xxxviii. 40.

CARDONA, de, Doña Catalina, Rel. iii. 12.
Carmel, the Order of, vision concerning, Rel. iii. 14; advice to, Rel. x.
Caterpillar of self-respect, xxxi. 24.
Catherine, S., of Siena, xxii. 10.
Censoriousness of the world, xxxi. 19.
Cepeda, de, Alfonso Sanchez, father of the Saint, fond of spiritual books, i. 1; gives his daughter Maria in marriage, i. 4, 8; places the Saint at school in a monastery, i. 8; would not consent to her becoming a nun, ii. 9; takes her to Bezadas to be cured, v. 5, 6: brings her to his house in Avila, v. 15; hinders her from making her confession in an illness, v. 17; persuaded by the Saint to practise mental prayer, vii. 16; makes progress therein, vii. 20; holy death of, vii. 20; seen in heaven by the Saint, xxxviii. 1.
Cepeda, de, Don Lorenzo, finds money for the new monastery of S. Joseph, xxxiii. 13.
Cepeda, de, Maria, sister of the Saint, ii. 4; sudden death of, xxxiv. 23; seen in heaven by the Saint, xxxiv. 24.
Cerda, de la, Doña Luisa, xxxiv. 1; attracted by the Saint, xxxiv. 4; visited by S. Peter of Alcantara, xxxv. 6; tries to amuse the Saint by showing her diamonds, xxxviii. 5; the Saint's watchfulness over herself in the house of, xxxix. 11.
Cheerfulness, importance of, xii. 1.
Cherubim, xxix. 16.
Choice of a director, xiii. 28, 29.
Church, the, ceremonies of, xxxi. 4;
the Saint's reverence for, xxxiii. 6.
Clare, S., encourages the Saint, xxxiii. 15.
Comforts, worldly, the Saint's fear of, xxxiv. 4.
Communion, effects of the Saint's, xvi. 3-10, xviii. 10-18, xxx. 16, xxxvii. 24, Rel. iv. 5, Rel. ix. 13; the Saint's longing for, xxxix. 31; graces of, Rel. ix. 20.
Complaint, loving, of the Saint, xxxvii. 13.
Confession, frequent, of the Saint, v. 17; matter of, Rel. v. 11.
Confessors, the Saint's difficulty in finding, iv. 8, 13; harm done by ill-instructed, v. 6, 20, vi. 6; one of them misleads the Saint, viii. 15; unskilful, xx. 28; wrong counsel of, xxvi. 5; of the Saint harsh with her, xxx. 15; obedience of the Saint to her, xxiii. 19, xxxiii. 4, 5, Rel. i. 9; the Saint rebuked for her affection to her, xxxvii. 6; names of the Saint's, Rel. vii. 5, 11, 12, 13.
Consecration, power of the words of, xxxvii. 30.
Consolations, xi. 21; not to be sought for, xxii. 15.
Contemplation, xxii. 1; why granted to imperfect souls, xxii. 22, 23.
Contempt, Satan shuns, xxxi. 10; the Saint directed to treat her visions with, xxix. 6.
Contradiction of good people, xxviii. 24, xxx. 6.
Conversation, worldly, vii. 10; danger of, ii. 6, vii. 12; delight of our Lord in spiritual, xxxiv. 20.
Conversion of a wicked priest, v. 12; of a sinner, xxxix. 5.
Courage of the Saint, viii. 10; necessity of, x. 8; effects of, xiii. 3; necessary in the way of perfection, xxxi. 19.
Covetousness, xxxiii. 14.
Cowardice, spiritual, xiii. 6.
Creator, the, traces of in things visible, ix. 9.
Crosses, xi. 8; desired by souls in the prayer of imperfect union, xvi. 9.
Cross, the, way of, xi. 8, xv. 17, 21; necessity of carrying, xxvii. 13.

DAZA, Gaspar, xxiii. 8; thought the Saint was deluded by an evil spirit, xxiii. 16 ; approved of the new foundation, xxxii. 21.
Delusion, a, into which the Saint fell, xxii. 3 ; the Saint always prayed to be delivered from, xxix. 6.
Delusions incidental to locutions, xxv. 3, 11.
Desires, good, xiii. 8, xxi. 9, Rel. xi. 5.
Desolation, spiritual, of the Saint, xxx. 10.
Detachment, blessing of, xi. 2, xxxiv. 19; necessity of, for prayer, xi. 16, xv. 17 ; of the perfect, xv. 18 ; an effect of raptures, xviii. 8, xx. 10 ; takes away the fear of death, xxxvii. 7 ; the Saint's, from kindred, xxxi. 22, Rel. ii. 5, Rel. ix. 11 ; from directors, Rel. iv. 3.
Detraction, avoided by the Saint, vi. 4, vii. 3 ; insensibility to, Rel. ii. 4.
Detractors, the Saint prays for her, xi. 11.
Devotion, sweetness in, never asked for by the Saint, ix. 10; but once, ix. 11 ; those who seek it censured, xi. 21 ; the Saint's, increased by difficulties, xxviii. 10.
Die, either to, or suffer, xl. 27.
Direction, unskilful, viii. 15, 16 ; importance of, xiii. 4 ; methods of wrong, xiii. 25 ; not to be the same for all, xxxviii. 16.
Directors ought to be experienced, xiii. 21 ; and prudent, xiii. 24 ; and learned, xiii. 26 ; choice of, xiii. 28 ; charity of, xiii. 29 ; should be secret, xxiii. 14 ; and humble, xxxiv. 15 ; should be trusted, xxxix. 35 ; necessary, xl. 12 ; the Saint preferred those who distrusted her, Rel. vii. 18.
Discouragements, xi. 15 ; must be resisted, xix. 6; certain causes of, xxxi. 21.
Discretion, xi. 23, xiii. 2 ; excessive, xiii. 8.
Distraction of the understanding in the prayer of quiet, xv. 10, xxx. 19 ; in monasteries not caused by poverty, xxxv. 3.

Distrust of self, viii. 18, ix. 3 ; necessity of, xix. 20.
"Domine, da mihi aquam," xxx. 24.
Dominicans, the, help S. Teresa, v. 8, Rel. vii. 11-14.
Dominion, true, xl. 21.
Dove, vision of a, xxxviii. 13, 14.

ECIJA, vow of the Saint in the hermitage of, Rel. vi. 3.
Ecstasy, xx. 1 ; how wrought, xx. 2 ; fear during, xx. 9 ; first, of the Saint, xxiv. 7.
Egypt, flesh-pots of, xv. 5.
Elevation of the spirit not to be attempted in union, xviii. 8.
Eliseus. See Jerome, Fra, of the Mother of God.
Enclosure, observance of, how important, vii. 5.
Endowments not accepted by the Saint for her monasteries, xxxv. 4, 5; offered for S. Joseph, xxxvi. 19 ; and forbidden by a Brief, xxxix. 20.
Envy, a holy, xxxix. 19.
Exorcisms, the Saint threatened with, xxix. 4.
Experience, more valuable than books, xiv. 10 ; a safeguard against delusion, xiv. 11.

FAITH, the, Satan was never able to make the Saint doubt, xix. 13 ; blessed effects of, xxv. 16.
Falls turn to our good, xix. 8.
Fear, xv. 22 ; of God, xxvi. 1.
Founders of religious Orders, xxxii. 17.
Francis, S., xxii. 10.
Francis, S., de Borja visits the Saint, xxiv. 4 ; consulted by her, Rel. vii. 5.
Friendship, advantages of spiritual, vii. 33-37, xxx. 6 ; with God, xv. 8 ; the Saint's detachment from, xxiv. 8.
Friendship, worldly, dangers of, ii. 4, v. 9 ; deceitfulness of, xxi. 1.

GARDEN, the prayer in the, ix. 5 ; the soul likened to a, xi. 10, xiv. 13.
Gifts of God, the, importance of discerning, x. 4 ; demand our gratitude, x. 7 ; supply strength, x. 8 ; a grace to understand, xvii. 7 ;

the Saint erroneously advised to conceal, xxvi. 5; given according to His will, xxxiv. 14, xxxix. 12; the Saint's joy when others received, xxxiv. 20.
God, sense of the presence of, x. 1; helps those who love Him, xi. 19; never fails those who trust Him, xiii. 15; munificence of, xviii. 5; the Saint has a vision of, xl. 13, 14; pain of absence from, Rel. iv. 6.
Grace, prayer the door of, viii. 13; comes after trials, xi. 18; the Saint's distress because she could not know whether she was in a state of, xxxiv. 12; vision of a soul in, Rel. iii. 13.
Guzman, de, y Barrientos, Don Martin, sudden death of, xxxiv. 23.

HARDSHIPS of the religious life, xiii. 30.
Health, anxiety about, vi. 3-8; importance of, in the spiritual life, xi. 24; to be made little of, xiii. 9.
Heaven, Queen of, xix. 9; revealed in raptures, xxxviii. 8.
Hell, a vision of, xxx. 14, xxxii. 1; effects of on the Saint, xxxii. 7-10.
Heretics, self-condemned, vii. 8; evil state of, xxxii. 9; resemble a broken mirror, xl. 9.
Hilarion, S., the Saint commends herself to, xxvii. 1.
Honour, point of, xxi. 12.
Hugo, Fra, Cardinal of Santa Sabina, xxxvi. 27.
Humanity, the Sacred, xii. 3, xxii. 1; mistake of the Saint concerning, xxii. 3; source of all grace, xxii. 9; never to be lost sight of in prayer, xxii. 11; the Saint directed to fix her thoughts on, xxiii. 18; the Saint renews her love of, xxiv. 2; vision of, xxviii. 4, xxxviii. 22.
Humility, advantages of, vii. 37, xii. 11; false kinds of, x. 4, xiii. 4; the foundation of the Christian life, xii. 5; worth more than all the science in the world, xv. 13; grows most in the state of perfect union, xix. 2; dangers of false, xix. 15-23; acquired in raptures, xx. 38; foundation of prayer must be laid in, xxii. 16; a false, the most crafty device of Satan, xxx. 12; asking for consolations not consistent with, xxxix. 21-23.
Hypocrisy, the Saint not tempted to, vii. 2, Rel. i. 18.

IBAÑEZ, Fra Pedro, x. 10, note, xvi. 10; consulted by the Saint about the new foundation, xxxii. 19; encourages the Saint to persevere, xxxii. 20; confident of success, xxxiii. 5; departs from Avila, xxxiii. 7; advises the Saint to accept an endowment for the new foundation, xxxv. 5; changes his opinion, xxxv. 7; and helps the Saint, xxxvi. 23; seen by the Saint in a vision, xxxviii. 15, 16.
Illness of S. Teresa, iv. 6, v. 4; extreme severity of, v. 14.
Image of our Lord not to be mocked, xxix. 7.
Images, devotion of the Saint to, vii. 3; effects of, on her, ix. 1-3; great blessing of, ix. 7.
Imagination of S. Teresa not active, ix. 6; wearisome to her, xvii. 9.
Imitation of the Saints, xiii. 5-8.
Imperfections, rooting up of, xiv. 14.
Impetuosities in prayer, xxix. 11-13, Rel. i. 3, Rel. viii. 13.
Impetuosities of divine love, xxix. 10, 11, 13, xxxiii. 9; physical effects of, xxix. 15.
Incarnation, the monastery of the, the Saint enters, iv. 1; the nuns of, complain of the Saint, xix. 12; the Saint tempted to leave, xxxi. 16; the rule not strictly observed in, xxxii. 12; the Saint's affection for, xxxii. 13, xxxiii. 3; nuns of, object to the new foundation, xxxiii. 2; election of prioress, xxxv. 9; the Saint returns to, from Toledo, xxxv. 10, xxxvi. 1; troubled because of the new foundation, xxxvi. 11.
Indisposition, bodily, evil effects of, on the spiritual life, xi. 23.
Ingratitude, delusion arising from the dread of, xxiv. 6; the Saint bewails her, xiv. 16.
Inquisition, the, threats of denouncing the Saint to, xxxiii. 6.

INDEX. 449

Inspirations, good, not to be resisted, iv. 3.
Intentions, good, no excuse for an evil act, v. 12.

JEROME, Fra, of the Mother of God, Rel. vi. 1-3, Rel. ix. 7, 21, 23, 26.
Jerome, S., xi. 17, xxxviii. 2; the Saint reads the letters of, iii. 8.
Jesus, the Society of, helps the Saint, v. 8; sought by her, xxiii. 3, 19; visions concerning, xxxviii. 18-39.
Job, patience of, v. 16; trial of, xxx. 12.
John, S., of the Cross, Rel. iii. 19.
Joseph, S., great devotion of the Saint to, vi. 9, xxx. 8; the teacher of prayer, v. 12; encourages the Saint, xxxiii. 14.
Joseph, S., the monastery of, purchase of the site of, xxxii. 22; not to be subject to the Order, xxxiii. 18; paradise of God's delight, xxxv. 13; foundation of, xxxvi. 4; destruction of, threatened by the council of the city, xxxvi. 14; obtains the good will of the people, xxxvi. 25; goodness of the nuns of, xxxix. 14.
Joys, of prayer, x. 3; of visions, xxvii. 13; of the saved, xxvii. 15.
Judas, temptation of, xix. 15.
Judgment, day of, xl. 16.

KINDRED, detachment from, xxxi. 22, Rel. ix. 11.
Kings, obligations of, xxi. 2, 4; wherein lies the power of, xxxvii. 8.

LABOURER, story of a, xxxviii. 26.
Laxity in religious houses, vii. 6-9.
Learning, accompanied with humility, a help to prayer, xii. 6; useful in directors, xiii. 24-26; the Saint wishes for, xiv. 9; not necessary in prayer, xv. 12.
Lie, a, Satan is, xxv. 26; the Saint's hatred of, xxviii. 6.
Life, the, of the Saint, under what circumstances written, x. 11.
Life, weariness of, xxi. 8; the illuminative, xxii. 1.
Light of visions, xxviii. 7, xxxviii. 3.

Locutions, divine, xix. 14, xxv. 2; delusions incidental to, xxv. 3, 11; efficacy of, xxv. 5, 12; human, xxv. 8; Satanic, xxv. 13; tests of the Satanic, xxv. 17; nature of, xxvi. 3; state of the understanding during, xxvii. 10; effects of the divine, xxxviii. 19-21.
Locutions heard by the Saint, xviii. 18, xix. 13, xxiv. 7, xxv. 22, xxvi. 3, 6, xxix. 7, xxx. 17, xxxi. 15, xxxii. 17, xxxiii. 10, xxxiii. 14, xxxv. 7, 9, xxxvi. 20, xxxviii. 4, 19, 21, xxxix. 29, 34, xl. 1, 21, 24, Rel. iii. 1, passim, Rel. iv. 4, 5, 6, Rel. ix. 1, passim.
Lord, our, accounted mad, xxvii. 15.
Love, joyous, in seeing a picture of Christ, ix. 7; servants of, xi. 1; wherein it consists, xi. 20; vehement in perfect souls, xv. 6; effects of divine, xxii. 21; makes itself known without words, xxvii. 12; impetuosities of, xxix. 10, 11; fire of, xxx. 25.
Loyalty, worldly, v. 9.
Ludolf of Saxony, xxxviii. 11.
Lukewarmness, vii. 1.
Lutherans, xxxii. 9, Rel. ii. 14; destroyers of images, Rel. v. 5.

MADNESS, spiritual, xvi. 1-8, xxvii. 15.
Magdalene, the, ix. 2, xxi. 9; her example to be followed, xxii. 19.
Mancio, F., Rel. ii. 18.
Mantles of the religious folded by the Saint, xxxi. 27.
Maria of Jesus, xxxv. 1; founds a house in Alcala de Henares, xxxvi. 29.
Martin, Don, Guzman y Barrientos, marries a sister of the Saint, ii. 4, iii. 4; sudden death of, xxxiv. 23.
Martyrdom desired by the Saint, i. 4.
Martyrs, the, sufferings of, xvi. 6.
Mary and Martha, xvii. 6, xxii. 13.
Meditation, advantage of, iv. 11; fruits of, xi. 20; example of a, xiii. 19; the perfect may have to return to, xv. 20.
Memory, the, in the prayer of imperfect union, xvii. 5, 9; troublesome, but not hurtful, xvii. 11.

GG

Mendoza, de, Don Alvaro, Bishop of Avila, xxxiii. 19 ; protects the new monastery of S. Joseph, xxxvi. 18.
Men, great, difficult of access, xxxvii. 7.
Mercies of God, the remembrance of, xv. 23.
Michael, S., the Saint commends herself to, xxvii. 2.
Misdirection, a, corrected by the Saint, xiii. 22.
Mitigation, the Bull of, xxxii. 12 ; disused in the new monastery, xxxvi. 27, 28.
Monasteries, courts in politeness, xxxvii. 17.
Munificence of God, xviii. 5, xxii. 26.

NEATNESS, excessive, ii. 2, Rel. i. 23.
Novices in S. Joseph's, xxxix. 15.
Novitiate of the Saint, v. 1.
Nun, illness of a, in the monastery of the Incarnation, v. 3 ; visions concerning a, xxxviii. 37, 38.

OBEDIENCE, the Saint writes under, xviii. 10 ; strict observance of, in the Society of Jesus, xxxiii. 9 ; of the Saint to her confessors, xxiii. 19, Rel. i. 9-29, Rel. vii. 14.
Objects, natural, moved the Saint to devotion, ix. 6.
Ocampo, de, Mary, xxxii. 13, note.
Office, the divine, the Saint's imperfect knowledge of, xxxi. 26.
Order, vision concerning a certain, xl. 18, 19.
Osorno, Countess of, Rel. iii. 16.
Ovalle, de, Don Juan, xxxv. 14, note ; providential illness of, xxxvi. 2.

PADRANOS, de, Juan, xxiii. 18 ; directs the Saint, xxiv. 1 ; removed from Avila, xxiv. 5.
Pain of raptures, xx. 11 ; sweetness of, xx. 19.
Paradise of His delight, xxxv. 13.
"Passer solitarius," xx. 13.
Passion, the, devotion of the Saint to, ix. 5 ; meditation on, xiii. 19, 20 ; xxii. 8.
Patience of a nun, v. 3 ; of the Saint, v. 16 ; of God, viii. 8.
Penance, necessity of, xxvii. 14 ;
of the Saint, xxiv. 2, Rel. i. 5, Rel. ii. 11, Rel. xi. 2.
Perfection, xxi. 10 ; true safety lies in, xxxv. 15 ; not always attained to because of many years spent in prayer, xxxix. 21.
Persecution, of the Saint, xix. 12, xxxvi. 13 ; blessings of, xxxiii. 5.
Perseverance in prayer, viii. 5 ; fruits of, xi. 6 ; reward of, certain, xi. 17 ; the Saint prays for, xiv. 17 ; and recommends, xix. 7.
Peter, S., of Alcantara, xxvii. 4 ; penitential life of, xxvii. 17-19, xxx. 2 ; power of, with God, xxvii. 22 ; understands and comforts the Saint, xxx. 5, 7, Rel. vii. 6 ; quiets a scruple of the Saint, xxx. 20 ; approves of the new foundation, xxxii. 16 ; and of the observance of poverty in it, xxxv. 6 ; in Avila when the Saint came back from Toledo, xxxvi. 1 ; death of, xxxvi. 1, note ; appears to the Saint, xxxvi. 20, 21 ; said that women make greater progress than men, xl. 12.
Phœnix, the, xxxix. 33.
Pilgrims, xxxviii. 8.
Pillar, the, meditation on Christ at, xiii. 19, 31.
Politeness, monasteries courts in, xxxvii. 17.
Poverty, effects of defective, xi. 3 ; of spirit, xxii. 17 ; the Saint's love of, xxxv. 3, Rel. i. 10, Rel. ii. 2.
Prayer, mental, viii. 7 ; blessings of, viii. 12 ; joys of, x. 3 ; the Saint's four states of, xi. 12 ; fruit of mental, xi. 20 ; vocal, xii. 3 ; doctrine of, difficult, xiii. 18 ; importance of persevering in, xv. 5 ; must have its foundations in humility, xxii. 16 ; of the Saint continued in sleep, xxix. 9 ; effects of intercessory, xxxi. 9 ; two kinds of, xxxix. 8-10 ; the Saint's method of, Rel. i. 1.
Preachers, xvi. 12.
Presence of God, the, xviii. 20 ; practice of the, xii. 4 ; effects of, in the prayer of quiet, xiv. 8 ; different from vision, xxvii. 6.

Priest, conversion of an evil-living, v. 13, xxxi. 7 ; vision concerning a, xxxvii. 29.
Progress made in the way of raptures, xxi. 11.
Prophecies made to the Saint, xxxiv. 22 ; fulfilled, Rel. ii. 6, 17.
Provincial, the, of the Carmelites offers to accept the new foundation, xxxii. 16 ; then declines it, xxxii. 18; sends the Saint to Toledo, xxxiv. 2 ; recalls her, xxxv. 8 ; reprimands the Saint, xxxvi. 13; allows the Saint to live in the new monastery, xxxvi. 23.
Purgatory, the Saint saw certain souls who were not sent to, xxxviii. 41 ; and delivers others from, xxxix. 6.

QUEEN of heaven, the, devotion to, xix. 9.
Quiet, the prayer of, iv. 9, ix. 6 ; disturbed by the memory and the understanding, xiv. 5 ; joy of the soul in, xiv. 7 ; few souls pass beyond, xv. 3, 7 ; great fruits of, xv. 6 ; how the soul is to order itself in, xv. 9 ; difference between the true and false, xv. 15.

RANK, slavery of, xxxiv. 6.
Rapture, xx. 1 ; irresistible, xx. 3, xxii. 20 ; effects of, xx. 9, 30 ; pain of, xx. 11 ; loneliness of the soul in, xx. 13 ; characteristics of, xx. 23 ; duration of, xx. 25 ; physical effects of, xx. 29, Rel. i. 26, iv. 1; made the Saint long for heaven, xxxviii. 8 ; good effects of, Rel. i. 8, 15.
Reading, spiritual, i. 1, iv. 12, 13 ; persevered in by the Saint, viii. 14 ; long unprofitable to her, xii. 10 ; impossible in the prayer of perfect union, xviii. 14 ; a delight, Rel. i. 7.
Recollection, prayer of, xiv. 2, Rel. viii. 3.
Recreation, xiii. 1.
Reflections, making, when dangerous in prayer, xv. 11.
Reform, the Carmelite, beginning of, xxxii. 13.

Religious must despise the world, xxvii. 16.
Resignation of the Saint, xxi. 7, Rel. i. 20.
Revelations, the Saint never spoke of her, when she consulted her confessors, xxxii. 19.
Rosary, the, of the Saint, xxix. 8.
Rule, the Carmelite, mitigation of, xxxii. 12 ; restored by the Saint, xxxvi. 28 ; observance of, xxxvi. 30, 31.

SALASAR, de, Angel. See Provincial.
Salazar, de, Gaspar, Rector of the Society of Jesus in Avila, xxxiii. 9 ; understands the state of the Saint, xxxiii. 11 ; bids the Saint go to Toledo, xxxiv. 2 ; vision of the Saint concerning, xxxviii. 17.
Salcedo, de, Don Francisco, xxiii. 6 ; gives spiritual advice to the Saint, xxiii. 11 ; fears delusions, xxiii. 12 ; helps the Saint in her new foundation, xxxii. 21, xxxvi. 21 ; hospitable, xxxvi. 1 ; gives Communion to the Saint when a priest, Rel. iii. 7.
Samaria, the woman of, xxx. 24.
Satan, subtlety of, iv. 14 ; an artifice of, vii. 17, 35 ; suggests a false humility, xiii. 5 ; and a carefulness for health, xiii. 10 ; afraid of learned directors who are humble, xiii. 26 ; efforts of, to deceive, how thwarted, xv. 16 ; tempted the Saint to give up prayer, xix. 8 ; a lie, xxv. 26 ; unable to counterfeit intellectual visions, xxvii. 4-8 ; tries to counterfeit imaginary visions, xxviii. 15 ; appears to the Saint, xxxi. 2 ; dislikes contempt, xxxi. 10 ; wiles of, Rel. i. 29.
Scandal, xxvii. 16.
Scorn, signs of, not to be made during visions, xxix. 6.
Self, contempt of, necessary in the spiritual life, xxxi. 23.
Self-denial, necessity of, xxxi. 25.
Self-knowledge, xiii. 23.
Self-love, xi. 2 ; strong and hurtful, xi. 4, 5.
Self-respect, harm of, xxi. 12.
Senses, the, suspension of, in the prayer of perfect union, xviii. 19.

Sensitiveness, xi. 4.
Sermons, viii. 17; without simplicity, xvi. 12.
Shame, good fruits of, v. 9.
Sicknesses of the Saint, xxx. 8.
Sickness sent for penance, xxiv. 2.
Sight restored at the prayer of the Saint, xxxviii. 1.
Sincerity of the Saint, Rel. i. 28.
Sin, occasions of, viii. 14; pain occasioned by the sins of others, xiii. 14; original, xxx. 20; the Saint, by her prayers, hinders a great, xxxix. 3; wickedness of, xl. 15; vision of a soul in, Rel. iii. 13.
Sins, the Saint consents to the divulging of her, x. 10.
Solitude, longings for, i. 6, vi. 5, Rel. i. 6.
Sorcery, v. 10.
Soto, de, the Inquisitor, Rel. vii. 8.
Soul, our own, the first object, xiii. 13, 14; likened to a garden, xi. 10, xiv. 13; in the prayer of quiet, xv. 1; growth of, xv. 20; powers of, in the prayer of imperfect union, xvi. 1, 4; beside itself, xvi. 1-5; crucifixion of, in raptures, xx. 14; detachment of the enraptured, xx. 33; strengthened in raptures, xxi. 14; effects of visions in, xxvii. 11; helplessness of, without God, xxxvii. 11; vision of a lost soul, xxxviii. 31; the Saint's vision of her own, xl. 8; and of, in a state of grace, Rel. iii. 13, Rel. v. 6.
Spirit, liberty of, xi. 25; poverty of, xxii. 17; flight of the, xviii. 8, Rel. viii. 11.
Spirits, evil, put to flight, xxv. 25; by holy water, xxxi. 4.
Spirituality influenced by bodily health, xi. 24.
Suarez, Juana, iii. 2; accompanies the Saint to Bezadas, iv. 6.
Sufferings, physical, of the Saint, iv. 7, v. 4, 14, vi. 1; of raptures, xx. 16; the Saint longs for, xl. 27.
Sweetness, spiritual, never sought by the Saint but once, ix. 11; seekers of, censured, xi. 21; of the pain of raptures, xx. 19; the Saint unable to resist it at times, xxiv. 1.

TEARS, gift of, iv. 8, xxix. 11; of the Saint before a picture of the Passion, ix. 1; in the prayer of quiet, xiv. 5; in the prayer of perfect union, xix. 1, 2; the Saint prays God to accept her, xix. 10.
Temptation, power of, xxx. 13.
Tenderness of soul, x. 2.
Teresa, S., desires martyrdom, i. 4; placed in a monastery, ii. 8; unwilling to become a nun, ii. 10; becomes more fervent, iii. 2; is resolved to follow her vocation, iii. 6; first fervours of, iv. 2; failure of health, iv. 6; God sends her an illness, v. 4; suffers grievously, vi. 1; afraid of prayer, vi. 5; leads her father to prayer, vii. 16; present at her father's death, vii. 22; perseveres in prayer, viii. 2; found it hard to pray, viii. 10; delights in sermons, viii. 17; devout to the Magdalene, ix. 2; never doubted of God's mercy, ix. 8; depreciates herself, x. 9; willing to have her sins divulged, x. 10; always sought for light, x. 13; complains of her memory, xi. 9; unable to explain the state of her soul, xii. 10; supernaturally enlightened, xii. 11; read books on prayer to no purpose, xiv. 10; writes with many hindrances, xiv. 12, xl. 32; bewails her ingratitude, xiv. 16; scarcely understood a word of Latin, xv. 12; understands her state in the prayer of imperfect union, xvi. 3; and describes it, xvi. 6; bewails her unworthiness, xviii. 6; writes under obedience, xviii. 10; confesses ignorance, xviii. 20; abandons her prayers for a time, xix. 8; evil spoken of, xix. 12; misled by false humility, xix. 23; prays to be delivered from raptures, xx. 5, 6; never cared for money, xx. 34; gives up her whole being to God, xxi. 7; unable to learn from books, xxii. 3; afraid of delusions, xxiii. 3; is directed by a layman, xxiii. 10; severe to herself, xxiv. 2; her first ecstasy, xxiv. 6; had no visions before the prayer of union, xxv. 14; told by her confessor

that she was deluded by Satan, xxv. 18 ; not afraid of Satan, xxv. 27 ; spoken against, xxvi. 3 ; prays to be led by a different spiritual way, xxv. 20, xxvii. 3, Rel. vii. 7 ; troubles of, because of visions, xxvii. 4, xxviii. 6 ; her defence when told that her visions were false, xxviii. 18, 19 ; afraid nobody would hear her confession, xxviii. 20 ; harshly judged by her directors, xxviii. 23 ; would not exchange her visions for all the pleasures of the world, xxix. 5 ; vehemence of her love, xxix. 10 ; her supernatural wound, xxix. 17 ; manifests her spiritual state to S. Peter of Alcantara, xxx. 4 ; bodily trials of, xxx. 17 ; finds no relief in exterior occupations, xxx. 18 ; buffeted by Satan, xxxi. 3 ; converts a great sinner, xxxi. 7 ; troubled because well thought of, xxxi. 13-17 ; her singing of the Office, xxxi. 26 ; commanded to labour for the reform of her Order, xxxii. 14 ; commanded to abandon her purpose, xxxiii. 1 ; her vision in the Dominican church, Avila, xxxiii. 16 ; goes to Toledo, xxxiv. 3 ; the nuns wish to have her as their prioress, xxxv. 8 ; restores a child to life, xxxv. 14, note ; begins the Reform, xxxvi. 4 ; her grievous trial, xxxvi. 6, 7 ; her health improved, xxxvi. 9 ; would suffer all things for one additional degree of glory, xxxvii. 3 ; her affection for her confessors, xxxvii. 6 ; supernaturally helped when writing, xxxvii. 28; obtains sight for a blind person, xxxix. 1; and the cure of one of her kindred, xxxix. 2 ; her spiritual state became known without her consent, xl. 28 ; submits all her writings to the Roman Church, Rel. vii. 14.

Theology, mystical, x. 1, xi. 7, xii. 8 ; the Saint says she does not know the terms of, xviii. 4.

Thomas, S., assisted at the deathbed of Fra P. Ibañez, xxxviii. 15.

Throne, vision of a, xxxix. 31, 32.

Trance, a, xviii. 17, xx. 1 ; outward effects of, xl. 11 ; gradual, Rel. viii. 10.

Transport, Rel. viii. 10.

Trials followed by graces, xi. 18 ; promised to the Saint, xxxv. 9 ; shown her in a vision, xxxix. 25.

Trinity, the, mystery of, revealed to the Saint, xxxix. 36 ; visions of, Rel. iii. 6, Rel. v. 7, 8, Rel. viii. 20, Rel. ix. 12.

Truth, divine, xl. 3-8.

ULLOA, de, Doña Guiomar, xxiv. 5 ; takes the Saint to her house, xxx. 3 ; helps the Saint to accomplish the reform, xxxii. 13 ; is refused absolution, xxxii. 18.

Understanding, the, use of in prayer, xiii. 17 ; disorderly, xv. 10 ; powerless in the state of imperfect union, xvi. 4 ; and of the perfect union, xviii. 19 ; the Saint speaks humbly of her, xxviii. 10.

Union, imperfect, prayer of, xvi. 1; a mystical death, *ib.*; the soul resigned therein, xvii. 1 ; how it differs from the prayer of quiet, xvii. 5, 6 ; another degree of, xvii. 7 ; the labour of the soul lessens in the later states of, xviii. 1.

Union, perfect, prayer of, xviii. 1 ; the senses wholly absorbed in, xviii. 3, 14 ; duration of, xviii. 16 ; fruits of, xix. 4.

Union, prayer of, iv. 9 ; followed by visions in the Saint, xxv. 14.

Union, what it is, Rel. v. 2 ; of the faculties of the soul, Rel. viii. 7.

VAIN-GLORY, vii. 2, 34, x. 5, Rel. i. 18, Rel. ii. 15, Rel. vii. 23.

Vanity of possessions, xx. 35 ; the Saint's watchfulness over herself herein, xxxix. 11.

Virtue, growth of, in the prayer of quiet, xiv. 6 ; and in that of imperfect union, xvii. 4.

Visions, our Lord seen in, vii. 11, xxv. 14, xxvii. 3, xxviii. 2 ; intellectual, xxvii. 4 ; different from the sense of the presence of God, xxvii. 6 ; joy of, xxvii. 13 ; imaginary, xxviii. 5 ; effects of, in the soul, xxviii. 13 ; Satan tried to simulate, xxviii. 14 ;

effects of, in the Saint, xxviii. 19 ; cessation of the Saint's imaginary, xxix. 2 ; of the Sacred Humanity, effects of, xxxviii. 23.

WATER, holy, puts evil spirits to flight, xxxi. 4, 5, 9, 10.
Water, the first, xi. 13 ; the second, xiv. 1 ; the third, xvi. 1 ; the fourth, xviii. 1.
Will, the state of, in the prayer of quiet, xiv. 4, xv. 2, 10 ; in the prayer of imperfect union, xviii. 16.

Women, great care necessary in the direction of, xxiii. 14, 15 ; make greater progress than men, xl. 12.
World, the, contempt of, x. 7, xxvii. 16; customs of, wearisome, xxxvii. 15, 16 ; hard on good people, xxxi. 12 ; vanity of, Rel. i. 21.
Wound of the soul, Rel. viii. 15 ; of love, Rel. viii. 17.

YEPES, Rel. ix. 1.

ZEAL, indiscreet, xiii. 8.

THE END.

CORRECTIONS.

Page 5, note ¹, *for* ch. xxxi., *read* ch. xxx.
Page 127, third line from bottom, *for* flights, *read* flight.
Page 202, thirteenth line, *for* over others, *read* over them.
Page 204, eighteenth line, *for* visions, *read* vision.

www.ingramcontent.com/pod-product-compliance
Lightning Source LLC
Chambersburg PA
CBHW051851300426
44117CB00006B/345